DATE			

BY ALBERT BERMEL:

CONTRADICTORY CHARACTERS
ARTAUD'S THEATRE OF CRUELTY
ONE-ACT COMEDIES OF MOLIÈRE
THE PLAYS OF COURTELINE
THE GENIUS OF THE FRENCH THEATRE
THREE POPULAR FRENCH COMEDIES
AUGUST STRINDBERG

A HISTORY FROM ARISTOPHANES FARCE TO WOODY ALLEN

Albert Bermel

SIMON AND SCHUSTER
NEW YORK

SIMON AND SCHUSTER and colophon are trademarks of Simon & Schuster
Designed by Jeanne Joudry
Manufactured in the United States of America

10 9 8 7 6 5 4 3 2 1

Library of Congress Cataloging in Publication Data

Bermel, Albert.
    Farce: a history from Aristophanes to Woody Allen.

    Includes bibliographical references and index.
    1. Farce. I. Title.
PN1942.B4   809.2'52   81-16672
ISBN 0-671-25148-1   AACR2

My thanks . . .

to Joyce, Neil, and Derek Bermel; Susan Bolotin; Barbara Bralver; Lynn Chalmers; Andrew Eller; Lila and Morton Kass; Morris Klein; Alice E. Mayhew; Harvey Mindess; Ron Moody; Brenda Newman; Carl Reiner; Saul Turteltaub; Kenneth Weiss; Anita and Shimon Wincelberg; Samuel Gill and the librarians at the American Academy of Motion Picture Arts and Sciences; Charles Silver and his staff at the Film Study Center of the Museum of Modern Art; The Research Foundation of the City University of New York for a grant that enabled me to visit Hollywood; the librarians at Lehman College; colleagues and students at Herbert H. Lehman College and the Graduate Center of the City University of New York; all authors quoted or referred to, dead or alive, and their publishers and translators; and others who encouraged, discouraged, suggested, warned, told jokes.

(A modified segment of Chapter 4 was published in the *Melodrama* Issue of *New York Literary Forum*, 1980, edited by Daniel C. Gerould, under the title "Where Melodrama Meets Farce.")

ALBERT BERMEL
The Bronx, New York, 1981

For Eric Bentley
and Stanley Kauffmann

As Chico says in *Animal Crackers,*
"I play you one of my own compositions by Victor Herbert."

Contents

10   *Contents*

PART ONE

◆

RECOGNIZING FARCE

♦

ONE

NOT THE FIRST WORD

Not a pig in a poke but a pig in the front of a car occasions roars of laughter in the fourth act of *John Bull's Other Island* by Bernard Shaw. In the rural town of Rosscullen a man named Barney Doran tells with Irish joy in the power of the word how an Englishman named Tom Broadbent offered to do a local farmer a favor by driving him and the pig he'd just purchased home to the farm. But the pig panicked as soon as the motor was cranked, threw the vehicle into fourth gear, and then got his tail caught between Broadbent's foot and the brake. The car careened through an outdoor market; it wrecked stalls, one of them laden with china; it knocked people down, one of them the man who'd cranked the car handle, and when the unfortunate pig managed to jump out, ran him over. In Doran's words, "it just tore the town in two, and sent the whole dam market to blazes." One of his listeners, a woman, wants to know how the others in the room can laugh at the incident. "Why not?" a mystic named Keegan grimly replies. "There is danger, destruction, torment! What more do we want to make us merry?"

This book celebrates the danger, destruction, and torment of farce, an ancient form of merrymaking. Short and long farces date back to men's and women's first attempts to scoff in public at whatever their neighbors cherished in private: standing in the community, habits, customs, affectations, eccentricities, weaknesses, virtues that are vices, friendships, enmities, work, play, the responsibilities and constraints of belonging to a family, a tribe, a clan, a race. But farce came into a new prominence in the past seventy years, thanks to early Hollywood. And then it ramified like mad. Since about 1912 the spirit of farce resurgent has squeezed into such other performing arts as dance and music, as well as painting, fiction, and poetry. Artistic movements and artificial groups like Dada, Surrealism, the Absurd, and Happenings, although annunciated with flourishes of theory and manifestoes about The Condition of Man, trade in farcical effects and would be unimaginable without them. As the early film farces demonstrated all over again, farce is by its nature popular: it makes a gut appeal to the entire spectrum of the public, from illiterates to intellectuals.

Being a destroyer and detractor, farce is a negating force, hard, if not impossible, to trap and pin down. I haven't come across a plausible definition, and I won't attempt one. Definitions in the arts are occasionally of some use, but they oblige a writer to start out by reinterpreting every word as he wants it understood and to end by defending the definition against encroachment—mending his fences to keep out poachers. If he's conscientious, he must revise his wording from time to time so that it covers new work which obstinately refuses to conform to definitions, compelling definitions to make the adjustments. If he's honest, he ultimately writes a new definition or forswears the old one. Rather than delimiting farce, then, this book will describe and analyze farces in the plural, mostly from theater and cinema. Each chapter contains a potted history of plays or films that were created during a certain period and seem to me to have features in common. The last chapter but one (15) suggests the pervasiveness of farce in the other arts.

The book, then, is a cumulative biography of farce. It draws on bits and stretches of both historical narrative and critical analysis. The only texts it concerns itself with are those that exist in English versions. To attempt a truly international survey would call for a brigade of writers who speak every language and dialect there is and ever was, and would take the book to an unmanageable length. All in all, there must be many more untranslated farces than the number now available to us in English. Even so, this number is staggering. While writing I kept thinking of a scene in *Laughter in Paradise*. Alastair Sim, a very proper gentleman, will inherit a chunk of a fortune left by a sadistic relative, but only on condition that he commit an act of larceny. He's now at the unattended jewelry counter of a department store. He glances in all directions and wears that frown of terror that corrugates his forehead and pulls his mouth into a Romanesque arch. Reaching for a string of pearls, he stuffs them into his pocket. But the chain is endless. As he loops up great handfuls of pearls and crams them away, more keep coming. His pocket is overflowing, but he can't stop and he dare not start putting them back.

Since farce infringes on the other principal genres of comedy, tragedy, melodrama, and tragicomedy (see Chapter 4), I felt I had to include quite a few partial farces, which are borderline cases. Over-the-borderline cases, however, have been omitted, among them the plays of Jean Anouilh, Jean Cocteau, Friedrich Dürrenmatt, Jack Richardson, Sam Shepard, and Thornton Wilder. Obviously, this is a matter of personal judgment, which may be influenced by the style of the productions I've seen. Just as obviously, I don't esteem these writers' plays any the less for their not being farces.

Farce seems to be favored by authors in their formative years. Once they have a reputation to uphold (or as they sometimes believe, to lose), their style grows more dignified, more punctilious, and their content more grave. They are attracted to stories of union and compassion, rather than dissolution, free sequence, and irrationality. They think about their "careers"; they want to leave posterity things of substance to gnaw on. If they do venture later in life into satire, it usually turns out bitter and strained, even misanthropic, rather than playful. It may hardly be funny at all, let alone farcical. Perhaps farce is a young person's game. To stay doggedly with it on into middle age and beyond may require a rare blend of arrested development and wide-open arteries from the soul.

The words "farce" and "farcical," which I employ recklessly here and there, do appear in critical discussions of films, novels, television, and other arts. But as a genre, farce has generally been considered a theatrical preserve. Films and fiction name their own genres or other categories (the Western, screwball comedy, science fiction, irony, black humor, and the like), and specialized scholars nurse them jealously. Stage farces, though, resemble movie farces as a rule more closely than they resemble stage tragedies, sometimes because the film farces are borrowed from stage farces. So it is too with films and fiction. An account like this one that ropes together samples of a genre from the different arts ought to—and I hope does—emphasize the affinities and similarities among these arts, and add to our understanding of an artist like Woody Allen or Jules Feiffer who works at several of them. I'd also like to think that an empirical book can provide material for criticizing some of the more gaseous forms of theorizing that go on in the name of aesthetics and semiology.

So far as I can discover, there are no other conspective books on farce. Some time after I began this one, I heard about *Farce* by Jessica Milner Davis of Stanford (London: 1978), a monograph that's part of a series entitled "The Critical Idiom." But I held back from reading it until my first draft was finished. Professor Davis has confined her application of the term farce to plays, and her book is a valuable one. I half-wish I'd read it sooner. To readers who notice that she and I have unavoidably crossed some of the same ground, I can only say that our copyright dates affirm that she was there first. Other critics were there a lot earlier with essays, chapters, paragraphs, and striking observations. If I knowingly plundered them, I tried to make partial restitution by putting in acknowledgments. Some thefts that have happened without my knowing are more than likely. The seminal statement on farce, the one that originally compelled me and, I believe, Professor Davis and others to take it seriously, but with a dash of frivolity too, is the "Farce" chapter in Eric Bentley's *The Life of the Drama*, every page of which resonates with wisdom and provocation. As a colleague once remarked to me, Dr. Bentley's book as a whole is the Aristotelian *Poetics* for our time—and maybe for all time.

In a piece of writing that has some factual history in it one can't help relying on many secondary sources. Theater history, however diligently sought after, is no more trustworthy than any other kind of history. Therefore, I can't in all conscience make the usual disclaimer about sources. My errors are almost surely theirs, and to anybody who knows better I apologize for perpetuating them and making life rougher for the coming generations.

Because of the popularity of farce, I address this book to an elusive figure, the apparition that haunts the dreams of authors and publishers—the average, intelligent reader. Whenever I ran into the choice of writing for specialists or for everybody else, I came down, if I could, on the side of everybody else. As a reader, I like criticism that's accessible to a person who's willing to give it a fair shake. I find terminology a distraction as well as a handicap to understanding; I give up on books that bat it around indiscriminately, as some do. Students of the arts are sometimes encouraged to assume that the more terminological a text or the more "scientific" the distinctions it lays down, the more profound it must be. I have an irrational contempt for the word "profound" and its priggish implications. Can somebody who dotes on Molière and Shaw, especially when they make us laugh at the "scientific" pretensions of some of their characters, allow himself to *become* those characters?

TWO

IN THE REALM OF THE UNREAL

Scene: A deserted street in Naples.

Time: The seventeenth century.

Characters: Scapin, a servant, and his employer, old Géronte.

Motive: Géronte told a lie about Scapin, who has sworn to have his revenge. In Scapin's world, when servants do wrong, their employers beat them. His vengeance, then, will consist of beating his employer.

Handicaps: Géronte won't stand still and let himself be beaten. He'll fight back; he'll cry for help. Besides, employers may beat servants as often, long, and hard as they wish, but servants do not beat employers. Scapin will be given a far worse beating in return and lose his job.

Odds: Scapin has two things going for him. First, he's cunning, as we realize from the play named after him, Molière's *Les Fourberies de Scapin,* which means something like *Scapin's Swindles* or *The Slick Tricks of Scapin.* Second, Géronte is not aware that Scapin means him harm.

Expedient: Scapin craves a personal satisfaction: he himself, with his own hands, must beat the old man. At the same time, somebody else, an unpunishable stranger, must administer the beating. Or appear to.

Action: In the play's most celebrated scene (Act III, Scene 2) Scapin starts out by frightening the old man: Bad news—a gang of enraged swordsmen are after you; they're going to cut you to pieces. You can't escape. They've posted men along the streets that lead to your house, and other men are searching for you right now, and—what was that noise?

Scapin darts away to the nearest corner, listens, creeps back. A false alarm.

Géronte is by now shaking. What can he do? Where can he hide? He promises that if Scapin can only come up with a plan to save him, there'll be a reward: possibly Géronte's suit, after he's worn it out.

A plan? Nothing easier. Scapin just happens to have a sack with him, a capacious sack. If the old man will only climb into it, Scapin can hoist it on his back and carry it "as if it were a bundle of something" through the enemy lines and into Géronte's house. Once there, they can barricade themselves in and call for assistance. But whatever happens, Géronte must take care not to stir or utter a sound.

As soon as the old man is halfway into the sack, Scapin pushes his head down and hisses that one of the swordsmen is approaching. Géronte hears heavy footsteps. A strange voice with a thick Gascon dialect demands the whereabouts of Géronte. The Gascon will find and kill him, "even if he tries to hide at the center of the earth." Scapin protests; he defends his employer. For his loyalty he is beaten with a stick. But the blows somehow connect with Géronte's shoulders as he crouches in the sack, blind and dumb with terror.

Outside the sack, Scapin continues the quarrel between his Gascon dialect and his natural voice. He wallops the sack as he gives out anguished cries. Géronte, denied the luxury of expressing his pain, doesn't know how much longer he can hold out. Then—blessed relief: he hears the footsteps recede, and Scapin muttering curses at the Gascon. Géronte ventures his head out of the sack.

GÉRONTE: Oh, Scapin, I can't take any more of this.

SCAPIN: Oh, Monsieur, I'm beaten to a pulp. I have this terrible pain in my shoulders.

GÉRONTE: What? When he was hitting mine?

SCAPIN: No, Monsieur, he landed the blows on me.

GÉRONTE: What do you mean? I felt them. I can still feel them.

SCAPIN: I tell you no. It was only the end of the stick that made contact with your shoulders.

GÉRONTE: You should have moved away and spared me—

SCAPIN (*thrusting Géronte's head down into the sack*): Watch it. Here's another of them. Looks like a foreigner.

And Scapin goes through his routine again, but he now plays the roughneck as a Swiss, whom he boldly defies. Once more Géronte takes the punishment on his back and emerges battered from the sack, complaining, "Oh, I'm in agony," only to find Scapin complaining, "Oh, I'm dead." Scapin gives him no chance to look around, but pushes his head down for the third time, as if to drown him once and for all in the sack's depths, saying, "Watch it. Six of them this time. Soldiers . . ."

Now Scapin overreaches himself. He must fake six pairs of footsteps, perform six roles in contrasting voices, and deal the sack-trapped Géronte six lots of blows. Whether Scapin's vocal artistry falters or whether Géronte finds the prospect of sixfold blows unendurable and thinks he might as well throw himself on the mercy of the merciless six, he rises fearfully from the sack while Scapin is still putting up a big fuss pretending to fight off the six soldiers. Géronte watches, dumb and aching with humiliation. Scapin turns to drub the sack again with his stick, freezes as he sees his employer's face, and—what else can he do?—scampers away as Géronte yells insults after him.

For Géronte the scene is a nightmarish experience. He went into it flustered, having just learned that while he was abroad recently his son married a poor girl, without permission, when he, Géronte, had almost sewn up a wedding for the boy with a wealthy bride, the daughter of a friend. Now, all of a sudden, the bad takes a turn for the worse. His life is threatened. He cannot get to his house. It's surrounded. So is he. He cannot go anywhere. And if he does nothing he will surely be set upon where he stands. Not one but many swordsmen are hunting him down. Swordsmen! What? In this quiet part of town? He doesn't have time to deliberate or question Scapin. He must vanish within the second, into that musty sisal probably used for carrying garbage or horse dung. One of the hooligans may jab at it with a sword just for fun. But Géronte has no choice: he must discipline his aged bones and trembling flesh, stay still and silent even when the blows whistle down on him. He can't see anything, can't hear properly. But he is also seething. He, a sober citizen, an elder of Naples, rich and respected, must squat in this cramped, undignified, and in every way hurtful position while scum, foreigners, social *nothings* whale away at him, and a servant witnesses his mortification. Isolated, incensed, unjustly put upon, aching, and holding his breath for the next assault, he feels not only on the brink of death but also cut off from his life.

Farce deals with the unreal, with the worst one can dream or dread. Farce is cruel, often brutal, even murderous.

For Scapin the scene provides satisfaction that is strangely mixed. After disconcerting Géronte, taking him by surprise, making him lose his equilibrium and bearings, so that he stumbles into the trap when he scrambles into the sack, Scapin must keep up his momentum; he must actually accelerate it. His motive is a flimsy one, but that doesn't matter: we've previously seen him as a man obsessed with getting his revenge, almost as if it were a birthright. The episode shows us a child flailing out at a helpless father, at class distinctions, at all authority, taking the law into his own hands. He is willing to risk everything: if he underplays or overplays his impersonations—as he eventually will—he is in trouble. But the risk seasons his enjoyment. The very danger intoxicates him and makes him strive and strike all the harder. He has driven himself into an ecstatic state which, in turn, drives him into taking greater risks: every moment of prolonging the punishment endangers him further out there on the open street. He's a clown on a high wire who progresses, like Chaplin in *The Circus*, from balancing to walking to dancing to handstands (on one hand) to somersaults. Chaplin is bedeviled by monkeys who swarm all over him and the rope he is on, get their tails in his mouth, put their fingers over his eyes, bite his nose, pull down his pants, and finally unfasten his safety belt. Scapin's monkeys are disembodied, but they are there. If the episode seems to Géronte like a nightmare, to Scapin it represents the fulfillment of a dream wish, but that dream verges on another nightmare.

Farce flouts the bounds of reason, good taste, fairness, and what we commonly think of as sanity.

The third participant in this scene, the spectator, shares Scapin's childlike delight in seeing the authoritative and miserly Géronte degraded. At the same time, the spectator shares Géronte's fears—we often wince at seeing somebody else hurt, and even when he's an unsympathetic character we want him to earn his punishment by fighting back and piling provocation on provocation. If he keeps getting pummeled and never retaliates, we begin to worry. (This must be why Molière, who could fine-tune himself into the feelings of audiences, stopped the beatings after two rounds and made Géronte cut off the third.) Still, the spectator doesn't share Géronte's pain or Scapin's risks. He is both enlisted in the scene and blessedly free of it. Finding himself in it, he can yield to its suspense; knowing himself out of it, he can appreciate Scapin's impudent skills and yield to laughter. He is not particularly committed to either of the figures onstage.

Farce has two main laughter-releasing mechanisms: characters who are only partially engaging, and the improbable situations in which they are caught up.

Indestructible People

However various, farces share several family traits: unreality (some farcical actions don't quite lend themselves to explanation, even to dream interpretation), brutality, and objectivity. These in turn modify one another. The unreality is objective. And to come closer to our point, the brutality is unreal. But what *is* unreal brutality? It seems to be what we mean when we speak of slapstick and knockabout humor, both of which are integral to farce and to Molière's scene. A slapstick, originally the blunt wooden instrument carried by certain actors of the commedia dell'arte, looked like a cudgel but was flexible. On impact it gave off a sharp cracking noise. This was not a natural sound but a sound effect. It was artificial.[1] Similarly, knockabout humor, including the old reliable

---

[1] In modern circuses the exaggerated noise made by the impact of a slapstick persists as a tradition. Every blow received by a clown, like every pratfall, is accompanied by the striking of a gong or a bass drum. This artificial sound doesn't magnify the blows; it magnifies the farce.

kick in the pants that causes a headlong plunge, belongs to the artifice of choreography, not to the reality of street fighting.

Scapin pounds Géronte with his slapstick so as to inflict the maximum punishment, but the actor playing Scapin does not hurt the actor playing Géronte, as we are well aware; otherwise, the production would need a new Géronte every night. But *inside the play* if these blows came down in actuality, Géronte would not rise from the sack once, let alone three times. Another character would have to carry him offstage with a broken collarbone, shoulder-blade and neck lacerations, shock, stomach cramps, and whiplash. As it is, after Scapin has bolted in Scene 2, the old man remains sturdily in view to perform in Scene 3.

In farce, characters seldom get badly injured, almost never die. Although a character doesn't merely clash with other characters but also collides with the scenery and props, he stays more or less intact. Blood flows like wine in a heavy drama or melodrama. In farce the victim, who is apparently bloodless, looks dazed after a collision, then shakes his head, picks himself up, and goes off to meet the next collision. Farce shows us human bodies that are indestructible, sponges for punishment.

One of the clauses in an unwritten contract between farceurs and their audiences used to state that the characters will, like Géronte, come out of their ordeals unscathed, because the audience must be permitted to laugh. When that clause was not honored, the play ceased to be a farce—for the moment, at any rate —and turned into something else. In recent times, and with the advent of film, the contract has undergone revision, and justly so: there are no rules in art. Death, like everything else, has become a legitimate subject for farce. Characters die and spring back to life. Or their deaths are bandied about farcically, like the succession of murders in *Arsenic and Old Lace* and *Kind Hearts and Coronets*. The director of *Kind Hearts and Coronets*, Robert Hamer, took the sting out of the deaths by casting Alec Guinness in the roles of all the members of the slaughtered family, a feat of mimicry that is the film's principal attraction. Each of Guinness's mischievous caricatures is certainly distinctive, but because they all have the same features, plus or minus some hair and putty, a spectator gets the impression of watching the same figure repeatedly cut down and revived. And this is a farcical effect. It represents not so much death as the unheroic defiance of death or the reluctance to die quietly: in the words of the old music-hall song, He's dead, but he won't lie down. The victims in Chaplin's *Monsieur Verdoux* are similarly farcical, most notably the almost unmurderable Martha Raye. In Mike Nichols' film of *Catch-22*, a "serious" farce, the body of Alan Arkin as Yossarian lies on the ground in its last agonies as his voice plaintively calls for help and the colors go bleached to suggest dying; but we see, intercut and superimposed, images of Yossarian alive—in a plane, on a bombing mission. The death is a dismissed nightmare. This sequence tells us that Yossarian has been wounded but will not die, and while it lasts farce goes into abeyance.

Incapacitated Victims

Why do we accept—and enjoy—the sight of characters who stumble into one physical indignity after another? In part because these characters, being indestructible, are more than mortal, and also less. All characters are their creators' puppets, but the ones in farce seem especially impersonal. Many of them have descended from stock characters or types. They are imitations of imitations, not of whole human beings. To enhance their unreality, the author of a farce will frequently put them under a spell, rob them of some of their senses or faculties, and make them behave like zombies who walk into trouble with their eyes wide open in a glassy stare. Such a victim, positively *stupid*—in a stupor—may be temporarily stunned from a beating, as Géronte is, or just awakened in the small hours and still asleep on his feet. He may be drugged or bound or blindfolded or earplugged. He may be ill or missing his pants or even naked. Or—the most popular variation of all—he may be drunk.

Instead of putting the spell on him, the author may put it around him by landing him on unfamiliar terrain where he appears odd and outnumbered, and where he feels fearful. He is different from everybody else. His clothes, or lack of clothes, his accent, his manners can make him look like an intruder or snooper or source of infection. A convict finds himself in a drawing room, a society swell in a jail cell or a junkyard. A man on the run charges onto a stage in the middle of a performance and must literally make a spectacle of himself. This sort of incapacity, being lost or not belonging, singles the character out when he would rather remain inconspicuous. It was Chaplin's genius to have settled on a tramp's outfit in which, no matter where he goes (with the exception of the fancy-dress ball in *The Idle Class*), he looks out of place.[2] Since the incapacitated character doesn't fully govern his own faculties, he is a natural target for aggression and mishaps.

Changing Fate

If we imagine the entire history and geography of drama and film spread out in a single panorama, we can separate its population into three main clusters of characters. The first, and cosmically loftiest, are the gods and goddesses of Greek, some Roman, and a number of Oriental plays. A subcluster came into being after these deities walked, or flew, out of Western theaters a couple of centuries before Christ, leaving behind them a supernatural residue in the shapes of ghosts, spirits, fairies, demons, and witches. The second grouping, which preoccupies professional and amateur critics, consists of human characters; these range from the indecipherable personalities found in Greek and Shakespearean tragedy, in the great tragicomedies of Shakespeare, Molière, Shaw, and Euripides, and in a few exalted comedies, all the way across the spectrum of mortality and beyond it to the incapacitated and hapless creatures of farce. The third collection of characters is the vast and heterogeneous community of objects, including machines. Objects as characters? The notion sounds bizarre; but as we will see, objects do behave like characters in certain plays and in most farces.[3]

---

[2] The Marx Brothers also look out of place; they seem even to resent being stuck with one another. But they almost never function in a plot as victims; they are either aggressors or, if they feel themselves provoked, powerful counterpunchers. Instead of behaving below capacity, they find endless stores of energy and insolence to expend. Instead of being intimidated by strange surroundings—a transatlantic liner, a state banquet, a commencement ceremony, a battlefield—they are driven manic by them. Instead of hoping to adapt to the surroundings, they offer the surroundings the option of adapting to them or being ravaged.

[3] Another subcluster, situated somewhere between people and objects, is animal, plant, and insect life. These characters are rare, except in animated films (see Chapter 9). Like the gods and other supernaturals, they are usually interpreted by human actors when they have more than a walk-on or stand-on part. This is understandable in view of the difficulty of training a lion for Shaw's *Androcles and the Lion*, a dung beetle for Aristophanes' *Peace*,

As characters, the gods may have abandoned the drama in Europe. But their manipulative abilities did not disappear; they were transformed into the abstraction that the Greeks had several words for. We refer to it loosely as Fate or Fortune or Destiny. Or plotting. Some post-Greek plays are more openly "fate-struck" than others. Seneca, Shakespeare, Racine, Chikamatsu, Ibsen, Miller, Hitchcock, Mizoguchi, and Bergman, to mention only a few outstanding artists, create foreboding dramatic atmospheres in which the characters are not quite in command of their own lives. They submit unwillingly to powers or psychological pressures they fail to understand: in *Thyestes* the horrifying vengefulness of Atreus toward his brother; in *Phaedra* the queen's feverish love for her stepson and in A *View from the Bridge* Eddie Carbone's for his niece; in *Othello* Iago's "motiveless malignity," as Coleridge named it; Mrs. Alving's determination in *Ghosts* to purify her son of his father's taints; the urge on the part of Norman Bates in *Psycho* to stab young women at the behest, as he thinks, of his mother; and so on.

In such stories, it's often said, "character is fate." The fate-doomed personage has what used to be known in Greek tragedy as a tragic flaw. Yet as we study these figures, we find that the flaw is not exactly *in* them but more like something outside and contrary, some external power that imposes itself and will be parasitic once it *gets* in. This power is far from the only ingredient of fate. Fate is multiple. It comprises, in addition to the external power, all sorts of circumstances plotted into the script by that terrestrial god, the author: such devices as coincidences, accidents, races against time, misunderstandings, and conflicts with other characters. But one ingredient of fate that has peculiar significance for farce is the third class of characters: objects. Yes, dumb objects, from small coins to enormous boulders, and mechanical contrivances, from modest wristwatches to unstoppable steamrollers, play not merely roles, but fateful roles, in farce.

---

butterflies and ants for *The Insect Play* by the brothers Čapek, and of finding beast-gods to perform in Kabuki and Sanskrit drama.

The Object as Antagonist

Farce shrinks the difference in consciousness between objects and people. If many human figures become incapacitated, many objects acquire intelligence of a sort; they appear malevolent; they are out to get the people. Paul Jennings, one of the finest comic essayists writing since World War II, noticed this phenomenon in his theory of Resistentialism, according to which objects balefully defy people in "real" life. In the unreal life of farce, the defiance shows up even more strikingly.

Scapin uses two objects against Géronte, and both are perfectly suited for the purposes of punishment. If objects were people, the inclusion of the sack and the stick could be considered typecasting. The stick does damage precisely because it's rigid, whereas the sack is harmful precisely because it's limp: had Géronte taken refuge in a barrel instead, his movements inside it would not be visible and its surface would protect him from the stick. These objects are friendly to Scapin—for a time. To Géronte they are undeclared enemies.

Sometimes such objects are simple, stationary items that are cumbersome in a given situation: a set of weights on a polished parquet floor or a pair of two-by-fours, twenty feet long, that must be removed from a greenhouse. Sometimes they look simple and then prove to be complicated and willful: a lace-up boot or a needle and thread or a bow tie.

As a rule, farce can do more with the object in motion than with the object that is stationary. As our victim goes his incapacitated way, he puts his head out an open window shortly before the sash cord snaps. Sleds, bicycles, cars, trains, speedboats, ice floes, and heavy articles of furniture slam into him. Sometimes he's aboard them while they travel. Sometimes they lie in wait. He passes through a landscape and—spontaneously, it seems—trees, telegraph poles, scaffolding, and girders topple, bridges and overpasses collapse. Tunnels cave in. Rafts capsize. Cliff edges crumble. Dams burst. Avalanches roll. If he hurtles down a ski slope, a log cabin will take up a position at the foot of the run. In *Animal House*, as soon as John Belushi mounts a ladder in order to peer into some girls' bedrooms, we know the ladder will turn treacherous; all it has to do is turn. Objects may lead inert, useful, and unassuming existences for years without disclosing their antagonism toward people. Then a farce energizes them: somebody remembers, say, that a chair, a vase, a book, a can of paint, or a custard pie is throwable.

In 1917, Guillaume Apollinaire, the author who thought up the name Surrealism, recognized the covert ambition of objects to become animated when, in *The Breasts of Tiresias,* he gave an actress the role of a living newsstand. By the early 1920s, other Surrealist playwrights, impressed by the stunts that objects had accomplished in silent film farce, gave them equal billing with the human characters. René Daumal's *en gggarrrde!* includes in its cast A Toothbrush, A Cigar (pure Havana, "Romeo and Juliet"), and A Pernod with Sugar. The rest of the characters in this three-and-a-half-page playlet are either unlikely (a lady named Mygraine, a "little angel" named Bubu, a "depraved young thing" called Ursule, Cleopatra, who is "a person not to fool around with," Napoleon, a part to be played by Napoleon, and The Author) or else animated only slightly (Some Snails, A Leech, and A Sociologist). In such company an animated toothbrush, cigar, and Pernod can feel at ease.[4]

The objects in most farces play a continuing role. They are thematic and wind into and out of the action, much as the characters do. In Eugène Labiche's *An Italian Straw Hat* (1851) and the film of it made by René Clair (1927), wedding guests, a large contingent of them, troop into and out of the scenes looking for the headgear of the title, which is the primary cause of the action. In Labiche's later play *Pots of Money* (1864), some provincials visit Paris, where they are arrested because of a misunderstanding. One of them, a farmer, has purchased a beautiful new pickax, of which he is proud. With it he hacks a hole in the station wall. When the prisoners learn that a police chief is coming in to question them before they have broken through the wall, they conceal some of the rubble—dust and rocks—by stuffing it into their pockets. They escape. With the police on their collective tail, they run into a

---

[4] Translations of *The Breasts of Tiresias* and *en gggarrrde!* will be found in *Modern French Theatre,* edited by Michael Benedikt and George E. Wellwarth (New York: E. P. Dutton, 1964).

high-toned salon. One member of the party pulls out his handkerchief to wipe away some sweat and smears his brow and cheeks
with dust. The farmer, who has managed to purloin a couple of
cream pastries, reaches into his pocket for one and bites it, only to
wince in anguish as his teeth connect with the stone.[5] In much the
same way, Harold Lloyd in *For Heaven's Sake* (1926) takes a leather
powder puff that has been making itself look like a cruller on a
plate of cakes and vainly chews it.

In *Sherlock Jr.* (1924), Buster Keaton plays pool with two gangsters who have hollowed out a "13" ball and filled it with high
explosive. Buster calmly puts away every ball on the table without
once touching the "13." Finally he aims for the "13." The gangsters
(and the audience) hold their breath. The "13" rolls quietly into a
pocket. Buster, it turns out, has substituted a regular "13" ball for
the explosive one, which he has put aside for an emergency. The
emergency occurs later in the film during a car chase. The gangsters are catching up with Keaton when he hurls the explosive "13"
at them and wrecks their automobile.

The thematic reappearances of objects, the ways in which they
sneak into and out of the plotting, point up yet another ambition
of objects. Not only do they wish to become animated and to foil
human purposes: they also think of themselves as being versatile.
They yearn to be used for purposes they never seemed intended
for. A plate of hot, wet food acts as a missile. A prison wall acts as
food. A table acts as a barricade behind a door. A door acts as a
toboggan.

Objects are would-be actors. And not only in farces. In a straight
drama, a bed sheet waits for its opportunity to act as a rope or a
gag or a screen or a bathrobe or a sail. A pair of scissors or a poker
catches somebody's eye and offers itself as a lethal weapon. Almost
every thriller depends on clues, usually objects, that will lead the
private eye to the criminal, or better, to an innocent person. And
in the tragedy *Othello* a significant role is enacted by a mere handkerchief which, for the hero, represents a priceless token of love.
But in farce, objects act more blatantly, more industriously, to

---

[5] *An Italian Straw Hat* is translated by Lynn and Theodore Hoffman in *The Modern Theatre*, Vol. 3, edited by Eric Bentley (New York: Doubleday, 1955); and *Pots of Money* is in
Three Popular French Comedies, translated and edited by Albert Bermel (New York: Frederick Ungar, 1975).

earn their places in the script. And they are not merely *there*. They impersonate other objects. We might say that the difference between a gun in melodrama and in farce is that while in melodrama the characters must beware of what it is, in farce they have to beware of what it may become.

Enter the Machine

A gun, however, is not an ordinary object. It belongs in an intermediate stage between things and people that is called machinery. Machines serve as extensions of human beings and also extensions of objects. They have to be switched on by a person; then they are animated until a person switches them off. This, at any rate, is what should happen. In practice, as farce has demonstrated time and again, machines start and stop occasionally—at the most awkward times—on their own initiative. Although they came into existence too recently to take part in ancient farce, in modern farce machines have assumed some of the tasks once entrusted to servants and slaves. Bergson noticed in his celebrated essay *Laughter* (1900) that some comic characters behaved mechanically. He could have been writing an annunciation of the film farce that would be unleashed a decade or so later, in which machines behaved humanly and took over the operative parts in incident after incident. The hardest-working machine performer is the automobile, which has become so pervasive that most contemporary films, farcical and other, are to some degree *about* cars.

Yet the artistic deployment in films and television shows of passenger vehicles is, well, pedestrian. One evening at about 11:30 I found that six channels out of seven in the New York area were replaying TV adventures that included fast car rides. The chariots and their trips had no dramatic significance either in their own right or for purposes of continuity or transition. They simply displayed people and metal and plastics moving rapidly from place to place, egged on by music hammered out *molto agitato*. In a good farce, on the other hand, a ride, like the machine that delivers it, has dramatic validity. It invigorates the motion in a motion picture. A farcical ride doesn't literally replicate travel at all. It is, to revert to that word, unreal. And by being so, it gives the machine, whether observed from inside or out, its opportunity to act, to be other-than-itself, to be poetic.

In farce, machines make trouble by opposing the human characters in any (or all) of four conventional ways. They break down when somebody depends on them to keep working; they go on working normally when it's important that they stop; they go at the wrong speed or go out of control; and they get destroyed. There are unnumbered variations possible on these four basic types of mechanical cussedness. But each of them corresponds dramaturgically to farcical events in which there is no machinery and the acting is done wholly by human beings and objects. For example, the nonstarting machine—a stalled car that coughs noisily but refuses to budge when the hero has to get away—can be compared to an escape staircase that leads to a dead end, or to a tree with no low branches that would give a handhold or foothold to a fugitive.

The machine that persists in working normally, such as a boat that plows into a pier when the captain gets into conversation with a pretty girl and forgets about the wheel—thereby fulfilling its regular function but in an inappropriate manner or at the wrong time—can be compared to people who act out of habit or inertia even when their circumstances change. At a given signal the members of a tug-of-war team pull hard, even though their opponents have just laid down the other end of the rope and are discussing strategy. A guest in a reception line, expecting to kiss the hostess, offers his lips and closes his eyes while the chihuahua she is holding licks his face. Sometimes it is not normal behavior that is machinelike. A disguise will be taken at face value. A borrowed cleryman's garb compels the wearer to lead a congregation in prayer and possibly to go on to improvise a sermon. In *Some Like It Hot*, Jack Lemmon in drag attracts a male admirer. Rosalind in *As You Like It*, pretending to be the youth Ganymede, finds that a shepherdess has fallen madly in love with her. (Is it coincidence that these two dissimilar works with similar titles both deal with transvestism?)

Of the third type of complication, the machine that goes out of control, a treasured example is the laborsaving gadget for feeding workers on the job in *Modern Times* (1935). It presents Chaplin with a corncob and a plate of soup, and holds his head in place while the cob turns sedately on its spindle and the plate rocks gently toward and away from his mouth. But then the machine speeds up until, like an electric belt sander going all out, it furiously buffs Charlie's lips and nose and hurls hot soup at him. This insane acceleration is reminiscent of a person who, for one reason or another—rage, maybe, or haste, or an urge or obsessive ambition—goes berserk. The Old Man and the Old Woman in Ionesco's *The Chairs* (1952) do this as they rush back and forth, faster and faster, through seven doors, bringing chairs onstage until they have left themselves no room to stand.

Machines, then, have made their incursions into the acting previously taken on by human beings and objects. But when we come to the fourth type of mechanical performance, the destruction of a machine, we notice a difference. Machines in farce are destructible; people in farces are not. Objects are also destructible; the history of farce is littered with torn paper, chairs broken over heads, shattered bottles, plates, and glasses, walls that have keeled over. But the destruction of a machine seems more awesome than that of an object. Its end is a kind of death. As wreckage it has lost its coordination, which is what made possible its animation. By losing its animation (its *anima*—literally its soul) it has lost its life.

Yet why, at such a moment of virtual death—a devastating car smash, for instance—do we laugh so freely? In part, that laughter may be a release for us, a childish glee; we have witnessed wanton demolition, but we have not ourselves been responsible for the act of destruction and we will not be penalized for it. But the laughter may also bubble up because of an unconscious realization, a sense of relief, that a human being has not perished. No legal murder took place. The machine died as a farcical substitute, as a sacrifice, for a person or people.

Machines are becoming more sophisticated, more "human" all the time. In the near future, farce writers will face the dilemma of whether to treat their androids and other anthropomorphic inventions as machines that can be destroyed for entertainment or as people who are indestructible and must, in the tradition of farce, be spared.[6]

---

[6] In nonfarcical works people often die wholesale. The authors of these works avoid the dilemma accordingly by making their androids heroes or villains. They can put an android on the good team, in which case it will be spared, or on the bad team, in which case it will

In and Out

These, then, are some of the ingredients of farce's unreality: objects and machines that not only play roles but change character; incapacitated human beings whose behavior sometimes verges on the spastic (Harry Langdon's, Stan Laurel's, Lou Costello's); activity conducted at stepped-up speeds. A further ingredient is the shaky environment. Farce unrolls in settings that keep the characters feeling unsteady. Their lives—as much of them as we see—add up to a series of surprises and shocks. Géronte is hardly back on land, in Naples, and trying to absorb the distressing news about his son's marriage, when he learns that mysterious swordsmen are after him.

The conventional device for creating farcical instability is a profusion of stage entrances and exits, swiftly executed. The cast onstage keeps changing. If the setting is an interior, it has doors and windows on all sides, and if it has windows they will be used to let in people, and not just light, sometimes without being opened. The drawing rooms of nineteenth-century French farces went so far in providing access to and from the stage that some of the sets appear to have more of their surfaces devoted to window and door frames than to walls, floors, and ceiling combined. But these plays were seldom content with means of entry and egress that were visible. They boasted, in addition, secret doors and passageways, sliding panels, nooks behind draperies and screens, and sundry other recesses, from wardrobes to small, tight closets. In Georges Feydeau's *A Flea in Her Ear* (1907), a Murphy bed closes into its wall, taking with it into very crowded quarters a pair of strangers of opposite sexes who will later be disgorged, stretched out and flattened on the bed, to their own and other people's chagrin.

Outdoor scenes in farce also are marked by human decor that is

---

be punished. Alternatively, villainous androids can be weaned away from evil by an adjustment of their controls. Some precedents here in nonfarcical films are 1) the computer Hal, a villain, in *2001: A Space Odyssey* (1968), who has his memory banks unplugged; 2) the androids C-3PO and R2D2 in *Star Wars* (1977), good "guys" who are kept "alive"; and 3) two early ancestors of the movie android, the female robot in Fritz Lang's *Metropolis* (1926) and the monster, memorably portrayed by Boris Karloff, in James Whale's *Frankenstein* (1931); both these menaces were destroyed; the monster won no reprieve for having behaved affably to a small child.

in flux. Exits and entrances are rife and unexpected. In *The Rope* by Plautus, two courtesans profane a shrine by taking refuge inside it from a pimp. In *The Navigator* (1924), Buster Keaton emerges from the sea onto a beach wearing a diver's gear; he puts the fear of a god into a tribe of island warriors. In the same film, as Buster and Kathryn McGuire are drowning, a trapdoor opens in the ocean and provides an escape hatch for them; it's the conning tower of a submarine. In *The Idle Class* (1921), Charlie Chaplin baffles a cop by dodging into and out of a clump of dense bushes. Géronte, strictly speaking, never leaves the scene with Scapin, yet he does disappear and reappear; the neck of the sack serves as an exit and entrance. Scapin summons and gets rid of imaginary swordsmen by imitating them; we might say that his mouth too is a two-way entrance and exit.

As the cast onstage keeps changing, so does the stage environment itself. Once Géronte has entered the sack, the street is no longer a place in his hometown where he can stop for a casual chat with a servant but a dangerous alley trodden by foreign killers. Farce's environments are made up of a seductive world of promises and a malign world of traps. These are not opposites or alternatives; they are obverse views, like contrasting scenes on a stage turntable. Just as an object can seem helpful and prove harmful, so the congenial environment can abruptly dissolve into a place of menace—or, as often happens at the end, the menace resolves into a scene of sunshine. The nightmare blows away. Géronte, after all, is a master, not a victim, and Scapin is a servant, not an oppressor. The world looks and feels real again. Naples has turned back into a civilized place, a known quantity; it's no longer a dreamscape of shifting images and people. As it happens, in *Les Fourberies de Scapin* a number of other short scenes must elapse before normality is fully restored. But when it comes, normality in farce seems abnormal, and the stage quickly goes dark.

THREE

DIONYSOS AT LARGE

The god Dionysos has come out of the east, down from the mountains of Asia and into Greece. For the starting point of his campaign to lay hold of the Greek soul he selects the city of Thebes. The former Theban ruler, old Cadmus, is his grandfather, parent of his earthly mother, Semele; and the present king of Thebes, in whose favor Cadmus abdicated, is young Pentheus, the god's cousin. But far from offering nepotic privileges to his mortal relatives or to the place of his birth, Dionysos is going to make a punishing example of this city.

Semele's sisters and other Thebans had mocked her when she was carrying Dionysos and said she'd been impregnated by Zeus. She had called on Zeus for proof, and either as a dubious sign of his love or as a gesture to appease his jealous wife, he had sent down a bolt of lightning to consume her, snatched the unborn Dionysos from her womb, and protected it until term by sewing it into his thigh.

Now, as Dionysos approaches, the new king, Pentheus, a puritanical, pragmatic, and quick-tempered youth of about sixteen, refuses to recognize his cousin—he addresses him as "Stranger" —and won't concede Dionysos' claim to divine powers. He treats him as a pretender, if not a usurper; puts him in chains; cuts off his curly hair; and orders him locked up.

Pentheus' skepticism isn't difficult to understand. Dionysos doesn't correspond to anyone's vision of a god on earth. "He is of soft, even effeminate, appearance. His face is beardless; he is dressed in a fawn-skin and carries a thyrsus [a stalk of fennel tipped

35

with ivy leaves]. On his head he wears a wreath of ivy, and his long blond curls ripple down over his shoulders [even after Pentheus has snipped them]. . . . He wears a smiling mask." And then, his supporters the Bacchae, a horde of wild, long-haired Asian women, hardly seem like the votaries of a new religion.

But ominous things happen. The women of Thebes, led by Semele's three sisters, the very ones who'd taunted her—Autonoë, Ino, and Agave—run off to join the Bacchae in an initiation ceremony on the slopes of Mount Cithaeron, nearby. Cadmus and the blind, ancient seer Teiresias get themselves up in Dionysian paraphernalia to show their devotion to the new religion. The tomb of Semele gives off smoke as if just struck by Zeus' lightning bolt. The palace of Pentheus, where Dionysos is held prisoner, collapses, his chains fall away, and the god walks out of the ruins unscathed. A herdsman from the mountainside reports that the Bacchae wrought miracles there out of their kinship with nature. They caused water, milk, and wine to spring from the earth; they suckled baby deer and wolves; they brushed lethal snakes against their cheeks and caressed them. But when provoked by the Theban herdsmen, the Bacchae turned into creatures with superhuman strength. They tore and clawed the herdsmen's animals to pieces, huge bulls included; could not be injured when stabbed with spears; wounded the herdsmen by touching them with their sprigs, the thyrsi; and finally wiped out the mountain settlements where the herdsmen lived. All this destruction is a portent of what will happen to Pentheus for resisting the encroachment of the new religion.

But Pentheus continues to defy the god and make light of the danger signals. Thereupon Dionysos promises to let him witness for himself the secret rites of the Bacchae. Pentheus becomes suddenly and inexplicably submissive, as though enchanted. He wants to see the rites. He lets himself be dressed in women's clothing and directed to a tree overlooking the Bacchic ceremony. During their peaceful rites the women spot Pentheus in the tree, as the god meant them to do. Once again turning ferocious, they pull the lofty tree out of the earth and, urged on by one of the sisters, Agave, Pentheus' mother, rip him limb from limb, scattering the flesh and blood. In her frenzied state, Agave doesn't know her son. She takes him for a lion cub and proudly carries his head back to Thebes, where she presents it to Cadmus, saying, "You are blest, Father, / by this great deed I have done." Not until later does she emerge from her trance, to be stricken by the savage irony of her "great deed."[1]

In Euripides' posthumous play *The Bacchae* (406 B.C.), which is set at the dawn of Greek religion, Dionysos has returned to Thebes to claim a sort of patrimony as he seeks recruits for his religious cult. What does this religion entail? Not the exclusive worship of the one god—to require this would be to put himself at odds with the Olympian establishment, including his father, Zeus, and his formidable step-siblings, Apollo, Artemis, and Aphrodite. Dionysos at this time has already gone through enough misadventures from having earned the enmity of Hera, the first lady of Olympus, by simply being born. The assorted myths that add up to a record of his earlier years tell of one escape after another from her wrath. Only because of the protection of Zeus does he still live at all: he's been killed and revived at least once. No, what Dionysos wants is his entitlement to a place in the Olympian pantheon, his due share of tribute from humanity for the boons he has conferred on it: wine, the sole "medicine for misery," and fertility—of both the soil and the loins. Later, in the sixth century B.C., he will also become "the patron of a new art, the art of the theater," when, according to E. R. Dodds, he puts on a mask: "the theatrical use of the mask presumably grew out of its magical use"; and "the new god of the theater . . . had long been the god of the masquerade."[2] The first Greek theater, the Theater of Dionysos, still exists, though in a form modified by the Romans and ravaged by history and tourism, at the foot of the Acropolis in Athens; and his altar had a prominent place in every theater built during the sixth and fifth centuries before Christ.

Wine and the pleasures (and perils) of intoxication, with its lib-

---

[1] The quotations above are from William Arrowsmith's translation of *The Bacchae* in *Euripides*, Vol. 5 of *The Complete Greek Tragedies* edited by David Grene and Richmond Lattimore (Chicago: University of Chicago Press, 1959).

[2] *The Greeks and the Irrational* (Boston: Beacon Press, 1957; paperback edition, Berkeley and Los Angeles, Calif.: University of California Press, 1968), p. 94, fn. 82. Professor Dodds's remark is a footnote to his chapter "The Blessings of Madness," pp. 64–101. See also Appendix I, "Maenadism," pp. 270–82, and Dodds's magnificent introduction to his edition of *Euripides' Bacchae* (New York: Oxford University Press, 1944).

eration of the spirit; fertility, the gratitude for which he shares with Cybele, otherwise known as Rhea, the earth mother; and the theater, incorporating its sister arts music and dance and their varied derivatives in our own time: these are only three of the godsends of Dionysos. For he has other gifts drawn from his other attributes, as well as other names (Bacchus, Iacchos, Bromios, Zagreus, Nyctelios). The deity we call Dionysos is actually a composite of mythical figures, male and female, who migrated to Greece from Asia Minor and the Mediterranean basin, each with his or her own biography. Since to the Greeks the drinking of wine symbolized the drinking of Dionysos' blood, there is a link between Christian and Dionysian myths, too.

Dionysos not only serves as the patron god of the theater: he is also taken to be the theater's inspiration. The tragedies of Aeschylus, Sophocles, Euripides, and other fifth-century-B.C. playwrights possibly represent a development of rituals held in honor of the god a century or more earlier. Euripides, whose *Bacchae* is the only tragedy extant that has Dionysos among its characters, introduces into the play Dionysian rituals enacted by the chorus. But scholars like Gilbert Murray, F. M. Cornford, Jane Harrison, and A. W. Pickard-Cambridge have persuasively related the Dionysian rituals equally to the Old Comedy of Aristophanes, one of the prime sources of farce, and of his contemporaries. Dionysos has the leading part, as a buffoon, in Aristophanes' *The Frogs* (see Chapter 5), his only role in ancient drama other than the one in *The Bacchae.*

A number of features of *The Bacchae* are worth noticing. First, it is named after the chorus (not an unusual practice in Greek drama) and other celebrants, not after the god or Pentheus; that chorus, like the celebrants on Mount Cithaeron, consists of women. Second, those women abandon themselves to peaceful impulses that are released by the wine and their ritual—peaceful, that is, until the celebrants are antagonized. Third, the four principal male characters—two young, two old—practice transvestism: Dionysos has an effeminate appearance and costume; Pentheus dons a woman's garb in order to spy on the bacchanalia; and Teiresias and Cadmus also dress like women to affirm their devotion to the god. Fourth, the dismemberment (or *sparagmos*) of Pentheus suggests a parallel to an episode in the life of Dionysos when he was torn apart by the Titans, who acted on orders from Hera, and then made whole again by Zeus.

These observations have some bearing on the nature of farce:

• The women in farces, from Aristophanes to Chekhov, have roles that make them less the prisoners of tradition or convention than the men are.

• The state of release from everyday behavior and reactions, analogous to a trance or spell, pervades farces; outright inebriation from wine or spirits recurs with farcical results in Aristophanes, Molière, Feydeau, Chaplin, and innumerable recent films and plays.

• Men in drag are a staple of farce—*Charley's Aunt, Some Like It Hot,* music-hall and vaudeville acts (Milton Berle!), Sennett shorts galore, Fatty Arbuckle, English pantomime, Benny Hill, *Monty Python's Flying Circus.*[3]

• The unequal contest between Pentheus and Dionysos for control of Thebes and her citizens ends predictably enough with victory for the god. But not content with being the victor, the god also absorbs his victim, his opposite. The two began as contrasts —the excitable, opinionated warrior versus the soft-spoken, relaxed sybarite. Pentheus then moves physically toward his opponent after he puts on the Dionysian outfit, comes to resemble his cousin outwardly, and says he wants to watch the ritual. His later rending at the hands of Agave and the other Bacchae makes him an understudy for Dionysos. Dionysos runs the show; Pentheus never rises to a more exalted state than being a Peeping Tom; but he dies in place of the god. For Dionysos, as a god of fertility, is ritually torn to bits and consumed every spring so that his followers may ingest his characteristics. Not literally, of course: a corn-spirit

---

[3] Women sometimes take offense at effeminate male acting, considering themselves ridiculed, but needlessly, I think. Farce means to puncture social pretensions; and just as drunkenness mocks formal poise, so men in drag mock the posturings of masculinity, fixing our attention not so much on women's flouncing as on male gawkiness. Women in men's garb, on the other hand, almost never come across as farcical. (Perhaps it's no more than coincidence, but the bravest, most heroic characters in Greek tragedy are all women: Iphigenia, Hecuba, Cassandra, Antigone, two Electras, Andromache, Medea, Alcestis, Macaria. In most of the plays of Ibsen and Shaw the women are bolder than the men; and when the men perform bold deeds, they're often egged on by female visionaries.) The women in Shakespeare's plays who impersonate men were surely more farcical in the original productions, when the roles were undertaken by young men playing women playing men, than they appear today.

—a live horse or bull—is sacrificed in effigy. Pentheus, the human corn-spirit, through his ordeal and death, dies to spare Dionysos, who is reborn again and again without ever dying. (Christ "dies" similarly in every performance of the Oberammergau Passion Play, much as He "died" every spring during the Medieval cycle plays that dramatized His Passion.) Now, Dionysos has not passed as a character into farces, except in the one play, *The Frogs*. However, the indestructible characters in farces, Dionysos' substitutes or understudies, might be said to mimic his born-again act as they emerge humiliated and bruised—but whole—from their terrible batterings and collisions.

• Dionysos is no modern, sweet-talking evangelist. He doesn't offer the Thebans the option of joining; he *demands* that they worship him, that they enjoy themselves or else. And because Zeus went to much trouble to create and preserve this illegitimate son, the monarch of the gods must have approved in advance the tenets of Dionysianism. In other words, the Greeks themselves, who had gradually created and preserved the figure of Zeus, believed that for the sake of their spiritual well-being Dionysian worship was not merely advisable or desirable, but necessary.

Laughing

Theories of comedy abound and intertwine with theories of laughter. Many of them also deal—directly, incidentally, inadvertently, or inadequately—with farce too, although for the most part they subsume it under comedy, rather than treating it as a genre in its own right.[4] Daniel C. Gerould, a playwright, translator, teacher, and scholar of high repute, recently lent me the bibliography of comedy he has compiled. It consists of seventeen separate categories which list, altogether, over four hundred writings— books, dissertations, articles, essays, anthologies, introductions, biographies, reference works, memoirs, and reflections: Bibliogra-

---

[4] I must, however, single out a book that may subordinate farce to comedy, but does so with discretion and wit, and gives farce its due: Maurice Charney's *Comedy High and Low: An Introduction to the Experience of Comedy* (New York: Oxford University Press, 1978). Professor Charney has also edited an issue of *New York Literary Forum* entitled *Comedy: New Perspectives* (New York, 1978), an excellent collection, much of which is enlightening about farce.

phies; General Studies and Collections; Classical Theories and Criticism; Christian Theories and Criticism; Psychological Theories and Criticism; the Grotesque; Fools and the Praise of Folly; Marxist and Soviet Theory and Criticism; Myth; Nonsense, Surrealism and the Absurd (Tragic Farce and Black Humor); Comedy of Manners; Eighteenth-Century Positive Theories; English Comedy; Shaw; Nineteenth Century (Feydeau and French Comedy); Neil Simon and American Comedy; Film Comedy. The compilation is far from exhaustive. Dr. Gerould has drawn it up as a guide for Ph.D. candidates in theater. A specialist in any of the seventeen categories could easily quadruple or quintuple the number of entries there, even without adding the thousands of names of plays, poems, novels, films, and other "creative" documents on which the critical theories and histories are based.

As it is, the compilation offers more than four hundred analyses and explanations of what makes us laugh, and why. There are difficulties, though, in regarding laughs as being the objective of comedy or of farce:

1. We may each laugh more or less or not at all at the same sketch, play, film, joke, verse, song, pratfall, or chance remark.

2. When we sit through a play, film, or show for the second or the third time we're likely to laugh either more or less, and possibly in new places as we catch amusing lines or bits of business we missed the first time around, or we may find corny, heavy-handed, or limp something that broke us up before. To put it formally: the amount, intensity, and distribution of one person's laughter can vary from viewing to viewing.

3. Our merriment may depend on the time of day, the company we're in, the setting, our readiness (or openness), the weather, our state of health, matrimony, parenthood, the upholstery, the people sitting nearby, and other given circumstances.

4. Different audiences, as distinguished from individuals, laugh differently at the same farce on different nights, as every farceur realizes. Previews and out-of-town tryouts are of only limited help in telling a producer whether he has a winner, a dud, or a package of mystery.

5. Canned laughter fed onto the sound track of a television show always sounds inordinately generous. Either the producers have overestimated the laughs from actual audiences or they hope

the canned laughter will prove contagious. Now, it often happens that hesitant laughers are warmed up by the hearty laughers, but it also happens that spectators who don't find the show as funny as the hearty laughers do or the canned laughers are supposed to are apt to become irritated by what they consider overreacting. They frown and sit more firmly on their hands. They groan, when they would otherwise have maintained a forgiving silence.

6. Performers play differently before audiences that laugh differently. Guffaws and shrieks, waves, *gales* of laughter may excite the performers into a hysteria of funniness. Through this mutual feedback, or "firestorm" effect, the farce grows funnier yet and the audience laughs itself into convulsions. A cool audience usually earns only a tepid performance.

7. No two performers will manage a single gag or a brief activity, let alone an entire work, identically. Imagine Stan Laurel substituting for Fatty Arbuckle or Woody Allen understudying W. C. Fields. Nor will any two casts identically manage a show. The laugh patterns at a summer-stock revival of a Neil Simon or a Thornton Wilder may hardly resemble those of the original production.

To sum up the difficulties: These and other variables of response and performance don't depend on anything intrinsic in the work being enacted. Between the objectives of the performer and the objectives of the writer there exists a hiatus. Actors and directors of farce rate themselves successful roughly in proportion to the laughter they garner; the more abundant the mirth—whether measured by a meter or by trained ears—the better the material "works." When playwrights and novelists bother to justify their efforts, they put forward motives that are broadly social; their writings have satirical and critical substance, are humble attempts to affect—or intrepid attempts to reshape—the thinking and manners of society. Preston Sturges, a social critic and satirist of a high order, gives the hero of *Sullivan's Travels*, a movie director, the film's last words: "There's a lot to be said for making people laugh. . . . That's all some people have. It isn't much, but it's better than nothing in this cockeyed caravan." A certain disenchantment overtakes even this brief declaration, which begins by suggesting that "there's a lot to be said," and concludes that laughter "isn't much," only "better than nothing." The visuals that accompany these closing lines recapitulate laughing faces seen earlier in the film, but these give way to an image of the director's face, superimposed and bemused.

I contend, simply as a matter of observation, that laughter is not the motive behind farce, only its principal by-product.

Good Health

A by-product can have considerable value. Laughter does us good, doesn't it? When we laugh, we love life. Loving life, we feel better. A laughing jag that physically depletes us and brings tears seems to refresh us, although some people prefer a crying jag. The words "I laughed myself sick" or "I could have died laughing" invoke fond nostalgia. Many pop numbers recommend laughing as an antidote to the blues, along with whistling a happy tune, singing a song (out loud and strong), and directing our feet to the sunny side of the street. Laughing may cure some of what ails us. As therapy, it gets high marks from psychologists and psychiatrists; they award the highest marks of all for learning to laugh at our own woes and worries, to differentiate *them* from *us*. Laughter is often said to be a safety valve. We laugh away fears, envy, guilt, antagonisms, and other noxious matter accumulated in the psyche. Harvey Mindess, a teacher and clinical psychologist, writes about laughter as a means of "coping." It can help us free ourselves from conformity, the sometimes absurd dictates of morality, inferiority, the tyranny of reason, the deceptions of language, naiveté, redundancy, seriousness, and egotism. This is a formidable array of things to get away from, if only sporadically.[5]

Laughing alone at a book or magazine article or a comedian on television is not quite the same as laughing in a theater. We savor a special satisfaction when we share a laugh with others, perhaps because their laughter in concert with ours confirms our taste and fosters sensations of brotherhood and sisterhood. When we laugh, singly or collectively, we shake off our inhibitions and conventional courtesies. We vent dislike for the figures, groups, institu-

---

[5] *Laughter and Liberation* by Harvey Mindess (Los Angeles, Calif.: Nash Publishing, second edition, 1978). Dr. Mindess illustrates at least some of the benefits of developing a sense of humor about oneself when he relates some neatly turned jokes about psychiatry and psychiatrists.

tions, thoughts, actions, words that are being ridiculed. Laughter may be enjoyable precisely because it lets us, as audiences, off the hook; it relieves us of the obligation to do anything about people and things we dislike. A Marxist might say that as a safety valve, laughing sanctions unjust situations by letting them persist. Like mild reforms, which ease pressures for radical change by making oppressive conditions in a society slightly less unacceptable, laughter breeds toleration. But in Eastern Europe, where the authorities pay devout lip service to Marx and in practice pervert all nineteenth-century ideals of socialism, playwrights and their collaborators have been driven into paroxysms of ingenuity to disguise the true objects of their farces. They must transpose any semblance of realism into allegory, fable, or historical parallel, sometimes with results that are all the more subversive for being partly secretive. The authorities would have less to worry about if they allowed free play to realistic farces. The population would laugh itself into toleration.

As farces strengthen dislike and then dispel it through laughter, they may make individual spectators feel better; but if social criticism is salutary, farces don't particularly contribute to the health of the community. Farces that make us laugh more than comedies do may endanger the current social framework less by letting more resentment melt into laughs and thin air. A satirical farce that makes an audience rock with laughter defeats one of its author's purposes. Should farcical writers and actors, then, sacrifice laughs? Doing that really goes against the grain. If it's intoxicating for audiences to laugh at officials and people a few rungs up the social ladder, to feel free and irresponsible like Bacchae, it's also intoxicating for artists to put an audience *into* that condition of intoxication. Only, in the case of the artists the intoxication proceeds not from a sense of enchanted ecstasy but from a sense of power. We refer to that power when we say that a play or performer "holds" an audience, when a comic "has them eating out of his hand." But another power, a competing power, emanates from farces: the power of revelation. In the twentieth century, more and more farce writers have exerted this power in preference to the other one. Tragifarces, grotesque farces, and other recent half-breeds of drama and film move right away from happy, laugh-drenched, stabilizing and reassuring endings. They conclude by unsettling the audience. They leave it dismayed, bewildered, or shocked. No outlet. No relief. We are finally stung, not mollified, by Vian's *The Knacker's ABC* and *The Empire Builders*; Ionesco's *Jacques, The Chairs,* and *The Lesson*; Simpson's *One Way Pendulum*; Pinter's *The Birthday Party* and *The Homecoming*; and Mro-żek's *Tango,* to seize on a few examples. The last act doesn't blithely paper over cracks in the universe pointed out by the previous acts. Not that the downbeat ending belongs exclusively to the twentieth century. It was anticipated by such isolated farces as Kleist's *The Broken Jug* (1801), Grabbe's *Jest, Satire, Irony, and Deeper Significance* (1822), Gogol's *The Inspector General* (1835), and much earlier still by Molière's *George Dandin* (1668). But are these plays farces? Predominantly, yes; their mingling of farce and grimness goes to prove that their authors are somehow alert to the twentieth century, as well as to the nineteenth or seventeenth.

If an author wants to teach, inform, or alert his audiences, why does he pick farce as a genre over comedy? One reason may be that farce is more bitter, more cruel, more downright unfair. The dislike that farce arouses has stronger components of violence and contempt. Therefore, it more tellingly reflects and echoes the corruption, treachery, hypocrisy, brutality, and injustices of life. Or not so much reflects and echoes as refracts and distorts. For farce doesn't try to reproduce life; it selects, manipulates, exaggerates. But is it possible to exaggerate the parade of calamities that reaches us in the newspapers every morning and afternoon and on the TV set every evening and on the radio every twenty-two minutes?

Equalizing Impulses

If theater, film, and television drama did nothing but acquaint us with the evils of life without processing them through art—if, that is, all drama were documentary—it would have the same effects on us as the news does. Most of us already feel impotent in the face of corporate profiteering, governmental abuses, and other institutional activities within and outside the letter of the law. A tiny number of us are driven into the obsessiveness of revolutionaries. To some writers farce appears needlessly irrational; yet farce's irrationalities cannot begin to match those of life. But they can make us laugh, and if they don't they're not farcical: farce and laughter are inseparable. In some farces laughter sweetens the pill; in others the pill is entirely sugar, or maybe saccharin. Authors of the more durable farces show us the difference.

As a by-product, our laughter may signify contempt for the victims of farcical events. But what is the *product?* Farce's overturning of decorum, the order of things, satisfies an unspoken, unwritten pact between us and the farceur. His work will play up to our democratic impulses; it will fulfill our desires for political and social leveling. Farce takes the smugly successful and eminent down a few pegs. We laugh when a campaigning politico falls off his platform. Or when a warrior trips on his sword. Or when a dowager gets a pie in the eye and custard drips onto her décolletage and diamonds. We enjoy equally watching farce elevate the humble, servants and slaves outwit their masters. The fool in all his guises, from clown and jester to Harlequin and village idiot, delights us when he beats out the unbeatable opposition.[6] Most of the film clowns of the Twenties give us variants of the fool. Ben Turpin, Harold Lloyd, Buster Keaton, Harry Langdon, and, preeminently, Charlie Chaplin set the pattern in movies for the timid, incompetent, or otherwise outclassed boob who trades on our sympathy for the underdog and then dips into some unsuspected reservoir and pulls a reversal, overpowering giants singlehanded, thrashing criminals, running harder, swimming faster, leaping farther, climbing higher than we or he had any right to expect, steering crazy buses and streetcars, taming ferocious animals, bringing obstreperous boats and trains and planes to a halt, and finally displaying the unattainable heroine stuck on his arm like a badge.

Scheming servants like Scapin and other *zanni* come out of a different tradition from the fool's, that of the trickster, as Paul Radin calls him, although the two have at times become confused in certain cultures.[7] Radin's trickster derives from the myths of

---

[6] Enid Welsford's *The Fool: His Social and Literary History* (London, 1935; reprinted, Garden City, N.Y.: Doubleday Anchor, 1961) is as nearly a full and definitive account as anyone could wish for.

[7] Radin writes: "The Trickster myth is found in clearly recognizable form among the simplest aboriginal tribes and among the complex. We encounter it among the ancient Greeks, the Chinese, the Japanese, and in the Semitic world. Many of the Trickster's traits were perpetuated in the figure of the medieval jester, and have survived right up to the present day in the Punch-and-Judy plays and in the clown . . ." *The Trickster* (London: Routledge

various North American Indian tribes: the Winnebago, the Assin-
iboine, the Tlingit, and the Wakdjunkaga, principally. He's part
animal, part supernatural being, a spirit of mischief like Puck,
Mercury, or Hermes, who can alter his appearance as deftly as
Yeats's "shape-changers." Sometimes the trickster plays tricks—on
animals as well as people—and sometimes the tricks are played on
him. Whichever the case, he appeals to us because he lives by no
rules and takes wicked delight in breaking the rules of others. He
too is a leveler.

But farce goes a step further. Before the onslaught of the farcical
events, characters are at the mercy of the inanimate world, those
malign objects everywhere that wait for the most propitious—the
most devastating—moment to spring to life. In *The Blacksmith*,
which takes place at a time when the old smithy was in the process
of becoming the repair garage, Keaton has removed the motor
from a jalopy and suspended it on a pulley. Every time he unthink-
ingly pushes the hanging motor aside, it crashes like a wrecker's
ball into another car. This is a handsome, expensive, white landau
owned by a haughty, impatient customer and waiting nearby for
an unnecessary wash. The landau is ruined not by Buster, who is
a mere agent of the forces of destruction, but by the jalopy which
resents the landau's upper-class pretensions and pleases the audience by demolishing a fellow machine.

In *John Bull's Other Island*, Broadbent, the rich English archi-
tect on whom the local Irish folk look with suspicion, becomes
suddenly acceptable to them after he undergoes his ordeal in the
car with the unfortunate pig. He has been brought unarguably
down to their level—to below it, because any of the natives of
Rosscullen could have handled the pig more adroitly. Now they
choose Broadbent to represent them in the British Parliament.
Admittedly, he has wealth and connections. But he had them
before. It's the incident with the pig that clinches Broadbent's
nomination. As if to make this clear, Shaw has one of the Irish-

---

& Kegan Paul, 1956), p. ix. In an extraordinarily suggestive afterword to Radin's book,
C. G. Jung writes: "The so-called civilized man has forgotten the trickster. He remembers
him only figuratively and metaphorically, when, irritated by his own ineptitude, he speaks
of fate playing tricks on him or of things being bewitched. He never suspects that his own
hidden and apparently harmless shadow has qualities whose dangerousness exceeds his
wildest dreams. . . ."

men, Doran, who recounted the pig story, raise three cheers for "Tom Broadbent, the future member for Rosscullen." Immediately, Doran congratulates Broadbent personally and adds, "May you never regret the day you wint dhriving wid Haffigan's pig!"

The gory ceremony in *The Bacchae* is both a literal and a figurative act of lowering or leveling. When Pentheus went to Mount Cithaeron, Dionysos "worked a miracle. / Reaching for the highest branch of a great fir, / he bent it down, down, down to the dark earth . . . / Then he seated Pentheus at the highest tip / and with his hands let the trunk rise straightly up, / slowly and gently, lest it throw its rider. / And the tree rose, towering to heaven. . . ." When "every effort failed" to uproot the fir with branches torn from an oak tree, Agave gave the order and "thousands of hands / tore the fir tree from the earth, and down, down / from his high perch fell Pentheus, tumbling / to the ground, sobbing and screaming as he fell, / for he knew his end was near. . . ."[8] Pentheus the king opposes the god's will, which is the will of the people of Thebes. He is raised to the highest tip of the fir and looks down on the Bacchae, godlike but in his farcical drag costume, before they dash him "down, down" to the ground with their maniacal strength.

---

[8] Arrowsmith translation, *op. cit.*, lines 1063–65, 1070–73, 1109–13.

◆

FOUR

THE SHADOWY EDGES
OF FARCE

A turbulent river dashes Buster Keaton over rapids and through white water toward a sheer drop. He is tied to a log. At the edge of the waterfall his log catches on a rock. He plunges over, but the rope and the trapped log yank him back. He bobs like a cork in the downpour.

Buster snaps into action. He goes hand over hand up the rope, hooks his heels over the log, scrambles on top of it, and tries to unfasten the rope. Water has tightened the knot. It won't give. He wants to cut the rope, but has no blade. The log now starts to ease itself away from the rock. Buster glimpses a notch in the cliff—a ledge—at the side of the falls. He swings across to it on the rope, which is still tied to the log. When the log breaks loose it will pull him off the ledge. Before he has time to deal with the prospect, he spots Natalie Talmadge floating downstream. The current has already swept her to within several yards of the fall. He makes a futile gesture: Get back! Then he dives boldly into empty air at the literal end of his tether. In one pendulumlike motion he scoops her into his arms with perfect synchronization as she goes over, and brings her back with him to the ledge. Within seconds the log finally comes free. It should drag Buster with it. But his acrobatics have scraped the rope back and forth across the rock's abrasive edge until, as the log plunges over, the rope parts, leaving Buster safe but drenched, high but not dry, on the cliff face.

Is this sequence from *Our Hospitality* (1923) farce? Or melodrama? The supporting cast—a log, a rope, a rock, a cliff ledge, and a limp heroine—inanimate objects all—plus the river and waterfall, two forces of nature, might persuade us that we are watching farce, as do the presence and virtuosity of Keaton, as well as his signal to Natalie to go back (by reversing the current, maybe?). But what we are watching is not so much funny as almost intolerably tense. The laughter may be in our mouths, ready to break free, like the log. But so are our hearts.

On a battlefield in Shropshire, the Earl of Douglas, a ferocious Scottish rebel, has been searching for the king he wants to overthrow, Henry IV, and has finally caught up with him. They fight. The King is in danger of losing when his son, Prince Hal, heir to the throne, bursts onto the scene, engages Douglas, and drives him off. The King and the audience marvel at this. Hal seemed like a playboy who divided his waking hours between escapades and taverns, hanging out with a bunch of commoners led by that fat braggart of a knight, that "knotty-pated fool," that "whoreson, obscene, greasy tallow-catch," that "huge bombard of sack, that stuff'd cloak-bag of guts," Sir John Falstaff. In a soliloquy much earlier, Hal has resolved to put Falstaff and his scapegrace past behind him, and to live up to his rank and his destiny so that, in a subsequent play, he might become a warrior-hero, England's salvation, Henry V. But the King did not overhear the soliloquy and is now overjoyed, not merely at being rescued from Douglas but also in finding that the Prince has redeemed himself.

Hal's reformation, however, has only begun. As the King leaves, elated, another rebel, far more formidable than the Earl of Douglas, enters the scene. This is Harry Percy of Northumberland, nicknamed Hotspur because of his fierce temper and prowess as a fighter. After exchanging threats, he and Hal square off; their verbal duel gives way to the real thing. Battling furiously they move out of sight, but not before Falstaff has seen them and shouted encouragement to Hal. The plump old knight has been roaming the battlefield looking for a hideout. Events move swiftly. The Earl of Douglas returns, still stalking the King. He comes upon Falstaff, whom he attacks and who collapses on the spot, as if mortally wounded. Exit Douglas, just as Hotspur and Hal, still dueling, reenter the scene. After several attacks and retreats, Hal delivers the telling thrust. Hotspur falls. As he dies, he laments the loss of "those proud titles thou hast won of me. / They wound my thoughts worse than thy sword my flesh." Death doesn't give Hotspur time to finish the speech, but Hal completes his last sentence and pays handsome tribute to him.

This is a moment of intense sadness, very close to tragedy. Hotspur was a redoubtable, colorful man of honor who had genuine grievances against the King, whom he had helped to the throne. He had a tragic stature. Hal's father, on the other hand, has been a deceitful, selfish political climber. The good die, we feel; the wicked live on and thrive. The sadness sharpens when Hal notices Falstaff lying among the dead, his companion of many years. He wonders, "Could not all this flesh / Keep in a little life?"

Hal leaves the scene musing over the high cost in life of that day's "bloody fray." Falstaff promptly clambers to his feet, talking as always. He stabs the corpse of Hotspur in the thigh and gets the body over his shoulders. When Hal returns and is amazed to find him alive, he claims that Hotspur recovered. Both of them, he says, were only "down and out of breath." They rose and "fought a long hour by Shrewsbury clock. I'll take it upon my death," Falstaff goes on, "I gave him this wound in the thigh." How can Hal possibly believe that the old impostor outfought Hotspur? It stretches credulity that he managed to hoist the corpse onto his shoulders. But Hal lets Falstaff bear away the body in triumph, "if a lie will do thee grace."

This scene from the last act of *Henry IV, Part One* is one of the trickiest in Shakespeare, and in dramatic literature. It represents the play's triple climax: a threat to the King's life, followed by a threat to the life of the heir apparent, followed by a single combat that will determine the outcome of the Battle of Shrewsbury and the future of England. It is the one scene in which all four principals take part—the King, the Prince, Hotspur, and Falstaff. It marks Hal's renunciation of Falstaff, the false father, who lives for pleasure, in favor of the true father, the King, who lives for conquest. Further, Hal, who in his soliloquy said that he had been deliberately playing the prodigal son so as to make his transformation look more impressive ("My reformation, glittering o'er my fault, / Shall show more goodly and attract more eyes / Than that which hath no foil to set it off"), has now demonstrated his princely qualities, his royal worth, his fitness for the throne. He slays Hotspur, delivers a graceful eulogy for him, and in a magnanimous gesture allows Falstaff to take credit for the kill.

Into this high drama Shakespeare has scattered handfuls of broad comedy and farcical byplay. But not merely for relief. Falstaff has to be present during the battle; he is essential to the play's conclusion. As he stands with Hotspur's gratuitously mutilated corpse across his shoulders, he creates a stage image in which the playwright epitomizes the futility of war. To the same end, Shakespeare seems to have vitiated the seriousness of the battle sequence beforehand by giving Falstaff his celebrated speech on honor ("What is honor? A word. What is in that word honor? What is that honor? Air. A trim reckoning! Who hath it? He that died a' Wednesday. Doth he feel it? No. Doth he hear it? No. . . ."). The farce in this scene is an essential ingredient of the high drama, just as the melodrama in *Our Hospitality* is an integral part of Keaton's farce.

Farce, then, can animate other kinds of drama, and they can animate farce. It is even hard to find a play or film that belongs wholly to one of the four main formal genres, tragedy, comedy, melodrama, and farce. Thus, when we say that a work is a farce we mean that the farcical effects predominate. Its most vivid moments, its most forceful impressions are farcical, and these are what we remember it for. It may well contain moments that are purely tragic or melodramatic or comic, but they are secondary.

In that case, where can the territory of farce end and the other territories begin? Farce might be said to exist on the lunatic fringe of comedy and on the ludicrous fringes of tragedy and melodrama. The four continents could then be schematically subdivided into countries (the continent of farce would include such kingdoms, principalities, and provinces as adventure farce, bedroom or boudoir farce, "screwball movies" of the 1930s and 1940s, and farcical fantasies). Between the continents, and even between the countries on this undrawn map, would lie borderline areas that are artistic no-man's-land, taking their mixed characteristics from the territories they adjoin.

In order to visualize the *shifting* connections between the four genres we might better imagine them as shapes of more than two dimensions (preferably four), without fixed definition or domain

and never at rest, drifting together and apart, colliding and infring-
ing one on another, combining their individual qualities without
surrendering them. If melodrama were blue and farce yellow, a
collision that produced a farce with moments of melodrama would
be not green but yellow with blue added, and all the more
heightened, all the more strikingly yellow because of the contrasting blue.

Farce and Comedy

Although farce has its own personality and traits as a full-grown
genre, it is sometimes taken as just one more country in the continent of comedy. Over the centuries, comedy has spun off subspecies as prodigally as a spider plant drops spiders. Among the
subspecies identified and named so far are the three types distinguished during the Renaissance: comedy of manners, comedy of
intrigue, and comedy of character. To supplement these, we now
have in addition the comedy of ideas, comedy of humors, problem
comedy, situation comedy, domestic comedy, high and low comedy, romantic, sentimental (or tearful), and realistic comedy, burlesque, satire, and mime, as well as tragicomedy, which today is
generally considered a genre in itself. Critics in this last quarter of
the twentieth century like to coin their own terms, and so new
species spring up all the time.

In order to differentiate between farce and comedy, we should
start by looking at the distinction between wit and humor. Wit is
usually verbal, while humor is generally physical and visual. It's
true that most characters in comedy get their laughs from their
lines, while characters in farce generally get theirs from their antics. We may as well start with the lines—that is to say, wit.

A character is witty only if he is drawn as a wit. That is, he
throws off clever remarks. Wit can direct itself at individuals,
professions, institutions. The law, the military, medicine, businessmen, bureaucrats, politicians, and mothers-in-law have long
been favorites. A witty character may attack contemporary manners, or the whole world, or life itself. In *The Importance of Being
Earnest* (1896), Algernon says, "More than half of modern culture
depends on what one shouldn't read." His friend Jack counters
with ". . . I don't propose to discuss modern culture. It isn't the

sort of thing one should talk of in private." The ballerina Terry in *Limelight* (1952) says to the comedian Calvero, "I thought you hated the theater." He replies, "I do. I also hate the sight of blood. But it's in my veins." These are samples of verbal wit; they belong to comedy and are *intentionally* amusing.

In farce we laugh *at* the characters, not with them. We may be entertained by what they say, but they didn't mean to be entertaining. In Labiche's *Pots of Money* (1864), the farmer with the pickax (see Chapter 2) tries to coax his young son into marrying an old lady. She has an enormous dowry but only one eye. He says, "You see the same things with one eye that you see with two. It's not as if she's blind." This is verbal humor; it belongs to farce and is *unintentionally* amusing. But what about the borderline cases, which are legion? Take a famous remark made by Britannus in Shaw's *Caesar and Cleopatra* (1899): "Blue is the color worn by all Britons of good standing. In war we stain our bodies blue; so that though our enemies may strip us of our clothes and our lives, they cannot strip us of our respectability." This would seem to be verbal humor, since Britannus is a solemn figure and after he says that we laugh *at* him. But I would classify it as partly witty too, because it is meant to make us laugh at modern Britons in Shaw's turn-of-the-century audience, and especially at their prissy middle-class morality. A different sort of borderline case emerges in a remark made by Sganarelle in Molière's *The Doctor in Spite of Himself* (1666). Posing as a physician, Sganarelle prescribes as a cure for a patient dying of dropsy a piece of cheese supposedly fortified with gold, coral, pearls, and other precious substances. But he then instructs the patient's husband that in case she dies, he must be sure to give her a splendid funeral. The remark seems at first to be humor, a comment by Sganarelle on his own incompetence, but the barb actually ricochets off him and hits the medical profession. Will its impact be witty or humorous? That will depend on how the actor delivers it. If he says it in all seriousness (without meaning to be funny), it will be taken as humor. If he delivers it with a knowing smile, it will be wit.

Nonverbal wit, like its verbal counterpart, implies a funny *intention*. In Mack Sennett's *The Knockout* (1914), Fatty Arbuckle is about to take off his trousers and change into boxing shorts. He stops, thinks, then beckons to the camera to move upward. It does, cutting off our view of him below the waist. Buster Keaton provides a glowing example of nonverbal wit, achieved by editing, at the end of *College*. After going through all kinds of torments in order to rate as an athlete and satisfy his jock-happy girl, he shows us three quick and astringent tableaux: the young couple, married, in a house aswarm with children; two decrepit old folks by a fire; and then two gravestones side by side. The succession of shots says in effect that Buster and his woman lived happily ever after. (And died.)

Such nonverbal wit can make at least as devastating a comment as verbal wit can. And just as verbal sarcasm is the lowest form of verbal wit, so nonverbal sarcasm—an upraised middle finger or a stuck-out tongue—is low-grade nonverbal wit, the cheap laugh, which irritates more people than it amuses.

The distinctions between the physical and the verbal, and between wit and humor, offer two unreliable ways of separating comedy from farce. A third, no more reliable distinction has to do with the dramatic situations of the work. If these seem normal or life-like, the work is a comedy; if they seem abnormal or unreal, chances are the work is a farce. But what is normal or abnormal? And to whom? And in what circumstances? The reality of a sailor on watch during a storm at sea is a nightmare for a passenger with a rocky stomach or for a stowaway. Moving about on the bare bones of an unfinished skyscraper is normal activity for a construction worker, but for Harold Lloyd in *Never Weaken* (1921)—trying to crawl toward a secure spot and slipping on a grease-covered wrench, then sitting on a hot rivet and scrambling onto a girder that a crane happens to remove—those heights are the depths of hell.

We might say, then, that farce specializes in making circumstances that are normal for some characters abnormal for others, or that in a comedy characters remain rooted in reality while in farce they keep venturing out of reality. And they often do so in everyday settings. Never mind the hyperbolic feats associated with skyscrapers and mountainsides and expanses of rolling ocean: to a fumbling noncook, a run-of-the-mill kitchen equipped with knife racks and hanging saucepans, a food processor and closets stacked with china is a deadly environment. I have mentioned that in most farces moments of comedy (reality) intervene, and that some comedies glide into and out of farce. During the transitions from one to the other, a play may be both comic and farcical, the degree of either being determined by the eye of the beholder.

One more distinction, which is pretty clear-cut, is the acting. Comic actors try to appear natural. A wise director reminds his cast in a comedy to "play the character," not the situation, or else they will seem to be pushing for laughs and will lose them. No overreacting. No neck-cricking double takes. Voices muted as much as possible (suppressed rage is usually more frightening and less predictable than ranting).

On the other hand, farcical acting has little use for such restraint. Because his capital effects are physical, the farceur quickly learns to act unabashedly with his entire body. If he is playing in Molière's *The Flying Doctor* and has to leap from a second-floor window and climb back through it at top speed several times in a row; if he has to stop himself from falling backward while on roller skates, as Chaplin did in *The Rink* (1916), keeping his balance by trying to get his feet behind his weight; if he is the protagonist of Aristophanes' *The Wasps* and must slither off a roof without being seen by the servants who are supposed to keep him from getting away, he is going to spurn subtlety. Buster Keaton may wear a somber face that hardly alters its expressions, but watch his arms, legs, and torso (and his head) in movement! His acting looks heightened to the point of caricature. His physique is more than articulate: it is eloquent.

The farce actor doesn't play the character; he "plays the situation," for all it's worth. If he can at the same time contrive to stay in character, so much the better, but this will be a secondary consideration. Besides, farce often ordains that time is limited; the character is in a panic as he pursues or is pursued; clocks are his adversary. In silent films the urgency becomes excruciating when the action speeds up; and the wonder of this acceleration lies in its unearthly beauty. Slow motion analyzes a moment and shows up its flaw or virtues, but fast motion blends them into a smooth flow.

Farce, in other words, takes leave of comedy not only in its written material but also, and more manifestly, in its enactment. It is primarily a performer's art, not a writer's. An effective staged reading of a farce, spoken with skill but stripped of its business or "shticks," is almost unimaginable. The farce actor as a rule either writes his own material or employs writers he has worked with repeatedly until they know what he can do and what he is willing to attempt; and farce writers who are free-lance like to use the same actors over and over; they often have them in mind while they compose a play or screenplay.

Farce, Tragedy, Melodrama

"From the sublime to the ridiculous" aptly describes the atmospheric separation between tragedy and farce. How, then, can farce and tragedy mingle? One difficulty in answering this question arises from the interpretations that have been put upon the two words, rather than from any necessary irreconcilability between the two forms. Farce, to repeat, is often a term of disdain, if not abuse. Tragedy, rather than being seen as a type of drama, a genre like the other genres, has become an ideal. Tragedies are, according to most critical writings about them, supreme, the very peaks of dramatic art. The word "tragedy" has acquired a halo, a mystique. Through the two and a half millennia since Aristotle tried to discern in the *Poetics* what tragedy was and how it arose, there has grown up a formidable body of criticism on the subject. Most critics (notably Aristotle himself, and Hegel) base their arguments and deductions on one or two plays. But almost every critic who has attempted to define tragedy has identified some plays (the ones he or she admires most) as tragic and locked the others out. Plays that do not conform to the ideal are said to be *near*-tragedies or *flawed* tragedies or *failed* tragedies or (the ultimate disgrace) melodramas.

Thus we need a fresh start in the criticism of tragedy if the term is to serve any purpose in referring to a genre; it must be divested of its corona of approval. We ought to be able to say that a play is both a tragedy and a lousy piece of writing as casually as we say that a Broadway comedy is feeble or a melodrama sloppy.

A tragedy deals with a leading character, the protagonist, who, consciously or unconsciously, wills his or her own downfall, and then, because of certain temperamental deficiencies (the "tragic flaw"), brings that downfall to pass. Self-will is at the heart of the formula, not high seriousness, which is superficial, an author's ornamentation. If a protagonist brings about the downfall of somebody else—an antagonist, say—or if the antagonist brings about the protagonist's downfall, then the work is not a tragedy, but a melodrama.[1] And not inferior for that reason. Further, when a work has a comic slant but in all other respects conforms to the tragic genre, it is a tragicomedy, and so forth. The point is that these genres need not be mutually exclusive and, specifically, tragedy and farce can coexist in one work.

The protagonist of a tragedy, because of a prevailing state of anguish, often approaches madness. In certain tragedies, such as *King Lear* and Sophocles' *Ajax* and Euripides' *Herakles*, madness actually possesses the protagonist for a time. It is an alien spirit inhabiting his soul. Euripides personifies it as a female figure in *Herakles*, and gives her a name, Lyssa, and a function: she is a servant of the gods and obeys the orders of Hera, the wife of Zeus. The upshot of such madness in tragedy is that the protagonist does something frenzied and foreign to his nature (Ajax slaughters cattle and sheep; Herakles slays his wife and children); he seems to go out of control and to be at odds with the world around him and with his sane self. This relationship between him and his world is akin to the farce character's with *his* world. He may not be mad; much of the time he will act with clearheadedness and even *politesse*, as when Harold Lloyd, partway up the side of a tall department store in *Safety Last* (1923), gets entangled in a net, frees himself from it with great difficulty, hears the crowd on the sidewalk far below applauding, and lets go with one hand to raise his hat in acknowledgment. He is merely, doggedly trying to be himself. No, it's the world around him that is abnormal. What counts here is the *disparity* between the character and his surroundings. In farce, that disparity is laughable; in tragedy, heartrending. We don't laugh at the tragic protagonist: he lacks the protective shell

---

[1] Some questions follow from this distinction between tragedy and melodrama. Does Hamlet cause his own downfall, or is it caused by the combined efforts of Claudius, Gertrude, Ophelia, Polonius, Laertes, Rosencrantz and Guildenstern, and the ghost of Hamlet's father? In the latter case, *The Tragedy of Hamlet* would be a melodrama, even though it's still the same play. Who causes Othello's downfall—Othello, or Iago (or Desdemona)? Is Iago as important a character as Othello is—that is to say, a protagonist? If so, his fate is tragic while Othello's is melodramatic. Who causes Willy Loman's downfall and death? He himself (tragedy), or society at large, including his wife and sons (melodrama)? It will be noticed that if I seem to be demoting tragedy, I am also expanding the compass of melodrama so that it takes in not only horror plays and *guignol* at one extreme but also what the French call serious drama (*le drame sérieux*), our "high drama," at the other.

of his farcical counterpart, the indestructibility. We are always looking ahead fearfully to his downfall, which colors our responses. But if the tragic actor proves defective, if he loses one jot of the total concentration and conviction that tragedy demands, he may slide into ludicrousness. And then the laughs will come: not the friendly laughter of relief, but the hostile laughter of scorn. The actor playing Macbeth dare not allow spectators so much as a smile during the episode when his madness has conjured up the smiling ghost of "blood-bolter'd Banquo," or the effect will be artistically lethal. The tragedian performs on the slippery edge of a pit, and its name is farce.

So does the melodramatist—only closer yet to the edge, if that is possible. The great French actor Frédérick Lemaître tells an anecdote about how, instead of avoiding the pit, he plunged recklessly into it. Some authors had brought him a script called *The Inn of the Adrets*. Reading through this "gloomy melodrama," he could not think of a way to induce the public to accept its "mysterious and melancholy plot"; nor could he believe in the character he was to portray, "a highway assassin, frightful as the ogre of any fairy tale, and carrying his impudence to the extent of curling his whiskers with a dagger, while eating a bit of Gruyère cheese!" Then the idea occurred to him of treating the work as a farce, without substantially altering its dialogue. The transformation would depend on the acting. The play turned out to be so successful as farce that it gave rise to a sequel featuring the same leading character, written by Lemaître in collaboration with two of the three original authors, and entitled *Robert Macaire*, which became one of the smash hits—if not the biggest—in the French theater of the nineteenth century.[2]

How did the actor achieve this result? Did he go into mugging and hamming? Unlikely. The audience would have resented this, and let him know; besides, Lemaître was an uncommonly intelligent artist who respected his public's discernment. He must have

---

[2] The two authors were delighted with their play's new personality and with the royalties therefrom. The third author, a Dr. Polyanthe, strenuously objected to Lemaître's interpretation—but then, as the actor writes, "if he had not been most fortunately stopped short, he might have managed to murder as many melodramas as he did patients." The anecdote is related in full by another renowned French actor, Constant Coquelin, in *Papers on Acting*, edited by Brander Matthews (New York: Hill & Wang, 1958), pp. 22–24.

brought to the part a farceur's concentration and conviction that compared with his fervor in a tragedy like Victor Hugo's *Ruy Blas* or in a cape-and-sword melodrama. Lemaître saw that ultimately the genre of the play depends on the creator of the dominant role or roles. If he feels sympathy for the central character, the play will come out melodrama; if he feels amused contempt, or affectionate contempt, the play will come out farce.

The meeting of melodrama and farce, a feature of many Hitchcock films, recurs in the James Bond series, which run sedulously along Hitchcock tracks. In *Moonraker,* for instance, a couple of water chases begin as melodrama and rapidly turn into farce. In the first chase, Bond (Roger Moore) is loafing along the canals of Venice in a gondola when the employees of the archvillain Drax tail him in a fast launch and try to machine-gun him. Bond twiddles with levers that convert the sedate vessel into a high-speed motorboat. Then, as his pursuers gain on him, he comes up with another mechanism that turns the gondola amphibious. Crawling out of the canal, it crosses St. Mark's Square—to the consternation of the crooks, the crowds in the square, and a pigeon that wags its head in amazement. In the second chase, Bond is racing along the Amazon in a boat followed by the man with the iron mouth called Jaws (Richard Kiel), and finds himself hurtling toward a waterfall at about sixty knots. At the last second he ejects himself into the air, attached to a hang glider, and coasts to a safe landing in the jungle, while his boat and Jaws and *his* boat go over the falls.

Both times, as well as in other parts of the film, the farcical intentions of the creator (screenplay by Christopher Wood; direction by Lewis Gilbert) are made plain by a series of side incidents; sly quotations from, and references to, other films (among them, *Close Encounters of the Third Kind* and *The Rules of the Game*) at tense moments; and names like Drax. The pursuit boat in the first scene cuts right through another gondola, the two halves of which drift apart. In one half, a pair of embracing lovers don't notice they're going under. A "corpse" raises the lid of his coffin, mounted amid wreaths on a funeral barge, takes aim at 007, and receives a knife in the chest; the coffin is bumped off the barge by a low bridge and floats away like another boat on the canal. In the second scene, Jaws mugs extravagantly as he sees he can't avoid the waterfall.

I imagine that in the future we will see many a melodrama that farcically kids itself and its audience as it reaches for thrills and at the same time muffles their impact with laughter.

Types of Farce

The word "farce" comes from the French *farci* or *farcie*, and thence from the Latin *farsa*, or "stuffed." In cooking, *farcie* retains its old meaning; more or less any food, from a pepper to a chicken, that can be hollowed out, leaving a firm skin or shell, can be stuffed. The stuffing is a mixture of ingredients. Forcemeat, still known sometimes as farcemeat, contains fish or meat chopped together with egg whites, herbs, and bread crumbs or flour to form a culinary mosaic. Possibly the use of the word farce in the arts recognizes that this genre will accommodate distinctive kinds of content, from snappy cross talk to gymnastics and mime. The playwright simply stuffs them into his framework, and if each holds up in its own right, it adds to the overall amusement.

Certain types of farce—for instance, those devised by Georges Feydeau in the drama and by Billy Wilder and his screenwriter I. A. L. Diamond in films—look so tightly plotted that while we're in their grip, every link in the chain of events clings to the one before and the one after; it's hard to envision them as separate ingredients. Yet later we remember each farce for precisely its individual turns or shticks, not for its continuity. Our memory, like Little Jack Horner, pulls out a plum from here, a plum from there: the bit with the cleft palate, two strangers waking up in the same bed, Jack Lemmon changing from a pimp to an English lord on a sidewalk elevator.

Farce not only is stuffed with ingredients, and invaded by other genres; it also breaks down, as comedy does, into four principal types: realism, fantasy, theatricalism, and the well-made play (the W.M.P.). Realistic farce, the youngest of these types—only about a century old—might be said to have the time of its life mimicking the life of its time. In any of the genres, realism can go only so far in mimicking life. In its extreme form, realistic farce would not have a fictitious subject but consist of life unedited. Some random examples might be a lecture or a free-for-all debate that goes awry, a wedding between two people who are grossly incompatible, or a snowball fight between old ladies. The ideas have farcical potential, but in actuality, the boring and unnecessary moments would be there together with the engaging and entertaining ones. Such a work would have no structural embellishments—no divisions into scenes or acts or shots; no alterations of camera angle; no narration or other telescoping of time. No willful falsification could be permitted in the name of a higher or artistic truth. Documentary realism or literalism of this kind is almost unheard of in farce. But some farces do imitate life with enough fidelity to be classified as realism.

Fantasy, at the other end of the farce spectrum, is all falsification, drawn not from life but from an imagined life. Fantasies of science fiction may occupy constellations beyond our universe or ken; or prehistory; or, as in the last play of Shaw's *Back to Methuselah*, a period as distant in the future "as thought can reach." In fable fantasies, animals talk and perform like human beings. Some fantasies are populated by immortals, such as gods, ghosts, sprites, or unslayable monsters; their settings may lie at the end of the rainbow, at the top of the beanstalk, in a land of heart's desire, in heaven, in hell, a limbo with no exit, or in an Athenian wood by night in the mythical days of Theseus, when the order of magic (or black magic) holds sway.

Somewhere between realism and fantasy is theatricalism, which reminds the spectators that they're present at a performance. This is self-conscious art; if not done with discretion, it's liable to turn self-consciously arty. There may be a play within the play with the inner play commenting on the outer one, or the other way around. The actors will then be playing characters *and* actors-playing-characters. Irma the whorehouse proprietor in Genet's *The Balcony* plays a queen; the hero of Cummings' *him* takes on several additional roles; the characters in Gelber's *Rehearsal* are not jail inmates but actors working on a play about jail inmates. Several directors have made films about the difficulty of making a film—Truffaut's *Day for Night*, Sjöman's two-part *I Am Curious*, Fellini's *8½*—although these are comedies, not farces. In comedy, theatricalism can resemble realism: a play set in a theater about a

play set in a theater and reconstructing the conditions of a performance is true to life, the life of the theater; but authenticity of this
sort is rare in farce. Theatricalism can also lean toward fantasy: in
Sherlock Jr., Buster Keaton as a projectionist falls asleep and
dreams he walks into the film he's screening; two critics in Stoppard's *The Real Inspector Hound* go up onstage and take part in
the play they're supposed to be reviewing.

The well-made play, a close relative of realism, has an ancestry
that goes back to the New Comedy of Alexis and Menander in
Greece, the farce of Plautus and the comedy of Terence in Rome;
and it continues, with interruptions, on down through the plays of
Molière, Beaumarchais, Labiche, Pinero, Feydeau to the West
End, Parisian, Broadway, Hollywood, and television audience-
pleasers of today. It conforms to one or another dramaturgical
formula that can be studied in courses or textbooks on writing
plays, and it lives by the slogan *No effect without cause*—otherwise
known as *No loose ends*. In its contrivances, the W.M.P. can become tiresome; in its shameless borrowings, trite and third-hand,
imitations of imitations. In Bernard Shaw's reviews in the 1890s he
generally admired the W.M.P.s of Labiche (mostly revivals by
then) and Feydeau for their zest, but he panned the "adaptations
from the French" of Sydney Grundy and labeled Sardou's sometimes bloodless and mechanical efforts "Sardoodledom."

The four principal types of farce are further complicated by the
intrusions of symbolism, satire, burlesque, parody, expressionism,
surrealism, and other stylistic treatments—occasionally two or
three or a cluster of them at the same time. In the course of
Modern Times, one of the peaks of farce and of film making, Chaplin switches from symbolic realism in his opening clip of sheep
crowding through a pen to straight realism as workers stampede
out of a subway to work; to expressionism as the workers enter the
factory and we view them from behind the looming shapes of
machinery; to parody and satire as we watch Charlie on the assembly line trying to keep up with the flow of metal plates on which he
must frantically tighten two nuts in opposed directions; to surrealism when, still jerking his wrenches, he chases a lady in the street
who has two buttons on her dress, or when he goes for a smoke
into the men's room, where, on a gigantic screen, an image of the
boss orders him back to work, or when he pirouettes and capers

with a squirting oilcan. He returns to realism in his depiction of unemployment, strikes, and strike-busting of the Thirties; ventures into a dream fantasy in the sequence when he tells Paulette Goddard about their future home where oranges and grapes grow by open doorways, waiting to be plucked, and a cow stops by to supply fresh milk for breakfast; and after trips to other kinds of fantasy, he ends with a symbolic realism that harks back to the sheep at the start when he and Paulette walk off arm in arm down the endless center line of a highway toward a mountainous vista. This farce also gives way to moments of comedy and melodrama: comedy when Paulette is trying to convince the owner of a café (Henry Bergman) that Charlie, who needs a job, knows how to wait on table and sing; and melodrama when she kneels, stricken, over the body of her father, who was shot during a riot. Yet for all its wealth of types and genres, *Modern Times* reverts again and again to the unifying theme on which it plays its variations: the need to eat in order to survive.

No genre sustains itself consistently through a work, and farces are internally less consistent than comedies, melodramas, and tragedies are. By interacting with the other genres and calling on a variety of writing styles, farce may have developed weak edges, but these allow for better absorption. Its very receptiveness has given it more to work with.

PART TWO

◆

IDENTIFYING FARCES

FIVE

A HURRIED TOUR FROM GREECE TO THE TWENTIETH CENTURY

(I) Aristophanes to Shakespeare

The character Lysistrata has found renown as a personification of women's resolve to keep men from fighting. This is not surprising since her name means literally "dismisser of armies." When Lysistrata induces the women of Athens and some other city-states, including Sparta, with which Athens is then (411 B.C.) at war, to refrain from having sex with their husbands until the men draw up a peace treaty that's fair to both sides, she anticipates by well over two thousand years every modern feminist movement from women's emancipation in the nineteenth century to ERA a hundred years later and, most appropriately, the organization of the 1960s called Women Strike for Peace. As a play that pushes for women's rights in the polity, the *Lysistrata* of Aristophanes has enjoyed attention in recent years equaled, or exceeded, only by the spate of revivals of *A Doll House*. Ibsen's drama, for all its sly charm and character comedy, is a scrupulously serious work.[1] But

---

[1] *A Doll House* is often misinterpreted, as Ibsen himself pointed out. Nora's walking out on her husband, Torvald, reveals not so much her defiance and abandonment of him as her misgivings about her ability to be a good mother and to set a worthy example to her three young children.

Lysistrata is a farce, almost nonstop—one of the most delectable samples of the genre. The women under the command of Lysistrata seize the Acropolis, or citadel-cum-treasury, at the summit of the city, and so make themselves doubly impregnable. An official and his men who try to storm the citadel are routed by the women. A chorus of old men carrying green logs, fire jars, and unlit torches totter onto the scene to burn or smoke the women out; but a second chorus, consisting of old women, bring on water and douse the flames and the old men. The women in the citadel grow restless under their regime of self-denial. They want their men. But Lysistrata rallies them when she reads a scroll prophesying that they will defeat the men only if they remain a united force. One voluptuous young matron tempts her erect and suffering husband into hauling a cot, mattress, and blanket out into the open; she will join him under the covers if he does what he can to end the war. He stalls, and she refuses. After some weeks of nationwide coitus interdictus, delegates of men from Sparta and Athens are eager to meet for what one translator ingeniously calls a "sexual congress."[2] The delegates wear their *phalloi* at the high port, revealing that they are under erotic duress, and Lysistrata inflames their appetites by introducing a shapely, naked young lady who is called Peace (or Reconciliation). The Athenians and the Spartans come to territorial agreements about who will take over which bodies of land by referring to the promontories and peninsulas on the anatomy of Peace. The choruses of old men and old women declare a truce, and everybody celebrates with music, song, and dance—a *kordax* celebration lubricated with wine. As for Lysistrata herself, we never discover exactly who she is. She speaks to the other women of "our husbands," but hers doesn't appear, and there is no mention of him by name, nor of her age or background. This farce incorporates a mystery.

It also incorporates—as do most of Aristophanes' plays—a fantasy. The prospect of Greek women in the age of Socrates getting together with the wives of the enemy and putting an end to warfare seems wishful, if not unbelievable. But some of Aristophanes'

---

[2] Douglass Parker, who also translated *The Wasps*. For the same series, the Mentor Greek Comedy, published in paperback by New American Library, William Arrowsmith and Richmond Lattimore have also contributed vividly colloquial and poetic translations of Aristophanes' plays.

farces make much bolder excursions into fantasy. A farmer flies to heaven on the back of an overgrown dung beetle to look for peace. He finds it buried up there, exhumes it, and brings it back to Athens *(Peace)*. Two Athenian citizens form an alliance with the bird kingdom, and one persuades the birds to construct a gigantic barrier in the sky called Cloud-Cuckoo-Land between earth and heaven; the birds will take over from the gods, receiving sacrifices from men and, in return, serving mankind more conscientiously than the delinquent gods have done *(The Birds)*. *The Frogs* tells of a trip made by Dionysos to hell to bring back his favorite playwright, Euripides; down there he hears a debate between Euripides and Aeschylus, changes his mind, and comes back with Aeschylus, leaving Euripides in the darkness. Aristophanes' theater casually ignores the boundaries between life and death, humanity and animals, mortals and immortals, the likely event and the unlikely in a fashion we sometimes consider exclusively modern, although his farces are all that remains of the "Old Comedy" of Greece.[3]

Aristophanes also makes use of two of the other types of farce, theatricalism and realism. The presence of the chorus, probably amounting originally to twenty-four members (in *Lysistrata* they would be split into twelve women and twelve men), with their outlandish costumes, masks, and headgear and their jaunty *phalloi*, enhances the theatricalism as they sing, dance, cavort, and exchange quips, questions, and answers with the principal actors. At the same time, the playwright dips into realism. His farces, however fantastic their sets, deal with current political and social issues, and at least once during the performance an actor, or the whole chorus, or its leader speaks bluntly to the audience on be-

[3] Because of the paucity of information about Aristophanes' life and work, other than the eleven plays that have come down to us and fragments of data from Plato and other sources, scholars spar diligently over the facts. He was probably born between 447 and 445 B.C. and lived until 386 or possibly as late as 380. He is believed to have written about forty plays altogether. The extant eleven are *The Acharnians* (425), *The Knights* (424), *The Clouds* (423), *The Wasps* (422), *Peace* (421), *The Birds* (413), *Lysistrata* (411), *Thesmophoriazusae* (411 too, a productive year), *The Frogs* (405), *Ecclesiazusae* (392) and *Plutus* (or *Wealth*, 388). The only play named after the leading character is *Lysistrata*; most of the others take their titles from the chorus (dressed as wasps, birds, frogs, clouds, or whatever). We know that there were more dramatists of the Old Comedy through references to them in Aristophanes' plays and other writings, but although some of them beat Aristophanes in the yearly festivals of comedy—one held in January, one in March—their plays, like the missing three-quarters of Aristophanes' output, have vanished or been destroyed.

half of the playwright about these issues or about other matters the playwright has on his mind, such as whether they will vote him the winner of the playwriting contest. (A production of a play was always part of a competition.) One issue that haunted Aristophanes was the costly and debilitating Peloponnesian War. It began when he was about fourteen and persisted on and off for twenty-seven years until he was in his forties, ending in the defeat of Athens, which he had dreaded, in 404 B.C. That strife was the overwhelming public fact in his adult life. One of the most admirable features of his plays is his ability to deal with it farcically, and yet in all passionate seriousness, as he proposes outrageous strategies for bringing it to what current politicians would call an honorable settlement.

The plays draw additional strength from satire and parody. Aristophanes mimicked and bedeviled Athenian leaders for their weaknesses, the people for allowing themselves to be herded like sheep, and an assortment of public figures, from his playwriting rivals to gluttons, toadies, misers, and men he considered false prophets—most notably (in *The Clouds*), the extremely influential philosopher Socrates. Because he reserved some of his most caustic criticism for the less autocratic leaders, such as Kleon (whom he made a fool of in *The Knights*, playing the role himself as though to salt the injury), and did not attack the strong leaders, such as Alkibiades, he is often said to have been a political conservative. This, I think, is a misleading conclusion. A satirist picks on those figures (and customs) that offend him; he may dislike people less for their titles—what they stand for—than for what they are as personalities. It is common to find somebody with whom we are politically in sympathy obnoxious as a human being, and perhaps even harmful. This sort of private rancor is the lifeblood of satire.

Before and After Aristophanes

Aristophanes wrote toward the end of the great outpouring of Greek drama. Of the three tragedians some of whose work has survived as whole plays, Aeschylus died about ten years before Aristophanes was born, but the lives of Sophocles and Euripides, both of whom died in 406 B.C., overlapped with that of Aristophanes by forty-odd years; and so for about twenty of those years the three of them were active contemporaries.

Tragedians may have composed their plays in trilogies. Aeschylus' *Oresteia*, for example, the only complete trilogy remaining, consists of *Agamemnon, The Libation Bearers*, and *The Eumenides*, tracing a pattern of murder and revenge through two generations of the House of Atreus and serving as the model for Eugene O'Neill's *Mourning Becomes Electra* (1931). The three plays were presented on the same day, but the playwright appended a fourth drama for comic relief—a satyr-play, or boisterous treatment of one of the weighty themes from the trilogy. The one satyr-play we have inherited, *The Cyclops* of Euripides, is similar in tone to some of the Old Comedies of Aristophanes, although it has a firmer story line, with fewer distractions from the main plot, and is not nearly so broad in its humor and wit. It is more like a comic adventure than a farce. But some critics believe that both the satyr-play and the Aristophanic farce (which was played alone, not as part of a tetralogy) grew out of parodies of tragedy. The origins of both forms of entertainment remain open to conjecture. But by the time Aristophanes staged his first play, the arts of dramatic parody and satire were solidly established.[4]

Meanwhile, out in the provinces, less formal types of theater flourished: in Sparta, in the town of Megara, not far from Athens, and in Sicily and the heel and toe of the Italian peninsula, where they were known as *phlyakes*. Each of these companies, which performed mostly or entirely in mime, had its local topics and mannerisms, but in many of them Zeus is a pathetic creature, Heracles a crude barbarian, Apollo effeminate, and the ordinary folk are either dimwits or rascals. In *The Origins of Attic Comedy*, Cornford says that these plays contain three fools to every knave.[5] Aristophanes knew at least some of the Megaran farces and lifted material from them.

However, when he came to his late plays, such as *Plutus*, he

---

[4] At least one playwright, Kratinus, author of *The Archilochoi*, is believed to have written parodies and satires in dramatic form as much as seventy-five years before Aristophanes' first play appeared. He would therefore have been an older contemporary of Aeschylus'. We still lack conclusive evidence that comedy and farce either arose from parodies of tragedy or predated it.

[5] First published 1914. Reprinted in many editions.

was moving away from the rambunctious farce of Old Comedy and in the direction of what is now known as Middle Comedy, a more stately genre. With the moderation in taste and style of the phase after that, New Comedy, farce had dropped out of the Greek drama, its spontaneous-seeming delights replaced by love affairs between wellborn young Athenians and slave girls who, in the last scene or thereabouts, turn out to be the social equals of their swains. These virtually diagrammatic exercises have reached us in varying conditions of repair and authenticity—as bits and pieces; as one complete, salvaged work called *Dyskolos (The Grumbler)* by Menander (born 343 B.C., date of death uncertain); and as the plays of Terence (195–159 B.C.), which are presumed to have been adapted from Menander's for the delectation of Roman spectators a century and a half later. The well-made play had apparently vanquished farce.

But farce lived on in the dogged *phlyakes* which, over the next hundred or more years, crawled like ants in no hurry up the ankle and shin of Italy to the town of Atella in Campania (not far from Naples), from which they eventually took the name *fabulae Atellanae*, or Atellan farces. In this form they were known to, and plundered by, Plautus.

The Plautine Predicament

Lysistrata and other women's roles in the Greek, Roman, Elizabethan, and Japanese theaters were played in the original productions by male actors. Women may have taken part in predramatic rituals in Attica and elsewhere, and even in the choruses of the earlier Greek plays; they could also, for all we know, have performed in local troupes. But according to Rosamond Gilder, "the first professional actress of whom we have any definite record" appeared as late in theater history as the sixteenth century. An Italian woman named Flaminia had, by 1565, "already achieved a marked success" in the commedia dell'arte.[6] A quarter of a century later another Italian comedienne, Isabella Andreini (1562–1604),

---

[6] Gilder, *Enter the Actress* (New York, 1931; reprinted New York: Theatre Arts Books, 1960), p. 57.

became the first internationally acclaimed actress. In the Italy of Plautus' time, though, exclusion of women from the stage and, in all likelihood, segregated seating in the auditorium must have resulted in some caricaturing of the female roles in comedy and even more in farce. Despite this convention, which meant that audiences didn't *expect* to see actresses, the caricatures probably appeared most blatant in the playing of desirable, not to say irresistible, girls like the ones who adorn most of Plautus' plays.

The first real playwright of the Roman era happens to be the first prominent author writing in Latin, whether prose, poetry, or drama. He called himself Titus Maccius Plautus. Since Maccius or Maccus is the name of one of the standardized characters of rustic farce, while "Plautus" means flatfooted, he had a sense of humor about himself, as well as about others. During his lifetime (254–184 B.C.) there were no permanent theaters in Italy. Rome had not yet swollen into an empire, as Athens had done during the lives of Sophocles, Euripides, and Aristophanes. Plautus' plays were put on out of doors on simple wooden structures, a platform with maybe a wooden screen for a background and an upper level, or gallery. There was no movable scenery. The setting (three doors at the back, one at each side—farce's need for plentiful entrances and exits dates back to Plautus) denoted two or three houses. Nobody had yet thought of displaying interiors on an *alfresco* stage. The *fabulae Atellanae* had crept north of Rome to Umbria, where Plautus was born, by the middle of the third century B.C. Besides helping himself to material from them, he snatched plot devices, characters, and ideas from the Greek New Comedy and stirred together the literary and nonliterary elements, much as Aristophanes had done before him and as Molière was to do more than eighteen hundred years after him.

Plautus, who had a more vivid and venturesome theater sense than his sources, transforms them into dynamic episodes about the straightening out of financial and other misfortunes; children restored to their parents (he is one of the few playwrights who can give us a recognition scene between a father and a lost child without trying to play a whole concerto on our heartstrings); the freeing of slaves; quarrels settled thanks to justice and wisdom; romantic affairs threatened, even broken, and then mended. The principal figures are the clever slaves who operate intrigues ("play-wrights within the plays"), sighing young lovers and unworldly maidens (helpless until the slaves advise them how to coalesce), good-natured courtesans, and foolish, gullible, sometimes lecher-ous and sometimes lovable old bachelors and widowers. (Why did Plautus and the farceurs who imitated him avoid giving us widows as characters? Perhaps widowhood was not thought to be funny.)

Many of the Plautine characters, incidents, and whole stories went into later plays, including the more sedate and sententious comedies of Terence, who was eleven years old when Plautus died. *The Menaechmi* gave Shakespeare his separate but unequal twin brothers for *The Comedy of Errors*. Euclio in *The Pot of Gold* inspired Molière's Harpagon in *The Miser*, as well as Hieronymus in Ghelderode's *Red Magic* (the "red magic" being, of course, gold). Lysimachus in *The Merchant* is a direct ancestor of Molière's Sganarelle in *The Forced Marriage*. The action of *Amphitryo* in-spired plays by Rotrou and Molière in France, Dryden in England, Kleist in Germany, and more than thirty other works, according to Jean Giraudoux, who in the late 1930s christened his version *Amphitryon 38*. In all of these plays, as in Plautus, Jupiter swoops down to earth disguised as the Theban general Amphitryon. At-tended by Mercury, who has made himself up to look like Amphi-tryon's batman, Jupiter takes advantage of the general's absence to visit and enjoy his wife, Alcmena. To prolong his night of pleasure, the god makes time stand still. The offspring from this adultery, the demigod Heracles, provides a model for Superman, the Hulk, and other galvanized slabs of meat who carry out their conscien-tious labors in the funnies and on children's television. Of the character *types* who have been lifted repeatedly from Plautus, his braggart soldier, the *miles gloriosus*, has passed on as a staple figure of farce, comedy, and melodrama: the bully who threatens force but won't stand up to it (Falstaff and Pistol belong to this type, and so does the youth in one of Michael Palin's *Ripping Yarns* who, when he picks up the phone, identifies himself as "School Bully"); while the Plautine slaves do later service as valets in France, *graciosos* in Spain, butlers in Britain (the admirable Crichton), and operators in the United States (the hero of *How to Succeed in Business Without Really Trying*).

Plautus created mostly plays of domestic life; not many of them have much to do with history or myth.[7] They take place generally in Greece, although they do introduce some local Italian jokes and color. In his early plays Plautus is fond of using cumbersome Greek and mock-Greek names, such as Ptolemocratia, Megaronides, Pyrgopolynices, and Philocomasium, and he will occasionally let fly an uncomplimentary dart at Athens and its people. In the original performances, the actors played, it seems, not to each other but facing the audience, like pairs of vaudeville comedians, sometimes asking the spectators questions or addressing remarks to them so that this give-and-take (if there was any take) had an agreeable air of self-conscious theatricalism not unlike that of Aristophanes.

However, these plays comprise, for me, at any rate, one of the theater's conundrums. The brisk action; the intrigues, coincidences, misunderstandings; the punning, rapid patter intercut by humorous, often self-deprecating soliloquies; and the stock types among the characters led me to accept for a long time the idea put forward by just about every theater historian that these plays were specimens of rollicking farce. For their enactment they would therefore need the energy and impudence we associate with Aristophanes, even if they lack his fantasy, exaggerations, and scatological invention, as well as lacking that versatile instrument of theater, a chorus. When A *Funny Thing Happened on the Way to the Forum* telescoped many of Plautus' plots, scrambled together characters from various plays, added show-biz wisecracks and music, and burst open on Broadway in 1962, the old impressions were confirmed. Yet a production later in the 1960s of *The Pot of Gold*, acted by a French company and made into a film for television, showed how stylization—a combination of mime, dance, and lines sung to the accompaniment of a flute—could add up to an interpretation of surprising power that coordinated several different arts. I don't recommend such a staging of Plautus—few directors and actors could bring it off so elegantly—nor do I suggest that it is superior to the good-natured frenzy of A *Funny Thing Happened*. But the beauty of that French version explained,

---

[7] Plautus may have composed as many as one hundred thirty plays, twenty-one of which are extant. Even some of these are not intact. The end of *The Pot of Gold* is missing but for a few stray lines, which are sometimes pieced out by translators and editors, not always convincingly. My generalized remarks above are thus guesses based on the surviving scripts.

as no theoretical argument could do, that what we choose to name a genre such as farce depends as much on performance as on the malleable text. One director's farce is another's ballet.

Medieval Interludes

The interlude was a Medieval performance, usually farcical in nature—dinner theater that would be either sandwiched in between less frivolous material or served up between courses of a meal while spectator-diners groaned, belched, or otherwise responded to the dishes. But the word "interludes" aptly describes the whole assortment of Medieval theater which, for more than a thousand years, formed tenuous links between the degenerate excesses of the Roman spectacles in the fourth and fifth centuries of the Christian era[8] and the outpouring of new theater in the Renaissance and Baroque eras. During those middle ages, when Christianity gave birth to a Church that dominated the lives of its adherents—the higher clergy, the lower ranks of clergy, and the people—churchmen were at first appalled by the moral crudeness of many performances at the lag end of the Roman Empire. The Church tried to kill off the theater, which had spread like a disease or taint, in its official view, all over the Empire, especially western Europe. Centuries later, the Church went about reviving theater of a new kind, for propaganda. It hoped to bring the holy word more forcefully and palatably to "the vulgar and the unlettered" by dramatizing stories from the Old and New Testaments. In the third phase, after having remade theater as a liturgical drama, episodes tucked into the services, the Church surrendered control of much of it to the trade associations called craft guilds and to other sorts of private enterprise.

Religious worship and the theater have always been intertwined competitors. Most scholars accept the proposition that theater originally *was* religious ritual, and the Medieval experience seems

---

[8] These Roman excesses might include parades of captured armies (with their elephants) across a stage between acts of a play. Cicero complained about having six hundred mules introduced into a production of *Clytemnestra*. Horace mentions that "squadrons of horses and men are seen flying" back and forth across the boards for four hours at a stretch. The Romans also had *naumachiae*, or lake-theaters, in which two fleets fought on water; this was not a rehearsed show, but a staged massacre, a murderous "happening," in which the actors, surviving and killed, were coerced slaves.

to confirm this. When the Church, in the productions it sponsored in and out of houses of worship, appealed to feelings other than a savoring of indecency—such feelings as awe, reverence, and a desire to meditate on theological questions—it was, perhaps unknowingly, arousing comparable impulses to the ones the lewd theater had called on, if we concede that religious conviction is one form of sublimation. The most striking difference between these two great institutions was that while the Church wished to inculcate faith, the theater has (with notable exceptions) tended to promote skepticism, religious *and* political.

The earliest Medieval dramas must have been written and acted by priests and some nuns. Outside the Church and below the upper ranks of the aristocracy and a few scholars, there was almost universal illiteracy. Gutenberg is said to have invented movable type by 1440, and Caxton was printing in English by 1475,[9] thereby ushering in what Marshall McLuhan calls the "alphabetical culture" and "lineal sequences as pervasive forms of psychic and social organization." Before Gutenberg and Caxton, news, information, gossip, theater, narrative, and songs were for the most part transmitted by word of mouth—oral repetition. The line of type signifies, as McLuhan points out, the breaking up of information into orderly, uniform, *visual* units. But even after printing had begun, two primary sources of the word in Medieval times were the strolling player and the Church. The player's objective was to supply entertainment in exchange for food or money. The Church's objectives were to teach and to recruit souls; its reward was enrollment, larger followings, an extension of its bases of power until the pontiff became Europe's leading emperor.

Strolling players were descendants of the Roman *histriones*, who traveled about Europe with their partially improvised, partially rehearsed shows, and they, in turn, had come from the Atellan mimes. Medieval players corresponded to almost every kind of individual performer we know today. They included jugglers, jongleurs, joculators,[10] minstrels, mimes, gleemen, nude dancers, troubadours, female impersonators, magicians, acrobats, puppe-

---

[9] Printing was invented long before this date in Korea, although it did not reach the Western world.

[10] The words "juggler," "jongleur," and "joculator" come from the same root as the Italian *giocare* or the French *jouer*, "to play."

teers (with dolls or monkeys), conjurors, and instrumentalists. The minstrel was the ancestor not only of the wandering poet, but also of the vaudeville and Borscht Belt comedian, the TV and night-club star, and the popular singer. The players were actor-authors. Some wrote their own material; some borrowed it from others. Since they were vagrants whose paths occasionally crossed and then separated, there must have been an inordinate amount of borrowing. They earned a shaky living by doing their turns in village squares and taverns, or pushing into banqueting halls and begging for payment. They risked getting kicked out if they failed to please. Their work was usually farcical, often satirical. Both the Church and the State disliked them. Political leaders believed that they wasted the time of honest workingmen, as well as their own, and that they spread sedition. They were masterless, unattached. They carried news from place to place at a time when there was no other way of discovering what was going on elsewhere. Some-times the news was distorted and based on hearsay. In that respect it isn't much different from the news we get today. But the lam-poons these strollers sang against unpopular people in high places may have modestly contributed to, say, the Peasants' Rising in 1381 or the revolt led by Jack Cade in 1450, and other local riots. From the time of the Black Death, in the years after 1349, they were constantly threatened with the stocks, the whipping post, and jail. Thomas de Cabham, Subdean of Salisbury and later Arch-bishop of Canterbury, classified minstrels into two broad groups: those who were damnable and those who were tolerable. The damnable ones were the mimes, impersonators, ribald singers, and mask wearers. They included satirists and wits, some of whom had once belonged to the Church and then abandoned it, as well as Goliardi, wandering scholars whom Cabham regarded as being no better than scandalmongers. Other damnables were tightrope walkers, knife throwers, tumblers, or people who worked in part-nership with trained bears. The group Cabham did not disapprove of, the tolerables, were mostly respectable minstrels whose songs praised saints, royal figures, and lords, since they were sometimes employed permanently by the last, kept on assignment like a king's jester. They would probably, Cabham felt, not go to hell—at least, not for their performances. Their modern equivalent might be a cross between a writer of press releases and a poet at the Library of

Congress. If such fellows were kept on by a patron and settled down in one place, they might rise from being tolerable to being respectable; some troubadours attained fairly high social rank. But the strolling players were quasi-outlaws. Doubtless some of them had multiple talents. Most of their shows would be given in the open air, at a crossroads, a fair, a market, or an open street; but they would obviously prefer, when they could, to play indoors to a captive audience. Later, some of them banded together into pairs or threes or troupes, not necessarily to do plays with dialogue, but to offer a variety of acts, what in England is still called a variety show, although Americans use the French term "vaudeville" (from *chanson du Vau de Vire*, or song of the Valley of Vire, which was in Normandy). But whether played out in a marketplace or inside a banqueting hall, these performances cannot be compared to those given in a modern playhouse where patrons pay handsomely (except when the show is "papered") and maintain an attentive and respectful hush. The Medieval actor had to compete with unwanted noise and visual distractions. He had to outdo them. Farce was his tool.

The liturgical drama in churches started as another story. The dialogue was in Latin, like the rest of the service. Within the sanctified precincts the congregation felt intimidated by the priest-performers. However, a priest-actor is an actor. He appreciates an audience that appreciates him. It could be that he started to push for audible reactions—that is, laughs. Or that, since a villain is almost invariably more of a scene-stealer than a hero is, a devil more enthralling than an angel or a saint, and blasphemy more provocative than sincerity, the plays took on a coloring that would have horrified their originators and did trouble the Church sufficiently to make it force the performances off the premises—first out onto the steps at the west door, where many churches and cathedrals had a spacious courtyard for spectators, and then away from the grounds altogether. In some parts of Europe the entire production took place on an immense outdoor stage with many different "simultaneous" sets visible at the same time: the actors moved from one to another. Elsewhere, especially in Britain, the cycle was broken up into individual sets or "mansions," each mounted on a pageant wagon and movable. A spectator settled down with his family and food at some point, or hired a window, and the entire cycle came to him. If he lived at a good point of vantage on the route he might even rent out a window to others. The event must have been rather like a forty-act piece of theater which, instead of being staged in a Broadway playhouse, made stops, act by act, at Fiftieth Street and Broadway, at Columbus Circle, inside Central Park, outside Saks on Fifth Avenue, and finally in Bryant Park.

Even before these cyclical dramas left the churches, their episodes were spoken less and less in Latin and more in local dialects —regional French, British, Italian, Spanish, Swiss, Austrian, and German—and the mansions had grown elaborate and complex until they overpowered the meanings, the propaganda value, of the plays. Liturgical drama had become popular and, in some of its segments, downright farcical. It therefore thwarted the Church's original intentions. Some productions, the ones that had not evolved into entertainment, remained under the auspices of the Church, but the tendency toward secularization of religious drama was under way by the fourteenth century. In Britain the cycles of thirty or forty or more playlets, performed in the spring (although not every spring), told of the history of man from the creation of the world and Paradise lost, the eviction of Adam and Eve from Eden, to the resurrection of Christ and the Last Judgment. Many of these playlets were comedies, some spectacles (the descent into hell), and others farces. The best-known farce comes from Yorkshire's Wakefield Cycle; it is the *Second Shepherds' Play* —still frequently revived, although nowadays as a Christmas evocation.

A rustic named Mak steals a sheep. When three shepherds stop at his cottage to look for it, Mak and his wife, Gill, hide it in a cradle and pretend it's their baby. One shepherd lifts the covers for a peek and exclaims, "What the devil is this? He has a long snout!" Mak, after feebly claiming that Gill gave monstrous birth to this sheep, and that it is not the one stolen from the flock, is tossed in a canvas sheet for punishment. An angel flies in. The play turns devotional as the three shepherds receive the annunciation that "He is born" this night. They leave Mak's cottage and arrive, by the grace of stage geography, at the manger. There they express their adoration to Mary. The two halves of the play complement each other: the first being a homely, farcical treatment of an unnatural birth, the second falling into line with the glorification of the Virgin Birth. Farce in the symbolic vein, with flashes of satire, melts into a drama of faith. In this brief work its unknown author, identified as the Wakefield Master in acknowledgment of his dramaturgical skills, enriched his dialogue by means of songs and an intricate pattern of meter and rhyming. He probably composed several more of the episodes from this cycle, which precedes Shakespeare's apprentice writings by something like two hundred years.

Before farce was driven out of the churches, though, it had shown up in other clerical guises. The *Festa Asinaria,* or Feast of the Ass, interrupted the liturgical performance during the announcement of Christ's coming. A priest represented Balaam, the Mesopotamian prophet who is ordered to curse the people of Israel but, after being reproved by his ass, decides instead to bless them. He entered on the ass, was welcomed at the door, and proceeded up the aisle. In the early years a real ass was hired or borrowed for the occasion; later the role was played by a priest in costume and a hood with long ears—a predecessor of Bottom in *A Midsummer Night's Dream* and the horned devil and the cuckold. Other priests knelt to the ass in obeisance, chanted, and gave off braying noises. The display of asininity—letting off steam or letting down hair—became confused and amalgamated with the German and French Feast of Fools. This New Year celebration followed the recital of the verse in the Magnificat that runs, "He hath put down the mighty from their seats." At that point the lower orders of the clergy, led by the subdeacons, took charge of the service. They burlesqued the Mass by waving sausages and black puddings as if these were censers, let out a chorus of drinking songs, and generally made asses of their superiors and themselves. The superiors came to resent this show of insolence, which grew more daring and outspoken. For four hundred years the Church tried to quash the Festival of Fools. The theology faculty of the University of Paris once complained that "priests and clerks may be seen wearing masks and monstrous visages. . . . They dance in the choir stalls dressed as women, panders, and minstrels."

The "fools" ultimately left the Church and became strolling players, partly because the upper echelons got disgusted with their pranks, partly because the low-ranking priests came for all kinds of reasons to prefer the life of a traveling comedian. "Companies of fools" were formed; some of them may well have taken part in the banqueting-hall interludes. They wore motley garments, with one sleeve that served as a pouch. They sported phallic shapes around their waists on a belt, sometimes with bells and the head of a cock or an ass on it. There are backward resemblances here to the choruses of Aristophanes, as well as anticipations of the fools and jesters in *As You Like It, Twelfth Night,* and *King Lear.* In France the companies of fools did short farces called "stupidities" *(soties)* and "joyful sermons." One of these, *Pierre Pathelin,* written in the later fifteenth century, might be subtitled "The Swindler Swindled," since Pierre, a crooked lawyer, advises a simple shepherd in the techniques of how to avoid paying his bills and, as a result, loses his fee. In Germany the shoemaker-poet Hans Sachs (1494–1576), on whom Wagner's *Die Meistersinger* is modeled, wrote scores of farces called "Shrovetide plays," many of them domestic anecdotes based on squabbles between peasants and their wives.

Sachs selected his casts from his neighbors in Nuremberg, using the same people year after year. The distinction in Medieval theater between amateur and professional was no sharper than it is today in the fringe theater Off Off Broadway, where members of Equity often lend their services to showcase productions for no pay, only for opportunities. One would have to call the strolling players professionals, for they did hope for rewards. But the actors in the cycle plays are hard to classify. Many were artisans, members of the guilds that sponsored the separate playlets. Some, who may have been not guild members but hired actors, did receive money. The star roles were the ones to which were entrusted the greatest number of lines, the loudest ranting, the juiciest characterizations, and/or the most farcical activities. In an extract from the salary list of one cycle we find that Caiaphas and Herod each received three shillings and threepence (thirty-four cents), God got two shillings (twenty-one cents), and Judas and the Devil eighteen pence each (sixteen cents).[11] In these circumstances, a Me-

---

[11] The modern equivalents given here in cents are strictly arithmetical sums derived from British currency before the pound went metric, when there were twelve pence to a shilling and twenty shillings to a pound. They bear no relationship whatever to today's negligible

dieval actor would hope to start his career as the Devil, progress to
God, and hit the peak of the profession as King Herod.

In the final quarter of the fourteenth century a distinctive type
of farce interlude took shape on the far side of the world. Two
playwrights in Kyoto, Kan'ami Kiyotsugu (1333–84) and his son
Zeami Motokiyo (1363–1444), were codifying religious dances,
music, recitation, and the tenets of Zen Buddhism, some of them
native to Japan, others imported from Korea and elsewhere in
Asia, and bringing them to an exalted level of theatrical accom-
plishment, the Noh. The word *noh* actually means "accomplish-
ment" or "skill." Much as a tragic Greek trilogy was succeeded by
a satyr-play as an emotional letup, so an evening of quasi-religious
Noh plays was, and still is, punctuated by interludes called *kyōgen*.
The name means "wild words," according to Arthur Waley, who
translated and published a sample in his Noh collection.[12] The
kyōgen, although quite stylized by our standards of farce, are
much less formal than the plays they relieve, and may parody
them. Most of them last no longer than ten or twelve minutes.
Waley's translation of *The Birdcatcher in Hell* is a farcical fantasy.
It tells of Kiyoyori, who has died and landed in hell, but is looking
for the way to heaven. At first some lower-rank demons want to
keep him down there as punishment for his having earned his
living by killing birds. But he explains to Yama, the lord of hell,
that the dead birds were used to feed other birds, falcons. He goes
on to catch a bird, roast it, and present it to Yama, who smacks
his lips over the delicacy. Result: Kiyoyori is dispatched back to life
for a few more years. The little play, although no rip-roaring farce
in a Western tradition, does have some affinities with Western
drama. Kiyoyori is reminiscent of Papageno in *The Magic Flute*.
There is a comic chorus, small and abbreviated, but analogous to
the one in Aristophanes' *The Frogs*. And one of the sentiments
spoken by a demon ("Hell is ever at hand, which is more than can
be said of heaven") is almost a transliteration of a remark by

---

purchasing power of the amounts quoted. As a very crude real-income equivalent we would
have to count every shilling as worth about fifty dollars today or, at the present rate of
inflation, one hundred fifty dollars by next year.

[12] *The Nō Plays of Japan* (paperback edition, New York: Evergreen, 1957). Twenty-two
kyōgen are translated by Shio Sakanishi in *Japanese Folk Plays: The Ink-Smeared Lady*
(Rutland, Vt.: Charles E. Tuttle, 1960).

Mephistopheles after he arrives on earth in Marlowe's *Dr. Faustus:* "Why, this is hell, nor am I out of it." The *kyōgen* illustrate an indisputable principle, psychological and theatrical, as valid in the East as in the West, namely: Don't put the spectator's serious attention under too much of a strain.

Improvisation and Masks

Two friends approach each other. But they are looking and walking backward. Each fears that someone is following him. They bump into each other and retreat in fright. They don't dare to look around; they'd rather not know what is happening. They come together again, still facing in opposite directions, this time more tentatively, experimentally, knees knocking, to see whether another collision will take place. It does. One of them turns his head, but sees only the other's back, which he doesn't recognize. The second one then turns his head and sees an unfamiliar back. But they are still afraid of their pursuers, real or imaginary. They bump yet again. Now, very cautiously, they turn their heads at the same time. Recognition! Relief! They fall into each other's arms.

This primitive routine may date back to antiquity. In one or another of its variations it drew laughs in nineteenth-century vaudeville and in twentieth-century silent films. Perhaps it still does. But we know it from the commedia dell'arte of the 1500s and 1600s, of which it formed a staple turn. It was described as one of "the *lazzi* of fear." *Lazzi* were set pieces in dumb show. In the commedia they combined with *burle,* or verbal set pieces (jokes, anecdotes, quarrels, monologues), to make up scenarios that were like patchwork quilts in that they consisted of lengths of ready-made material that could be rapidly basted together into new patterns. The two men could be neighbors meeting in a wood at night. Or shipwrecked sailors tossed ashore separately on an island. Or servants in a garden guarding their master's property from burglars. Or burglars. All the actors needed for a performance was a) the given circumstances—the setting, the time, the events that led up to this and what was due to happen after it; and b) the cues that brought on this episode and the cues that ended it and led into the next sequence of *lazzi.*

The commedia dell'arte, or professional comedy, was a trade, not a vocation. In any troupe, every actor knew every other actor's special turns, and used three types of signal to cue him. The *uscite* (openings) served to announce an entrance by calling another player onstage; the *chiusette* (closings) provided a line or two for an exit; and the *concetti* (transitions) introduced new turns that did not require entrances to or exits from the stage. This is a style in which theatrical improvisation flowered. But improvisation doesn't mean invention of new material from scratch, verbal and physical free association. It implies the rearrangement of material that has already been worked out. Even in the 1960s when improvisation revived in the United States and became a code word of the Second City company from Chicago, the Premise, which started in St. Louis, and the Proposition from Boston, the actors had a pretty good idea of what they were going to do beforehand. They might ask spectators to suggest a situation or a couple of characters for them to toy with, but they had enough prepared and rehearsed skits on hand; what they did on the spur of the moment was adapt them. Such adaptation calls for exceptionally quick wits and fertile imagination; but it also calls for long, grueling practice, knowing the material so well that the performer can depart from it and return to the point of departure.[13] Improvisation is not wholly spontaneous.

The reason the commedia actors knew their parts so well was that they each did nothing else. They took the same characters on circuits from place to place, through big and small towns and to country markets and fairs, much as the strolling players and companies of fools had done before them, and before *them*, the Roman and Greek farceurs. Beginning in Italy, they branched out into France, Spain, Britain, Germany, Scandinavia, and Russia. They were invited for visits by Henri III of France and by Queen Elizabeth to England as early as the 1570s. Some of them settled abroad and established commedia traditions there. Jean Renoir's film *The Golden Coach* (1953) has to do with a commedia troupe traveling as far afield in the eighteenth century as Peru. But wher-

---

[13] Involuntary improvisation sometimes happens in nonimprovisational theater. Actors who go "dry" and forget their lines in, say, *Othello*, have been known to fill in smoothly with a passage from *The Winter's Tale* or *Cymbeline* until their memory returns. Spectators rarely notice the switch.

ever they went, the commedia actors hardly varied their roles. A performer might stay with one part all his working life and, if he was particularly good, become famous for it. Tiberio Fiorelli, who spent the later part of his career in Paris, sharing a theater with Molière's company, immortalized the part of Scaramuccia (Scaramouche).

Most of the actors wore masks, and since they were stock types, personalities who changed little, if at all, from play to play, they were identified by those masks and by their conventional costumes, which were like a body-length extension of the masks. The commedia characters themselves are usually referred to as "masks." Arlecchino (Harlequin), for example, is called a comic mask and Colombina (Columbine) a serious mask, even though the serious characters didn't in fact wear masks. The masks were made of leather and had various embellishments—a wart, a mustache, a bald scalp, reddened cheeks, a beard, or whatever. They were caricatures, intended for instant recognition and quick laughs. They must have been uncomfortable to wear. The very act of wearing them threw a great responsibility on the actor's body and limbs and voice; but then, the commedia was noted for its broad humor and speed and agility, not for the expressive subtlety of the faces.

Not that all the roles *could* be played for an entire career. A young actor whose "mask" was that of a heroine or lover would sooner or later have to graduate to something more mature, or else retire—even though, as everyone knows, actors do not age. Thus a handsome and heroic but not very bright or colorful youth —a Lelio, Flavio, Ottavio, or Orazio—would be studying the more seasoned members of the troupe and, if he had comic gifts, might hope to take on the more rewarding mask and accent of one of the servants, who need not be young, although they had to be spry, or one of the older men. Similarly, a heroine, or *comica innamorata* —Lucinda, Isabella, Flaminia, Ginevra, or Aurelia—would keep her eyes on the older maidservants' masks.[14]

Arlecchino would be a desirable mask for an ambitious young

---

[14] A *comica innamorata* who mostly sang ballads and other songs was known as a *cantarina* (a forerunner of Italian opera singers), while from the comedienne who danced we take our word "ballerina."

actor to aim for. He was a rascally servant from Bergamo, but he might be a beggar taken on by a master because of his cunning. He wore a black mask, a hare's tail (for luck?), a wallet in which he deposited the loot from other people's pockets, and a patched costume. In the course of time the patches became systematized into red, blue, and green triangles, and the triangles later became diamonds, sometimes cut by vertical yellow stripes. His jacket came down to his mid-thighs; it was about the length of a modern suburban coat. He had bulky pants to match, not unlike Buster Keaton's in shape. He was smart, but not always smart enough to escape a beating, and not always wise enough to get what he wanted, although he usually did get Colombina. Arlecchino was the best-known of the *zanni,* or comic servants.[15] He carried a wooden sword, which evolved into the slapstick. Translated into the British theater he became a dumb character, Harlequin, as interpreted by the British clown John Rich (1692–1761), who specialized in pantomime.

Another servant mask that a young actor might covet was that of Brighella. He had an olive-green mask (the commedia did not go in for realism in complexions or anything else) with protruding, greedy lips, little eyes, a prominent nose. He wore a real dagger—made of metal, not wood. The dagger symbolized the difference between Brighella and Arlecchino. Arlecchino was fairly good-natured as crooks go. Brighella was a brutal villain or brigand. He wore a short jacket laced up with green braid, sometimes green stripes running east and west on his vest, wide pants, and a brief Roman cloak over his shoulders. He too was a valet, but he hailed from Naples, not from Bergamo. Other servant characters derived from Brighella: Scapino, taken straight into French drama as Scapin in Molière's play (see Chapter 2), came from Milan, but Molière made him a Neapolitan, like Brighella. Molière also borrowed Coviello, another descendant of Brighella, and gave him an important role in *The Bourgeois Gentleman.*

Pulcinella likewise came from Naples. He was a contentious

---

[15] *Zanni* was taken into English as "zany," a noun, and used by Shakespeare, among others. It has since become an adjective as well. One scholarly view derives the singular Italian form, *zanno,* from the Latin *sannio,* meaning "clown." A rival opinion has it that *zanni* comes from the Venetian dialect for John or Giovanni—Zan. Both derivations are plausible.

older servant distinguished by his hump, his hooked nose, and a cock's feather (or two) in his hat. A famous drawing of him by Callot is entitled *Cucurucu*, which may have been his name in a certain production or location and seems to be an onomatopoeic reference to the cock's feather. Pulcinella was a nasty piece of work; he beat his wife and spent much time evading justice on earth and the Devil when he found himself in hell. He was certainly not as amiable as the versions of him that turned up in other countries: Kasperle in Germany, Polichinelle in France, and Punch, of the Punch-and-Judy seaside show, in Britain. Much the same is true of Pedrolino. Exported to France, he turned into the melancholy and sentimentalized Pierrot, wearing a white costume with large buttons or pompons. Throw in a bald wig, a blob of a nose, a gaping slot of a mouth, and ghastly white skin, and you have the prototype of the circus clown, as well as the image of the modern mime, as incarnated by Marcel Marceau and his imitators. Pierrot's Colombine, for whom he pines, was sometimes known as Pierrette; she wore matching costume, so that they appeared as a stark white his-and-hers act.

The stock commedia villain, who drew automatic jeers and whistles, was derived from the Roman *miles gloriosus*, the blustering soldier given a Spanish pedigree and known as Il Capitano, with a boastful name like Captain Blood-and-Fire, possibly because the Italians resented the ambitions of imperialist Spain in the sixteenth century. The Capitano mask had an imposing nose, an angry mustache, and a ferocious expression. This captain favored a fancy dress uniform of which he was unreasonably proud, like the very model of a modern bemedaled general; he had a ruff around his neck and a perpetual growl in his voice. When challenged to a fight, he blustered or ran. At other times he swore elaborate oaths.

There were many other stock types: magicians and rulers of remote domains (Prospero in *The Tempest* is a Shakespearean reconstruction of one), fat and greedy sloths, and an assortment of shepherds and shepherdesses rejoicing in such bucolic names as Silvio, Silvia, and Silvano. But the two who survived most doughtily and would have offered careers any young actor might aspire to were Pantalone and the Doctor. As the butt of many jokes and the principal victim of most scenarios, Pantalone played the despotic father whose daughter got away from him in the end or the aging husband whose young wife cheated on him. He wore a black beard, a black cloak (originally red, but this color may not have proved somber enough for his social standing or enough of a clue to his parsimony) with a red or yellow jacket beneath it, a Greek cap and Turkish slippers, spectacles, and broad pantaloons, a garment to which he gave his name. He was a merchant of Venice, a moneygrubber. Among Shakespeare's characters, not only Shylock but also Polonius in *Hamlet* and Justice Shallow in the second part of *Henry IV* are versions of Pantalone. So are most of Molière's overbearing fathers.

The Doctor, *Il Dottore*, might be a pedant, a medical doctor, a lawyer, or a philosopher, who reeled off yards of erroneous Latin and sometimes attributed it to the wrong sources. He had studied either at the University of Bologna, which specialized in law, or, less often, at the University of Padua, where medicine was taught. He dressed as a professor with a dark cloak, his most serviceable prop as it whished about and emphasized his words, and a flattish hat, often of black velvet. His mask was dark, with a short pointed beard, a heavy brow, and red cheeks to signify his short temper and impatience with those incapable of understanding his flow of language and gibberish. Invariably he was a figure of fun who got thrashed because a beating was the only way to make him stop talking about the Latin roots of words and about his scholarly reputation.

These comedians with defined personalities, each dominated by one obsession (a determination to win that girl, get out of this father's clutches, save money, plot an escapade, brag about one's virtues and achievements), not unlike what Ben Jonson meant by a "humor," were beautifully suited to the age-old demands of farce. In the more than eight hundred scenarios that have been preserved as little more than curt stage directions, substantially the same set encounters and developments keep recurring. During a period when the commedia was the sole entertainment for most of the public, people delighted in watching almost identical turns time and again—probably, though, no more than once a year, or whenever a troupe passed through. But as the commedia became the darling of court circles, adjusted its farce to courtly tastes, and succumbed to the temptation of security, it softened, working for pathos and tears, rather than continuing to project its blunt—even gross—wit and humor. In dispersing physically, it became dispersed artistically and lost touch with its traditions and conventions. Still, the commedia routines had resolved themselves into a series of farcical myths that would be thankfully tapped by subsequent generations of performers, writers, and film directors. Generous slivers were kept virtually intact by being written into the plays of such men as Lope de Rueda, Molière, and Goldoni. And at the dawn of this century the Spanish dramatist Jacinto Benavente wrote his tribute to the commedia. In his prologue to *The Bonds of Interest* (1907) he has Crispin, a scion of the house of Arlecchino, say:

> Here you have the mummer of the antique farce who enlivened in the country inns the hard-earned leisure of the carter, who made the simple rustics gape with wonder in the square of every rural town and village, who in the populous cities drew about him great bewildering assemblages. . . . It was the common heritage of great and small. Its rude jests, its sharp and biting sentences it took from the people, from that lowly wisdom of the poor which knows how to suffer and bear all, and which was softened in those days by resignation in men who did not expect too much of the world and so were able to laugh at the world without bitterness and without hate. . . .
>
> This is a little play of puppets, impossible in theme, without any reality at all. You will soon see how everything happens in it that could never happen, how its personages are not real men and women, nor the shadows of them, but dolls or marionettes of paste and cardboard, moving upon wires which are visible even in a little light and to the dimmest eye. They are the grotesque masks of the *commedia dell'arte*, not as boisterous as they once were because they have aged with the years and been able to think much in so long a time. The author is aware that so primitive a spectacle is unworthy of the culture of these days; he throws himself upon your courtesy and upon your goodness of heart. He asks only that you should make yourselves as young as possible. [Translated by John Garrett Underhill.]

Shakespeare and His Planets

The way in which directors nowadays like to imprint themselves on plays from the Elizabethan, Jacobean, and Caroline drama is to dress up their productions with physical business, most of it mime or farce. They evidently believe that doing this enlivens texts that are difficult and, in places, incomprehensible to a modern auditor, what with their spilling emotions; wild, partially obsolete vocabulary; strange oaths; networks of wordplay; extended metaphors; agile verse rhythms alternating with driving prose; metaphysical discourses; and locations that dissolve in a wink from Britain to Italy, Italy to Cyprus, Scotland to England, Verona to Mantua, a palace to a wood, a castle to a cave. Most of the time the embellishment by the director does little damage; the plays are big and sprawling enough to swallow up all kinds of additions—as well as suffer rude cuts—without losing their identity. They may even benefit if the director is ingenious. Peter Brook's A *Midsummer Night's Dream*, played inside white wooden walls, lofted Titania and Bottom on a couch up into the flies to imply the transports of their bestial love; and when Lysander tried to run from Hermia, she hurled herself into his arms and lay horizontally across them like a barrier that would not let him through the doorway, as if to demonstrate that what held them in this nightmare was their own thwarted intoxication.

It could be argued that the plays written in this period, from the early 1580s to 1642, themselves encourage tampering. Comedies, tragedies, histories, allegories, portraits of contemporary life, and admixtures of all of these, they consist of main plots that trail festoons of subplots; sextets and octets of principal characters that give way now and then to the piping and booming of the secondary voices. *The Tragedy of Antony and Cleopatra* has thirty-seven identified characters, plus clusters of officers, soldiers, messengers, and attendants. Some of Shakespeare's history plays have well over forty identified characters. In most of the many hundreds of surviving works written in those years up to 1642,[16] when Cromwell

---

[16] This Elizabethan-Jacobean-Caroline period, which we think of as being preeminently Shakespeare's, was populated by at least a score of other first-rate talents, with some of whom he collaborated. It is a tribute to their abilities that some of their contributions cannot be definitively separated from his. They include George Gascoigne (1542–77), John Lyly (1554–1606), Thomas Kyd (1558–94), George Peele (1557–96), Robert Greene (1558–92), George Chapman (1559–1634), Christopher Marlowe (1564–93), Thomas Middleton (1570–1627), Ben Jonson (1572–1637), Thomas Dekker (1572–1632), Thomas Heywood (1574–1641), Samuel Rowley (1575–1624), Cyril Tourneur (1575–1626), John Marston (1576–1634), John Fletcher (1579–1625), John Webster (1580–1634), Philip Massinger

closed the theaters by edict, a director finds such staggering abundance of event and personality that when he is let loose on almost any work he must feel rather like a five-year-old admitted for the first time to an enormous adventure playground. As further encouragement to the director, a great many of these plays already contain farce. Of Shakespeare's thirty-seven plays only fifteen, by my count, do not have any farcical scenes or characters in them.[17] These are mostly history plays, either British or Roman. But even among the fifteen, three offer us villains who are all the more sinister for being playful: Richard III, Iago in *Othello*, and Aaron the Moor in *Titus Andronicus*. Two outright comedies, *The Merry Wives of Windsor* and *The Comedy of Errors*, are heavily dosed with farce. And most of the other plays support farcical figures who range from servants, go-betweens, tradesmen, rustics, craftsmen and their apprentices, constables, amateur actors, schoolmasters, jailers, clowns, and jesters to bawds, harlots, and panders. Among them we find loons and rascals who, if their minor roles are brightly enacted, vie for remembrance with the heroes, heroines, and heavies: Christopher Sly, Holofernes, Launcelot Gobbo, Touchstone, Dogberry, Sir Toby Belch and Sir Andrew Aguecheek, Feste, Parolles, Elbow, Pistol, Lucio, Owen Glendower, Mercutio, and Puck. Even two of the great tragedies have their farcical breaks. Hamlet plays the clown now and then *vis-à-vis* Polonius, Claudius, Ophelia, and Rosencrantz and Guildenstern. *Macbeth* has occasioned much carping over the scene in Act II with the Porter and the knocking at the gate, an episode that became the theme of a defensive essay by Thomas de Quincey justifying the farcical interruption at a moment of high tension, right after the murder of King Duncan.

As for Shakespeare's contemporaries, we notice the same disposition in them to write farce into their subplots. *The Changeling* by Middleton and Rowley, a grisly story of a gentlewoman who

---

(1583–1640), Francis Beaumont (1584–1616), William Rowley (1585–1642), John Ford (1586–1639), Richard Brome (1590–1652), James Shirley (1596–1666). Many of these dates are approximate.

[17] The fifteen plays in question are the three parts of *Henry VI*, *King John*, *Richard II*, *Henry VIII*, *Richard III*, *Titus Andronicus*, *Julius Caesar*, *Othello*, *Antony and Cleopatra*, *Coriolanus*, *Timon of Athens*, *Pericles*, *Cymbeline*. *The Two Noble Kinsmen*, which Shakespeare is thought to have co-written with John Fletcher, also contains no farce.

hates a servant but allows him to kill for her and then becomes masochistically involved with him, has a subplot that takes place in an insane asylum and veers between farce and horror. Ford's *'Tis Pity She's a Whore*, dealing with a grim and incestuous love affair between Giovanni and his sister Annabella, has as one of Annabella's suitors a simpleton who tells her with superb tactlessness that he has recently met a girl "who had a face, methinks, worth twenty of you," and who, when he is later stabbed, cries out ridiculously, "Here's a stitch fallen in my guts" and "I am sure I cannot piss forward and backward, yet I am wet before and behind." In Marston's *The Malcontent* there is a fawning, foppish, Polonius-like courtier named Bilioso ("Bilious") whose loyalties swing about farcically in favor of whoever is currently riding high; he says at one point, "I had rather stand with wrong than fall with right," revealing an attitude known as "policy" (today we would call it "pragmatism") that seventeenth-century writers strenuously condemned and satirized. Massinger's *A New Way to Pay Old Debts* has a character in it called Master Greedy, "a hungry Justice of Peace," who spends his life looking forward to gigantic meals— tasting them, as it were, in advance. Shirley's *The Lady of Pleasure* presents us with two wealthy, idle, fashion-mad figures, Kickshaw, who is "fat like Christmas," and Littleworth, "lean like Candlemas"; a bawd named Madame Decoy; and a barber named Haircut. In these and other instances the farcical interlude from Medieval times has undergone changes, through the intervening Tudor period, and now, instead of standing as a separate work, has been incorporated into the larger drama.

Farce will sometimes enter, and even take over, the main plot. Marlowe's Dr. Faustus, once he abjures God, sells his soul to Lucifer, and can do anything he pleases, seems intent on indulging in pranks and nonsense. A distinguished critic, Harry Levin, writes that we might have expected more from Faustus than "jaunty hocus-pocus," such as tricking a horse dealer and then letting him appear to pull off one of Faustus' legs, or playing hob with a papal banquet and boxing the pontiff's ears. Dr. Levin observes that "such conjuring tricks may be mildly amusing, but are they worthy of the inspiration or worth the sacrifice?" He goes on to suggest that Marlowe's "refusal to believe in miracles may well have hindered him from making sorcery altogether credible in his plays. . . ."[18] But it could also be that Faustus, like the son of a billionaire, swimming in cash, doesn't know how to make the most of his freshly acquired power-without-responsibility. Such a situation is almost inevitably farcical, and supplied more than one film romp for Harold Lloyd and Buster Keaton. The main plot of Jonson's *Volpone: or, The Fox* is also built on farcical premises. A flamboyant con man, together with an equally unscrupulous aide, pretends to be rich and dying. Other predators with Italian names that mean Crow, Vulture, and Raven (all carrion-eating birds) visit him at his bedside and leave expensive gifts, each hoping to become Volpone's sole legatee.

Although far from dominating the written drama in this period, farce stayed alive and seethed. Almost every textbook used to state as a matter of course that the playwrights in the reigns of Elizabeth, James, and Charles I wrote their serious scenes for the aristocrats and courtiers, who occupied the expensive seats, and the farcical brawls and low comedy for the hoi polloi, the groundlings, most of whom stood in the pit area in front of the stage. But Henri Fluchère dismisses this cliché, remarking that we need not suppose that Shakespeare, for one, "alternates high poetry and farce in order to please *successively* the Court and the Pit. The Court equally with the Pit required clowning of him, and the Pit . . . appreciated, as did the favorites of Elizabeth and James I, Hamlet's soliloquies, the precious verbal fencing of Rosalind and Orlando, and the lyrical outbursts of Romeo."[19] Farce surmounts class barriers. The theater writers and practitioners of the period seemed instinctively aware of this, and would usually forgo a glossy finish in favor of a rough edge and texture in order to give their work an inclusive, class-free appeal. But at their hands farce underwent alterations and extensions. They may have taken it into their writings for the sake of contrast, but it acquired some of the high style of the surrounding prose and verse. In some cases, it remained sheer farce; in others, it developed into quite sophisticated games of wordplay, sexual innuendo, choplogic, and character assassination, crossing the invisible boundaries between humor and wit

---

[18] *The Overreacher: A Study of Christopher Marlowe*, by Harry Levin (Cambridge, Mass.: Harvard University Press, 1952), pp. 120–21.
[19] *Shakespeare and the Elizabethans* by Henri Fluchère (New York: Hill & Wang, 1956), trans. by Guy Hamilton, p. 23.

and preparing the way for the Restoration comedy of manners. One sign of these alterations was the increasing popularity of descriptive, comical names after 1600. As a summation of the effects of these plays on farce, one can say they gave it an intellectual and a verbal tonality more marked than in the farce of any writer since Aristophanes.

(II) After the Restoration

In 1642, when the Puritan spirit took over in Britain, Oliver Cromwell and his Roundheads brought to a boil the dispute between official religion and the theater. The Roundheads despised theater for being licentious and immoral. To some extent it was, and not only because of its subject matter: theater has always found new energies by reaching out beyond the pale of custom and acceptable taste. There had been all kinds of scandals. One kind in particular arose because of the association between male actors and the boys who played women's roles. Under official proscription most public playhouses, including all those in London, went dark, and remained so until the restoration of Charles II in 1660, although some performances took place in wealthy homes. Farce too went dark, at least in the written drama. Traveling players may still have plied their popular wares in the British provinces, but the records are scanty. The next farcical impulse was to come from France in the year after the English ban was imposed.

In 1643, Jean-Baptiste Poquelin dropped a possible career as a lawyer, for which he had qualified and registered the year before; left his home and the family business; and, renaming himself Molière, helped to incorporate a new acting troupe, the Illustrious Theater. After several years of tepid success and crippling debts acquired in Paris and Rouen, the company of about twenty players went on tour and stayed away from the capital for over twelve years. During the exile, Molière became its principal director, actor, author, and producer.

In the border country of southern France, and probably elsewhere, the Illustrious players undoubtedly crossed paths with commedia troupes from Italy. Most of Molière's early plays contain scenes and characters that lay French names and interpretations on commedia farce routines. They also consist, as do the commedia scenarios, of distinctive turns or acts written for the individual members of the company.[20] In his later, longer, more ambitious plays, written and staged, after he had won royal patronage, in Paris and various châteaux, Molière revisits those brief farces. An episode like that of the man who locks his flirtatious wife out of the house and is then tricked into letting her lock *him* out is taken nearly intact from an early one-act *The Jealous Husband* and replanted in *George Dandin*, a three-act, almost twenty years later. The servant who impersonates a physician in the farcical skit called *The Flying Doctor* becomes a pseudo-medical woodcutter in the three acts of *The Doctor in Spite of Himself;* at first this impostor tackles medicine reluctantly, but he begins to revel in it once he discovers that it takes no special learning to give patients advice that will kill them. *The Miser* and *Don Juan* and *The Bourgeois Gentleman,* all five-act plays, are splashed with farce, as when Harpagon the miser finds he's lending money at an extortionate interest rate to his own son; or when the Don has to confront simultaneously two girls both of whom he swears he loves; or when Monsieur Jourdain, the prototypical snob, goes through the ceremony of being elevated to the rank of a Turkish mamamouchi, a title that doesn't exist. In Molière's more formal verse plays, such as *Tartuffe,* farce keeps rearing its meddlesome head: the devout businessman Orgon crouches under a table and listens while the preacher he believes to be chaste and unworldly makes advances to Madame Orgon. Molière not only rescued the commedia farce—some of it—from oblivion and gave it new life: he also gave it respectability. Currents of it run, deep and hardly detectable, below the resilient alexandrines of *The Misanthrope, The School for Wives, The Learned Ladies,* but it gushes up again through his late plays *Scapin* and *The Imaginary Invalid.*

As early as 1663, while Molière was still finding his way as a dramatist, his farcical verse play *Sganarelle, or the Imaginary Cuckold* was adapted into English—freely, in both senses of the word, in that precopyright era. By the end of the seventeenth century no fewer than twenty British playwrights, among them the

---

[20] Shakespeare likewise wrote in parts that would show off the special talents of the actors at the Globe Theater. To do so is one of a resident playwright's understood obligations.

cream of Britain's playmakers (Dryden, Otway, Vanbrugh, Shadwell, Wycherley, and Aphra Behn), had more or less rewritten sundry Molière plays at least thirty-eight times. And the polite pillaging has continued ever since.[21] From Molière, however, the Restoration playwrights wanted to mine not his farce but his dramatic situations, as well as his caricatures of Court and society froth, male and female.

Because they are often brash in their attacks on social pretensions, vapidity, intrigues, and sexual frolics, these authors occasionally snap into and out of farce, leaving us with such images as that of the Frenchman Dufoy running onstage attached to a bathtub (in Etherege's *The Comical Revenge*); and Bayes the playwright (in Buckingham's *The Rehearsal*) instructing his actors on how to rise from the dead, gracefully and to music; and a love scene between Mrs. Sullen and Archer (in Farquhar's post-Restoration play *The Beaux' Stratagem*) in which she is fending him off and screaming bloody murder out loud while praying in asides that he not stop wooing her. Many of the characters have farcical tics and tag lines, as their names suggest—Sir Novelty Fashion, Lady Fidget, Sir Fopling Flutter, Mrs. Squeamish, Captain Bluffe, Mr. Careless, Sir Willful Witwoud, and Mr. Tattle, who marries Mrs. Frail. But these plays cannot be claimed for the farcical canon.[22] We cherish them for their glorious wit, for their intellectual substance expressed in glittering monologues and in verbal fencing between people who know how to place a simple word that turns a sentence into a sword. ("The woman's misfortunes and mine are nothing alike: her husband is sick, and mine, alas! is in health.") During the Restoration and the early years of Queen Anne (roughly 1665–1710) a debate went on between those playwrights who thought comedy should be humorous and those who thought it should be witty. Thomas Shadwell claimed that it was funnier when it depended upon humor, by which he meant something like the humors propounded by Ben Jonson: personal, innate attitudes

---

[21] The same period in British theater was tremendously indebted to another French dramatist: the tragedies of Corneille served as models for the English "heroic tragedies," consisting mostly of plaster sentiments and wooden verse that traduced Corneille's impassioned conflicts and noble style.

[22] Edward Ravenscroft explicitly called his plays (such as *The London Cuckolds*, 1661, and *The Anatomist*, 1697) farces, and they did prove to be rapid and reliable vehicles for farcical actors, but seem today like well-made comedies.

and external mannerisms. Dryden countered that the essence of comedy resided in wit, the deliberate cleverness on the part of speakers. As is always the case in literary disagreements, both contenders argued in favor of what they respectively liked (or hoped) to write; their theoretical statements were based on self-justification. Restoration comedy actually avails itself of both humor and wit. Almost every one of its plays with witty characters also has humorous ones who don't mean to be amusing when they say, for instance, "Oh, pray, Sir, spare all I have and take my life."

Laughing Through Sobs

Farce did not die out in the eighteenth century, but neither did it throw up anything like a successor to the many-sided Molière. In France, Alain-René Lesage, the novelist, wrote a sharp satire on businessmen in *Turcaret*; and by the end of the century Beaumarchais had become famous for his political activities (among them, providing funds for the American Revolution) and his comedies *The Barber of Seville* and *The Marriage of Figaro*, which have led double lives as plays and operas. In Italy, Goldoni resuscitated stories and characters from the commedia in modified form, although his later plays were written and staged in France by the Italian Comedians. Any of the foregoing works (say, *The Servant of Two Masters, Il Campiello*, and *The Hostess* by Goldoni) can be, and have been, farcically mounted; they seem to thrive nowadays on such directorial embroidery as the introduction of slapstick. In England, a number of authors (Susannah Centlivre, Samuel Foote, John Gay, and others) wrote farces or comedies with some farce ladled into them; Henry Fielding (1707–54) was responsible for several such riotously farcical pastiches as *Tom Thumb*, and Tobias Smollett (1721–71) for *The Reprisal*. Oliver Goldsmith and Richard Brinsley Sheridan contributed to the stock of outstanding comedies that one can watch and read repeatedly with increasing pleasure. But in the main, the taste of the century was for comic satire and lampooning, rather than for farce. And for a new species of play.

By the time Congreve, the master of witty *and* humorous comedy, had had his last play, *The Way of the World*, staged in 1700, Restoration drama had started to give way to sentimental, or "weeping," comedy. British and French stages alike were overrun with it in the next hundred years. And like a weed, it has since shown itself to be astonishingly hardy. In our time it has infested the theater capitals of the world. Broadway capitulated to it long ago and may never recover. Hollywood did too, and where Hollywood went, television lamely followed. Since sentimental comedy stands opposed to the insurgent spirit of farce, and of most other kinds of comedy—is, in fact, their enemy—it calls for a brief discussion here.

Farce laughs at the foolishness of men and women, and at their bad luck. Laughing may make a spectator feel better, or better disposed toward the world, or even better informed on how not to behave—that is, how to avoid becoming a figure of fun. The effects last, as a rule, only for a uselessly short time, or else foolish behavior would have died out centuries ago. But farce doesn't rely for its effects on just deserts (wrongs righted) or the smoothing out of differences between characters. If farce has often resorted to these devices, they have served merely as ways of bringing performances to a conventional close; they have signaled to an audience that the curtain will shortly come down or the lights in the auditorium go up. However, in sentimental comedy and its complement, the so-called "bourgeois drama," reconciliations have become not endings but ends, the very intentions of the plays. A wife forgives a husband for his philandering or for having contemplated divorce by murder. A father graciously concedes his child in marriage to somebody he disapproves of. Feuding families shake hands, the womenfolk exchange impulsive kisses, the offspring smile at one another shyly. The seventeenth and eighteenth centuries are to blame for this. The reconciliations themselves go back to Greek plays, but in the late Baroque theater, authors were not content to amuse people: they wanted to "move" them or "touch" them. Moving and touching played into the hands of writers with limited means.[23] In the twentieth century they have practically

---

[23] In 1772, Oliver Goldsmith, complaining about "the weeping sentimental comedy so much in fashion at present," declared, "there is one argument in favor of sentimental comedy, which will keep it on the stage, in spite of all that can be said against it. It is, of all others, the most easily written." Oliver Goldsmith, "An Essay on the Theater: or, A Comparison between Laughing and Sentimental Comedy," *Westminster Magazine*, Vol. 1, p. 4. Reprinted in *Goldsmith: Two Plays* (New York: Hill & Wang, 1958), pp. 99–102.

industrialized the performing arts, corrupting not only television sitcoms but also, at a far remove, the otherwise admirable miming of an artist like Marcel Marceau.[24]

Denmark and Central Europe

While commedia dell'arte and the French and English traditions persisted, farceurs sprang up throughout Europe. One of the most gifted was Ludvig Holberg (1684–1754). Born in Norway when that country was ruled by the king of Denmark, Holberg settled after a few years of European wandering in Copenhagen, where he became a leading history scholar and Scandinavia's first playwright of international stature. In the 1720s he rapidly wrote a series of vivacious plays for a newly founded private theater. He is sometimes referred to as the Molière of the North, doubtless because he populated his farce and high comedy with characters who are at the same time universal types and striking, unduplicable individuals. But although he knew, admired, and adapted some of Molière's plays, he might as justifiably be called the Baroque Plautus or the One-Man Commedia, since he ingeniously transplanted into Danish settings hybrid versions of the Latin author's and the Italian comedy's people and plots. Not that it matters exactly who his theatrical progenitors were. Plautus, the commedia, Molière, and Holberg form a continuous strand through the history of farce. And Holberg has his own imaginative verve.

Most dead authors remain alive to us through only one or two works, thanks to college survey courses and textbook anthologies of the same items. So it is with Holberg, who is most frequently identified with his early five-act play *Jeppe of the Hill*, a mixed comic-and-farcical portrait of a drunk. Jeppe is a peasant with a nagging wife who whips him with a switch she calls Master Eric. The play leaves open the question of whether she punishes him because he drinks or whether he is driven to drink by her torments, by his poverty, and by the greed of the local innkeeper, who drops

---

[24] The equivalent of moving and touching in the serious or bourgeois drama is the arousing of pity on behalf of certain characters. Pitifulness came into its own, not unexpectedly, at about the same time as sentimental comedy did, and derived from "tragedies of pathos," which in turn dipped away from the "tragedies of renunciation" written by Corneille, such as *Polyeucte* and *Cinna*.

salt into his beer and brandy to aggravate his thirst. Jeppe's part gives an actor large and varied opportunities. In one solo scene after he leaves the inn without having satisfied his thirst, he has to act out a dispute between his belly and legs, which want to return for more, and his back, which dreads another harsh taste of Master Eric. A later moment when the character is again at farcical odds with himself shows us Jeppe waking up in a lord's bed, like Christopher Sly, lapped in fine, embroidered linen and listening to soft music as he wonders whether he is still Jeppe or somebody he doesn't remember being, in paradise or merely asleep, and he alternates between laughing and crying.

In Germany more than sixty years earlier a Silesian-born older contemporary of Molière, Andreas Gryphius, had written a number of estimable tragedies, but also two rousing farce-comedies called *Absurda Comica, or Herr Peter Squenz*, a sort of reversal of the wooing-and-swooning pastoral play, spoken in peasant dialect (unusual for that time), and *Horribilicribrifax, or Choosing Lovers*, which mocked declarations of love at the other, upper end of the social register and supplied the most suggestive title in German literature. This pair of plays forms the most noteworthy link between the *Fastnachtsspiele*, or festival plays, of Hans Sachs and Jacob Ayrer in the sixteenth century and the stray farces of a few mid-eighteenth-century dramatists. For when Holberg died in 1754 a number of young German writers had recently produced farcical comedies, which were then often thought of, and still are, as being potboilers, quick and easy, not to say "cheap," routes to recognition. However, Johann Christian Kruger's *The Candidates* (1747), with its neatly turned political comments, and Johann Elias Schlegel's *The Dumb Beauty* (1748), a verse play, both had friendly, respectful receptions. Gotthold Ephraim Lessing, who twenty years later would become one of the most influential dramatic critics in history with the publication of his *Hamburg Dramaturgy* (1767), and would give a new impetus to the native German drama with his subsequent plays (especially *Miss Sara Sampson*, *Emilia Galotti*, *Minna von Barnhelm*, and *Nathan the Wise*), began his playwriting with several semifarces that were indebted to —once again—Plautus and Molière; they included *The Young Scholar* (1748), *The Misogynist* (also 1748), and *The Old Maid* (1749).

The two most imposing creators of German theater, Goethe and Schiller, never experimented with farce; but in the closing years of the eighteenth century and the opening years of the nineteenth, while these majestic poets lifted first romantic and then classical drama to its most exalted achievements in German, farce persisted. August von Kotzebue, a play-spinner who unburdened himself of commercial comedies as effortlessly as some executives today dash off memoranda, used farce here and there in his work as a counterpoint to the sentimentality that everybody in his time disparaged and everybody went to see. Ludwig Tieck, whose name has come down to us as the supreme translator of Shakespeare into German, delved into such varied types of farce as fantasy, fable, satire, and self-conscious theater in his dramatizations of fairy tales, such as *Puss in Boots*, *The Knight Bluebeard*, and *The Upside-Down World* (all 1797), *Zerbino: or, the Quest for Good Taste* and *Little Red Riding Hood* (both 1799). Tieck's buoyant plays not only avoid the obvious moralizing that sinks so many fables; they also are plausible psychological studies, even of his animals—the wolf, for example, who ingests Red Riding Hood. They would be worth reviving for their own sake, as well as in gratitude to Tieck for his devotion to Shakespeare. In the realistic vein, Heinrich von Kleist's *The Broken Jug* (1808) is a farcical trial play, still frequently done, in which the judge turns out to be the culprit, thus anticipating the denouement of *Ten Little Indians* by about a century and a quarter.

A playwright with the daunting name Ernst August, Count von Platen-Hallermünde derided the puffier tragedies of his time with a fine, sly sense of satire in, for instance, *The Romantic Oedipus* (1829). Von Platen's short-lived fellow countryman Christian Dietrich Grabbe feverishly wrote historical epics about Napoleon, Frederick Barbarossa, Hannibal, and the German king Henry VI; but these were preceded by a youthful effort, what a once-revered German historian called a "play of brilliant humor, profound contempt for the world and insolent arrogance"—namely, the iconoclastic *Jest, Satire, Irony, and Deeper Significance* (1822), which "cannot be staged at all."[25] It can be, of course. And has been.

---

[25] *Witkowski's German Drama of the Nineteenth Century*, trans. by L. E. Horning (New York, 1909), p. 39. *Jest, Satire, Irony, and Deeper Significance* is translated by Maurice Edwards (New York: Frederick Ungar, 1966).

Written when Grabbe was only twenty-one, it consists of a series of disconnected and sometimes hallucinatory scenes—which add up to a rivalry among three suitors for an heiress, complicated by the intervention of the Devil, his grandmother, and, for a few lines, the emperor Nero—that predate Surrealism by a hundred years. Another outstanding playwright of prophetic vision, Georg Büchner, who died at the age of twenty-three and whose *Woyzeck* and *Danton's Death* did not come into prominence until this century, wrote one comedy, *Leonce and Lena*, that is not exactly farcical but, like some of Shaw's and Wilde's plays, might be called intellectual farce in that its sumptuous dialogue makes sense out of nonsense. Its hero, a languid prince, does not want to be a prince; he gets married, although he doesn't want to marry; at the same time, he does fall in love with the princess he has been betrothed to; and therefore, after meeting her he tries to commit suicide. The play parodies the habit of work, the habit of play, the habit of living, and the customs of ruling and being ruled.

Frank Wedekind, who squeaks into the nineteenth century, even though his work, which foreshadows Expressionism, belongs conceptually to the twentieth, had a sardonic, even satanic outlook that shocked his audiences and was most hospitable to farce. *Spring's Awakening*, written in 1891 but not staged until 1906, and then (and many times since) expurgated for the stage, describes both cruelly and lyrically the heartbreak of adolescence and the stirrings of sexual impulses; but it has one scene of caricature-farce in which a group of schoolteachers sit in judgment on a student of fourteen who has written "a treatise twenty pages long in dialogue form, entitled *Copulation*, equipped with life-size illustrations and teeming with shameless indecencies."[26] The teachers' real preoccupation during the session is whether or not to open one of the windows in the room. Wedekind's *The Marquis of Keith* (1900) tells of a swindler who almost builds himself a financial empire by flim-flam tactics; after being caught, he concludes with a line that could be uttered by any fallen tragic hero: "Life is a roller coaster."

Many Austrian authors wrote farce into their plays. Two early ones were Philipp Hafner, in *Megara, the Terrible Witch* (1758),

---

[26] Translation by Eric Bentley in *The Modern Theater*, Vol. 6, (New York: Doubleday, 1960).

and Emanuel Schikaneder, whose libretti served the operas of eight different composers, the most celebrated work being Mozart's *The Magic Flute* (1791). Johann Nestroy, an actor and bass singer (who, by coincidence, played Sarastro in *The Magic Flute*), wrote more than sixty folk plays and magic stories, such as *Eulenspiegel* (1830), based on the adventures of a traditional German scamp and from which Richard Strauss drew a symphonic poem; *Lumpazivagabundus*, the name given to a wicked spirit (1833); and *He Wants to Go on a Spree* (1842), which was the source of Thornton Wilder's play *The Merchant of Yonkers*, which became *The Matchmaker*, which became *Hello, Dolly!* Ludwig Anzengruber wrote some farces, also based on Viennese and other Austrian folk tales but more realistic in tone than Nestroy's and in keeping with his period, the later nineteenth century, when the realism of Hebbel and Ibsen flew across Europe and remade the drama once more. Anzengruber's *Writers of the Cross*, portraying a conflict between clergy and peasants whose wives go on strike, has inevitably been compared to *Lysistrata*. Finally, in tracking down bits and pieces of farce in plays that do not fully subscribe to the genre, one should not overlook episodes from Arthur Schnitzler's *Anatol* (1893), *The Green Cockatoo* (1899), and—perhaps in part because of the British movie version—his best-remembered comedy, *La Ronde*, or *Reigen* (1903); still, in *The Green Cockatoo* the farcical moments are like paper screens through which the characters smash only to find themselves tipping over into an abyss of bloodshed and horror.

Russia

Farce came to Russia late, but when it arrived it exploded. Before the plays and brief skits of Nikolai Gogol, the most daring farce writer of the nineteenth century in any language, Russian authors had accomplished several high comedies, which have become classics.[27] Gogol, however, introduces new notes of ridicule in his drama and neurosis in his characters, which resound down to the present day.

---

[27] Most conspicuously Denis Fonvizin's *The Brigadier* (1766), *The Minor* (1782), and *Choosing a Tutor* (1790), and Aleksandr Griboyedov's *Wit from Woe* (1831, first production).

The critic Belinsky claimed Gogol for the nascent school of Realism; and it's true that he wrote about ordinary people, as well as aristocrats and high functionaries; ordinary life, rather than the cossetings and artificialities of society behavior. Other Russian commentators have maintained that Gogol was not so much a Realist as a Naturalist (exposing the evils of his time) or a Romantic, a satirist or a fantasist. Vladimir Nabokov calls him simply, or not so simply, "the strangest prose-poet Russia ever produced."[28] Gogol can certainly wear any of these labels. Just as certainly, he had a penchant or (as he himself might have put it) a nose for farce. In *The Inspector General* (1835) the mayor of a hick town summons his "cabinet" of local officials and starts a panic when he warns them that a government snooper either is coming from St. Petersburg or has already settled among them, incognito, to check up on their probity. But even before this gathering of petty crooks and nitwits ("I tell everyone openly that I take bribes," says the judge, "but what bribes? Wolfhound puppies"), we see from the program that some of the characters have farcical names; the judge is Liapkin-Tiapkin, and there is a pair of hardly distinguishable landowners called Bobchinsky and Dobchinsky. If we happen to read the play, instead of watching a performance, Gogol's notes to the actors about his dramatis personae cajole us into a receptive mood. The judge, for example, is "a man who has read five or six books, and so is something of a freethinker," while the postmaster is "good-natured to the point of simplemindedness."[29]

These dud souls are so gullible that they take the first stranger they hear about for the inspector. He happens to be an impoverished, unprincipled, "scatterbrained" clerk, Khlestakov by name, who has put up at the local inn. Having gambled away his income, he can't move out until he pays for his room. They flatter him. They bring him their compliments and grudges. They rat on their friends and fellow townspeople. They drop him money and chattels. Khlestakov, astonished at this turn in his fortune, plays up to them for all he's worth. He keeps his hand out, palm upturned; concocts stories about his connections in Petersburg ("I'm in lit-

---

[28] *Nikolai Gogol* (New York: New Directions, 1944), first line.
[29] The quotations here are taken from the English translation of Constance Garnett, revised by Leonard J. Kent, in *The Collected Tales and Plays of Nikolai Gogol* (New York: Pantheon, 1964).

erary circles . . . on friendly terms with Pushkin. I often used to say to him, "Well, Pushkin, old man, how are things?"); makes advances to the mayor's wife and daughter; and although he likes the wife better, promises to marry the daughter as soon as he returns. He leaves town, rich and magnificently sent off. Shortly before the curtain falls there is an announcement: the inspector general has arrived, this time the genuine article.

Through farce Gogol depicts the weaknesses and vulnerability in his people, who are also Russia's, and ours. When Khlestakov brags, "Tomorrow I am to be made a field marshal," he unaccountably loses his balance and almost falls to the floor, as if he can't stand up under the weight of his boast. This is our modern scourge of the Steppes and terror of the East, Genghis Khan reborn as a pretentious, grasping civil servant. Khlestakov is also a modern equivalent of the parasite in Plautus' farces, the self-invited dinner guest who battens on rich patrons. Food and other objects, dreams, insane reflections crowd in on the characters and obsess them, from vodka, fish, salted cucumbers, suitcases, and bits of paper to nightmares about rodents and playing cards. The patterns of these humble lives conform with somebody-or-other's law of probability that is the first rule of farce: if anything can go wrong, it will. Or: whatever is most unlikely is most likely to happen.

In *The Marriage* (1842), a "quite incredible incident" in two acts which is all too believable, another clerk escapes from his intended. The wedding arrangements have been made through a marriage broker, and the bride is about to walk in in her gown when the trembling groom, Podkoliosin, leaps out a window, hits the sidewalk with a thud, hails a cab, and orders it to take him to "Kanavka, near Semenovsky Bridge." Is he injured by his landing? Was the window jump a rehearsal for going off the bridge? Is the bride, who didn't care much for Podkoliosin, more relieved than disappointed? The gist of this play is, as in *The Inspector General*, not so much the events as the portraits, the gallery of quirky figures whose brains are bombarded by thoughts that emerge incomplete from their mouths. *The Gamblers* (1842), on the other hand, is a tidily plotted anecdote about a fleecer who gets well and truly fleeced. Yet Gogol, while holding here much more resolutely to his characters' main attributes, and not allowing their lines to drift off on winding streams of consciousness so that they come to seem less farcical than comic, nevertheless keeps up a farcical pace by means of unceasing exits and entrances. This substantial one-act again demonstrates the equivocal meaning of "realism" in Gogol. His antiheroic creatures utter noble and brave sentiments, announce driving ambitions, and proclaim themselves satisfied with their lot, but a certain faltering tone betrays them.[30]

This effect was matched in nineteenth-century drama by the work of only one other farce writer, who might almost have deduced a creed from Gogol and taken it as his own: Anton Chekhov. Half a dozen of Chekhov's early one-acts consist of farce of the realistic type.[31] Four of them are subtitled "a joke in one act," but they all work up a sweat of desperation as some characters try to convey their anguish to others who are too busy with their own anguish to listen. In *The Bear* (1888) a man calls on a fetching young widow to demand a sum of money owed him by her late husband. They insult each other at the tops of their voices and work up enough rage to begin a duel with pistols. But then, to his surprise, he falls madly in love with her eyes and her courage and her inept handling of a gun. They finish up in a crushing embrace, and we can assume that the debt is never paid. *The Proposal* (1888–89) is more or less *The Bear* in reverse. A man wants to marry his neighbor's daughter, but the three of them get into blustery arguments over the ownership of some meadows and over whose hunting dog is fiercer. The suitor, like many of Chekhov's younger men, is a hypochondriac. (This was not the only farcical gimmick that Harold Lloyd's scriptwriters were to pick up from Chekhov.) He imagines his heart is shrinking, his legs turning paralyzed, his eyes giving off sparks, and, for one moment of disbelief, that his shoulders are coming away. When the suitor passes out, the father joins his hands hurriedly to the daughter's. The young man comes to only to find himself engaged (and numb in one leg). *The Reluc-*

---

[30] In addition to these three plays, Gogol wrote a few dramatic sketches cannibalized from an earlier play that he decided to suppress, and also an afterword to *The Inspector General* in dialogue form.

[31] These six plays are included in *Ten Early Plays by Chekhov*, translated by Alex Szogyi (New York: Bantam, 1965).

tant Tragedian (1889) tells of a country dweller oppressed by having to do favors and errands for his wife, relatives, and neighbors. Every time he comes into town he has to travel home with an unmanageable load of packages. When the friend from whom he has asked to borrow a pistol to end his misery also asks a favor, the unwilling messenger goes off his head and chases his friend around the room yelling, like some daytime Dracula, "Blood! Give me blood!" *The Wedding* (1889–90) presents a reception messed up by one of the guests. He was supposed to be a general who would lend some class to the affair, but he turns out to be a decrepit lower-ranking former naval officer who reminisces sea-doggedly and incomprehensibly about his nautical past—"Top sheets, jib sheets laxed . . . taken to starboard"—in an "exalted tone" that bores everybody to distraction. *The Anniversary* (1891) amounts to another ruined ceremony (a recurring feature in Chekhov's plays). The chairman of a bank is being honored for fifteen triumphant and profit-laden years at the helm. He has himself made all the arrangements for the tributes and written the speeches that glorify him. But he cannot get rid of two talkative women. One is his wife, half his age, who insists on talking about the charming young men she met on vacation. The other, a lady whose husband lost his job, cannot seem to understand that he was never employed at the bank. In the early monologue *On the Harmfulness of Tobacco* (1886) an old man who smokes, Nyukhin, is supposed to give a lecture on the dangers of smoking. Instead he unloads a confession about how he has let his wife and daughters browbeat him. This little classic embodies one kind of unfulfilled longing expressed in Chekhov's full-length plays. His characters long for love and yet direct their affection at others who cannot reciprocate (*The Seagull, Uncle Vanya, The Three Sisters*, and *The Cherry Orchard* are mostly *about* unrequited, futile love); or they long nostalgically for a past that cannot be recaptured and may never have been as golden as it appears in retrospect; or else they are frustrated mystics who long for a state of communion with nature and the impersonal universe. So it is with Nyukhin.

In the middle of his rambling confession he suddenly says that he dreams of running away from his wife and six daughters (or are there seven?), to stand still in a field like a tree or a post or a scarecrow and gaze all night at the moon and "forget, forget." This is a longing for the release of death, as the order of the imagery suggests: first the living tree, then the inert post, then the scarecrow, a mere effigy of a man. He wants to run out of life into what he calls the night. Yet this play remains one of the funniest, for its length, ever written. It is charged with a pathos that is all the more pathetic for being interspersed with farce. And precisely because of Chekhov's farcical treatment, it is at the same time at the far end of the dramatic scale from sentimentality.

France Again

For many people the words "French" and "farce" belong together like "English" and "muffins." But when they use the term "French farce" they are thinking not of Molière, but of the nineteenth century and specifically Feydeau. As it happens, the French romantic and realistic outpourings of drama threw up a dozen or so playwrights who tried their hands at farce in either a desultory or a wholehearted manner, among them Guilbert de Pixérécourt, Eugène Scribe, Alfred de Musset (a poet-playwright of extraordinary range), Victorien Sardou, Édouard Pailleron, and Edmond Rostand. But the three who gave farce its modern lineaments and, because their plays enjoyed acclaim, its middle-class respectability were Labiche, Feydeau, and Courteline.

Labiche was embarking on a career of writing middle-class farces five or six years after the premiere of *The Inspector General* had displayed farce as a fast-rolling vehicle for satirizing the middle classes, rather than as "low comedy" that made fun only of the gawkiness of peasants and other poor, unlettered folk. Labiche was to stay with this career for close to forty years and produce over one hundred and fifty long and short plays, most of them written in collaboration. But when he came, late in his life, to collecting his "complete" works, he published only fifty-seven, the bulk of them (thirty-four) in one act. Labiche does satirize the merchants and minor officials among whom he grew up—*les bons bourgeois*, and their wives and families—and he might have taken as an overall epigraph the Russian saying Gogol attached to *The Inspector General*: "Don't blame the mirror if your mug looks twisted." Yet his satire is good-natured, reflecting his ability to laugh at himself and not only at others.

An expansive writer, Labiche sends his characters traveling from setting to setting in all of his multiact plays. The reason may be that the commercial theater in the third quarter of the century liked to uncover one contrasting decor after another that would knock the customers' eyes out, a deep stage set followed by a shallow one that masked the preparations for the next deep one. The boulevard houses for which he wrote, notably the Palais-Royal, were designed in neo-Baroque style to be emporia of magic and *luxe* whose proprietors could show off their technical wonders and have recognizable locations faithfully reproduced. In *Monsieur Perrichon's Trip* (1860) a prosperous coach builder takes his wife and marriageable daughter to a resort near Mont Blanc, and returns to Paris. But even as the play ends he is being forced to make another trip to the resort. In *Pots of Money* (1864) three men and two women who go to Paris to celebrate Mardi Gras are hounded from one spot to another by the police. *An Italian Straw Hat* (1851) takes the guests at a wedding party traipsing all over town when the hat that the bridegroom must find is back in his house among the wedding gifts. The four acts of *Gladiator's Thirty Millions* (1874), in which an American millionaire falls for a call girl under the impression that she is a society lady, take place in two handsome salons, a dentist's office (the first ever onstage?), and the open square in front of the Châtelet Theater, crowded with stalls and vendors. But the effect of the changes of scenery when we read or see the plays today is something different from exposure to one gorgeous stage picture after another. Labiche seems to be keeping his characters off balance; he doesn't let them settle down anywhere or feel at home. His plays are restless, itchy, slightly disconcerting, even while we laugh at them. People are not in their own domain for much of the action. When they are, something happens to make them feel out of place, as if the premises belonged to somebody else and they were intruders.

Despite the verisimilitude of his scenes, Labiche plays with deliberately theatrical effects, some of them inherited from earlier generations of playwrights, for he is no particular innovator but, rather, an improver of tried-and-true dramaturgical techniques. The characters use asides and occasionally speak to the audience.

Other signs of Labiche's traditionalism are his opening lines spoken by servants in many plays, and the brief quatrains at the end of an act, sung by the actors in chorus to popular tunes. [32]

Labiche's deftness in manipulating objects and making them virtually characters plotted into and out of the action has already been referred to (in Chapter 2). When a servant drops and breaks a salad bowl at the beginning of the short play *Grammar* (1867) we can feel confident that the author is not simply getting the play going with a crash but that the fragments of salad bowl will reappear. As they do. The servant buries them under an apricot tree to hide them from his master, but later they are exhumed by an amateur archeologist who is convinced that he has found some remains of Roman civilization. When the out-of-towners in *Pots of Money* enter a palatial restaurant, are handed elaborately framed menus, and are pleasantly surprised by the reasonable tariff, those menus will mean trouble. The frames conceal additional zeros, and the group will order dishes that are ten times as expensive as they seemed to be.

But Labiche (with his collaborators) doesn't depend solely on stage business for laughs. He has great facility with dialogue. He favors lines that add comic touches to the characterizations, self-deprecating humor (almost never wit) of a kind that would have gladdened Shadwell's heart. And some of his exchanges are pure illogic. In *The Man Who Set Fire to a Lady*, the culprit, who had smoked a cigarette that set off some firecrackers that destroyed a coach with a woman inside it, wonders why the victim didn't cry out for help. It will turn out that the "woman" was a wax dummy, but her husband, who is trying to collect compensation, speculates: "Her skirt had probably gone up in flames. She would never have dreamed of showing herself in that state. Ah, what virtue!" At the beginning of *An Italian Straw Hat* we are introduced to Félix, a flirtatious servant, and Virginie, a maid:

---

[32] These sung verses come from French vaudeville of the eighteenth century, which may have come indirectly from the Elizabethan practice of closing scenes with a series of rhyming (but unsung) couplets to mark the transition to a new setting. They are not quite the same as the British ballad-operas of John Gay (*The Beggar's Opera* and *Polly*, for example), in which the songs are set to familiar airs (thereby saving composers' royalties), but are integral to the action, like arias—not used for rounding off an act.

FÉLIX: Just one kiss?

VIRGINIE: I don't want to.

FÉLIX: Because I'm from the same place as you; I'm from Rambouillet.

VIRGINIE: Oh, now, look! If I had to kiss everyone from Rambouillet . . .

FÉLIX: The population's only four thousand.[33]

Labiche, for all his geniality, doesn't scruple to extract humor from subjects we would now consider in doubtful taste. Deformities, for example. These days there is more and more of what might be called the poetry of pathology in theater, utterly serious scrutinies of people who are depressed, dying, undergoing surgery, malformed, mutated; their conditions are discussed in sometimes clinical, sometimes elevated language. The last thing a recent playwright would dream of doing is laugh at a cripple, although several decades back Ionesco did introduce a young lady in *Jack, or the Submission* who had two noses. Nor does Labiche laugh at cripples exactly, but he does get humorous mileage out of deaf characters, such as an old uncle in *An Italian Straw Hat*, who remain oblivious to the conversation that goes on around and behind them, and continually offer the wrong replies to questions. His people have all kinds of other handicaps, real or (not altogether) imaginary, and these make them into unorthodox marriage partners. Behind the joshing about mismatches, though, there lurks a quasi-moralist, or at least, someone who, while making fun of marriage and its appanages, defends it indirectly. Marriage is normal. A family is normal. It's normal to have no disfigurements or hang-ups. It was normal for Labiche to retire when he felt written out, become a gentleman farmer, and live harmoniously on his estates with his family and livestock.

[33] There are no collections of Labiche's plays in English. Eric Bentley has included two, *Perrichon* (translated as *A Trip Abroad* by R. H. Ward) and *Célimare* (translated by Lynn and Theodore Hoffman), in *Let's Get a Divorce! and Other Plays* (New York: Hill & Wang, 1958); the Hoffmans have also translated *An Italian Straw Hat* in Bentley's *The Modern Theater*, Vol. 3 (New York: Doubleday, 1955); *Pots of Money (La Cagnotte)* appears in *Three Popular French Comedies*, translated by Albert Bermel (New York: Frederick Ungar, 1975). *The Man Who Set Fire to a Lady* translated by Fred Partridge is in *Tulane Drama Review*, T-6, Winter 1959. *Dust in Your Eyes (La Poudre aux yeux)* and *Ninety Degrees in the Shade* are both translated by Emanuel Wax (New York: Dramatists Play Service, 1962).

But Georges Feydeau, who wrote his first play (at eighteen) a few years after Labiche's retirement, seems to have gone untroubled by norms. He was far more pitiless in his portraiture. He positively dwelt on physical and mental aberrations. In *Keep an Eye on Amélie!* (1908) there's a page and a half of whispering about a growth on somebody's forehead. A *Flea in Her Ear* (1907) has a character in it who must use a false palate without which he can utter only incomprehensible sounds. Naturally, he knows a piece of information that is vital to the story, and when he leaves his palate soaking in a glass of water, somebody else innocently drinks it down, so that the information is left unsaid. In that same play the leading man goes to see a doctor because he fears he is impotent—a topic the censors had not had to contend with before, and which they let pass. As for marriage and the family, Feydeau makes hay with them. In his farce world, well-mated bed or marriage partners exist only in visions. That is, delusions. He writes first and foremost about adultery. He may not condone it, quite, because his characters, especially his middle-aged men, land in hot water, not to say boiling acid, every so often as a result of chasing other men's wives; but trysts and fleeting rendezvous are what wind them up and keep their lives catastrophic. Sometimes four or more affairs are going on simultaneously, each with its subplots.

Yet onstage a Feydeau farce, which trades on its profusion of characters—women of pleasure, painstaking lechers, shrewd wives, fumbling servants, sundry old people well past their dotage, and bewildered scapegoats, some of them doubles or look-alikes —is absolutely clear in its intentions and movements, a many-faceted crystal that throws off a barrage of gleams every time it turns. In spite of the coincidences and gimmicks that straighten out a cluster of near-calamities in the last act, nothing has happened by accident. All has been methodically prepared, and the audiences do not feel cheated. A letter, a character, a property that had been forgotten about in the rush of events restores sanity to the proceedings, and they realize that the author has played fair with them.

Feydeau must have studied not only Labiche but also Sardou and other engineers of the well-made and well-oiled play, those generations of stage artisans who preceded him in the boulevard theater and whom he supplanted by going them one better, one funnier. If it was Labiche who raised cross-plotting and multiple crises to a fine art, it was Feydeau who organized them into a science. He used the old devices of misunderstanding and freakish coincidence, but he increased the speed by imposing time limits and so compelled his characters to race the clock. A great sum of money will be lost if a marriage ceremony is not completed by a certain hour. A man must get a message to his mistress before his wife learns about the liaison. Ribadier, who lends his name to *The Ribadier System* (1892), hypnotizes his wife each time he has a date with another woman; he tells the secret to his best friend— who, by chance (and in Feydeau chance is always destiny), loves Ribadier's wife. Once Ribadier has left, the friend comes back and awakens Madame from her trance. But then Ribadier comes back too. Can the friend rehypnotize Madame in time?

It seems only just that several recent American directors have staged Feydeau with some scenes flickering under strobe lighting, as if played during an electric storm. The pulsing urgency of silent movies, which showed only sixteen frames per second, was transferred into that slightly earlier period in which much of the groundwork was laid for movie farces. Feydeau did go on writing until 1916, overlapping the early Sennett years and bringing his total of plays to thirty-nine in thirty-six years. Some of them remain unknown to English-speaking audiences, but a spate of English versions in the past fifteen years has lifted more than a dozen of them over the language barrier.[34] The British Broadcasting Corporation once sponsored a series of crackling, if drastically short-

---

[34] Some English translations and adaptations of other Feydeau plays, with the names of the translators or adapters in parentheses, are *Keep an Eye on Amélie!* (Brainerd Duffield; also translated by Noël Coward as *Look After Lulu*); *A Flea in Her Ear* and *Cat Among the Pigeons* (John Mortimer); *A Gown for His Mistress* and *The Happy Hunter* (Barnett Shaw); *Wooed and Viewed, On the Marry-Go-Wrong, Not by Bed Alone,* and *Going to Pot* (Norman R. Shapiro, published together with a substantial introduction to Feydeau's themes, Chicago: University of Chicago Press, 1970); *Hotel Paradiso* (Peter Glenville), *13 Rue de l'Amour* (Mawby Green and Ed Feilbert), *The Lady from Maxim's* (Gene Feist), *Chemin de Fer* (Suzanne Grossman and Paxton Whitehead).

Shapiro has recently published a second collection of mostly short plays by Feydeau called *Feydeau, First to Last* (Ithaca, N.Y.: Cornell University Press, 1981). The most comprehensive and discerning criticism in English of Feydeau's theater is *Georges Feydeau and the Aesthetics of Farce* by Stuart Baker (Ann Arbor, Mich.: University Microfilms International Research Press, 1982).

ened, adaptations of Feydeau. They were replayed on American public television, but with little fanfare.

Georges Courteline's dramatic output is slimmer than Feydeau's, twenty-eight plays, of which only *The Frolics of the Squadron* (1895) and *The Blockhead* (1909), both written in collaboration and not among his best work, are full-length. Courteline made his reputation as a prose humorist and continued to write essays and stories in a beautiful, stylish French after he became a playwright. But he fretted about his inability to develop more involved patterns. "My plots stop short after one act," he once complained, accusing himself of a lack of sustained imagination. Feydeau, who wrote his share of one-acts, is remembered for his three-hour farces that make up a full evening of excruciating amusement. But the distinctions between the two dramatists (who were friends) cut deeper than mere questions of length and complication. Feydeau oppresses his characters, then lets them off. He finishes a play so neatly that he doesn't usually leave much of a sting in the tail. Courteline does. He wants his work to go over well with his audiences, yet is incapable of appeasing them, cannot bring himself to forge happy, closed endings. There is in Courteline an unresolved and ambiguous note, something disquieting and bleak that resembles more the Molière of *The Misanthrope* and *George Dandin* than the Molière of *Scapin* and *The Bourgeois Gentleman*. His farces look forward to the "antifarces" of Adamov, Ionesco, and Beckett, not back to the *comédies-vaudevilles* of the nineteenth century and earlier, even when he does occasionally revamp some of the *vaudeville's* formulations.

Of all his plays, the two-act *Boubouroche* (1893) most subtly lets pain strangle laughter. Its hero, a kind, complacent bachelor in his late thirties, who lets everybody sponge off him, has supported a mistress, Adèle, for eight years in an apartment of her own. And for eight years Adèle has supported another lover in the same apartment. Whenever Boubouroche visits her, she hides the lover in a nice-sized closet, which in turn is outfitted like a tiny apartment with its own cramped furniture and candle. A neighbor of hers, an old man, tells Boubouroche about the deception. The lover is uncloseted; he leaves in leisurely, dignified fashion. Boubouroche rounds on Adèle, but she swears that she has been faithful, only she cannot disclose who the man is; it's a "family secret." Boubouroche not only swallows this barefaced lie; he not only weeps when she says she'll leave him unless he trusts her in the future; but he also goes on to beat up the old neighbor for slandering Adèle. Boubouroche's final spasm of rage caps his humiliation. But what exactly does it represent? Is he trying to assert himself after his contrite, not to say abject, surrender to Adèle? Has it at last dawned on him that his eight years of lovemaking were overheard by the lover and the neighbor? Does he suddenly realize that he will go on being similarly gulled all his life, that to be easygoing and generous is to offer oneself as a sacrifice? Can he suddenly see himself as the first unmarried cuckold?

A play in one scene performed the next year, *Afraid to Fight* (1894), also ends with an outburst of frustrated anger. A young husband and wife have returned from a dance, where she allowed an army officer to flirt with her. He rants about the way she behaved ("no better than a streetwalker"), while she taunts him for his cowardice. He would not confront the officer then and will not do so now—she has the man's address on a visiting card. By the end he is abusing not only her, but also her mother, her maid, and the cat ("the unnatural beast, emptying himself every morning all over the umbrella stand"). Obviously, though, he is having this tantrum because he is incensed at himself for not challenging the officer. This is farce with a thorn in the heart. In other words, Chekhovian drama.

In 1897, Courteline's *Hold On, Hortense!* seemed to be no more than a playful anecdote with music. A young man and his wife are expecting a baby within minutes. But they are about to be evicted from their apartment for rent arrears within a minute and a half. The moving men have arrived; they consist of a singing quartet. The landlord stalks in; he won't listen to pleas or hear of delays. All of a sudden, the tenant pulls out of the air a little-known law. It decrees that a pregnant woman may not be moved for at least nine days. But the landlord has already contracted with another tenant to take over the apartment. Too bad for him: if he moves the pregnant woman he will be sued, and if he doesn't admit the new tenant he will be sued. Exit landlord, bowed and baffled. The young people have nine days' grace—which, in Courteline's drama, is tantamount to living happily ever after.

But this variation on the old "I can't pay the rent / You *must* pay the rent" situation is enlivened by the introduction of a character and theme that were to make Courteline nationally famous. The tenant's name is Jean-Philippe La Brige, and he figures in a number of subsequent plays in which he points out the irrationality of what Frenchmen assumed to be their medley of most rational precepts, the law, including the bureaucratic civil code. La Brige tells his landlord, "You threatened me with the law. Now the law is on my side. That is how it happens nine times out of ten: the only way for a meek man to get satisfaction is to act like a tyrant. And then, to his astonishment and delight, he finds that the law is on his side."

In *Article 330* (1900) La Brige declares himself to be a "philosopher on the defensive," and observes that "Justice and Law are two entirely different things. Law is the caricature, the parody of Justice"—a sentiment that doesn't go down well with his hearers, since he is in court. He has been indicted for exposing his bare backside to 13,687 witnesses. The fact is that the Electric Transportation Company of the Paris World's Fair of 1900 has built a "moving boardwalk," a predecessor of the Disney World monorail, that passes La Brige's window. At the time when the thousands of witnesses saw him he was bending forward in his living room to pick up a coin. It is hard for La Brige to prove that he has not "offended against public decency," under Article 330. In vain does he protest that his privacy has been violated; that the animated frieze of spectators passing his windows has hurled cherry pits, olives, peanuts, and popcorn into his room; that he's been mocked, abused, and subjected to a constant barrage of noise; that, in short, Article 330 doesn't apply. The law, states the Judge, "does not intend to permit defendants to show up its contradictions, errors, and absurdities"; and therefore, although La Brige has "thoroughly established his case," he is to be fined, imprisoned for over a year, and made to pay court costs. La Brige ends the play with a cry, "I appeal to posterity!" As far as the law is concerned, he might as well appeal to posteriority.

Courteline called La Brige "the friend of the law," a title that caught on and stuck; but in later plays he did not always win in his brushes with his "friend," no matter how persuasively the hero argued from his lawyerlike familiarity with the civil code. In *The*

Scales of Justice (1901) he finds himself trapped between two opposing laws. One decrees that he must get his defective roof re-
paired so that slates don't drop on innocent passersby and brain
them. But as soon as he summons the roofing men, a local official,
backed by a local ordinance, enjoins him from making any alterations to his house that may bring it out of line or out of character
with his neighbors' houses. La Brige is stymied. So much so that
he, the formidable because unprofessional legal mind, is driven
for advice to a lawyer. The latter can recommend only that La
Brige willfully break the law and commit arson by setting fire to his
house, collecting the insurance and settling elsewhere on the proceeds. But while explaining his plight La Brige has been failing to
light one cigarette after another. Bits of hot sulfur have lodged in
his fingernail, scorched his palm, and flown into his eye. Who
could depend on 1901 matches to set fire to a piece of paper, let
alone a house?

After Feydeau and Courteline, farce in the French drama
needed recharging. Feydeau's imitators and outright plagiarizers
—and there were plenty of them—went into the used-bedroom-
furnishings business, where they pushed for easy, hand-me-down
laughs. Courteline seemed constricted by farce and to be trying to
escape into anecdotal satire of the literary kind practiced by Anatole France.[35] Two or three years after the turn of the century,
while both men were still actively writing, the next big impetus
came not from theater but from films, and most imaginatively
from a former stage magician, Georges Méliès, and a comedian,
Max Linder, who both saw and seized all kinds of fresh opportunities in the newborn medium.

But a poet named Alfred Jarry, one of those almost-demonic
figures in the line of Lautréamont and Rimbaud, whom the
French call *cursed*, had already unleashed a strange work, couched
in outlandish dialogue and bizarrely shaped scenes and acts, which

---

[35] Ten of Courteline's plays have so far been translated into English. *Article 330*, translated
by Jacques Barzun, and *Boubouroche*, *Afraid to Fight*, *Hold On, Hortense!*, and *Badin the
Bold*, translated by Albert Bermel, all appear in *The Plays of Courteline* (New York: Theatre
Arts Books, 1961). Mr. Barzun's translations of *The Scales of Justice*, *The Torn Transfer*, and
The Registered Letter are in *The Tulane Drama Review*, Vol. 3, No. 1, Oct., 1958. *The
Commissioner Has a Big Heart*, translated by Bermel, is in *Three Popular French Comedies*
(New York: Frederick Ungar, 1975). *These Cornfields*, translated by Eric Bentley, is in *Let's
Get a Divorce! and Other Plays, op. cit.*

set off a gigantic literary scandal. When *King Ubu* had its first night at the Théâtre Nouveau in Paris on December 11, 1896, and then its second night on December 12 (after which it vanished from the stage for twelve years), it flouted every known tradition with obscene thoroughness. I can think of only one earlier piece of theater to which it might be compared, and that not too closely, Grabbe's *Jest, Satire, Irony, and Deeper Significance*, written seventy-four years earlier. (Either Jarry knew and admired Grabbe's play, or else somebody brought it to his attention soon after *Ubu* was done, for he translated portions of it into French.)

Iconoclastic in form and content, *King Ubu* is a farce to end all farces. After a few lapses in time, it turned into a landmark play, and inspired wave after wave of peculiarly twentieth-century farces, starting with Dada and Surrealism, continuing with the farces of Ghelderode—composed mostly in the 1920s and 1930s, but hardly known outside Belgium until the 1950s—and culminating in the antifarces of Vian and Ionesco and the "ridiculous" theater of Off Off Broadway. As an insult to the French, German, and British classics, *King Ubu* has five acts, each broken into discontinuous scenes many of which run to only ten or twelve lines. It consists of a glorious conglomeration of theatrical parody, satire of French life, broad sight gags, masks that cover not merely the actors' faces but their entire bodies, off-color exclamations, and vaudeville. Jarry liked to think of it as being a specimen of *guignol*, or melodramatic horror; at least, he said so. But to a contemporary American it seems like a crazily warped version of a history play put together by a gag team consisting of Shakespeare, Calderón, Corneille, S. J. Perelman, and Lenny Bruce.

It tells how the pear-shaped, cowardly peasant Papa Ubu kills off his rivals for the throne of Poland, which is the kingdom of Nowhere. (The name of Poland was removed from some European maps in 1896, as if that country did not exist.) Ubu is aided and hindered by his unfaithful helpmeet, the equally pear-shaped Mama Ubu; and after mock battles, intrigues, treachery, and other grotesqueries and entertainments, he is dethroned by the crown prince of Nowhere, whose name, Bougrelas, innocently recalls such Polish names as Wenceslas and Ladislas but actually means Lazy Bugger. Ubu finally sails away for France, where he promises to begin another reign of terror. In the course of this perverted epic Jarry drops disrespectful allusions to sundry writings in French and other languages, but especially to *Richard III*, *Julius Caesar*, *Hamlet*, and *Macbeth*. Ubu, the ruthless, bungling lout who lusts after power and disposes of his foes by putting them through a debraining machine, is a laughably grotesque version of such military dictators as Caesar, Tamburlaine, and Napoleon. But he also anticipated the fascistic "folk" leaders of the twentieth century. I use the word "fascistic" advisedly. In one of a number of follow-up writings about Ubu, Jarry mentions the building of a platform supported on four shafts which are upraised and "united into a fascicle by the vigor of our [Ubu's] fist." Did Mussolini ever hear about this? Did Stalin and other practitioners of brainwashing know about the debraining machine? Before Freud isolated the id, Ubu personified it unhampered by an ego or a superego, giving himself up to appetites filched whole from dreams. He has a habit not so much of entering a scene as of smashing through a partition into it. He can be viewed as the greedy, snobbish French bourgeois citizen of Molière and the miserly French peasant of Balzac or Maupassant rolled into one as an earth-wrecker. Cyril Connolly, in a famous phrase that stuck, called him the Santa Claus of the atomic age, while Roger Shattuck describes him as Jarry's "Other, the flesh of his hallucination," and it's probable that Jarry did dredge this monster out of his own unconscious desires, everything he loathed about himself.

Hardened as we are today to scatology, we would not be startled, as the original French audience was, by the play's opening word, *Merdre!* ("Shitr!"), nor by the erotic and anal exclamations and wordplay, such as "By my green candle!" and "Hornsass, I'm dying!" When I saw the play at two different stagings Off Off Broadway the spectators were hard put to it to stay awake, partly, it's true, because the productions were bad and partly because the play's references went up into thin air or were edited enough to make them unintelligible. To remain alive as a play in its own right, and not simply survive as a document, *Ubu* needs fresh theatrical interpretations that will convey something akin to the shock aroused by its first production. Jarry was young, twenty-three, when he saw this play staged, and there is in it the adolescent's joy in uttering the forbidden, breaking the rules. But why do adolescents relish the forbidden and object to rules? Why, they seem to ask, do their elders wish to keep certain things unsaid? What exactly do the rules protect? Farce has always challenged the masks of adulthood.

(III) Nineteenth-Century Britain, Ireland, and America

Farce had a checkered life in nineteenth-century Britain. Playwrights continued to take out loans on French plays, as they had done in the previous two centuries. Sydney Grundy (1848–1914), for one, wafted *The Little Birds* by Labiche and Delacour into a suburban London setting, renamed it *A Pair of Spectacles* (1890), and tamed its few flights of fancy; Grundy was one of those commercial winners pumping out assortments of writings "adapted from the French" and "new and original plays" for whom Bernard Shaw reserved his most acidic critical notices. Isolated, homemade farces included J. M. Morton's *Box and Cox* (1847), later borrowed for a one-act comic opera, *Cox and Box*, by Arthur (subsequently Sir Arthur) Sullivan on a text by Sir Francis Cowley Burnand, and *Charley's Aunt* (1892) by Brandon Thomas, that earth mother of countless tales of a man in drag wooed by another man, which still rears its wigged head these days in regional and university theaters. Arthur Wing Pinero (1855–1934) launched himself as a playwright with farces about the horses-and-hounds set (the environment Shaw would later call "Horseback Hall"), such as *The Squire* (1881), *The Magistrate* (1885), and *Dandy Dick* (1887, revived a few years ago in London with Alastair Sim overworking his eyeballs as a compromised clergyman). But Pinero went on into well-made sentimentality about fallen women and other distressed people in upper society.

The century cast up only one dramatist, W. S. Gilbert (1836–1911), whose perseverance as a farceur compares with that of Labiche or Feydeau. Gilbert's theater was lapped at by currents of fantasy and ironic nonsense and satire that drifted through the century's British literature: fantasy from the hundreds of lavishly mounted fairy-tale plays of J. R. Planché (1796–1880) to the children's comedies of J. M. Barrie (1860–1937), *The Little Minister* (1897) and *Peter Pan* (1904), with their affable, writer-to-reader confidences in the stage directions; ironic nonsense of the kinds that saturate Lewis Carroll's fiction, the verses and drawings of

Edward Lear (1812–88) in *The Book of Nonsense* (1846), and the *Ruthless Rhymes for Heartless Homes* (1899) of Harry Graham (1874–1936);[36] and satire that extends from Edward Bulwer-Lytton's *Money* (1840) to Tom Robertson's blunt castigations in *Society* (1865), *Caste* (1867), *Progress* (1869), and *War* (1871). Not one of these plays is farcical, but Robertson (1829–71) advised and sponsored Gilbert, and the latter's chosen mode of satirical farce can be regarded as an extension of the former's satirical comedy.

Gilbert's plays and libretti for the operettas composed by Sullivan use age-old dramatic situations of mistaken identity, thwarted love, and misunderstandings, buffed to a nineteenth-century gloss. His juvenile leads are blank young swains with strong voices that belie their fearfulness about whether or not they are eligible, but the girls they ache for have more spirit and may even utter an epigram or two. The memorable characters are the older men, uncertain authority figures all, and the older women who tell the men what to do. Gilbert didn't bother to believe in the conflicts he created; rather than disagree or debate formally, his characters cheerfully expostulate at one another. But then, almost all his scripts are satires of the Victorian English (as well as modern Americans and just about everyone else), and they parody other writers. *Princess Ida* (1884) takes aim at *The Princess* by Tennyson, who had just become Poet Laureate; while Reginald Bunthorne, the "fleshly poet" of *Patience* (1881), is recognizably Oscar Wilde. Some of the settings are directly England—*The Sorcerer* (1877), *Trial by Jury* (1875), *Patience*, *The Pirates of Penzance* (1880), and *Ruddigore* (1887), the last two in Cornwall, England's westernmost peninsula. *H.M.S. Pinafore* (1878) takes place aboard ship, and *The Yeomen of the Guard* (1888) in the sixteenth century. Others have an exotic ambience: *Thespis* (1871) on Mount Olympus; *Iolanthe* (1882) in "an Arcadian landscape," a fairyland; *The Gondoliers* (1889) in Venice; *The Mountebanks* (1890) in Sicily; *Utopia, Limited* (1893) in "Lazyland"; and *The Mikado* (1885) in a Japan of the mind.

Since Gilbert makes no attempts at realistic geography, his au-

---

[36] Graham is the author of such plundered and altered four-line farces as: "Making toast by the fireside, / Nurse fell in the fire and died. / But, what makes it so much worse: / All the toast got burnt with Nurse," and "Into the well / The plumber built her / Aunt Jane fell. / We must get a filter."

diences have the best of two worlds. They can revel in absolute escapism (release from the workaday world) and at the same time savor his very pointed home truths. But Gilbert is more justly celebrated for his facility with language and his occasional glints of poetry than for his satire, even though his satirical barbs were the most pointed ones produced by an Englishman since Pope's. The quips—the actual lines and verses that deflate people and institutions—form a quoter's treasury. They were taken in large part from the "Bab Ballads" he had earlier contributed to the magazine *Fun* and then repolished. Not all of them fall under the heading of wit. Many are humor, and belong more to farce than to comedy, among them the half-deprecating, nearly nonsensical lyrics with which certain characters introduce themselves: "I am the very model of a modern major-general," "Oh! my name is John Wellington Wells, / I'm a dealer in magic and spells," King Gama's "If you give me your attention, I will tell you what I am: / I'm a genuine philanthropist—all other kinds are sham," and Sir Joseph Porter's "I am the monarch of the sea, / The ruler of the Queen's navee" (assisted by his sisters, and his cousins, and his aunts). The same kind of humor recurs in the dialogue. In *The Mikado*, Katisha, "a most unattractive old thing, / Tra la, / With a caricature of a face," tells Pooh Bah, "But I have a left shoulder-blade that is a miracle of loveliness. People comes miles to see it. My right elbow has a fascination that few can resist. . . . As for my circulation, it is the largest in the world." Lord Tolloller of *Iolanthe* says to Lord Mountararat, "You are very dear to me, George. We were boys together—at least *I* was."

As one of his few concessions to realism, Gilbert catches the inflections and affectations of upper-class speech, which, because of him as much as anybody, passed into the vocal mannerisms and vocabulary of the middle classes and have remained oppressively there ever since.[37] The "fear" adverbs in particular—frightfully,

---

[37] The popularity of—the craze for—Gilbert and Sullivan has been approached since only by that of Rodgers and Hammerstein. (From the idea of popularity I exclude recordings, films, and other types of exploitation that had not appeared in the 1870s to 1890s.) This is all the more startling in view of the G & S lampooning and hard hitting—newspaper reviewers were scandalized by the mere title *Ruddigore*—which are emotional worlds away from the nursemaidlike reassurances of R & H, almost every one of whose musicals contains at least one lugubrious number that encourages us to whistle a happy tune or climb every mountain or walk on, walk on through the wind and the rain.

awfully, shockingly, abominably, dreadfully, horribly, fearfully, terribly—became mannerisms in the plays of such later "sophisticates" as Noël Coward: slapdash, worn substitutes for wit and humor.

The four legitimate heirs of Gilbert in verbal dexterity happen to have had an affection that was not a weakness for farce. For one of them, Oscar Wilde, farce proved to be a culmination. For another, Bernard Shaw, it was a reservoir from which he siphoned off whatever quantities he needed through more than half a century of playwriting. For Lady Gregory and J. M. Synge, it served as a useful, middle-range weapon in their armories. All four wrote with a keen sense of the ridiculous and the therapeutic value of exposing it that characterizes the plays and fiction of a line of Irish authors stretching from Swift, Congreve, Goldsmith, and Sheridan to Lennox Robinson, Joyce, O'Casey, Beckett, and O'Brien.

Wilde's earlier plays, written between 1882 and 1895, strike us today as being better than competent, but if we read or see them in chronological order they don't begin to prepare us for the tornado that is *The Importance of Being Earnest* (1896). I hasten to mention that *Earnest* is not a finer play *because* it's a farce. In fact, it lacks one of the leading attributes of the genre: it doesn't bristle with stage business. And its main plot, that of a misplaced infant, which demands a recognition scene to round it off, is a standard ploy that goes back to the nonfarcical Greek New Comedy. Further, its milieu and its adroit, snip-snap dialogue come right out of comedies of manners and remind us stylistically of Restoration plays, not all of which had any farce in them. Objects do not figure significantly in the action, although there is a little byplay with cucumber sandwiches and a cigarette case in Act One, crumpets in Act Two, and a black leather handbag, the token of Jack's true birth and lineage. Nevertheless, the play moves like farce because of the quicksilver exchanges between its thoroughly artificial characters and because of the connecting up of dissociated ideas in an impudent, sometimes breathtaking fashion: "CECILY: But I don't like German. It isn't at all a becoming language. . . . I look quite plain after my German lesson." Or: "ALGERNON: I hope tomorrow will be a fine day, Lane. LANE: It never is, sir. ALGERNON: Lane, you're a perfect pessimist. LANE: I do my best to give satisfaction, sir." Or: "GWENDOLEN: If you are not too long, I will wait here for

you all my life." Or: "MISS PRISM: Cecily, you will read your Political Economy in my absence. The chapter of the Fall of the Rupee
you may omit. It is somewhat too sensational." Wilde, too, catches
accents of upper-class speech by adding words that stretch the
sentences and give them a casual, drawling sound that belies their
farcical intent and punctuates their rapidity: "*at all* a becoming
language . . . *quite* plain . . . a *perfect* pessimist . . . not *too* long
. . . *somewhat* too sensational." This effect has also been overused
since Wilde (and without his sharpness) until it sounds less imita-
tive than strangulated.

We are bound to wonder why *Earnest* displeased Bernard Shaw.
Privately "he thought it immature, inhuman, mechanical, old-
fashioned, funny but hateful," according to Hesketh Pearson,[38]
and in his *Saturday Review* notice said that although it amused
him, "unless comedy touches me as well as amuses me, it leaves
me with a sense of having wasted my evening. I go to the theater
to be moved to laughter, not to be tickled or bustled into it."[39] Yet
only six weeks earlier, in reviewing *An Ideal Husband*, Shaw had
perceived that Wilde, "in a certain sense . . . our only thorough
playwright . . . plays with everything: with wit, with philosophy,
with drama, with actors and audiences, with the whole theater."[40]
Shaw could here have been describing his own dramatic and other
writings, for he had a sportive streak that never allowed him to
take even his more hortatory passages seriously. He called this
quality

> a curious psychological thing. It has prevented me from being
> a really great author. I have unfortunately this desperate temp-
> tation that suddenly comes on me, just when I am really rising
> to the height of my power that I may become really tragic and
> great: some absurd joke occurs and the anti-climax is irresisti-
> ble. . . . I cannot deny that I have got the tragedian and I have
> got the clown in me; and the clown trips me up in the most
> dreadful way.[41]

---

[38] *George Bernard Shaw: His Life and Personality* (New York: Harper, 1942, reprinted Atheneum, 1963), p. 167.
[39] *Dramatic Opinions and Essays*, edited by James Huneker, Vol. 1 (New York: Brentano's,
1916), p. 33.
[40] *Op. cit.*, p. 12.
[41] *Shaw on Theater*, edited by E. J. West (New York: Hill & Wang, 1959), p. 194.

In trying to account for Shaw's distaste, one of his many biographers, St. John Ervine, another Irishman, quotes Dr. Johnson, who "remarked that the Irish are a fair minded people: 'they never speak well of each other.' "[42] But this incompatibility between fellow countrymen (and exiles by choice) doesn't explain why Shaw praised *An Ideal Husband,* nor why he tried to help Wilde after the latter's trial and imprisonment. I prefer to ascribe the distaste for *Earnest* to an aesthetically competitive feeling on Shaw's part. Wilde had pulled off what he himself had been reluctant to attempt: an altogether facetious play untrammeled by weighty themes, sustained speeches, or psychologizing. Shaw did indulge his clown (who had haggled him from the beginning), to the delight of his audiences, and allowed the tormentor to take charge of whole scenes at a time in the full-length plays *Arms and the Man* (1894), *You Never Can Tell* (1896), *The Devil's Disciple* (1897), *Caesar and Cleopatra* and *Captain Brassbound's Conversion* (both 1899), *Man and Superman* (1903), *John Bull's Other Island* (1904), *Major Barbara* (1905), *Androcles and the Lion* (1911), *Pygmalion* (1912), *Back to Methuselah* (1921), *The Apple Cart* (1929), and thenceforward as far as *Buoyant Billions,* written in 1947, when the playwright was ninety-one. Shaw's saddest work, *Heartbreak House* (1916), tingles with farce throughout; and that story of martyrdom *Saint Joan* (1923) opens with a farcical scene in which Robert de Baudricourt is intimidated by Joan's apparently supernatural powers. But only in his one-acts did this mighty intellect of the theater let rip and give his clown the freedom of the house —in *The Admirable Bashville* (1901), *How He Lied to Her Husband* (1904), *The Dark Lady of the Sonnets* (1910), *Overruled* (1912), *Augustus Does His Bit* and *O'Flaherty V.C.* (both 1917), *The Six of Calais* (1934), and most rampantly of all in *Passion, Poison and Petrifaction* (1905). This playlet, subtitled "a brief tragedy for Barns and Booths," begins with a cuckoo clock that strikes sixteen (some forty-five years before the "English clock" in Ionesco's *The Bald Soprano* opened that play by striking "seventeen English strokes"). Lady Magnesia Fitztollemache goes to bed in a converted bookcase, while a choir of angels sings her to sleep with

---

[42] *Bernard Shaw: His Life, Work, and Friends* by St. John Ervine (New York: William Morrow, 1956), p. 273.

"Won't you come home, Bill Bailey?" Her husband enters stealth-ily with a dagger, but her lover also arrives on the scene wearing evening dress of black on one side, yellow on the other so that he will never again be mistaken for a waiter. The lover drinks whiskey and soda, but the husband has poisoned the soda. When the lover squirms in agony, he endeavors to neutralize the poison by gorging on lumps of plaster, which contains lime, torn from the ceiling. But the plaster sets inside him and he rigidifies. A sudden storm brings on lightning, which destroys a policeman, a doctor, and the landlord, who had been summoned on short notice and depart on even shorter notice. They are swept out of the way by Lady Mag-nesia's maid and her broom. The lover, now a statue, raises his hands to bless the renewed union of man and wife. The curtain falls to the angelic strains of "Bill Bailey," which melt into the national anthem. The play was written for an Actors' Orphanage benefit and performed in a booth of the Medieval kind in the open air at Regent's Park, which has been the site of many productions of Shakespeare. Shaw, no doubt aware of the heavy proportion of actors in the audience, includes skits on *Othello* and sundry melo-dramas in his dialogue, as well as a sprinkling of famous quotations misquoted. Even in this little madcap exercise, his humor is at least as much verbal as physical.

Synge's six plays, although verbally agile, have little in common with those of Wilde or Shaw. His name is pronounced "sing," and that is what his plays do as they celebrate the blessings and travails of living in the western outposts of Ireland, next to an ocean of poverty on one side and, on the other, visionary meadows of free-dom. Synge's melodic dialogue invokes a pathos that grows out of genuine, transmitted suffering, rather than concocted sentiment. His short *Riders to the Sea* (1904), a grim story, rich in symbolic content, about a widow's loss to the sea of the last of her six sons, stays well away from comedy, let alone farce. It is one of the high dramas of the modern era, matched in its dramatic intensity, and for its compactness, only by Giovanni Verga's *Cavalleria Rusti-cana* (*Rustic Chivalry*, 1884). Synge's last play, a three-act, *Deirdre of the Sorrows* (1910), his reinterpretation of an ancient Celtic myth, also makes no concessions to wit or humor. But three of his four remaining plays swerve periodically into a lyrical style of farce that is unique in the drama, tinted as it is with a brogue that Synge knew how to fashion into active poetry. In *The Tinker's Wedding* (1903, revised 1906) a mercenary priest will not confer respectability on a brawling vagabond woman, Sarah Casey, who calls herself "the Beauty of Ballinacree," by marrying her to the tinker she lives and roams with, because she can't pay enough. The priest gets gagged and bound with sacking (reminders of Géronte and Scapin) by the pair, aided by the tinker's old souse of a mother. Sarah swears, "It'll be a long day till I go making talk of marriage or the like of that."

The Playboy of the Western World (1907) tells of a humorous spiritual rebirth. Timid young Christy Mahon thinks he has murdered his father, a tough old peasant, because "it was a bitter life he led me till I did up a Tuesday and halve his skull." The village where Christy takes refuge from the "Peelers" welcomes him as the Thebans did Oedipus. Treat a fellow like a hero and, in this case, he behaves like one, winning the local races and the adoration of the village girls. But the old father, far from dead, is in pursuit, with his skull bandaged and looking like a ghost. Christy tries to brain him a second time, and again fails. The villagers, disappointed that Christy is not an authentic murderer, tie him up and torture him. The very girl he falls in love with, Pegeen, burns his leg with a lump of hot peat from the fireplace. It's his father who unties Christy, and the two of them depart, reconciled but with their original relationship reversed, "like a gallant captain with his heathen slave," thanking the villagers sourly because they've turned him, as he puts it, into "a likely gaffer in the end of all, the way I'll go romancing through a romping lifetime." Pegeen, regretting her haste and cruelty, wails, "Oh, my grief, I've lost him surely. I've lost the only playboy of the Western world." Thus, Synge seems to be saying, has Ireland always treated her heroes, driving them into exile, in this case Christy Mahon, a "Christ Man."

But Synge's most triumphant incorporation of farce into his plangently affecting pathos occurs in *The Well of the Saints* (1905), a short three-act in which the principals are a couple of blind, middle-aged beggars, Mary and Martin Doul. A saint sprinkles their eyes with water from a holy well. But when these pitiful souls who believed themselves fine and impressive figures see each other for the first time, weathered and decrepit, they squabble, accuse each other of deceit, and separate in anger. Treated no longer as beggars but as able-bodied people, they must now earn their keep. Luckily or unluckily for them, the miracle is short-lived: the blindness returns. When the saint offers to sprinkle them again with the water, they refuse, choosing beggary and blindness over the ugly realities of sight and work. Like Christy and his father, they are driven out of the community. They will go south with mixed feelings (reflecting the mixed feelings engendered by the play) from this eastern settlement to "where the people will have kind voices maybe, and we won't know their villainy at all," as Martin says. Mary is less sanguine: "It's a long way itself . . . where you do have to be walking with a slough of wet on the one side and slough of wet on the other, and you going a stony path with a north wind blowing behind." She is talking in the twentieth-century accents of farce-undermined-by-despair.

The person who did more than any other two or three people to found and nurture the Irish drama and its voice, the Abbey Theater, was that prodigy, Lady Augusta Gregory (born Isabella Augusta Persse). Not only a full-time manager and an encourager of dramatists from Yeats, Synge, and Edward Martyn to O'Casey and Denis Johnston, she also was herself a formidable playwright of comedy, tragedy, and farce, and an essayist, historian, and translator of Molière and Goldoni.[43] Of her half-dozen or so farces— including *Spreading the News* (1904), *The Jackdaw* (1907), and *The Image* (1909)—two, set in the tiny town of Cloon, exhibit her skills with language, character, and situation. *Hyacinth Halvey* (1906) is named after a youngster who has come to work in Cloon as a sub–sanitary inspector and brought a clutch of glowing reference letters written, like most such documents, by people of standing who hardly know the subject. The townsfolk he meets so revere him that "in no way wishful to be an example" and "a credit to the town," Hyacinth first steals a dead sheep from a butcher's shop and then plunders the local church. But his efforts to blight his good name turn against him. He is coerced into giving a public lecture on virtue and temperance, marched through the town

---

[43] Her translations of *The Doctor in Spite of Himself, The Miser, The Bourgeois Gentleman,* and *Scapin* are collected in *The Kiltartan Molière* (Dublin: 1910). Like *Mirandolina,* taken from Goldoni's *La Locandiera,* they move the action into Irish settings and the supple Irish dialect of County Galway, where she grew up.

seated in a chair at shoulder height, and called "the preserver of the poor," one of "the holy martyrs." *The Workhouse Ward* (1908) shows us two old, sick men in adjoining poorhouse beds. They have bickered and fought since they were boys, and now spend their days wrangling over their reputations, their families and bloodlines, their faults, their infirmities. When the sister of one offers to take him home to live with her on a farm that sounds idyllic, he is at first enraptured. But then he realizes that he will be miserable without his lifelong friend-enemy. The sister refuses to take in two men; she remembers their altercations from years before. The brother will not go with her. The playlet ends with the two curmudgeons hurling at each other pillows, mugs, prayer books, and anything else they can lay their arthritic hands on in their old, incorrigible way. Lady Gregory writes in an idiom that has an unforced richness to it; it sounds less "composed" than the dialogue of Wilde, Shaw, or Synge. One blessing from *The Workhouse Ward* runs: "The height of the castle of luck on you!" She was no bland realist, but she did want her plays to draw to the Abbey popular audiences who would have a good time there and recognize—no, not themselves exactly, for audiences never do that, but at least their neighbors.

Burlesques, et Cetera

Through the latter half of the 1800s and on up to the outbreak of World War I, farce continued to lodge wherever it could find a berth. Besides taking up residence in legitimate plays by American authors, such as Edward Harrigan (1845–1911), Augustus Thomas (1857–1934), and Clyde Fitch (1865–1909), who adhered to the European formats of well-made plays, it entered theatrical entertainments of many other kinds. Early burlesque (parodies and travesties of famous novels, poems, and plays) gave way to a later species, often ending in a *k*, instead of a *q-u-e*, which traded on its thinly—or even transparently—clad women; striptease as such came in later still, perhaps not by accident at the beginning of the Great Depression, and it may have been the comedians and other farceurs taking part in these shows who coined the term "a hard act to follow." Farce popped up at different times in honky-tonks, musical plays, extravaganzas, revues, nightclub cabarets, the circus, vaudeville (in the United States), or music hall (in the United Kingdom), always consisting, like the Medieval traveling show, of disconnected turns, sometimes linked together by a weak theme. The Rogers Brothers, Max and Gus, for example, did a series of "vaudeville farces" set in Wall Street, Paris, Central Park, or Washington; and the *Ziegfeld Follies*, which were launched in 1907, did one show on the history of the world, a topic open enough to include anything or everything, but especially dozens of Anna Held Girls (Miss Held was Mr. Ziegfeld's wife).

The British music hall started out in the middle of the nineteenth century as singing and instrumental acts done by amateurs in public houses, taverns where performers and spectators got well lubricated before and during the show. In some pubs a special room was set aside in which hired professionals came to do their own numbers and to lead communal singing. Some pub owners eventually opened theatrical premises next door for the divided benefit of those who wanted to concentrate on singing or drinking. In this "hall" set aside for "music" other types of artist appeared: dancers, solo comics, actors doing skits or even short plays, impersonators. By the 1880s, music hall had evolved into an institution in its own right, depending on performers who plied the circuits much like touring theater troupes. These performers had a few staple routines which they stayed with most of their working lives; in this respect they resembled the actors of the commedia dell'arte. Their audiences might each see them once a year or less and *expected* the same old act, looked forward to it. As a result, the individual performer might become famous for one song or skit if he or she was lucky, unusually talented, or foxily promoted. The craving for novelty, a constant supply of new material, arrived only with the advent of radio and television and the mass audience. Singing in pubs has persisted as a separate recreation to the present day; on Saturday nights somebody may come in to accompany on the piano or the piano accordion, and a few of the more adventurous and mellow patrons will dance. But music halls, in which customers drank at tables while they listened, waved their beer glasses in tempo, and sometimes consulted song sheets or books, were supplanted by variety.

In the United States, vaudeville took over from the honky-tonks. There customers had once sat at tables with hostesses who enticed them to drink more and more whiskey-flavored tea. These hostesses, who collected a modest percentage on each drink, would then join forces for a chorus—movements and gyrations, rather than dancing—while the customers threw money at them. The girls must have been hit by appreciable sums, because eventually honky-tonk managements organized the choruses into shows, charged admission, and paid the former hostesses wages. These were the forerunners of shows that would "bill" the big-timers of the 1900s (who played only two shows a day, instead of three, four, or more) at Hammerstein's, Loew's State, and the Palace in New York, at the Olympia in Paris (or just possibly the Folies-Bergère), and the Palladium (sometimes by way of the Windmill) in London. Vaudeville/variety *was* show business, that scintillating confusion of popular arts.

By 1913, according to a *New York Times* survey, there were 2,973 theaters in this country that booked vaudeville acts.[44] Many of the top names playing these houses transferred into films, radio, and television. Mae West, Marie Dressler, George Burns and Gracie Allen, Jack Benny, George Jessel, Will Rogers, Milton Berle, and W. C. Fields, among others. But Walter Huston, Barbara Stanwyck, William Demarest, Penny Singleton, Leon Errol, Victor Moore, James Cagney, and Cary Grant also went into films from vaudeville; while dramatic actors of the caliber of Alla Nazimova and Ethel Barrymore did vaudeville stints in sketches between their "legit" assignments.

Many of the sketches were deliberately sententious, moral anecdotes, and not funny, much less farcical. They aped the popular drama in relying on coincidences of name and appearance, misunderstandings, forgiveness, and noble gestures. The solo acts, or "singles," for the most part confidential monologues or storytelling, resembled the duos (comic and straight man) in retailing ethnic and misogynistic gags. Blacks, Irishmen, Jews, Italians, and "Dutchmen" (Germans) were favorite targets, and the comics

[44] Fifty-three of those theaters were in the borough of Brooklyn, fifty-one in Philadelphia, thirty in Boston, thirteen in Cincinnati. These *Times* figures are cited in *Once Upon a Stage* by Charles and Louise Samuels (New York: Dodd, Mead, 1974), p. 248. Shortly before World War I, a high proportion of the theaters had been taken over or built by one of two chains controlled (mostly west of Chicago) by Martin Beck or (in the East) by B. F. Keith and his partner-successor, Ed Albee.

dressed in strictly conventional outfits.[45] All the talking acts traded heavily on wordplay that now seems bewhiskered, if not moldy, but took life from the timing and accompanying hand movements. "TEACHER: Give me a sentence with the word *delight* in it. PUPIL: The wind blew so hard it blew out delight." "WOMAN: The man I marry must be straight, upright, and grand. MAN: Say, you don't want a man, you want a piano." The dialogue moved rapidly from topic to topic by means of perfunctory transitions: "by the way" or "incidentally" or "that reminds me" or "talking of people . . ."

But women, and particularly wives, came in for the most abuse. "A woman has twenty-four ribs and an umbrella has thirty ribs, and yet see how much easier it is to shut up an umbrella. . . . Can you imagine a barber trying to shave a woman's chin? All he would have to do is hold the razor to the chin and she would talk so much that the chin would shave itself," says a comic playing a preacher in blackface.[46] An Irish comic tells how "my wife and her mother tuck the horse out fur a drive in the park the other day; the horse ran away, the buggy upset, and my wife and mother-in-law war thrun out and kilt. Now, ayther you belave me or not, more than five hundret min have been after me thrying to buy that horse."[47] In a typical sketch between a man and a woman the man garners almost all the good lines and effortlessly tops the few good ones allotted to the woman, so that she serves as both a feed and a mark.[48] A "two-woman act" pits somebody from the carriage trade, the straight woman, against an eccentrically dressed heroine: "STRAIGHT WOMAN *(Looking at ring on comedienne's finger)*: Say, that's a nice emerald you have there. COMEDIENNE: That's a diamond. STRAIGHT WOMAN: Who ever heard of a green diamond?

---

[45] In *Vaudeville* by Joe Laurie, Jr. (New York: Henry Holt, 1953), an invaluable source of information, especially for its reconstructions of different types of turns, a "Double Dutch Act" has a straight man who is tall and wears a "large-checkered suit, with the coat short and with large pearl buttons" and a "derby hat, large collar, loud tie, big squeaky tan shoes." The comedian has a "belly-pad," wide-striped suit, brown derby, big shoes. "They both wear chin pieces" (pp. 444–45). In "The Double Wop Act" the "comedian has long mustache and bandanna handerchief around neck. Straight man wears celluloid collar, red tie, big watch chain, yellow shoes that squeak, and is sort of sporty in an Italian way" (p. 448). In "The Straight and the Jew" Mr. Cohen has "hat over ears, short beard, and misfit suit" (p. 454).
[46] Laurie, *op. cit.*, p. 439, "The Stump Speech."
[47] Laurie, *op. cit.*, p. 452.
[48] Laurie, *op. cit.*, pp. 423–27.

COMEDIENNE: Give it a chance; it isn't ripe yet."[49] In this duologue women get some of their own back on men (not much), but they spend more time making fun of each other. It would be interesting to know the sex of the writer of the original script.

Almost every act, though, had its moments of shucking off the comedy of stereotypes and moving into farce, physical or verbal. Most comics were multitalented; did their songs in a farcical style, often striking up conversations with the orchestra, the conductor, or the audience between verses; and specialized in their own kinds of pratfalls and other antics. Joe Smith played a fireman who comes into a burning house, with smoke and flames visible in the next room as he sits down calmly, takes out a sample case, and discusses with the homeowners what size and quality of ladder they would like him to use.[50] A Viennese named A. Robins played a violin that shrank down to almost nothing but kept giving out music. He would also take out from under his coattails a cornet, a trombone, a bass violin, drums, flowers, a music stand, and a campstool, proceeding to play each instrument in turn. His secret: all the props were false models which either folded up or were inflatable; Robins did not actually play the instruments, he imitated the sound of each by humming.[51] In a typical schoolroom shtick the teacher would tell a troublesome pupil to hold out his hand and, when the youngster obeyed, hit him on the head with an umbrella.[52] Again like the commedia actors, vaudevillians had to be alert in order to improvise when necessary. Jack Durant came into a sketch in which a live dog had urinated by accident on a desk and on the floor. Durant deliberately did handstands and cartwheels in the urine and kept offering to shake hands with another performer; the audience, according to Durant, went hysterical.[53]

Some comics, like Jean Carroll, had an aptitude for verbal farce. "I used to do that routine about my daughter being a hippy with

[49] Laurie, op. cit., p. 459.
[50] Bill Smith, The Vaudevillians (New York: Macmillan, 1976), p. 245. Two more recent sources of gags and routines from vaudeville have been stage productions: the Broadway musical Sugar Babies, which opened in 1980, and Will B. Able's show Baggy Pants, which has been touring the U.S. since 1973.
[51] Samuels, op. cit., p. 161.
[52] Laurie, op. cit., p. 428.
[53] Smith, op. cit., p.111.

the dirty sneakers and dirty blue jeans, but why a beard? And you know people would actually come to me and say, 'Does your daughter really have a beard?' I'd say, 'No, I made her shave it, but I let her keep her mustache.' "[54] Eve Sully of the Block and Sully team reports that "I'd say to Harry Richman, 'What time is it?' and he'd say, 'Eight-thirty,' and I'd slap him right and left. Then he'd yell, 'What's the idea?' and I'd answer, 'All day I've been asking people what time it was and everyone has told me different.' "[55] In a two-man act the straight man would ask: "Of course, you know what a miracle is?" The routine went on: "COMEDIAN: Well, if you see a bull in a field . . . STRAIGHT MAN: Yes, if you see a bull in a field? COMEDIAN: That ain't no miracle. STRAIGHT MAN: Of course not. COMEDIAN: And if you see a thistle in a field, that ain't no miracle. STRAIGHT MAN: Of course a thistle in a field is no miracle. COMEDIAN: And if you hear a lark singing, that ain't no miracle. STRAIGHT MAN: Of course hearing a lark sing is no miracle. CO-MEDIAN: But if you see a bull sitting on a thistle singing like a lark, *that's a miracle.*"[56]

What are the overall changes that took place in farce between 411 B.C. and 1900? It moved indoors. It played to smaller houses. It acquired technical paraphernalia that enabled it to depend on stage wizardry. But aesthetically it did not advance; it retreated. Vaudevillians of the turn of the century may have had more specialized polish, and therefore less versatility, than their counterparts in the *phlyakes* of Megara and Sicily—and here I am speculating—but so far as we can judge, the material they used didn't improve. In written drama, *Lysistrata's* brash feminism gave way to the morally tepid bedroom farce, a slick, mindless evening out. The journey had been long and roundabout, forward in time, backward in artistry. If we revert for an instant to the theme of women's attempts at emancipation, we realize that more serious drama, comedy included, did not come off so badly. The heroines of Ibsen and Shaw compare favorably as dramatic portraits with those of Sophocles and Euripides. But farce lagged. It breathed

---

[54] Smith, *op. cit.*, p. 258.
[55] Smith, *op. cit.*, p. 80.
[56] Laurie, *op. cit.*, p. 457.

stale air, needed an intake of fresh ideas. Some of these the twentieth-century theater would uncover by breaking away from the degeneration of Plautus' plots and looking for its leads to Jarry, Grabbe, and the movies.

◆

SIX

SENNETT AND FARCE ON FILM

Out in the countryside somewhere, a burly maiden of uncertain years called Tillie Banks tosses a brick over a hedge as carelessly as one might toss a message to the wind. Cut to Charlie, a "city slicker" in dandified clothing, who, for reasons ungiven, is passing the hedge on the other side. He receives the brick on the head. His injury introduces guileless Tillie to the mustachioed rascal who will rob her of her innocence and money. In a series of snappy misadventures, Charlie, abetted and frustrated by his jealous girlfriend Mabel, courts Tillie, hauls her out of her rural element and into the city, gets her drunk, steals her pocketbook, and abandons her. There she must demean herself by drudging as a waitress and entertaining the diners with frenzied and clumsy bumps and grinds. After he hears she has inherited a fortune and a town house from her uncle, Charlie returns to Tillie, proposes, and is accepted. But it dawns on Tillie that he is deceiving her when she catches him embracing Mabel. Followed by a line of Keystone Cops and brandishing a pistol loaded with inexhaustible ammunition, she chases Charlie and Mabel to Sunset Pier, where she sets off a riot and gets dunked several times in the scummy Pacific. Charlie is arrested by the Cops, and Tillie and Mabel commiserate with each other over their escape from a fate worse than spinsterhood.

Into the making of *Tillie's Punctured Romance*, released in late 1914, Mack Sennett (1880–1960), the producer-director of Key-

stone Studios, poured copious resources. It featured his brightest
male and female comics, Charles Chaplin and Mabel Normand.
Its supporting cast included established "types," Mack Swain,
Chester Conklin, and Charles Murray (who had each starred in
his own series as respectively Ambrose, Droppington, and Hogan);
Alice Howell and Alice Davenport, recognizable from their portrayals of wives and sweethearts in many short films; the draco-
nian, mother-in-law-ish Phyllis Allen; trusties of the Keystone Cop
brigade who would later distinguish themselves individually as
farce artists, such as Hank Mann, George (Slim) Summerville,
and Al St. John; Edgar Kennedy and Harry McCoy, who had
already graduated from the anonymous ranks of the Cops into
roles that carried names or titles ("proprietor," "pianist"); and
Minta Durfee, the pretty, diminutive wife of Roscoe (Fatty) Arbuckle—Arbuckle himself happened to be working on some shorts
and was the only Keystone celebrity who did not appear in the
film. To play Tillie, Sennett secured Marie Dressler, popular on
the vaudeville and Broadway stages, for a fee of two thousand five
hundred dollars, a princessly and almost unheard-of sum for the
time. As further insurance he appointed Hampton Del Ruth, one
of Hollywood's most proficient writers and editors, to adapt for the
screen *Tillie's Nightmare* (1910), a Broadway play in which Miss
Dressler had been a hit. On the average, Sennett's studio turned
out ten to twelve half-reel and one-reel pictures a month; *Tillie*
took him three and a half months to complete.

The film proved to be one of the high points in Marie Dressler's
career; she went on to play in some Tillie sequels, none as successful as the punctured romance. For Chaplin it was his thirty-third
film (in less than one year) and gave him his plummiest and
lengthiest part to date. It must have been instrumental in winning
him a contract shortly thereafter from a rival concern, Essanay,
together with a salary that jumped him from two hundred dollars
a week to six times that sum plus a ten-thousand-dollar bonus.
Mabel Normand's standing as the foremost young film comedienne of the time looked less challengeable than ever. And Sennett,
Mabel's lover in private life, and in many movies, earned unprec-
edented grosses for the financial backers of Keystone, Adam Kessel
and Charles O. Bauman, and earned himself the title King of
Comedy. By the following year, Sennett was on a par with Amer-

ica's two top producer-directors, D. W. Griffith and Thomas Ince, when he became the third corner of the Triangle Film Corporation.

The picture that made so much money for so many people—I have not even mentioned the exhibitors—is exiguous as a work of art by the standards of Feydeau's or Labiche's farces, let alone those of Chekhov, Molière, or Aristophanes. But it does mark a great stride forward in the progress of farce as a genre. It is the first humorous film of feature length (six reels, or six thousand feet, which run for something over one hour); earlier film farces had been not much more than extended sketches. It displays farce in action out of doors amid bucolic settings and on the street and on and below the pier at Venice, California. It provides a chase that has apparent continuity over a long distance, in place of a series of dashes out through exit doors and windows and back in through entrances. We see Marie Dressler hoisted from real water, then dropped back into it, taking a couple of Cops and the rescue rope with her. In addition, there are those "magical" effects of movies that fracture time and space: cutting and editing, especially cross-cutting between scenes to link the subplots. The camera changes its shot or angle in the middle of a scene so that the spectators can witness the action from both near and far, from more and better vantage points. Those sequences in which the hand-operated camera is deliberately "undercranked" result in abnormally rapid motion when the frames are projected at normal rates. Vehicles travel at breakneck speed. There is even some farce of the theatricalist sort when Mabel and Charlie slip into a movie house where the current offering has a plot that resembles their own machinations against Tillie and the title instructs us, "Little do Charlie and Mabel realize that they are about to see their own types on the screen."

But *Tillie*'s vaudeville origins stick out like overlong undergarments. The actors stand about in pairs or lined up in threes and fours before the fixed camera and face it while they trade insults. They mug for the back row and the balcony. They kick asses, collapse and rise again in double time, keep their eyes goggling and their mouths agape. They talk—no, shout—with their arms, legs, and whole heads. They work too hard. They squeeze out laughter. They are exhausting to watch. All the same, the film they're in sums up the condition of farce as it plunges into the cinematic century.

Pioneers of Film Farce

When Sennett started out as a producer of film farces in 1912, just over two years before he launched *Tillie*, the career of his most illustrious predecessor, Georges Méliès (1861–1938), was coming to an end. Sennett, during his more than twenty years in Hollywood, was to rack up an output that exceeded seven hundred films—mostly farces, with a few commercial assignments thrown in. Méliès managed to turn out close to five hundred in a shorter period, sixteen years (1896–1912), and although all of them were short, and many not farcical, he directed every one himself.

Méliès is a visionary and a wonder. He could justifiably claim to be the parent of the cinema. Georges Sadoul calls him "the Giotto and Uccello of the Seventh Art,"[1] for he gave movies form by telling stories with them. The few film pioneers before him, and notably his fellow countrymen the Lumière brothers, had been principally inventors and recorders. The Lumières built and refined a mechanism, the Cinematograph, for both filming and projecting. With it they photographed real events: processions of workers leaving a factory, riots and parades overseas, people on the street or happenings around the house, such as Louis Lumière's baby child taking a meal and being waited on by his parents. Today most of the Lumière films look like home movies and vacation memories in eight millimeters, but today it's a little too easy to be smug about them. As early practitioners of *cinéma vérité* and film journalism, the Lumières caught life on the wing. Seldom did they *set up* a film. Méliès always did. He must rank as an artist rather than a technician-cum-reporter. He painted his own sets in his studio at Montreuil, outside Paris. He acted in and directed his films. He initiated science-fiction pictures, fantasies, and serious short documentaries.

Méliès had worked as a stage magician, and in 1888 had pur-

---

[1] *Dictionary of Film Makers* (Berkeley, Calif.: University of California Press, 1972), p. 172. Sennett and Méliès each lived on for a quarter of a century after his film-making career had ended. But both men died poor; so did D. W. Griffith and Edwin Porter, two other great American film innovators.

chased a playhouse, the Robert Houdin, which he kept in business until 1914, putting on vaudeville shows that specialized in conjuring acts done by himself and others. When he began making films he put them on the programs. As in America, early screenings in France were combined with stage routines. According to Jacques Deslandes, Méliès' "fantastic scenarios reveal that the prime source for Méliès, man of the cinema, is the work of Méliès, the man of the theater."[2] The Méliès films do look like stage performances. The camera doesn't shift out of position, although sometimes—in the hand-drawn sequences—it appears to, and the sets look exactly like the stage scenery they are. But on that tiny platform at Montreuil, Méliès reinvented farce in short bursts. His films circulated abroad, and he made a fortune. He probably lost another fortune when exhibitors pirated his prints and screened them without paying him a royalty; he didn't police the showings —he couldn't have done that without having a tightly controlled system of distribution—and it took him years to learn that he must insert a copyright notice on the frames of each film. Even then he continued to be swindled, for at that time, before World War I, film distribution was itself farcical.

In his pictures he modernized myths and legends, such as those of Faust and Mephistopheles, Pygmalion and Galatea, the Oracle of Thebes, Rip Van Winkle, and Baron Münchhausen, the tall-story teller of all time. He revived his own versions of famous literary figures: Hamlet, Gulliver, Tartarin de Tarascon, and Figaro, the barber of Seville, as well as historical personages, among them Christ, Joan of Arc, Shakespeare. In *The Dreyfus Affair* he defended the falsely accused Jewish officer at a time when only a few courageous people like Zola dared to do so. Imaginary beings also populate the Méliès footage: gnomes, goblins, fairies, creatures from other planets. His characters explore exotic corners of the world and of history. The scientists in his best-known films, *A Trip to the Moon* and *Journey Through the Impossible* (1902 and 1904), venture through space to the moon and the sun.

Critics have occasionally charged that Méliès' films suffer from static camera angles; the images move, of course, within the

---

[2] *Le Boulevard du Cinéma à l'époque du cinéma* by Jacques Deslandes (Paris: Éditions du Cerf, 1963), p. 34.

frames, but the lens monotonously views them all head-on as if it were a spectator in a center front seat of the orchestra. The charge reeks of hindsight; it is rather like complaining that Newton did not anticipate Einstein. Another accusation, that Méliès' special effects are little more than a bundle of tricks, is equally true. But what a bundle! Méliès brought narrative to the cinema. He experimented with animated line drawings and the massing of shapes. He worked with color, tinting his frames by hand. He superimposed one image on another and dissolved one image into another to create a gradual transition between scenes. Instead of going directly to a new shot he initiated the fade-out to a black screen and the fade-in to a fresh picture. He was the first director to attempt underwater filming in glass tanks, in, for example, his adaptation of Jules Verne's *20,000 Leagues Under the Sea* and his picture about building a tunnel to link Britain and France beneath the English Channel. In his *Gulliver* film and some of his fairy tales he showed Lilliputians and huge Brobdingnagians in the same frames as human beings. He varied his shooting speeds so as to portray abnormally fast or slow motion when the film was projected. Most strikingly, he demonstrated all kinds of "magic" in his photography by stopping the film and restarting it with one or more of the characters missing or with new characters suddenly present. Every child who gets his or her hands on a movie camera is familiar with this gimmick today; but at the turn of the century, audiences thrilled to these instantaneous appearances and disappearances, just as they did to the sight of characters who abruptly lost their heads and instantly grew new ones, also thanks to Méliès' stop-and-go camerawork. All these discoveries opened up a language that served film makers from Edwin S. Porter, who directed the first real American farce, *Dreams of a Rarebit Fiend* (1902), down to the razzle-dazzle directors of the Seventies and Eighties who, like high school seniors, delight in showing off their vocabularies and quoting the work of earlier directors. I have often heard it said that the overworked "freeze frame," which stops a movie's motion and resolves it into a still picture, especially at the end, dates back to Truffaut's *The 400 Blows* (1959); in fact, it goes back almost sixty years earlier to Méliès, who used it with a strictly farcical intent.

Méliès was an independent. His compatriot Ferdinand Zecca

(1864–1947), another adept at both live-action and animated farce, worked for the Pathé company, and it took longer for his contributions to the burgeoning film arts to be acknowledged. Zecca turned out a number of advertising shorts and documentaries on assignment from Pathé's clientele during his period as a director, 1898 to 1914, which roughly coincided with that of Méliès. People who have seen a great many of the Pathé farces made by Zecca (as I have not) maintain that Sennett and other later film makers freely lifted themes, situations, and characterizations from them. This sounds plausible, since Pathé had outlets in those cities where films were screened, and since plagiarism of all kinds, technical as well as artistic, has always been considered a sign of professionalism in the movie business. If you know what the others are up to, you know where you're going.

In Zecca's *The Legend of Polichinelle* (1907) he picked for the lead a comic named Max Linder (1882–1926), who was to become what one writer calls "the motion picture's first truly international star"[3]—and incidentally, the first film farceur to achieve a reputation other than Méliès (who was, and is, rightly viewed as being more a director than an actor). Linder had been straining at the leash in four or five different bit parts each week at the Pathé studio in Vincennes. Previously he'd studied at the Bordeaux Conservatoire and had carried off at the age of sixteen that institution's first prize for acting comedy and second prize for acting tragedy, so that his direction as a performer seemed predestined. Refused admission to the Paris Conservatoire (like another eminent artist before him, the director André Antoine), he nevertheless worked Paris nightclubs; undertook some grimly serious but inconsequential parts onstage for the best part of a year; found his way to Pathé by 1905, to Zecca less than two years later; and so onward and upward to the top of the Pathé roster within months thereafter, at a time when very few film actors received credit in France and none did in this country.

Linder tried out an assortment of characterizations before settling on the one that became familiar and gave him the artistic scope he needed. As a suave but improvident boulevardier in a silk

[3] Jack Spears in *Films in Review*, May 1965: "Max Linder Was the Motion Picture's First Truly International Star," pp. 272–91.

top hat, a black cutaway sometimes concealed by an opera cloak, silver tie, pearl tiepin, white gloves, striped pants, spats, and black boots, with an elegantly wielded cane for a slapstick, he stood five feet two inches tall. He had good features enlivened by a finely carved triangular mustache. In many of his films he confronted an outsized villain but won the heroine for himself after undergoing for the sake of this taskmistress the sort of trials, mental and physical, to be endured later by Harold Lloyd, Fatty Arbuckle, Buster Keaton, and Harry Langdon. In the four hundred–odd films he made for Pathé between 1907 and 1914 he played astonishing variations on his basic role. He was a jockey, office worker, podiatrist, painter, landlord, photographer, airplane pilot, gas man, novelist, musician, and matador—at least one of each. He scaled mountains, teetered on skis and skates, blew away in a collapsing balloon, overwent and overcame waterfalls in canoes, doing all his own stunts, including the skilled ones like flying. He was married, he was single; obliging and reckless; nearsighted like Magoo and as gentle as Jacques Tati; sometimes slow on the uptake like Langdon, sometimes ingenious with the reluctant cunning of Chaplin, as when, in *Max, Victim of Quinquana* (1911), he quarreled with several swordsmen in turn, accepted their cards, and then defiantly handed the cards as his own to other swordsmen and let them enjoy the ripened fruits of their aggression. If Max (and by 1914 to the public at large the name Max meant only one man) resembled a string of dissimilar comics who came after him, that was their good fortune and proved their discernment. By 1910 he was directing his own films, using among his actors Maurice Chevalier and Abel Gance, who was later (1922) to direct Linder in a picture called *Help!* and later still (1927) be responsible for the historical and historic epic *Napoléon*.

World War I, in which he enlisted, ravaged his body, his confidence, and his career. Wounded, suffering from pneumonia and then a breakdown, he could not quite recover. Nor did he ever recoup anything like his prewar fame. A rich offer from Essanay lured him to Chicago, but he stayed for only a few months. He returned to the United States when the war was over to make several pictures, including *Seven Years' Bad Luck* (1921), dealing with the consequences of a smashed mirror, and *The Three Must-Get-Theres* (1922), a parody of Douglas Fairbanks' ragingly popular

Three Musketeers (1921) in which Max romped through the D'Artagnan role. But the labored wordplay and phallic innuendo of the title and of his character's name, Dart-in-again, suggest that he didn't adapt comfortably to the explicitness of Anglo-Saxon farce, even though his earlier films had earned him and Pathé a lot of money here. Max's farce was his face. He liked to dream up excruciating situations, but not to bull his way through them in the American tradition exemplified most blatantly by Sennett. A certain turn of the head, a curve to the mouth, a quiet glance, a Gallic flick of the fingers—these had become his language. He'd forsworn roughhousing, falls, pushing. He was moving toward a *farce de l'esprit*—a contradiction he might have resolved if he'd had time, but which it was left to Chaplin to realize glancingly in *The Kid, The Gold Rush, The Circus,* and *City Lights,* though it appears several decades later in more sustained forms in the early plays of Beckett and of Pinter and in Woody Allen's films.

For by 1926, Max Linder was dead. He and his young wife had fulfilled a gruesome suicide pact. Thirty-two years after his death, his daughter, who had been an infant in 1926, collected scenes from some of Max's feature-length films into a tribute entitled *In the Company of Max Linder* (1963), which, however, has never had a general release in the United States.

Most film histories remark on Chaplin's borrowings from Linder. Chaplin did once acknowledge such debts, though he later repudiated them. He and Max were even next-door neighbors for a while in Hollywood; they used to show each other their scripts and exchange ideas. "Chaplin called me his teacher," said Max during an interview, "but I am glad enough myself to take lessons from him." Chaplin, it seems to me, did not really encroach on the Max persona. He did borrow (and transform) ideas, and especially situations, that had appeared in Linder's films; but then, so did—so does—just about every subsequent farceur. Max's example was unavoidable. He stood less as a performing model than as a goad to others in the fact that a success like his was achievable; his vivacity on screen, his willingness to take chances—these were imitable and imitated. Once he had established himself, he tried to grow by working at the outer limits of his abilities and of farce. He was restless, questing, never complacent. He surmised correctly that as soon as artistry sits on its laurels, the audience starts to sit on its hands. Nobody learned this lesson more thoroughly than Charles Chaplin.

Finch Pecks Bunny

Two more comics, both Americans, John Bunny and Alkali Ike, also had a vogue in the pre-Sennett years. Bunny tended toward comedy rather than farce. His family sitcoms have supplied the outlines and many of the particulars for unnumbered plays, sketches, films, and television episodes ever since his burst of glory from 1910 to 1915. Harold Dunham describes him as being "the screen's first comic fat man and the first American film comedian of note,"[4] who in a 1912 poll taken by *Motion Picture* magazine came out as the screen's seventh-most-popular artist. (Later comics like Arbuckle and Chaplin were to rank much higher.) Bunny was also the male half of the first fat-and-lean film team, his wife being played by the slim, sharp-featured, and effervescent Flora Finch, who could not seem to get going again on her own after Bunny's death in 1915.

John Bunny's spry locomotion took him through well over one hundred fifty short films, most of them one-reelers or split-reelers.[5] He came into movies at a much later age than most of his successors; he was forty-seven and had put in more than twenty-two years in vaudeville and stage comedies when he sought a job with the Vitagraph Company. He then walked blithely away from a hard-earned and assured stage career, but he was prescient: he did even better in films and turned into Vitagraph's strongest box-office attraction. Still, he remained an actor, a "type" character, rather than a clown. In the film adaptation of *A Tale of Two Cities* he took on a serious role; in *The Pickwick Papers,* shot in England, he became convincingly John Bullish as Mr. Pickwick. But to most spectators he was the best-known husband and father in the world, harassed, humiliated, likable, and, when he flirted with girls, a roué who looked more elderly than his age: a Cyril Ritchard gone to seed and fat. Despite that age, and despite his girth, he was

---

[4] "John Bunny" by Harold Dunham in *The Silent Picture*, No. 1, Winter 1968–69, p. 12. Bunny theorizes about his work and past in "How It Feels to Be a Comedian, by John Bunny, Himself" in *Photoplay*, October 1914, pp. 111 *et seq.*
[5] John Bunny's filmography is listed in *The Silent Picture*, Summer 1972, pp. 8–15.

nimble, although never athletic in the manner of Keaton, Chaplin, or Lloyd. In his bumbling and timing—his delayed, thoughtful reactions—he anticipated Oliver Hardy and at times W. C. Fields, who had similar jowly expressions of disgust and a similar pumpkin of a nose; but there is no hint in Bunny of Fields's satirical edge or of his subdued ill will toward men, boys, beasts, and babies.

Alkali Ike had been Gus Carney during his vaudeville days, just as Linder had been Gabriel Leuvielle, his real name. But after a series of Alkali Ike one-reelers, in which he played a seedy cowpuncher or hick, he struck a short-lived gusher of fame at Essanay in 1910, when Bunny made his first pictures. Ike was the humorous counterpart to one of his bosses, G. M. (Broncho Billy) Anderson, the "A" of S & A, and for a time he "rivaled John Bunny and Max Linder in popularity."[6] A bony-faced shrimp of a man, Carney habitually triumphed over his larger rivals thanks to his stupidity. Carl Laemmle of Universal (previously IMP, the Independent Motion Picture Company) hired Carney away from Essanay and changed his name to Universal Ike. Whether because of the change of name or because he ran afoul of his producer and director, Carney suddenly had to make way for somebody who was certainly not his son but received the name Universal Ike, Jr., and the fame and career of the original Ike petered out.

Meanwhile Sennett had gone into action. By 1915, when Méliès and Zecca had retired from directing, Linder hit a slump, Bunny died, and Ike become a memory, Sennett ruled over a dozen production units at Keystone and had eclipsed the competition.

Sennett in Hollywood

In the seven years before the outbreak of World War I, heady opportunities loomed for people who could persuasively claim film-making experience. In January 1908, Mack Sennett, aged twenty-eight, took a job as an extra at Biograph Studios in New York, where he earned five dollars a day, mostly for walk-ons. The following year Sennett sold scenarios to Biograph at five dollars each, although his payment went up to twenty-five for *The Lonely*

---

[6] *Clown Princes and Court Jesters* by Kalton C. Lahue and Sam Gill (Cranbury, N.J., and New York: A. S. Barnes, 1970), p. 77.

Villa, directed by the young D. W. Griffith and starring Gladys Smith—not yet known to the public as Mary Pickford because, like all actors of the time, she received no billing. In 1910, Sennett took over many leading roles. Less than a year later he became a director, heading his own Biograph unit and making fifty dollars a week, a healthy salary for the time.

By August 1912, Sennett had left Biograph, taken most of his unit with him to Edendale, on the outskirts of Los Angeles, and was directing the Keystone Film Company, an independent producer that used another independent, Mutual, as its distributing outlet. Three years after that, Sennett went into a three-way partnership with Griffith and Thomas Ince, the Triangle Film Corporation, sponsored by an operator who had been one of the founders of Mutual, Harry Aitken. By now, Sennett and Keystone were world-famous names. Griffith was, if anything, even better known. By early 1915 he had screened and been reviled for the longest and most controversial film yet made, *The Birth of a Nation.* In six years these two men soared from obscurity to renown at a pace usually traveled only by lucky or extraordinary film stars.

Hollywood itself had not yet taken on its distinctive personality. When Cecil B. De Mille went west in 1913 to film *The Squaw Man* for Jesse L. Lasky's Feature Play Company, he considered Flagstaff, Arizona, as a locale, decided it was "no good for our purposes," and wired Lasky to ask for "authority to rent barn in place called Hollywood for seventy-five dollars a month." Lasky's son remembers the "place called Hollywood" in 1914–15, when he was a small child, as having "pepper-tree-lined streets," wild hills nearby, sunflowers in "empty fields of weeds," and "a handful of wooden bungalows in an orchard realm."[7] The first movie people (from the Selig Company in Chicago) who checked out Hollywood had gone there as recently as 1907, when it seemed to be nothing more than a "sleepy little suburb of Los Angeles," to repeat a favorite phrase from histories and memoirs; it then had a population of roughly three thousand. The following year, the first film made entirely in California was shot on a small Hollywood lot.

---

[7] *Whatever Happened to Hollywood?* by Jesse L. Lasky, Jr. (New York: Funk & Wagnalls, 1975), p. 6.

Thenceforward the colony expanded—by fits and starts to begin with; then, from about 1914 on, explosively. But the movie "Hollywood" had already spilled out of the administrative boundaries of Hollywood proper. Griffith was shooting at San Juan Capistrano, in the Sierra Mountains, and elsewhere; Sennett had set up his studio at Edendale; "Broncho Billy" Anderson, the first popular cowboy, was running off a one-reel Western a week at Niles, outside San Francisco, and with his partner George K. Spoor would establish new Essanay studios there; Thomas Ince had taken over a twenty-thousand-acre lot in Santa Ynez Canyon, on the way to Santa Monica, which he would later call "Inceville"; and sundry other big and small producers were either engaged in producing or looking at property elsewhere in the Angeleno hinterland.[8]

The instability of Hollywood reflected the instability of the country as a whole. Perhaps there has never been a stable age in America, and disorder was always the order of the day. Some politicians look back to the years preceding World War I and discover a settled, even a halcyon, time when Americans knew where they stood in the world and in their own communities, had beliefs (in today's jargon, called "values") in common, and shared a confident, not to say complacent, sense of expectation and of the rightness of "progress." This nostalgic view can be ascribed to a desire to contrast those times with others—our own, for instance. But when we scan the national scene in those years, we find strikes; attempts to limit immigration; trust-busting; the exposure of political bosses; slums and starvation in the cities; and brutal measures aimed at enforcing Prohibition—and defying it.

There was turmoil overseas, too. Imperial struggles among the European powers (Britain, France, Germany, Holland, Russia) and America led to the carving up of the Middle East, Africa, the Pacific Islands, and China in the contests over raw materials and outlets for manufactures; they also led to the Great War. When *Tillie's Punctured Romance* opened in November 1914, the assassination of the Archduke Franz Ferdinand was three months out

---

[8] The information here is drawn from a number of sources, but principally from *D. W. Griffith: The Years at Biograph* by Robert M. Henderson (New York: Farrar, Straus & Giroux, 1970) and *Sixty Years of Hollywood* by John Baxter (New York: A. S. Barnes, 1973).

of date; Lenin had just reached Zurich; and the informal inauguration of the Panama Canal had begun to rewrite dozens of shipping routes.

The arts were undergoing their own drastic formal alterations. In 1913 Proust published *Swann's Way*. When the Armory Show in New York served up its stew of Postimpressionist painting that same year, and Duchamp's nude descended her staircase without moving, in what looked like a travesty of film superimpositions, the opening salvos of Dada, that arcane attempt to assassinate art and enthrone abstract mockery in its place, were only a year or two in the future. Stravinsky's *Firebird* and *Petrouchka* had been performed in 1910 and 1911, and a year later, Schoenberg's atonal *Pierrot Lunaire* song cycle. By 1914 Yeats and Pound had published some of their most venturesome poetry and, in Yeats's case, plays. The year 1912 marked the death of that most radical, versatile, and prescient of nineteenth-century artists, August Strindberg.

Hardly any word of these insurrectionary events could have leaked into the consciousness of Mack Sennett, whose brushes with literature and the arts seem to have been at most incidental, as when he once plagiarized a story by O. Henry for a screenplay which was rejected—he'd read it in a newspaper, not a book. Nor does Sennett appear to have shown any curiosity about national or international affairs, or any familiarity with them. To the two biographers in whom he confided[9] Sennett spoke almost entirely about his upbringing, his work, his employees, and about life in the movie colony. And yet it seems obvious now that, consciously or not, Sennett, who is thought of as being little more than a merchant of nonsense and some dribs and drabs of satirical fantasy, was affected by that spirit we call with convenient vagueness the *Zeitgeist*, for his farces do reflect the instability of America, the world, and young Hollywood.

In its first decade of life, the movie colony witnessed fistfights and running gun battles between thugs hired by established production companies and independents. Conflicts broke out be-

---

[9] *Father Goose* (New York: Covici and Friede, 1934) by Gene Fowler, who interviewed Sennett tenaciously and drew most of the firsthand information from him; and *King of Comedy* (New York: Doubleday, 1954) by Sennett himself, "as told to" Cameron Shipp.

tween residents who had settled down for a quiet retirement in a Mediterranean climate and feverish movie colonizers; these conflicts were summed up in that ubiquitous boardinghouse slogan, "No dogs or actors." Real estate kept changing hands at wildly inflated prices. New movie stars ascended from nowhere, propelled by publicity budgets, then as now; they shone with unnatural brilliance for a year or two and lit up society. At the same time, superstars would blink out without warning. The rocketing and plummeting of reputations symbolized that Hollywood instability, the elbowing for places in the relentless sun, for profit, pleasure, power, property, and properties. About ten years earlier, the underlying San Andreas Fault had delivered its warning to San Francisco. And the Pacific kept nibbling away at the California shore, portions of which might rumble, founder, and roll away into the water.[10] Perhaps Hollywood, in its turn, symbolized the instability of the new century in America and elsewhere.[11]

Early film farces provide an unexpected portrait of that community which was not a community. The portrait is neither complete nor realistic, for they perceive and refract Hollywood from an artistic remove: farce is even more dispassionate and cool than comedy is. They offer us less the factual detail, much of which is on record elsewhere, than the atmosphere, the jarring rapidity of change, the awkward juxtaposition of contrasts. In so doing, they preserve for us images of the larger disjunctions of the United States, a country with no center then, or only an empty one, an ocean of land between two coastlines with a few dispersed islands of population.

To cross from coast to coast, moviemakers had to shuttle back

---

[10] Gavin Lambert called his fictional "scenes of Hollywood life," published in 1959, *The Slide Area* after the SLIDE AREA signposts along the coastal highway. In one of the scenes he describes the aftermath of a slide: "From a great pile of mud and stones and sandy earth, the legs of old ladies are sticking out" (p. 18).

Even today residents of the Hollywood Hills, like settlers at the foothills of a dozing volcano, live dangerously. They build their dream homes, infinite variations on the hacienda, hanging off the edges of cliffs, supported by stilts on the sheer side and ringed by sentinel cypresses and palms. Spiky cacti are meant to anchor the surrounding grounds. But the rains come every winter, and the grounds slip, and houses tumble into the canyons.

[11] Two excellent books deal with this topic indirectly: Hortense Powdermaker's *Hollywood, the Dream Factory: An Anthropologist Looks at the Movie-Makers* (New York: Little, Brown, 1950) and Robert Sklar's *Movie-Made America: A Social History of American Movies* (New York: Random House, 1975), especially Chapter 5, "Hollywood and the Dawning of the Aquarian Age," pp. 67–85.

and forth on four-day train trips. They had shipped large consign-
ments of talent and equipment west, but much talent—playwrights and name actors—remained in the East to be courted.
So did all the money. The separation between financing in New
York and producing in Los Angeles kept the industry a divided
one through the interwar years of prosperity and on into the
1950s.

The studios themselves by their very nature lacked coherence.
They looked like sprawling, outdoor lofts into which artists had
dropped jumbles of paintings, each canvas having then turned
three-dimensional and its figures come alive. In late Medieval
times, the "simultaneous stages" of France and Switzerland
housed many sets on a single platform, and the actors moved from
one scene to the next. On Keystone's shooting stages, the fifteen
units worked back to back on different productions. Not yet fully
elaborated, the studios were growing fast.

A quarter of a century later, in the riper days of Hollywood,
Nathanael West was to create a character who was both fascinated
and disconcerted by one of these dreamscapes. In *The Day of the
Locust*, Tod Hackett, a painter, finds himself on an open lot where
a film entitled *Waterloo* is being shot. He seeks shelter from the
fierce sun by standing in the shadow of an ocean liner made of
cloth; crosses a stretch of artificial desert to a sphinx, forty feet tall
and built of papier-mâché; sits nearby on a rocking chair outside
"The Last Chance" saloon on a Western street; notices a nearby
jungle and an Arab on a white stallion, as a truck hauls snow and
some malamute dogs past him. Pushing through the saloon doors,
he discovers a Parisian quarter. Not far off, people are "eating
cardboard food in front of a cellophane waterfall." Just beyond
this picnic scene he comes upon a Greek temple; a Trojan horse;
a decaying Zeppelin; a fort; a windmill; "a flight of baroque palace
steps that started in a bed of weeds and ended against the branches
of an oak"; dinosaur bones; "part of the Fourteenth Street elevated
station"; another temple, this one Mayan; a Venetian barque; and
a cleaning lady on a stepladder "scrubbing with soap and water the
face of a Buddha thirty feet high." Before leaving, Tod watches a
reconstruction of the battle of Waterloo featuring hundreds of
authentically uniformed French troops. As they charge up the
slope, Mont-St.-Jean collapses under them. "The whole hill folded

like an enormous umbrella and covered Napoleon's army with painted cloth."

A Hollywood studio stood prepared to serve as the world, with all the extensions in space and time its screenwriters and designers could conceive of. But, like a film, its fragments were spliced together. They lacked connecting, intervening tissue. If only they had all become disused at the same time!—then they'd at least have had the internal congruity of a junkyard. But because a studio was every place, it was no place.

The analogy between a studio's parts and a film's succession of shots, which West implies in his description, was anticipated, however, by Buster Keaton. In *Sherlock Jr.* (1924) he plays a moviehouse factotum who sweeps floors, sells tickets, shows patrons to their seats, runs the projector, and, in secret, pores over a book entitled *How to Be a Detective*. Once he has fulfilled his several duties and started the film rolling, he falls asleep in the projection room. An image of Buster detaches itself from the sleeping body. It is Buster the dreamer, the private eye. On the screen the actors have mysteriously turned into people he recognizes: his girl, her father, and the girl's other admirer, Buster's rival. The Buster-in-a-dream wants to get into that picture. He rushes into the auditorium and up onto the stage and tries to enter the picture. His rival boots him out of it. He tries again, and this time succeeds in staying on the screen. But the shot has changed from a living room to a locked front door. He is in the film but out of the house. When he tries to cope with this new shot, it changes again. And again. In a series of matched cuts he seems to walk, stagger, fall, somersault, and otherwise land in one new landscape after another, each presenting some fresh danger. He stands on a rock in the ocean battered by waves; he dives off and plunges head down into a snowdrift. Or a train roars at him. As he dodges, he sits down for relief—on a desert cactus. He escapes from the traffic in a street by leaping onto the sidewalk—which treacherously becomes the top of a sheer cliff. At last he contrives to get wholly into the dream picture, defeats his rival, and wins the girl. But the sequence of obstacles he has first to overcome correspond closely to the settings—desert, heights, street, jungle, ocean, snowfield, and so on—that West would lump together fifteen years later to make up the incongruous movie studio in his novel.

West—the pen name could not be more apt—is one of America's finest writers, and bibliographies galore list *The Day of the Locust* as "the best novel ever written about Hollywood." *Locust* shows him off at the height of his power and refinement both as a storyteller and as a shaper of prose. His account of Tod Hackett's stroll through a movie lot's clutter of history and geography constitutes an outstanding passage of funny, low-keyed narration. But it doesn't measure up to Keaton's sequence of cuts in *Sherlock Jr.* There may be little validity, if any, in comparing two media, but in Keaton's case the medium really is the message. "This is the point of movies," he says in effect, "and a movie is being used to make the point." West is a subtle writer; Keaton is both subtle and broad. But aside from its movie theatricalism, a never-excelled sample of film as film, Keaton's chosen genre is active farce. West's is descriptive comedy. There are times when farce will do more, much more, than comedy. West himself apparently realizes this. He saves his most graphic moment for last, when the hill of painted cloth tears under the rush of troops. Here he has left comedy behind and gone triumphantly into farce.

Neither Mack Sennett nor his principal competitor, Hal Roach, ever came up with a film that catches the flavor and identifies the essence of Hollywood—and of the gloriously chaotic American dream—as sharply as Keaton does. But Sennett, for all his deficiencies, got there first. He made the way plain, and possible.

Improvisation and Collaboration

When Sennett arrived in Edendale and started filming under the Keystone banner, he had seduced four other people away from Biograph. Fred Mace, an established comic, then ranked in popularity only just below Max Linder and John Bunny. Ford Sterling, an immensely versatile face-puller who wore "Dutch" getup, supported Mace and later took over from him as leading actor. Mabel Normand, an ex-model whom Sennett had directed and encouraged at Biograph, could mug, act, swim, and dive beautifully; billposters and advertisements were subsequently to feature her as the Diving Venus. Henry Lehrman, whom D. W. Griffith had nicknamed "Pathé" when Lehrman, an Austrian, promoted himself into a job at Biograph by pretending to be a veteran of the

French studio, proved to be one of the most treacherous figures in the history of Hollywood, although at the time Sennett trusted him enough to take him along as cameraman and assistant director and later to put him in charge of a production unit.[12] Sennett himself wrote, acted, directed, and administered. His four original actors constituted the casts of all the twenty-eight split-reelers and one single-reeler turned out by Keystone between September and December of that year, although two extras were taken on for small parts.

Two related characteristics of Sennett's early style of producing represent a break with farces then done in the theater: improvisation and collaboration. Plays and vaudeville sketches invariably relied on scripts. A playwright might, and probably would, alter his lines or stage business in rehearsal, perhaps at the behest of an actor, in order to extract the farcical utmost from the enactment. In vaudeville, gags and shtick were tested and added or dropped; the comics adjusted their timing and attack, or swapped lines or gestures. But no old hand at vaudeville would dream of going before an audience with only the outline of an act. Yet this is more or less what Sennett's team did before the camera; and filmgoers, still enchanted by the novelty of the medium—more than eight million of them every day in the United States alone—devoured the results and cried for more. One of the original Keystone Cops, Wallace MacDonald, says that in the early days Sennett repeatedly "used one story—the plot of the girl, the man, and the Menace. The cops came in at the grand finale, the big chase. Hampton Del Ruth strung the different versions of this story together and worked out the incidents. In those days, any director who used a

---

[12] Lehrman ran afoul of Normand and Chaplin, among others, at Keystone. He left Sennett in 1914, at the same time as Ford Sterling, for Universal, where he formed his own outfit, L-KO Comedies, using Sennett-trained actors, Sennett material, and Sennett techniques. Years afterward, he played a damaging role in the sensational trials of Roscoe Arbuckle, who was accused of having murdered Virginia Rappe. Rappe had been Lehrman's lover, but he'd abandoned her. However, he did his best to capitalize on the publicity and reestablish himself as a director. He demanded revenge on Arbuckle, his former friend and colleague, in the name of his "brave sweetheart." He gave outrageous statements to the press about Arbuckle's morals and about the "murder" in San Francisco (Lehrman was then living in New York), which successive juries could not find to have *been* a murder. Rappe's death seems to have been caused by a combination of overdrinking, venereal disease, and pregnancy, the last two conditions contracted thanks to Lehrman. For a detailed account of the Arbuckle trials see David Yallop's *The Day the Laughter Stopped* (New York: St. Martin's Press, 1976).

script was considered effeminate."[13] Minta Durfee, sixty years later, thought back to 1914: "I don't recall that anybody paid too much attention to the script. Improvisation was the key. One-camera setups."[14]

Within a year Sennett was trying to rationalize his sprawling operation. He hired a business manager. He employed writers to confer with him and come up with brief shooting scripts. A visiting journalist found him rehearsing his actors within lines chalked on the floor. But Sennett still okayed every big decision. He still worked at a feverish pace, during punishingly long hours, because he loved what he was doing. He could be severe with his employees. He had his office in a modest tower that gave a view of the studio lot so that he could check up on slackers. He prowled the buildings and would butt in unexpectedly on his writers until they set up a primitive warning system—loose boards on the creaking stairs outside their quarters. He even fired Wallace MacDonald for loitering over breakfast in the company cafeteria until nine-thirty when everybody was supposed to have quit the cafeteria by nine. On the other hand, an interview with Roscoe Arbuckle, whom Sennett had trained as a director and who was running a separate unit for a time with Mabel Normand in Fort Lee, New Jersey, in "one of the largest glass-enclosed film factories in the East," depicts much more free and easy working conditions that correspond closely to the ones actors and directors recall at the Edendale lot. The performers in 1916, said Arbuckle, seemed to "make it up as they went along. Fresh ideas pop out, and we all talk them over. I certainly have a clever crowd working with me. Mabel alone is good for a dozen new suggestions in every picture. And the others aren't far behind. I take advice from everyone."[15] Even Chaplin, who by 1916 had strayed from Sennett to Essanay to Mutual, could say many years later, "I never worked with a script in those days," and show some brief cuts of himself directing a Mutual cast to prove it.[16]

---

[13] "Those Were the Good Old Days! Is Zat So?," A Sentimental Interview with Wallace MacDonald by Agnes Smith, in *Photoplay*, October 1925, p. 34. Robert Cox, another original Keystone Cop, also insists that no scripts were used.
[14] Yallop, *op. cit.*, p. 53.
[15] "Behind the Scenes with Fatty and Mabel," by Wil Rex in *Picture Play*, April 1916, p. 52.
[16] The quotation comes from a spoken introduction to three Mutual shorts that he combined under the title *The Chaplin Revue* in 1951.

To the notion of Keystone as a one-man enterprise, a fief under the domain of a lord and master, we can oppose two facts about Sennett: one, he went after the best talent he could find and made up his mind to get more than his money's worth out of it; and two, he enjoyed the give-and-take with his directors—one might say he needed it.

Talent: In addition to his acting discoveries of the first and second magnitudes, the roster of film makers who graduated from writing and/or acting under Sennett's tutelage amounts to a fair proportion of Hollywood's subsistence directors of the silent and early sound periods: Mal St. Clair, Eddie Cline, Eddie Sutherland, Del Lord, William Campbell, Hampton Del Ruth, Fred Fishbach, Victor Herrman, Walter Wright, Erle Kenton, Clarence Badger, Frank Capra, Richard Jones, Alf Goulding, Dell Henderson, Nick Cogley, and Harry Edwards. Sennett was, as Gene Fowler remarks, "a bloodhound for talent."

Give-and-take: By the time Frank Capra—later his most successful directing pupil—came on his payroll in 1924, Sennett was holding regularly scheduled conferences with his gagmen and directors. During these sessions they talked over new projects and cooked up additional business for films already in the works. There was much animated gossip and joke-telling and capping of one another's lines, which gave way to a hush whenever a verdict was required of Sennett. By then the "old man's" views had begun to harden into dogma. He had issued for studio and public consumption altogether too many dicta on what made people laugh and why; on theories, principles, and structures of laugh-provoking materials; and he regarded himself as something of a sage, thereby endangering his sense of humor.

Sennett had long since acquired a curious habit of taking frequent hot baths in office hours—in his office, in fact. Unlike most people, who take baths, if at all, before going to bed in order to sedate themselves, Sennett believed hot baths stimulated his creative fancies. The tub, "which cost several thousand dollars and was hewn out of marble with silver trimmings," rivaled that in which Claudette Colbert in *The Sign of the Cross* practiced her round-shouldered immersions in a liquid publicized as being asses' milk. It sat on an upper story of his tower, measured eight feet by five, weighed two tons, and must have required extra-sturdy floor joists underneath and heavy caulking all around. In it, he says, he "could bathe and soap and splash and shout any time of the day and simultaneously keep an eye on my outrageous employees." Sennett sometimes invited subordinates to join him in his ablutions, in the course of which, he claims, "I did my best thinking," but "no one ever took me up."[17] The adolescent self-indulgence may help to explain both his unwavering choice of farce as a genre and the twitting of authority that is the backbone of most of his plots.

But whatever the setting—tub, desk, set, or location—Sennett must be reckoned a pioneer of groupthink. In assembling his films by a process of accretion, rather than composition, he functioned less as the writer-producer than as the galvanizer, the idea man who energizes others. He provided the gale force in what subsequently was called brainstorming. Such collaboration, or cross-fertilization, was, of course, itself a performance—a series of turns or acts brought about by challenges and counterchallenges, reminiscent of amateur comedians at somebody's party or professional comedians on the David Susskind show trying to outjoke one another. It was, in a word, theater. Sennett's very *technique* of making films was in part farcical.

It was picked up by most of the other studios that turned out farces, including such majors as Paramount and, later, MGM when they produced the Marx Brothers pictures. And this technique has refreshed and, in some cases, opened up the performing arts of this century, beginning with the spontaneous impieties of the French Surrealists in the Twenties and continuing through the improvisations ("improvs") of Chicago's Second City troupe in the Fifties, the transformations of the Open Theater in New York during the Sixties, and the factual and fictional *cinéma vérité* practiced in the past thirty years (Ricky Leacock, Morris Engel, the Maysles brothers, Fred Wiseman, and all the movie and television teams that go out and shoot in what are called "available" settings on a main thoroughfare). As offshoots of groupthink in the arts we can cite much of the writing for radio and television: I've heard gagmen say that the preliminary bull sessions are usually a lot funnier, and sometimes better acted, than the finished show.

---

[17] The Sennett quotations are from *King of Comedy*, p. 93.

Sennett's Turbulence

One noteworthy feature of *Tillie's Punctured Romance* is that its heroine remains ridiculous throughout the six reels: when she dances, waits on tables, sighs over Chaplin, flies into a tantrum, bosses her servants around, or flashes looks of hatred at Mabel Normand. Tillie ends up bedraggled, fished out of the drink. Marie Dressler's size, deportment, and rowdy acting do nothing to endear the character to her viewers. She's a tough, funny woman without a speck of cuteness or phony modesty. Yet the film drew repeat audiences. So much for the hoary notion that for a picture to succeed, your average spectator must be able to admire, pity, or "empathize" or identify with a principal character. Tillie is unrelievedly a figure of fun. Chaplin bears hardly any resemblance to his later Charlie the lovable tramp, either in his looks or in his mannerisms; while Normand, who, given the chance, can switch on her star appeal and keep it glowing, doesn't have an assertive enough role here for the audience to feel strongly about her one way or the other.

That the picture did succeed should come as no surprise. The history of farce is studded with plays and films that have no likable or admirable hero or heroine. So is the history of the drama and cinema as a whole. Sennett reminded Theodore Dreiser during an interview in 1928 that people laugh wantonly at other people's troubles: "Something uncomfortable happening to the other fellow, but not *too* uncomfortable? Yes. Things must go wrong, but not too wrong. And to some fellow you feel reasonably sure can't be too much injured by it—just enough to make you laugh, not enough to make you feel sad or cry." Dreiser countered by saying, "But years ago, when you started, the type of comedy you produced was decidedly crude, wasn't it? I recall the hot stoves on which people fell, the hot soup that steamed down their backs, the vats of plaster or tar or soap that they fell into; the furniture, walls, ceilings, even houses that fell on them; the horses, wagons, trains that ran over them."[18] Whom did Sennett mean by "some fellow

[18] "The Best Motion Picture Interview Ever Written" by Theodore Dreiser, in *Photoplay*, August 1928.

you feel reasonably sure can't be too much injured" by "something uncomfortable"? Selected victims, heavies, the so-called "menace" in each film?

Ten years earlier, in one of the secrets-of-my-trade articles that magazines occasionally wheedled out of him, Sennett talked about the incidence of custard pies. He allowed that the best recipients of pie in the eye were comic cops and fat people. "Well-dressed, elderly men are headed straight for misfortune in the movies. But," he cautioned, "Shetland ponies and pretty girls are immune."[19] We can easily conceive of animal-lovers bearing down on any director who sanctioned pie assaults on a helpless dumb creature. But why only ponies? and why did he single out Shetlands? and why did he exempt pretty girls when many of them, including Gloria Swanson, had already been doused in his films with the ground-up raspberries and whipped cream that passed for custard and not a murmur had been heard from any society for the prevention of cruelty to young beauties? Whatever he says, every one of his dramatis personae was fair game for injury. He simply disbelieved in positive characters, as Feydeau, Courteline, Grabbe, and Molière had before him.[20] A Sennett farce has little to do with characterization at all. It collects its energies for the climactic chase, the rally, which brings everybody more or less together for a grand confusion of a finale; in other words, it's kids' play that stops with an "all fall down," or it's a chess match in which the end game consists not of a planned checkmate or even a hopeless stalemate but a sheer scattering of the pieces by a huge, godlike hand to the winds of chance. The jumble of racing figures, carts, automobiles with minds of their own, and maybe even a Shetland pony resembles the *poursuite* in a play by Labiche or a film by Linder, except that Sennett doesn't bother to follow it with a quiet wrap-up scene of reconciliation or explanation. He closes on a note of disarray. The film's currents run turbulently right to the end.

There are three such currents, the sources of turbulence, in a

---

[19] "The Psychology of Film Comedy" by Mack Sennett, in *Motion Picture Classic*, November 1918.
[20] Molière's reasonable characters who try to drive some sense into the obsessed heads of the unreasonable ones are either male platitude-mongers or mischievous maidservants; we are not meant to like or admire them but, rather, to see them as foils for the obsessives.

Sennett farce: disrespect, speed, and abuse of the human body. These give the film its main impetus, although they may be complicated by minor eddies, whirlpools, splashes, backwash, and other subplotting.

Disrespect first. Not only does the film maker show contempt for his characters, but they also make a point of deflating one another. Public officials, people in authority, snobs, and bosses are set up to be put down. High-society parties, formal balls, and other decorous celebrations, particularly those intended as pretexts for speechmaking, will ferment into anarchy. Tokens of social superiority like evening dress or bemedaled uniforms or a high hat must be crushed and defaced or, better, blotted out, preferably with the sort of sticky or squishy or fast-hardening substances of a contrasting hue that are the despair of dry cleaners. White shirts and pale robes call for lashings of tar or gravy or stew; black jackets, striped pants, and dark dresses exert their pull on live dough, mortar, and ceiling paint.

Sennett repeatedly spoke or wrote about the "fall of dignity" in his pictures. Most often he accomplished it by obliterating visible evidence of class differences. Tarred, floured, or drenched people look alike. Dignity might fall in a literal fashion, especially from a height into a liquid. The room in which the action of *Whose Baby?* (1917) takes place has a balcony hanging out over a fishpond, and most of the men in the cast will enter the pond from above more than once. A body hitting a sheet of water became a Sennett staple. One actress at Keystone said she didn't feel a part of the company until she'd been "initiated" with a Sennett baptism. Wallace MacDonald reported: "I rode in the patrol wagon five days out of every week. On the sixth day, that was pay day, all of us Cops fell in the lake. Every Saturday we had to go to the park and fall in the lake. Or sometimes, just for a change, we fell into the ocean —just off the pier at Venice. . . . Charlie Chaplin has kicked me into every lake in Los Angeles. Those were the good old days."[21] The actors playing Cops got smart. For those wet Saturday rehearsals they wore their dirty clothes for the week and had them laundered at company expense.

All of Sennett's early comedians save Chaplin began as Cops.

---

[21] MacDonald-Smith interview, *op. cit.*, p. 34.

Sennett was indulging a dream he'd had years before he directed. He yearned to film a gang of crazy policemen in order to humble them, to overturn each spectator's neighborhood token of law and order.

Why this precise ambition? Had the police ever mistreated him? Had he enjoyed seeing a dumb-cop act during his vaudeville days? Did he recall, as the comedians Wayne and Schuster once speculated, the burlesqued policemen in *The Pirates of Penzance*, one of the most popular Gilbert and Sullivan comic operas playing in the United States when Sennett was a child? Could he have noticed or read one of those rare farces in which policemen figure as chumps or dupes? (Courteline, who pitted himself untiringly against public servants, wrote such a one-act, *The Commissioner Has a Big Heart*, in which a sadistic commissaire gets his comeuppance by being locked in a coal closet.) However we try to account for Sennett's predilection, he put himself out to rob cops of respect by keeping a swarm of them futilely active while ordinary police work went undone. If they ever capture a miscreant, it happens by mistake. In *Fatty Joins the Force* (1913) they arrest one of themselves. As a rally heats up to its climax they pour from a vehicle, their own or commandeered, only to compound the confusion.

Next, speed. The Cops travel in a gaggle, but they also rush. Ford Sterling as the sergeant takes a phone call, overreacts with his eyes and torso; his followers unfreeze and leap into activity, usually going in different directions.[22] Meanwhile, other characters are running away from, or after, one another. Machine-gun editing mottles the screen with convulsions of accelerated, countervailing motion. Because of the frames cut out during the editing, an actor like Sterling appears to jerk his head and limbs about spasmodically as if he were a tufted titmouse. All Sennett film behavior comes straight out of impulses. He told another interviewer, "The way to write a good moving picture is first to get your idea; you will find that either in sex or crime. Those two fields are the great feeding grounds of funny ideas."[23] Sex attracts; crime repels. As the performers hustle toward their partners or put dis-

---

[22] Wallace MacDonald again: "Sterling was wonderful at registering horror . . . he was the best police sergeant I have ever known—before or since—on or off the screen." *Ibid.*, p. 35.
[23] "Mack Sennett—Laugh Tester" by Harry C. Carr, in *Photoplay*, May 1915, p. 71.

tances between themselves and their opponents—or try to close those distances—the frenzy invokes a sense of danger, for speed can end only in deceleration (unlikely in a Sennett movie; it would lead to an anticlimax, a result Sennett abhorred) or in collisions. One sort of collision, the soft one, lands a character in water, mud, or some other disfiguring cushion. A second sort combines the soft landing with a hard one: a tumble into a rain barrel; a dive into a cartful of cement or a wagonload of hay. A third sort exploits uncompromising material: a brick wall, a roadway, a tree.

Hence the remaining source of turbulence in a Sennett picture: abused bodies. The specialists in this line of stunt were Roscoe Arbuckle, Hank Mann, Al St. John, and Ben Turpin. They cheerfully accepted their fate; even volunteered to redo a take when they or Sennett didn't believe the impact was everything it might have been. Out of upper windows they sprang; off moving wagons and cars they somersaulted; behind trucks and horses they let themselves be dragged along in the dirt on their faces or backs, prevented from being altogether scraped away only by invisible roller-skate wheels. "My people competed with each other in murderous antics before the camera and got themselves so wound up that they seldom knew when to stop gyrating," says Sennett, remembering that on one occasion Hank Mann was "supposed to be yanked out of the driver's seat of a wagon and spread-eagled on the landscape." But the horses "cut loose like runaway ghosts and snatched Mr. Mann thirty feet through the air." He "descended into a plowed field, chin first, and furrowed a belly-whopping trench for ten yards before, with considerable common sense, he let go the reins. He returned to me in need of a face wash but without a limp. 'Boss,' he said, 'I think we'd better retake that scene.' "[24] A journalist watched Arbuckle directing himself and Mabel Normand in *The Bright Lights* (1916) and observed that "getting half-killed" was "second nature" to those veterans. He saw Arbuckle fall down a flight of stairs, bang his head on an open bureau drawer, slam a door on his fingers, and keep crashing heads with another actor, while the rest of the cast stood by and laughed.[25]

[24] *King of Comedy*, pp. 91 and 99–100.
[25] Wil Rex in *Picture Play, op. cit.*, pp. 46 *et seq.*

Under Sennett's direction the body may undergo abuse, but no damage is done to the mind—precisely because his madcap characters have negligible minds. Each is at the mercy of the four-year-old within. And we ourselves go to a Sennett farce expecting to give rein to our own repressed inner four-year-old, whose wicked enjoyment is regularly sanctioned by the noise of others' laughter. "In farce," writes Eric Bentley, "hostility enjoys itself."[26]

Masquerade

It follows that Sennett's actors had to be able to shake off their inhibitions. Since almost without exception, they had come to him from vaudeville, they'd trained themselves to do exactly that. Two desirable assets for any performer, in vaudeville or elsewhere, are unselfconscious playing, which permits direct contact with the inner four-year-old, and the ability to improvise by means of free association in order to cope with a false or missed cue, a lapse of memory, or a raucous interruption. But these assets become immeasurably valuable to a vaudeville entertainer, who mustn't appear to rely on a script.

Sennett actively sought out these abilities, unselfconsciousness and a gift for improvising. At the same time, his actors had to be readily identifiable "types." Typecasting made it easier for him to meet his schedule of two to three films a week, sometimes more, and to shuffle the actors among the different directors on his lot. Even when his film-making pace eased up, in 1917 and thereafter, so that he could give more attention to details of continuity,[27] subtle effects, and overall "quality," he liked to work with actors each of whom was a known quantity. As a result, each actor developed a fairly fixed appearance that was analogous to the masks worn by actors of the commedia dell'arte.

In Sennett's pictures, as in the commedia, the mask is not only the face but also the role, a guide to the whole persona. Chester Conklin collaborates with his walrus mustache, wide-open eyes,

---

[26] *The Life of the Drama* by Eric Bentley (New York: Atheneum, 1964), p. 255.
[27] As examples of imperfect continuity in some early Sennett films we can see that actors have occasionally reversed their positions in different shots within a single scene or are wearing different items of clothing. Bloopers of this kind were, and continue to be, common in film making, even in productions that boast a continuity staff.

and thin hair to play a little, put-upon husband. Ford Sterling's blob of a beard and spectacles and nervous hand-flutterings make him fussy and imperious; when he infrequently drops the beard and spectacles, as in *Tango Tangles* (1914), he comes across as a stranger. Arbuckle's mask consists of his plump muscularity, gymnastic prowess (he was also a heel-kicking dancer), and dopey, innocuous smile. Hank Mann is described by Wallace MacDonald as "the boy with the Theda Bara eyes and the Elihu Root haircut."[28] Ben Turpin's right eye, always trying to get a fix on the bridge of his nose, reduces the heroic stars he parodies—William S. Hart, Douglas Fairbanks, Erich von Stroheim, Rudolph Valentino—to his inane, grinning mask. Louise Fazenda wears gingham dresses, a country maiden's naiveté, and a circular spit curl dangling on her forehead like a misplaced monocle. Mack Swain's flattened, scanty hair, bulk, and popping eyes look like a throwback from Zero Mostel. The two groups Sennett made famous, the Keystone Cops and the Mack Sennett Bathing Beauties, which served respectively to break in and test new male and female talent, needed only their collective masks—their uniforms—to function as Aristophanic choruses. Two of his most successful graduates, Chaplin and Arbuckle, probably parted from him because their conceptions differed from his over what their masks should be, whether they could modify them, and not simply because they could squeeze more money out of his competitors. Sennett may not have reinvented the commedia mask—vaudeville did that—but he gave it wider currency and new colors; and rival farce studios like Hal Roach's, Al Christie's, Educational, and Lehrman's L-KO unit imitated him by typecasting as religiously as he did. Harold Lloyd's mask didn't evolve until after he had left Sennett and gone over to Roach (who had himself worked for Sennett for a time). Bing Crosby, whom Sennett brought into movies in the late Twenties, escaped into an entirely new mask, that of the romantic lead who sometimes doubles as a crooning priest; but he readapted the old mask to farce when he later played in the "Road" films opposite Bob Hope and Dorothy Lamour.

Sennett's own acting mask underwent changes. Early on, when he began as an actor at the Biograph studio in New York, "he did

---

[28] MacDonald-Smith interview, *op. cit.*, p. 35.

The Curtain Pole, wherein he played a mad French count and proved himself to be Biograph's best comedian. After that they had to keep him."[29] He took on other French (meaning dapper) characters at Biograph, as well as Indian and Russian roles, clergymen, hoboes, young lovers, old cranks. In modern and historical settings he was variously bearded, mustached, side-whiskered, clean-shaven. At Biograph alone he directed and acted in two hundred and sixty-six films.[30] In his duos with Mabel Normand, at both Biograph and Keystone, at a time when actors received no credit in movies, the pair of them had become popular enough in Britain to have earned for marquee identification the drawing-room names Muriel Fortescue and Lionel Marchbanks.

Subsequently he seemed to enjoy playing hicks. Sennett's acting has often been maligned. Watching his films today, we can't help noticing that even in the role of a rube with his features pulled into a cautious, idiotic mask of a grin, he has considerable discretion as a performer. He never attempts to steal scenes from Mace, Sterling, Normand, Arbuckle, Raymond Hitchcock, or other principals, even when he carries a lead role himself. He also pays devoted attention to the other characters, displaying an acting virtue not always evident in a more flamboyant clown like Ford Sterling. Sennett, however, will be remembered not for his performing, but for his reinvigoration of farce and for the stars of the Twenties on whom he helped to confer the gift or curse of fame.

---

[29] *When the Movies Were Young* by Linda Arvidson (reprinted New York: Dover, 1969). This is a significant tribute to Sennett's skills as a performer, for two reasons: first, Linda Arvidson, once Griffith's wife, was herself an actress at Biograph; second, she didn't much like Sennett, as her book makes clear.
[30] "Mack Sennett" by Robert Giroux, in *Films in Review*, December 1968, pp. 603–4.

SEVEN

SILENT FARCE IN THE JAZZ AGE

One judgment shared by most critics and historians of film is that the outstanding comics of the 1920s who worked for Sennett or some other mentor, such as Hal Roach, went on to make pictures that were better than farce. Those pictures were certainly better, for the most part—but better *as* farce. The decade from 1919 to 1929, roughly what Scott Fitzgerald called the Jazz Age, saw a richer gush of farce than in any comparable period in history. It started with the triumphs of Chaplin in *The Kid* (1921) and *The Pilgrim* (1923), and moved on to *The Gold Rush* (1925) and *The Circus* (1925); the cream of Buster Keaton, Harold Lloyd, and Harry Langdon; and the teaming up of Laurel and Hardy, as well as several classics directed in France by René Clair. Each of the American comics strove to combine a swiftly recognizable persona, like the "masks" in Sennett's pictures, with a good-natured and, in many ways, admirable hero who was down on his luck most of the time but resilient enough to survive a variety of misadventures. Farce, then, a genre that had never "needed" characterization in depth, acquired a fresh gallery of characters. Not until the W.C. Fields talkies, when that stout, be-spatted man let fall a mumble of misanthropy out of the left side of his mouth, and the advent of Marx Brothers pictures, in which Groucho insulted everybody in sight, and himself most bitterly, while Chico and Harpo swindled and assaulted with manic concentration, did film farce get around to accommodating the antisocial hero, the sub-

167

versive comic who had remained in abeyance since the great days of vaudeville. Chaplin had played saturnine figures in a few early films, most notably *Tillie's Punctured Romance, The Face on the Bar-Room Floor* (1914), and *The Idle Class* (1921), but forswore them in favor of, first, his lovable tramp and, later, his hero-critics.

Characterization, though, was only one of the accomplishments in which the silent farce of the Twenties excelled. Farce used the techniques of the medium with virtuosity, trying out nearly every kind of camera angle and movement and lighting resource. It experimented with indoor sets and outdoor environments, natural and studio-made scenery. It brought to the screen many of the finest sustained acting performances of the time and told some of the best stories. It often revealed formal and beautiful control of the medium, yet its plots had a startling, maybe eruptive, spontaneity. It seemed to be the genre that offered the most opportunities, and its practitioners investigated it with zealous abandon.

Chaplin

Even Chaplin, the Sennett graduate whose career as a farceur outlasted everyone else's, did not cross the threshold of a different, more sober genre—comedy: not, at any rate, until his very late films *A King in New York* (1957) and *A Countess from Hong Kong* (1966). And by then Chaplin and his Charlie had parted ways. With few exceptions (three out of eighty), Chaplin's short films and features alike are farcically conceived and underpinned.[1] Like most farces, they do relax into moments of comedy; and without jeopardizing his farce, he could ladle scenes of memorable pathos into *The Immigrant* (1917), *The Kid, The Gold Rush,* and *The Circus.* He brings *City Lights* (1931) to a close with the Little Fellow, a rose against his cheek as he confronts the girl who was

---

[1] Among Chaplin's films of the Twenties, only *A Woman of Paris* (1923) belongs to a genre other than farce. He made it in order to launch Edna Purviance on a new career as a "serious" actress, which it failed to do, although it did boost the reputation of her co-star, Adolphe Menjou. *A Woman of Paris* and *A Countess from Hong Kong* were the only two completed films directed by Chaplin that did not feature him as an actor. In the first he played the tiny role of a porter; in the second, a ship's steward. *A Woman of Paris* is an offshoot of melodrama, the *drame sérieux;* so was another film Chaplin produced (with Edna Purviance again) but gave to Josef von Sternberg to direct, *A Woman of the Sea* (1926), which was never released.

blind until he paid for her cure, wondering now if she will know him—a take that must be the very pinnacle of film acting as his eyes grow lustrous with terror, hope, love, and disbelief, all at once. In *Modern Times* (1936) and *Limelight* (1952) he indulges in nostalgia, but still without relinquishing his grip on the farce. *Limelight* actually jogs us with reminders of its farcical essence; the film's high point is a musical duet performed by Buster Keaton on piano and Chaplin, as the comedian Calvero, on fiddle, trying to make a comeback; the screenplay opens with a drunk solo that recalls the vaudeville acts in which Chaplin made his stage name, the early split-reelers and one-reelers (*Tango Tangles, His Favorite Pastime*, and *The Face on the Bar-Room Floor*, all 1914), and the reeling two-reeler *One A.M.* (1916), in which Chaplin played drunks with inspired frenzy; it also recalls his drunken interplay with a millionaire (Harry Myers) in *City Lights*.

What is there left to say about Chaplin as farceur? Biographies, reviews, retrospective critiques, and put-downs in more than a dozen languages have taken stock of his writing, directing, acting, public and private personalities, working habits, home life, sexual proclivities, and the probable dynamics of his unconscious, occasionally weaving them together for the sake of a rounded view. Pretty nearly everybody who was anybody during his lifetime—artists, critics, statesmen, philosophers, and distinguished others—made a point of meeting him and having a say about him to reporters, friends, and general audiences. For almost five decades Chaplin was one unavoidable topic of discussion and appreciation. His wives, mistresses, acquaintances, neighbors, co-workers, employers, employees, and peers have been extensively questioned and quoted. Other comedians made a living doing impersonations of him and filching his mannerisms, thereby adding to the burden of commentary: Billy West, Billie Ritchie, the Mexican Charles Amador, and Stan Laurel, who was Chaplin's friend and had belonged to the same Fred Karno troupe. Commentators have taken note of his bodily proportions (large head, narrow shoulders, short legs, small hands) and scrutinized his tramp's outfit, wresting symbolic implications from its totality and its component parts. The undersized derby is a balloon, a token of his aspirations; the fidgety mustache connotes his nobility, as do the wing collar and frayed tie; his cane turns the traditional slapstick into a magic wand; his loose, swallow-tailed jacket, occasional vest, and cylindrical pants imply that he is an ill-fitting member of society; his lumpy shoes (and waddle) weigh him down, keep him close to hard reality, thereby counterpoising his hat and stressing that his feet are weapons. Others have discussed the twitching of his nostrils and eyebrows, the way he stands, leans, scampers, brakes on one foot to round a corner, drops his head to one side and stuffs his hands between his knees as he throws off an ingratiating smile. We've all cherished his choreographed falls and somersaults, his miming, dancing, skating, and ass-kicking, besides the balanced concurrence in his persona of bum, ardent worker, and vestigial aristocrat. (A film made as a tribute to him in 1974 is called *The Gentleman Tramp*.)

Then there are the abounding contradictions. Charlie is cunning and he is innocent. He can be more cruel than any other comic character and he can be more considerate, especially to women, children, stray animals, young lovers, people down on their luck. He is shabby, but not grubby. He may sleep on dirt next to a hole in a fence (in *A Dog's Life*), but when he comes upon humble quarters (in *The Kid* or *City Lights*) he will make them snug and clean, a trim nest that preserves an image of decency, arrangement, and above all, respectability. He may go into assorted outerwear—the garb of a jail, a hospital, a restaurant, the army, or a hollow tree trunk—but his identity, whatever it is, remains firm, his silhouette somehow unaltered. He warms us with his familiar looks, gestures, moves; at the same time, we admire his unexpected turns, little bursts of novelty that prove him an actor who both lives in the character and surpasses it. He is Everyman, every one of us, and none of us, a synthetic and invented individual pieced together out of memories of vaudeville and memories from childhood. He incarnates the lonely seeker and the gregarious finder. He worships his freedom and cannot resist binding himself to others. He will always share food and goods with others, but—and I think that this is his most striking characteristic—he can never shake off his hunger. His stories take him from one unassuaged appetite to the next. That is why so much in his films is about eating.

Between Chaplin the creator and Charlie the creature, the businessman and the vagrant who finds bliss in the scent of a rose, the exacting boss and the menial who, for a needed buck, will tighten bolts or sweep up horse dung, there stretches a gulf, although not an unbridgeable one. How many Charlies are there, anyway? And how many Chaplins? Parker Tyler distinguishes a string of separate figures, all Charlies; he links the tramp with his successors, Hynkel (in *The Great Dictator*), Verdoux, Calvero, Shahdov (in *A King in New York*); calls the role played by Marlon Brando in *A Countess from Hong Kong* "Charlie Diplomat," and the Chaplin who made a triumphal return to America in 1972 "Charlie Oscar." Behind and above all these looms the "puppet master and master of life's labyrinth," whom Tyler christens "Charlie Daedalus," the artist-entrepreneur who "kept his identity best concealed behind the overall worldly mask of Charles Chaplin."[2] However one manages or doesn't manage or doesn't bother to reconcile the succession of Charlies sloughed off by Chaplin—and Tyler does contrive a most ingenious, if complicated, reconciliation—there is a hiatus between the early and the later artist that has puzzled critics and, as a result, provoked some of the best, most heartfelt writing about the nature of film performing. (For this by itself we are in Chaplin's debt.) How could the monarch of silent films have declined into a prater, a speechifier, a gasbag? In the early silents, only an infrequent line of dialogue written as a title is worth recall; one example is his reply in *Shoulder Arms* to the question how he managed to capture thirteen enemy soldiers: "I surrounded them." The young Chaplin demonstrated; he didn't explain. But as of his first out-and-out talkie, *The Great Dictator*, he began to elaborate on motives and causes, most egregiously when the Little Barber takes the place of his double Hynkel and trolls up from some shallow in himself a thundering peroration urging all little people to unite and "fight . . . to free the world." Was it the arrival of sound, as some commentators believe, that damaged Chaplin's art, and even induced him to replace the *Gold Rush* titles with a voice-over narrative that was at odds with the transitions of the original editing? Sound may have had something to do with it; and yet Chaplin used a sound track unconventionally and imaginatively in his first two features of the talking era, *City Lights* and *Modern Times*, pretty much as those two Russian masters, Eisen-

<hr>

[2] *Chaplin: Last of the Clowns* by Parker Tyler (New York: Horizon Press, 1972 edition).

stein and Pudovkin, said it should be used: not to duplicate or reinforce the camerawork, but to add to it or possibly clash with it. Nor, I think, is it primarily a matter of Chaplin's political convictions. These do ring out with some urgency in the later films, almost as though each film might be his last, and therefore his last chance to say what he felt must be said. Chaplin may have thought of himself as a political messenger, even as the chosen conscience for a confused world; and this would not be quite so egomaniacal a vision as it might appear because his films do all bear political declarations or implications, and they did go out to the entire world. At the same time, Chaplin can plausibly be regarded as one of the supremely self-conscious aestheticists of the century. From his youth he had a passion for the most formal of the arts, music. After he grew rich he became a tennis "formalist" too, saying that what attracted him most about tennis was "its form, its grace. . . . Tennis was dance: that was why he loved it, he said, and it had become for him both recreation and a search for beauty."[3] He was never the mere propagandist.

But his garrulity was most likely caused by his growing older and therefore different. He knew he could no longer rely on the skills of the past. He tried to experiment with new ones for which he did not have anything like the same dazzling aptitudes. As did his great literary contemporary Bernard Shaw, Chaplin kept working well beyond his prime, and kept trying new ways to reinvigorate his faltering art. Still, farce was the genre he had conquered and immeasurably amplified. Much as Molière, the all-rounder to whom Chaplin most persuasively invites comparison, had returned to farce with *Scapin* and again with *The Imaginary Invalid* (the play in which he collapsed onstage, dying that same evening), so Chaplin cannot resist one last stab at farce after another, even with an aging body and a more embittered outlook. In his sixties he is still nimble, *for his age*. He seems to be telling us this toward the end of *Limelight*, made when he was sixty-two. Calvero concludes his two-man act (with Buster Keaton, who is not given a fictitious

---

[3] John McCabe, *Charlie Chaplin* (New York: Doubleday, 1978), p. 176. This is Chaplin's own account, a confidence to his friend Konrad Bercovici. Other people who played tennis with him, among them the former world champion Alice Marble, said Chaplin always played to win, and sometimes would not scruple to call an opponent's ball out when it had gone in.

name in the film but simply called Calvero's Partner) by falling off the stage into a drum. He cannot get out of it. Hilarity in the auditorium. The laughter and cheers swell when he complains, "I'm stuck" and has to be hauled offstage in the drum. He has had a heart attack. He returns to the stage to speak his thanks. As he is carried out again, still in the drum, at the edge of the frame we glimpse one of the most poignant shots in Chaplin's films. Keaton is staring after him, bewildered but knowing that something is wrong. And then the curtain obliterates him. If Keaton had had a line here, it might have run: "But he's taken thousands upon thousands of falls like this before and they never hurt him." That dying fall of Calvero's into a drumskin marked Chaplin's final parting from farce.

Of course, he changed his mind. The two tamer films that followed do erupt into spasms of farce. Chaplin's later career was a series of final partings. Even so, and with all their hortatory and other defects, the last films don't stand up badly against the popular novels, plays, and pictures of their time. It is just that Chaplin had trained his audiences to expect better.

His output exceeds eighty film farces.[4] It is worth remembering, though, that Chaplin is a prodigy not only because of the volume and range of his natural skills and training but also because he forges a style that owes much to his outsider's status. His early movie years illustrate as vividly as do Griffith's or Sennett's that Hollywood instability referred to in an earlier chapter. In January 1914 he went on the Sennett payroll at Glendale. By the beginning of the next year he had left for Essanay's studios, first the one in Chicago overseen by Spoor, then Broncho Billy Anderson's in Niles, California. The year after that, 1916, he was working for Mutual, back in Los Angeles. In late 1917 he moved to First National. Each shift—four in as many years—brought him a larger

---

[4] Those films have been individually described and analyzed, shuffled into groups, variously rediscovered and reevaluated, and interpreted biographically, philosophically, historically, and even cinematically. I make no attempt here to deal with any individual works at length: there would be too much to say, and most of it would be recapitulation. In addition to McCabe's book, *op. cit.*, a recent entry, there are excellent works devoted to Chaplin by Louis Delluc, Donald W. McCaffrey, Roger Manvell, R. J. Minney, Robert Payne, Isabel Quigley, Georges Sadoul, Parker Tyler, and Gerith Von Ulm. Other writers whose books include valuable material on Chaplin are James Agee, Kevin Brownlow, Otis Ferguson, Graham Greene, Pauline Kael, Stanley Kauffmann, Walter Kerr, Dwight Macdonald, Gerald Mast, Andrew Sarris, and Edmund Wilson.

income and more discretion in making his films. He took this initiative further in 1919 when he joined Griffith, Mary Pickford, and Douglas Fairbanks in establishing United Artists, a company that was more of a distributing setup than a producer. But since he was still under contract to First National for a few pictures, he did not get around to releasing his first U.A. feature, A Woman of Paris, until 1923. His affiliation with U.A. at last gave him virtual independence. The price of this was the cost of his films. He had to raise his own capital or else pour profits from one film into financing the next. Chaplin grew rich, but he invested heavily all the time in his future.

Parker Tyler is not the only critic who has proposed that independence, when superimposed on the comedian's vanity, spoiled Chaplin by turning him away from the Tramp and toward "the beleaguered 'king' " and "the harassed big money-maker . . . the hard business man and the great celebrity." His later characterizations of Hynkel the dictator; Verdoux the dapper murderer; Calvero the neglected comic, once the prince of vaudeville, who loses faith in himself—for a time; and the misunderstood King Shahdov do suggest that Chaplin had misgivings over what had become of him.

And yet he was more prescient than any other farceur in tenaciously playing—being—his own boss. He may have fallen out of touch with popular taste, failing to listen closely enough to the changing cadences of the marketplace; but who can ride the popular swell for more than fifty years? At least, Chaplin never exhausted that taste; for even in the years when he was widely accused of being a fellow traveler, a do-gooder, an un-American, a corrupter of teen-aged girls and public morals, his new films were each eagerly awaited. No artist sets out to become unpopular. If Chaplin felt disappointed and resentful over the reception of Monsieur Verdoux and the films that followed it, he nevertheless went on courting his audiences in his own voice. To the very end he kept possession of himself. He could accept suggestions, but nobody told him what to do.

After 1923, the financial uncertainty inherent in his role as producer doubtless aggravated the instability of his personal life—his caroming among wives and mistresses until his marriage in 1943 to Oona O'Neill—and after that the Joan Barry trial, the abuse, and the other indignities that led up to his self-imposed exile to Switzerland. The instability may have affected his screenplays, which are even more episodic than Molière's or Labiche's plays. In Chaplin's full-length films, as in the shorts, the episodes take precedence over the story, which is sometimes little more than a linkage. But he makes a virtue of necessity. He links the episodes more by means of thematic repetitions and relationships than by the sweat-provoking suspense we find in Sennett, Keaton, and Lloyd. In *The Gold Rush* the big theme is greed; in *The Circus*, the nature of performing; in *City Lights*, generosity and blindness; in *Modern Times*, the tyranny of mechanization; in *The Great Dictator*, the abuses of power; in *Monsieur Verdoux*, murder as an outlet for a sense of suffocating injustice (a theme taken up twenty years later by Imamu Amiri Baraka in *Dutchman* and *The Slave*). *Limelight* recapitulates some of these themes—especially generosity and the agonies and rewards of performing—as well as introducing others, such as the encroachments of age on the body and spirit.

Chaplin's tramp comedian had roots in the theater; had become a standard act in vaudeville and music hall before Chaplin's career began. The theater-tramp embodied a romantic vision of the minstrel, living from hand to mouth but sustained by his wits—king of the outdoors, while remaining a figure of fun, so that spectators felt superior to him, reassured about their own settled lives, comfortable homes and worldly possessions, families and friends. Yet back of the tramp comedian stood the ingenious servant of farce, Pseudolus/Scapin, the sharpie of yore who wins a girl and often a fortune for his handsomer but less cunning master, a mongrel by blood but a mental thoroughbred.

Chaplin took the tramp but transformed him, made a new creation of him: the vagrant who is not necessarily more intelligent but decidedly more humane than his social betters. And his humaneness, his magnanimity, pass on to the Little Fellow's successors, the Little Barber, Verdoux, Calvero, King Shahdov, and the chivalrous diplomat Ogden Mears in *A Countess from Hong Kong*. Every Chaplin film after *The Tramp* (April 1915) has one or more sequences in which the Charlie figure performs a selfless act. Chaplin did mean him to be an exemplar of sorts. In *Modern Times*, Paulette Goddard as the *gamine*, "a child of the waterfront who refuses to go hungry," has stolen a loaf of French bread and run off with it. She bumps into Charlie. A woman has seen her take the bread, but Charlie insists that he is the thief, and offers himself to the police. The camera lingers on Paulette. She has a look of wonder on her face. In this harsh world her unemployed father was shot and killed and her younger sisters snatched away to an orphanage from which she herself is now on the run. Charlie's sacrifice is the first magnanimous gesture by a stranger that she has known.

Chaplin's private code of conduct doesn't much matter in a consideration of his artistry. He could have been what the British call "a right bastard," and his Charlie would still be the most appealing figure ever to appear on a screen. But the final verdict on Chaplin the man will surely be favorable, if only because of his loyalty. He kept Edna Purviance on his payroll until her death. He employed the same cameraman, Roland Totheroh, until "Rollie's" retirement, and even after that brought him back as a consultant. But if Chaplin's magnanimity remained to the end, it was curiously darkened. His aging and artistic restlessness led him away from farcical realism toward satire; hence his more explicit social commentary and detectably embittered tone.

Nor was satire altogether congenial to him. A satirist requires an unstated norm, an alternative scheme of things, possibly drawn from his background or upbringing, that is proposed by implication. In their satires of California, *The Loved One* and *After Many a Summer Dies the Swan*, Waugh and Huxley drew on their upper-class English backgrounds to drive home their barbs. In *Merrily We Roll Along*, Kaufman and Hart satirized Broadway treacheries by contrasting them with the virtues of idealistic undergraduates: loyalty to one's friends, honesty, the quest for truth. Chaplin's background, however, proved elusive, hard to recapture. He came out of English poverty and hoped to raise himself to the level of an English gentleman abroad. From what footing could he launch his satire? That likely was the most vexing question he faced as an artist after his fiftieth year. Rather than being an overseas Englishman, he was a man of mixed cultures, an early Hollywood colonist who had made his life there since his mid-twenties. He sensed that, and used his American-ness, the Hollywood pedigree he had earned, as background for his shorts and features up to and including *Modern Times*. But thereafter an estrangement developed between the artist and his sources, and the exile fell back on his obscure origins, or invented others. Thus his late films have a vague, unreal atmosphere; they are artificial and movie-studio-ish. In *The Great Dictator*, Hynkel's palatial quarters are stylized; but so are the Jewish Barber's, which almost demand to be more specific. The Barber comes out of jail after many years and finds himself in a movie lot that could be any Middle European or Ruritanian set out of the Hollywood files. *Monsieur Verdoux* is laid in a France that appears hypothetical, trumped-up, because Chaplin has no experience of the real France to communicate here and is trying, anyway, to satirize America. In *Limelight* his desire to rediscover an authentically personal background makes him revert to a gaslit London and its show-biz pressures of 1914; but he had known that world as a rising comic, not as a mature, disillusioned Calvero; and again the impression we get is of a fabrication—London as it might have been, rather than as it was. The hero of *A King in New York* is a monarch on sabbatical from the land of Nowhere, ill at ease in the United States but with no homeland to retreat to that sounds plausible. In *A Countess from Hong Kong*, Chaplin finally gives up his search for a base altogether and lays most of the action aboard a ship at sea.

Looking back at his silent films of the Twenties and before, one cannot help noticing that exile figured prominently as a Chaplin theme. The Tramp is usually homeless, uprooted or a visitor from out of town. Later the theme became naggingly obtrusive. When the Barber in *The Great Dictator* declaims about One World, in which, presumably, no one will be an exile, his speech seems to be an attempt to unmake the Tramp and the abundant farce he brought to life. But evidently Chaplin didn't think he was turning his back on his earlier hero, only articulating what he had always felt as an artist and a man.

Keaton

The figure of the superman-underdog did not belong exclusively to early Chaplin, nor did Chaplin exploit it to its limits. The three other leading film farceurs of the 1920s, Keaton, Lloyd, and Langdon, appropriated the formula too, adjusting it to their different styles and taking both the underdog and the superman to further extremes. From these characterizations they forged a new farce tradition, which was taken up by a string of comics from Eddie Bracken in the 1940s to Jerry Lewis and Woody Allen two and three decades later.

The cinema bunglers, goaded by impossible odds into displays of stupendous prowess, are travesties of two melodramatic heroes: one, the beast of Beauty and the Beast, the sentimentalized outsider who transforms his "differentness"—freckles, stammer, big ears, shyness, skinny physique—into the moral equivalent of charisma; the other, the latter-day Hercules or St. George—Tarzan, the Saint, Superman, Batman, Spiderman, James Bond, the Hulk —who pits himself against arch-villains, the enemies of all mankind.

This farce hero comes on slowly. Apparently outclassed by everything and everybody, he gradually reveals superhuman grit and stamina, and thereby carries the day. Thus, Keaton at the end of *Battling Butler* (1926) takes a terrible beating from the world's lightweight boxing champion and is almost on the ropes when he rallies by losing his temper, goes berserk, and knocks the champ out. Again, as a studious, unathletic undergraduate in *College* (1927), he races, leaps, and hurls with every track and field skill when he has to rescue his girl. Similarly in *Why Worry* (1923), when Lloyd, a wealthy hypochondriac, sees his secretary being mauled, a surge of adrenaline transforms him into a rock-fisted slugger. Harry Langdon, the floundering farce hero of *The Strong Man* (1926), has to be in dire trouble before he can overcome an entire, hostile theater audience by tearing down the building around them.

In the farces of Buster Keaton, the formula is further elaborated. Keaton doesn't extend himself to win the girl. Like the heroes of myth, saga, and legend, he sets out to prove his mettle to *himself.* Can he ride out a cyclone or a river in flood? Can he escape from platoons of cops or a tribe of Indians? Can he elude a horde of fleet women, every one bent on marrying him? Can he navigate a riverboat from its upper deck with the aid of a tangle of ropes connected to the engine room? Can he stand in the path of an avalanche and dodge every bouncing boulder? The face gives away nothing. No fright, no curiosity, no resolve, not even an expectation. At most, it says, "We'll see." Buster himself doesn't know. He was put into this farce to find out. Usually the girl turns out to be more hindrance than help. When they are racing along in a locomotive to get away from the Union Army in *The General* (1926), she stokes the firebox with twigs instead of logs. While he is saving her from floodwaters in *Steamboat Bill Jr.* (1927), she clasps her arms so tightly around his neck that she disables him and very nearly drowns them both. In some Keaton features she addresses him to his mission early in the story and then retires to the sidelines, reappearing in camera range only at odd intervals, now the agent of fate or angel of grudging mercy. Buster, meanwhile, takes the necessary buffetings as he pursues his real interest—impressing his father with his manliness or learning how to be a sleuth or saving an amiable cow from the slaughterhouse.

As commentators on Keaton never fail to point out, he is fond of the long shot. He uses it more inventively than any director did before him, Griffith included, and more potently than most directors have done since. It lets him play fair with his audience because a Keaton long shot, which is usually also held for a long take, shows the actor performing exactly what his character performs, without editing or other dissimulation. Thus we witness Keaton's deep falls and dives in their entirety, his motorcycle ride (seated on the handlebars) across a gap in an overpass that is filled in precisely as he crosses it by two trucks traveling on the highway below, and his insouciant pose when the wall of a three-story house keels over on him so that the frame of an open, upstairs window misses his shoulders by three inches on either side. (This last was his most suicidal stunt. Nobody else on the set expected to see him come out of it alive, let alone capable of walking calmly away from the rubble.) Buster is a conjuror who affirms he has nothing up his sleeve except a daunting supply of muscle and elbow grease. One of the real Keaton's heroes, after all—who worked in the same medicine show as his father, and who was responsible for the nickname Buster—was Harry Houdini.

Apart from their candor, those long shots confer cinematic benefits. They are beautifully composed, more than justifying themselves scenically. They also serve as backdrops for milling activity —a freight yard, tourist boats docked at a riverbank, a desert aswarm with bandits, a herd of cattle bulling through a busy street

—or else they are empty, and their grandeur dwarfs and isolates his figure. The sight of a lonely Keaton in apposition to an immense panorama oddly recalls the tragic characters of Ibsen (Brand, John Gabriel Borkman, Arnold Rubek) as they confront the majesty of Norway's mountains.

How can such a figure on such landscapes be farcical? The answer is that he is not. Keaton is giving us flashes of lyrical respite while the farce cuts in and out. The genre changes, then abruptly changes again, reminding us, as Chaplin so often does, that genres need not be hard and fast. Keaton himself balked at the word "farce" to account for what he did. He thought of his work as being comic, rather, or slapstick. In 1931, not long after Joe Schenck stopped producing Keaton's films and put him in the hands of MGM, the most mercenary of the major studios, Irving Thalberg bought him a stage property. Keaton looked at it and said, "It's a farce—not my kind of story."[5] The play was an old Broadway favorite, *Parlor, Bedroom and Bath* (1917), and the following year Keaton, despite his misgivings, did appear in the film adaptation. But evidently he, like so many others, thought of farce restrictedly as being that specialized, nineteenth-century type of boulevard play known as bedroom farce. He believed himself to be a realist, while "farce" was synthetic, phony. In some respects his pictures support that belief. Keaton insisted that his backgrounds look geographically and historically authentic. There is more to it than that, however. He was a parodist. Almost every one of his films parodies an earlier work by somebody else or some other film maker's mannerisms. If, as I remarked earlier, the waterfall rescue in *Our Hospitality* could almost be a melodrama, that is because Keaton seems to have felt convinced that in order to be effective, a parody must virtually become the subject it makes fun of; it mustn't indulge in needless hyperbole. *Our Hospitality* starts out as a melodrama; so does *The Navigator* (1924).

Here we run into a contradiction. Keaton is the complete farceur. He can whip up a frenzy of movement, risking—and once breaking—his neck in falls and somersaults that professional stunt men could not equal. He graduated from vaudeville's school of

---

[5] Rudi Blesh, *Keaton* (New York: Macmillan, 1966), p. 317.

hard knocks and became the big attraction of "The Three Kea-
tons," who consisted of his mother, his father, and himself. (Even
when he was a small child his father spent a lot of stage time
pummeling him—one of his most successful gags was the delayed
"Ouch!"—and flinging him into the wings.) In vaudeville every
gesture, every vocal inflection, every set of the features had to
carry to the back of the uppermost balcony. Yet Keaton on film
understates. He practices absolute economy of means. He is outrageously tasteful. Perhaps this restraint comes out of his predilection for "realism." When he runs he takes off directly for his
destination, never tricking up the pure activity of running, as
Chaplin so magnificently does. When he dives or tumbles from
cliff edge X to water surface Y, the line X–Y looks stylistically
straight, uncluttered by frantic waving of limbs or contortions of
the trunk. He gets laughs not because he is anguished or innocent
or guileful, but because he doesn't push for them. Much of the
time he appears oblivious to the danger he faces or the very exertions he is making to ward it off.

Keaton revived the tradition of the farceur's mask. In so doing,
he created a new tradition, that of the expressionlessly expressive
mime. Producer after producer asked him to smile—"just this
once." Being an obliging man, Keaton would put on a smile for a
special test at a preview screening. The audience invariably
groaned when it came on. And so for the public, Keaton never
smiled.

That "pan"! Anything but "dead," it allows a spectator to read
there whatever feelings the situation calls for. And more. It takes
the silence in silent movies further: all the way into imponderabil-
ity. If you can't tell from it what Buster thinks or wants, that's
because you don't have to be told. It travels into and out of manic
scenes, a barometer with no needle—but who needs a needle
when the whole instrument is visibly passing through the eye of a
storm? As the body goes to the limits of endurance, as the brain
concocts its outlandish solutions, as the artist plumbs the parody,
that face, defiant *and* put upon, aggrieved *and* aloof, seems more
like everything than like nothing. It has the conventional, chalky
complexion of the clown, although the blanched appearance may
owe as much to lighting as to makeup. It projects a steady gaze out
of eyes edged in the usual black and set well apart over unusually

high cheekbones. From a noble forehead the nose in profile drops away in a hardly broken dip to its point. Keaton's eyes do move. When they swing to one side, it's as if the whole man had turned. When they close in bliss, the whole man is transfigured. When he kneels to propose to a girl, the uplifted stare and the sinews of his bent body speak his entreaty more passionately than words could. His mouth moves too. It occasionally opens—not much—when he lowers his jaw. But he doesn't move his upper lip. This lip gives the Keaton face its immobility, its center of gravity. Fixed in a line that doesn't quite suggest a pout, it holds the narrow mouth firmly in place. Without knowing Keaton the man, who often smiled offstage, one couldn't be sure that the lip wasn't glued or riveted to his upper teeth until Buster grew old—when, for instance, he enacted Beckett's one-character *Film* in 1965, the year before he died, and the lip's shallow division from its center up to the nose had worn and hardened into a wrinkle.

Yet that constant, youthful face of the 1920s, ruled by the lip, has astonishing versatility in its stillness. In many sequences it displays unmistakable feelings. In an early scene from *Sherlock Jr.*, Buster is sweeping the trash out of a movie house. A girl comes along the street, notices the trash, and anxiously inquires whether he found a dollar on the floor. Buster gives her a long stare. Suspicion. Before he answers her, he wants to know what her dollar looked like. She tries to picture it for him, George Washington etching and all. His face softens—without changing, of course. Gallant concession. He takes a dollar out of his pocket and hands it over. Ruefulness. Next, an old lady appears. She is tearful; she too has lost a dollar and wonders if it's in the trash pile. Buster is about to ask her for a description, but then decides not to: her anguish makes it clear that she needs the money badly. Compassion. He takes out another dollar and hands it over. Relief: that was one bill he would not have wished to keep. Buster now has one dollar to his name—as we know, because in an earlier scene he wanted to buy his girlfriend a box of candies, which cost four bucks. He counted out his resources and had only three. It seems certain that he is going to lose that last dollar.

But the scene takes a new twist. A tough-looking character stops by. He says nothing to Buster but goes directly to the trash pile and searches through it. Buster is not about to mess with this character. He takes the remaining dollar from his pocket and holds it out to the man, who spurns it impatiently and goes on rummaging in the pile as though after something much better. Sure enough, deep in the trash he comes up with a wallet stuffed with bills, which Buster must have missed. Consternation. As the man walks away, Buster burrows into the pile wondering what else he could have overlooked. Unfortunately, not a thing. The face, still without any alteration, registers disappointment. End of sequence.

Keaton often shared the credit for directing his films, or gave it to Eddie Cline or Mal St. Clair or somebody else; and he had a team of screenwriters—Clyde Bruckman, Jean Havez, and Joseph Mitchell—on the payroll; but Keaton himself was the mastermind behind his films. He did not, like Chaplin, function as a producer —one reason for his artistic downfall after he went over to MGM. But once an idea had come up, possibly from one of the writers (a wealthy young man and a wealthy girl aboard an ocean liner set adrift, for *The Navigator*), or a stage property had been purchased for adaptation (*Seven Chances*, 1925, or *Battling Butler*, 1926), Keaton dreamed up most of the gags and plot variations, managed the budget, called the shots, and, when he wasn't happy with the rushes, ordered the retakes. On the set he took over because only he knew what he could do. His collaborators testify that his ideas were the most daring ones proposed, requiring the most strenuous feats and the most demanding precision.

Keaton had exceptional mechanical aptitudes. He could build fantastically intricate machines and systems of gadgetry for merely striking a match or setting off an alarm; his inventiveness had farcical purposes, among them the crashing anticlimax. In contrast to his contemporaries, including the Expressionists in Germany, he doesn't allow his hero to be overwhelmed by the machine; the man will plumb its meaning, ascertain the sources of its power, and tame it. Keaton belonged to the machine age. Machines were not his antagonists, but puzzles, challenges. He loved cars, trains, boats, bicycles, balloons, and escalators, and gave them starring roles. He was also devoted to cameras, as he showed in *The Cameraman* (1928). The Russians Sergei Eisenstein, with *Strike* (1924) and *The Battleship Potemkin* (1925), and Dziga Vertov, with *The Man with the Movie Camera* (1928), astounded the film world with the results of their mercurial editing, which investigated the dramatic force of successive, contrasting images, the montage effect. But by 1921 Keaton, with the aid of his cameraman Elgin Lessley, had made a two-reeler, *The Playhouse*, which presented the *composite image* with a flair that has never been matched; this short is, in its unpretentious fashion, as dazzling an advance as anything the Russians attempted. Not since the brief farces of Georges Méliès in the first decade of the century had there been such an innovation in the use of composite images. Directors had toyed with split screens, inserts up in one corner or over to the side of the frame, masking shots, irising in and out, and simultaneous foreground and background activities; but Keaton's contributions in this movie are virtually unduplicable.

The film began as a skit on Thomas H. Ince, a frighteningly efficient producer-director who organized his studio like a time-and-motion fanatic, had the final say on every decision, and took multiple credits for himself. In Keaton's opening sequence for *The Playhouse* he parodies this egomania by taking over every single role in a theater: the solo act, a duo, a lineup of nine minstrels, the various instrumentalists in the band—and the conductor—a performing ape, and the whole audience of men and women, young and old, in the orchestra, the balcony, and the boxes. How was it possible to film them together? Lessley had to mask his camera lens, section by section, and reshoot each matching moment—nine times, for example, in the case of the minstrels, who sang and danced as an ensemble. Meanwhile, Buster took up the necessary position for each repeat and moved in exactly the same rhythm as his other selves. In case this doesn't sound too difficult, it is worth remembering that cameras were then cranked by hand; Lessley therefore had to crank at precisely the same speed each time.

Apart from its virtuosity as acting and as technical achievement, this sequence is the most breathtaking example of theatricalism in the cinema. After his "collective" performances, Buster is seen sitting in a room, which might be a small cabin. Some burly men enter and take out the furniture and fittings. Then they remove the wall. We discover that Buster is situated on an open stage. He is a stagehand who has had a vainglorious dream amid the scenery.

David Robinson has remarked that "the form of Keaton's art was conditioned by the first principle: the need to get a laugh."[6] For the sake of that laugh the comedian would go to almost any length without ever appearing to have strained for effect. He would keep at it until he found the *how*. If Chaplin the Englishman sets himself up as an ethical model, Keaton the all-American boy offers himself as a different sort of model: the man who will not give up, who knows that there must be a way. He is the quintessential problem solver.

One would expect a perfectionist like Keaton to have behaved despotically. He did not. His mockery of Ince implies contempt for the working practices at the major studios, which were set up like assembly lines and where niggling questions had to be cleared with the front office. He enjoyed the camaraderie and the give-and-take of what is now called brainstorming. Other people relished working with him. The writing and filming *chez* Keaton were not separate or rigidly specialized tasks, but part of a relaxed group improvisation. Keaton did not train with Sennett, but his first boss, Roscoe (Fatty) Arbuckle, did. It was Arbuckle who tempted Keaton into the movies in 1917, and soon saw how much there was to learn from his pupil. Arbuckle was respected and envied in the profession for his improvisations. He tried to wheedle the same sort of extemporaneity out of his co-workers. Keaton needed no encouragement. He had been an alert, adaptable comic onstage since his childhood. His art is immeasurably more studied and finished than Sennett's, but it did observe the Sennett tradition in this respect (if Sennett can be said to have founded something as hallowed as a tradition): in letting farce flow from the inspiration of the moment.

Lloyd

Keaton may have set his heart on winning laughs, but in his autonomous years he never pandered for them, never needlessly explained. Keaton's films gather their own momentum and slip without excessive pumping into high gear. If Harold Lloyd has been treated with less awe and attention than were Chaplin and

---

[6] *Buster Keaton* by David Robinson (Bloomington, Ind.: Indiana University Press, 1969), p. 185.

Keaton—was even for a time neglected[7]—it may be because his films appear to be so anxious to please. Keaton and Chaplin keep their distance, let us make our own deductions, and encourage a sense of wonder. Lloyd is more explicit. He works harder in similar circumstances. He wants to get under our skin by making us get into his. He would take us, if he could, into the frame with him. It can be claimed that a film which is meant to be funny should be so, and to hell with the means. But the effect as we watch Lloyd is a sense of being cajoled, if not coerced; of having prompt cards held up to us. Lloyd is a great clown, and we'd laugh without the coaxing because his climactic scenes invariably pay off.

Yet they do sometimes require elaborate preparation: for instance, his most famous stunt, the scaling of the fourteen-story DeVore department store in *Safety Last*. Harold has come from a dead end named Great Bend to find his fortune in the big city. He strikes up a friendship with a cop who is also a Great Bender. He then tells his roommate, while the cop is busy with a phone call, to play a trick on the cop and see how he, Harold, straightens matters out. The cop, however, has strolled off, and a new one takes over the beat. Harold crouches behind him, and the roommate shoves him over Harold's great bend. The new cop doesn't appreciate the gag. He chases the roommate, who has a knack for clinging to buildings and goes vertically up the side of the store where Harold is employed. Now, in previous segments of the film Harold has written to his sweetheart that he is doing brilliantly in the city. She leaves Great Bend to visit him. He must make good on his bragging and dazzle her. He just happens to hear the store's general manager declare that anybody who can think up a gim-

---

[7] In an article reprinted in *Movie Comedy*, edited by Stuart Byron and Elisabeth Weis (New York: Penguin, 1977), pp. 10–18, Richard Schickel answers charges that Lloyd was "superficial" and made films that "say nothing about life." These and other faults in Lloyd's pictures are aired by Gerald Mast in *The Comic Mind: Comedy in the Movies* (Indianapolis and New York: Bobbs-Merrill, 1973), pp. 149–64. Schickel argues, among other things, that "one is struck by how purely [Lloyd's work] seems to be the product of the movies and nothing else," and also that "his pictures reflect the exquisite confusions of a time of vast environmental transition"—from farm life to urban life, from horse-drawn vehicles to internal combustion, from the low rural landscape to the jagged cityscape bristling with its skyline of towers. All of this is true. Lloyd does incarnate the small-town youngster dizzied by city heights before he conquers them. His films nevertheless look labored next to Keaton's or Chaplin's. Nor was he as graceful an actor. But standing below the peaks attained by those two is still a pretty lofty spot to occupy.

mick for attracting more customers will get a reward of a thousand dollars. Harold's brain starts clicking. He invites his roommate to impersonate him and go up the outside of the building, all the way to the top; they will split the reward. In 1923, Harold's share, five hundred dollars, was ample for a down payment on a house. The roommate agrees to the deal; the climb is publicized; a crowd gathers. Unluckily, the cop who was the pushover is on duty again. He spots the roommate and goes after him. The roommate manages to urge Harold to commence the climb; he will take over for him at the second floor, once he has eluded the cop. Naturally, the roommate cannot shake off the cop, who stays doggedly on his heels as they rush upstairs through floor after floor, and Harold, no human fly, eventually has to go it alone to the roof. But he wins the full grand for himself.

Perhaps it's mere carping or ingratitude to complain that two-thirds of a movie must serve to set up the other third when those preliminaries incorporate some excellent farcical maneuvers and when the final third ascends into the most thrilling sequence ever filmed. Yet, as with a Broadway hit play or musical (something by Kaufman and Hart, say, or Rodgers and Hammerstein), however delectable the fare, we cannot help feeling we're being spoon-fed and nudged in the ribs. Lloyd doesn't always trust us; he gives more vigorous help in understanding what is going on than we need.

In much the same way, whereas photographs of Keaton and Chaplin stare at us calmly, those of Lloyd intrude on our consciousness. The face actively seeks our gaze. It projects its high, fine forehead; its toothy, ingenuous smile; nicely brushed hair sometimes topped by a porkpie hat, a fedora, a Panama helmet, a cap, or, most often, a boater; the substantial jaw; the puckered mouth; and those conspicuous horn-rimmed, lensless glasses. (Horn-rims became a fad, and an appreciative manufacturer sent Lloyd twenty free pairs.) Through those open frames Lloyd is very good at looking startled, unnerved, agog, apologetic, shyly affable, or flummoxed. But he is not so good at listening to other actors. He even takes our eyes away from them when, at times, he cannot repress a smirk. He is concentrating not on them but on the camera.

If Lloyd is less than a convincing actor in repose, give him an activity and he compels us to undergo it with him more insistently than any other clown can do. When he takes some mothballs off a candy dish proffered by a girl in *Grandma's Boy*, rolls his eyes as if in imitation of the naphthalene morsels skipping around on his offended tongue, and then rinses his mouth with the contents of what turns out to be a gasoline can, we really taste those substances with him, much as we do when, in *For Heaven's Sake* (1926), he mistakes a powder puff for a doughnut and bites expectantly into the chalky leather. In *Hot Water* (1924) he carries a spilling pile of packages onto a crowded bus, and we *feel* the weight and disequilibrium of his load, not to mention his embarrassment. Lloyd's acting may occasionally slip below par, but he can squirm like nobody's business, and do it infectiously.

He is most fondly and justly remembered for his clambering, slithering, and scrambling on parapets, sills, ledges, and girders (which are not always riveted in place) hundreds of feet above street level. But Lloyd, the go-getter of all time, also pulled off some heart-stopping horizontal journeys across town or across country, races against time. These races owe something to his apprenticeship at Keystone, where just about every film ended with a chase—known as a rally since it brought together the entire cast in a helter-skelter pursuit on foot or on wheels or both. Lloyd's slowly cranked cameras capture even more excitement than Sennett's did. In *Girl Shy* (1924), nominally directed by Fred Newmeyer and Sam Taylor, Harold plays a stuttering author who becomes wildly voluble when he talks about his writing. He has to prevent the girl he loves, Mary Buckingham—not so incidentally, an heiress—from marrying a bigamist. He tries to thumb a ride, is unsuccessful. As one car goes by he pops a paper bag. The driver gets out to look under the hood, and Harold leaps in, but the car turns into the next driveway and stops. Another driver who passes is a learner; her car keeps jerking to a stop, starting again, backing up. Harold cannot decide whether he's being offered a ride. He finally grabs onto the spare wheel in the rear. The car turns in crazy circles, and then backs into a tree, Harold taking the impact. He sees a couple picnicking at the side of the road and steals their car. But the road is closed; he must take a detour. The car bounces over an unmade track; even when it reaches a blacktop surface it keeps jumping like a skittish horse, and lands in a ditch. Harold gets into another car, which is being towed away backward, he finds, to a service station. He boards a fire truck, holding on to the hose, which unwinds until he is stretched out in a straight line behind the truck and then dropped on the roadway, the hose still in his hands. He commandeers a trolley while the driver and con- ductor are talking beside it. The trolley picks up speed, smashes past a fruit cart, and spins people around. The trolley's arm then comes unhooked from the power cable. Harold gets on the roof and connects the arm, but he has left the trolley's motor running. It takes off and careens through the streets while he is still on the roof. He succeeds in disconnecting the arm again, but as he does so, he swings out over the side of the vehicle and dangles there, still traveling, until the arm snaps off and he is dropped into an- other car, next to the driver, so that his foot comes down on the accelerator. The driver is stopped by a motorcycle cop for speed- ing. Harold jumps on the cop's bike and takes off, straight through a street market, while chickens and feathers fly. Afterward he boards a cart drawn by two horses; he unharnesses them in order to be able to go faster, but he and the horses fall in a tangle: they really do fall. He reaches the Buckingham Estate on foot through private yards and gardens, scampers into Mary's house, and grabs her just before she says, "I do."

For Heaven's Sake lavishes on us not one but two races against time. For these Lloyd reverts to something like the old Sennett rally and its human stampede. Harold Manners, a carelessly afflu- ent playboy, wants to impress the girl (Jobyna Ralston) by recruit- ing a congregation for her father's mission hall, rather as Sky Masterson did in *Guys and Dolls* exactly a quarter of a century later. Harold darts through the broken-down neighborhood, smashing the hats of the street loafers and unleashing ass-kicks and other physical insults until he has a furious mob in pursuit. He loses them momentarily when they get distracted by a passerby dressed like him; but after all his exertions Harold is not about to let them go. Reappearing in front of them, and diverting them from the terrified passerby, he leads the way back to the mission hall with his distinctive knees-up, all-out run. By the time he and Jobyna are ready to be married, less than one reel later, Harold pledges that for the wedding, he will round up the gang again. The film ends with a second rally aboard a bus that has no driver.

In *The Freshman*, Lloyd turns the final touchdown into a variation on the race against time. Harold, yearning to become the hero of Tate, "a large football stadium with a college attached," doesn't get into the game until the final minutes, after most of the other players on the Tate team have been carried off and the coach despairingly calls on Harold, the water boy. Reeling from a bruising tackle, he accidentally achieves a thirty-yard advance. He unties the ball's leather lace, lets his opponents from Union State College grab for it, and then jerks it away. This yo-yo caper doesn't succeed in letting him through, but from then on Harold is a marked man. With only seconds left, he makes the run we have been waiting for, fumbling and dropping the ball, picking it up again, brushing off tackles almost unwittingly, and dragging a couple of heavy Union State men with him. The Tate coach has his head in his hands. He doesn't dare look up until he knows for sure that Harold is over the line. How could he doubt it?

Although Lloyd courted success and popularity as avidly as his heroes did, and is usually thought of as the American heroic prototype—the young man willing to do anything but a mean trick in order to come out on top—his most endearing attribute as actor and person is his ability to laugh at his own aspirations. Walter Kerr notes that Lloyd "often gave us something no one else would: the double climax."[8] After winning the football game for Tate, for example, Lloyd receives a note from the girl in the film (Jobyna Ralston again) saying that she always knew he could do it, and that she loves him. After being let down from the shoulders of his fans, he stands gazing at her note in a daze of joy, then closes the sequence by taking a shower in his football gear. Similarly, in *Safety Last*, when Harold has reached the security of the roof and strolled away with his arm around Mildred Davis, he walks into a patch of wet tar, steps out of his shoes, and continues walking, obliviously shoeless.

It took Lloyd several years and hundreds of short films to light on a character that suited him. In the course of those years he discarded a tramp named Willie Work and a nondescript wanderer named Lonesome Luke, both of whom he put through the standard repertory of farcical hoops and shtiks. Both figures estab-

---

[8] *The Silent Clowns* by Walter Kerr (New York: Knopf, 1975), p. 200.

lished a reputation for him as a known Hollywood comic, probably because they—especially Luke—appeared in dozens of films at a rate of two a week. But Lloyd felt more inventive and became more discriminating with what he referred to as "the glass character"—an apt description, as his motives are always transparent. The glass character is actually at least two separate creations. The first, a timid boy on the verge of manhood, goes through adventures in initiation. The structure of *Grandma's Boy*, *Girl Shy*, or *The Freshman* is Harold's uncovering manly powers in himself. *Never Weaken* goes further; it contains an abortive suicide attempt, after which Harold is "reborn."[9] He has overheard a conversation between his girl and a man who promises to marry her. He doesn't know that the man is her brother, a newly ordained minister. He meditates, then writes a farewell note, fills a tumbler with Peerless disinfectant, and is about to swallow it when he thinks he may have misspelled a word. He erases "sepulchre" in his note, tries it again with the "h" in different places, looks it up in the dictionary, sees that he was correct the first time, then reluctantly sips the disinfectant. It tastes awful; he adds sugar. As he is about to drink, a fly settles on his nose. By the time he gets rid of it he notices that one of his buttons is loose. As he pulls it off, he knocks over the disinfectant. Next, he decides to stab himself on a paper-holder spike, but after accidentally pricking his finger he changes his mind and opts for a painless ending by means of the gas pipe that feeds the lamp in his office. No good. The smell of the gas repels him. He has one instrument of destruction left, a revolver. But the mutilation would be too disquieting. He remembers that he can still leap out the French window behind him; his office is on an upper floor. He runs at the window, pulls himself up short at the last moment, almost falls over the edge, then sits down to brood in self-contempt. A higher power takes over. A girder manipulated by a crane swings in through the open window under Harold's chair and carries him out.

The other glass character is not an underdog but an overdog,

---

[9] Keaton included a very different suicide scene in his *Hard Luck*, made that same year, 1921. But whereas Buster is doing everything he can to do away with himself and not succeeding because of fluke and misjudgment, Harold is striving to *avoid* doing away with himself. Both sequences are funny; but Keaton's is also serious and haunting, another of his prefigurings of the drama written after World War II.

rich and assured and spoiled, who comes to care about others. In *For Heaven's Sake* he can afford to see two of his luxurious automobiles demolished in one day with no more regret than is conveyed by a shrug. In *Why Worry* he plays a slothful hypochondriac in a wheelchair, attended by a male servant and female nurse as he visits a South American republic called Paradiso (apparently off the coast of Chile) for a rest cure. But he lands at the start of a murderous uprising. By the end, he has put down the uprising with the aid of the nurse and a huge, bearlike caveman (John Aasen) called Colosso, who looks like an overgrown Michel Simon.

Between these extremes of the glass character there are the intermediate Harolds of *Safety Last* and *Hot Water*, neither as retiring nor as imposing as the alternate Harolds, but, like them, all resourcefulness, all intelligence and determination, once they know what must be done to win the day.

Langdon

Harry Langdon doesn't get himself out of farcical tangles; they let go of him. He emerges bewildered, a chick from its shell; he sizes up the world for the first time, since for Harry every emergence is the first one; and he knows he could figure it all out sooner or later. But he never has the opportunity. The next tangle is lying in wait. He will stall for as long as he can, advance on it a bit, retreat a bit, and hope to hold his ground. Then it will snare him. Langdon resembles Chaplin and Lloyd in that he would love to be liked. He resembles Keaton in being solemn, rather than mischievous. In expression he sometimes resembles Stan Laurel in those moments between hearing bad news and letting his face sag into crying. The dangers he faces resemble those faced by other heroes of farce and melodrama. But Harry Langdon has his own timorous personality. He looks out of place because he is out of his time. He belongs in the ranks of the heroes of antifarce—Ionesco's, Beckett's, Pinter's—who were not to come to light for another thirty years.

From 1924 to 1928, Langdon enjoyed a spell of unexpected fame. Then, all of a sudden, he burned himself out in popular esteem. Sennett had snatched him out of one of those vaudeville acts in which an automobile mysteriously breaks down and refuses to yield to repairs, threats, or prayers—the sort of sketch a stage comic could live off for years. In a succession of short films Langdon went through the Sennett paces with the pie-flinging, frenzied tempo, consorts of bathing beauties, rallies. And for a while it worked. Then it didn't.

Sennett, having acquired this freak among farceurs, despairingly handed him over to a team of people who might be able to fashion the right material for him. They included the director Harry Edwards and the writer-director Frank Capra, still a dozen years shy of his stride. With them Langdon made three features that were winners, *The Strong Man; Tramp, Tramp, Tramp* (both 1926); and *Long Pants* (1927). But Langdon longed to be a comic of pathos, to out-Chaplin Charlie. He went on to direct himself in *Three's a Crowd* (1927), *The Chaser*, and *Heart Trouble* (both 1928), leaning over so far into pathos that he almost lost his footing in farce. He seems to have been stretching himself in search of something new—perhaps an extended form of farce, or a satirical style of comedy, or, just possibly, melodrama. But he had little time to find out what it was before the industry and the viewing public dumped him.[10]

Langdon came closest to triumph in *The Strong Man*, his funniest film and the favorite of nearly everybody who has written about him. Although his name doesn't appear among its directing or writing credits (Capra directed and, with three other writers, was responsible for the scenario; the first cameraman was Elgin Lessley, who had worked for Keaton), in his dual role of star and producer Langdon must have had a lot of say in what went into it. What did go into it was something of Chaplin, of Keaton's parodies of heroics, and of the athletics-at-a-height of Lloyd; but it shows canny departures from their send-ups of Hollywood's romantic leads.

In the first place, the hero, Paul Bergot, is not American but Belgian, a soldier in World War I, said to be "out in no-man's-

---

[10] Langdon didn't vanish after releasing *Heart Trouble* in 1928. But his independent corporation dissolved, and from then on he acted only sporadically in shorts and a few features through the 1930s, with a hiatus between 1933 and 1938. He contributed gags to a number of farces and comedies, much as Keaton did in the same years. In 1939 he temporarily replaced Stan Laurel as Oliver Hardy's partner in *Zenobia*. He died in 1944, aged sixty.

land"—a quiet dig that opens the farcical attack on virility. The film begins with actual battlefield footage, then slips into fiction as the diminutive hero practices trench warfare with a slingshot while the enemy, Zandow the strong man, stalks him and snatches him up under one arm.

Suddenly the war is over. Harry and his captor emigrate to America, where Harry's wartime pen pal Mary Brown waits to be courted. The screenplay falls into two main parts. In one, Harry searches for his girl—and doesn't find her. In the second, he stops looking—and finds her. Accidents rule his life.

In the first part, Harry meets up with a blond Amazon, a Mary Brown impostor who plants a wad of stolen money in his jacket and then tries to get it back. When she starts to feel him up, he shies so strenuously that she takes him in her arms. Thwarted again, she pretends to faint, to get him up to her apartment, where, as he politely clears some cushions to make room for her on the sofa, she smashes a bottle over his head.

The next segment is a transition between the film's two parts. It takes place on a small, crowded bus traveling toward the town of Cloverdale. Harry has a cold, and his sneezes annoy the other passengers, who keep getting splashed. He takes out a Smith Brothers cough drop, places it on a spoon, and swallows it. His next dose is bad-tasting medicine; he pours it into the spoon and blinks at it,[11] then sneezes again and blows the spoonful over another passenger. He rubs some camphor salve on his chest, but deprived of his sense of smell, confuses the container with a pot of Limburger cheese that happens to have rolled next to him. At this, the other passengers rebel and toss Harry off the bus. He rolls and somersaults down some embankments while the bus is negotiating hairpin bends, and lo! again by accident, Harry rejoins it at a lower point on the hillside, returning to his seat by way of the open roof.

The second part consists of the film's climactic high jinks. Zandow, assisted by Harry, is supposed to do his strong-man act in Cloverdale, before an audience of out-of-state crooks and bootleggers. But the strong man has drunk himself into a stupor. Who

---

[11] Langdon's thoughtful, obtrusive blinking was imitated by a number of cartoon animators. It is especially noticeable in some of the Hanna-Barbera series' female characters, such as Wilma, Fred Flintstone's wife.

can take his place? Harry is thrust onto the stage with only Zandow's weights, cannon, and trapeze to help him out. He stands with one foot locked behind the other, like a first-grader in a year-end school musical. He blinks. He wonders. In lieu of bows, he introduces himself with tiny flourishes, spraying his hands open as though to say, "Here I am." And then what? He sees a poster of a woman doing a split; tries one. Jeers. Rotten fruit. Some weights descend from the flies. He slowly hoists them into the air. And then above his head. Applause. He goes up in the air with them. An old gag. More jeers. More missiles. More abuse. Now Harry's dander is up. He pelts the spectators with bottles of liquor; knocks the bung out of a barrel and drenches them with beer; flies back and forth on the trapeze over their heads, still hurling bottles. His crazy antics on the trapeze and his mounting delight in destruction are like a child's temper tantrum. But the destruction has hardly begun. Harry loads a stage cannon with weights and balls and fires the balky weapon by kicking it. He discharges shot after shot until the axle breaks and the front of the building caves in.

But what of Mary Brown? We meet her just before Harry goes onstage. He needs some water. A stagehand advises him to ask Mary Brown, who is outside. Mary Brown! Harry shudders, caught between fear and fervor, between reluctance to face the big moment and the impulse to rush out. The impulse wins—and he discovers that Mary is blind. The scene, with its hesitant greetings, Harry's realization that Mary cannot see him, and the mimed conversation, is so restrained and eloquent, so masterly in its mimicry of innocent first love, that one can easily understand how Langdon, seeing it, could feel that pathos was his strength. Almost any competent clown could have played the madcap climax with the trapeze, but in the meeting with Mary, Langdon set a new standard in courtly acting, venturing at one moment to take her hand only after placing his hat over it. Unfortunately, he never got the chance to rise to that standard again. It was left to Chaplin in *City Lights* to match, to transcend it.

Capra says in his account of his work with Langdon (in *The Name Above the Title*) that he "made" Langdon, created a screen persona for him, gave him every bit of business, shot and edited him flatteringly; but that Langdon dismissed him in a fit of ungrateful pique and thereafter couldn't go it alone. Capra did move on to a big career, winning the Oscars he yearned for, heading up the Motion Picture Academy, taking charge of film propaganda during World War II, and becoming for a time one of the most sought-after directors in Hollywood, while Langdon went steadily down. But it never seems to have occurred to Capra that maybe he wasn't dealing with a dummy, that Langdon ditched him because he didn't want to be fixed in a Capra mold like the narrow types cast in Capra's subsequent films.

Mo's, Heavies, and Fair Rowdies

In addition to Chaplin, Keaton, Lloyd, and Langdon, there were more than five dozen farceurs who, at one time or another before 1930, drew audiences. Nearly all of them came out of vaudeville, and a fair number went back into it or shifted from studio to studio. At least thirty of them, including Alice Howell, Jimmy Finlayson, Gale Henry, Charlie Murray, Charley Chase, and Billy West, starred in their own series of one- or two-reelers. In their better days Larry Semon, Snub Pollard, and Chase rivaled Chaplin and Lloyd in popularity, keeping watch on one another's screen novelties for professional reasons. Every new or revamped act provoked imitations, and within weeks. Every takeoff on William S. Hart or Rudolph Valentino (The Shriek of Araby, That Son of a Sheik) became an open invitation, a challenge to do better.[12]

From among this welter of clowns one can distinguish several types. The first consists of little men with mustaches. A mustache can cloak and rigidify the center of the face so effectually that it dwarfs the nose and does away with the mouth. Comics like Chester Conklin, Hank Mann, and Jimmy Finlayson, who were national favorites, could peel off the 'tache at the end of a day's work and walk home safely incognito through crowded streets. The one comic to whom the mustache made little difference was Ben Turpin; his obstinately crossed right eye and head tilted to the left rendered him unmistakable.

Mustaches became so critical for recognition that a comic's

---

[12] There are discussions of many of these figures in Clown Princes and Court Jesters by Kalton C. Lahue and Samuel Gill (Cranbury, N.J., and New York: A. S. Barnes, 1970) and in Walter Kerr's appreciatively critical The Silent Clowns.

complete outfit and makeup became known as his "mo." The actual swatches of hair came mostly in trapezoids and rectangles. Conklin's dropped some undisciplined wisps as low as his chin. Andy Clyde's fell away on both sides of his mouth; so did Snub Pollard's, but in points, so that it took on the shape of an inverted croissant. The two halves of Billy Bevan's split away from his nose at an angle of sixty degrees from each other. The separated halves of Fred Mace's aspired upward and outward, a pair of nose antennae. Turpin's looked like a misplaced bow tie. Syd Chaplin, Charlie's half-brother, often affected one that rose around either nostril before coming to its ends like a frustrated vine. Monte Banks and Charley Chase wore narrow, horizontal lines for a gigolo effect. Billy West and Billie Ritchie favored unassertive oblongs, diminutive military hairbrushes, similar to Charlie Chaplin's—not surprisingly, since West was Chaplin's most dedicated imitator and Ritchie claimed to have originated the figure of the tramp.

The roles consisted mostly of victims, rather than aggressors, but victims who, being put upon, swiftly turned into counteraggressors. Harried fathers and husbands, they could not prevent their mo's from quivering when a young charmer stood near. They underwent two basic types of adventure: the worm who turns and the solid citizen who steps out of line and is hammered back into submission, in both cases after a reel or two of lithely compressed but punishing horseplay. Few of them needed stand-ins for their falls, high dives, and head-on smashes; some could themselves have earned a living as stunt men, even though the fast-motion episodes make their exploits look more daring than they possibly were.

The second type, big men with a lot of eye shadow but without mercy, were the "heavies," frequently represented on the screen today by Eric Campbell and Mack Swain, thanks to the revivals of early Chaplin films. Campbell left his enormous mark on the Mutual shorts. In *Easy Street* he is the cock of the walk, conquered only when Charlie plunges that pear-shaped skull into a streetlight and turns on the gas and, that treatment not being sufficient, assails the skull with a stove dropped from a window. In *The Rink* he serves as Charlie's ricochet surface, a great cushion that skates nimbly. In *The Immigrant*, as an overbearing, coin-biting waiter-cum-bouncer, he works his upturned eyebrows like an impatient crow's wings. Swain, more comic than villainous, acquired some celebrity as Ambrose, the well-meaning principal of a bundle of short films, and as a bulky support in scores of others. As Big Jim, Charlie's prospecting partner in *The Gold Rush*, he painted his false mo up to the foundations of his nose and ringed his eyes, pheasant-style, with a wide application of black, while his hairline pointed down at his nose like the collapsed horn of a unicorn. Swain was brought back from semiobscurity by Chaplin, as Mann was later in *City Lights* and Conklin in *Modern Times*.

Vernon Dent did heavies opposite Bevan, Langdon, and Clyde, but never established himself in one guise. Kalla Pasha could contort his broad face and shaggy black hair into the most frightening mugs on film before Lon Chaney. Craggy Noah Young, Eddie Baker, and Ford Sterling sometimes played villains. So, in his early years, did Oliver Hardy, former boy soprano, before he found his lasting partner. These heavies threw their weight around not only at the pitifully sized heroes, but also at the women, although in an emergency those same women tenaciously fought back with pies, fists, and heavy objects.

The third comic type, powerful ladies, played either battle-axes (Fanny Kelly, Blanche Payson, Louise Carver), if they were older, or robust heroines, who were required to be good-looking. Alice Howell might pop her eyes, Gale Henry swing her mouth around in all directions, and Louise Fazenda settle into grossly unbecoming clothes, but photographs of them with their vivacious faces in repose don't hint at the danger of injury that continually threatened them on the lot. Mabel Normand and that early partner of Harold Lloyd's, Bebe Daniels, did not glow with the lacquered radiance of Garbo or Swanson or Louise Brooks, but they could do pretty good burlesques of Mary Pickford, everybody's sweetheart. Miss Pickford was not above burlesquing herself, perhaps as a defensive maneuver, but not until *Modern Times* and Paulette Goddard did any actress go Pickford one better at her own game. Pearl White turned up in some farces before surrendering to the slim characterization of the imperiled Pauline. Minta Durfee (married to Arbuckle) and Polly Moran cheerfully roughhoused with the roughest of the men. Both were winsome. Miss Moran is said by Bessie Berger in Odets' play *Awake and Sing!* to have "a nose from here to Hunts Point"—the "here" being the West

Bronx; but that was in the mid-Thirties, and over time, noses, even Cleopatra's, will grow.

Finally, there were the unclassifiables—a spectrum of artists, some pronounced personalities, some capable all-arounders, and most able to function as writers and directors. There were the rotund men who did not play heavies: Roscoe Arbuckle, a genial conjunction of weight and light-footed slapstick, whom scandal drove from the peaks to the troughs of international esteem;[13] Frank (Fatty) Alexander, a solid supporting comic; and Max Asher, the "Dutch" vaudevillian and makeup expert who occasionally played several characters in the same short. Among the memorable thin men of silent days are Stan Laurel (under his own name, Stan Jefferson), an actor, director, and idea man long before Hal Roach put him in harness with Hardy; Larry Semon, whose cropped hair, carving knife of a nose, and trustful eyes were almost as renowned as the faces of the Big Four; Al St. John, Arbuckle's nephew by marriage, a prime specimen of the lanky hayseed who also specialized in losing control of fast cars; and Slim Summerville, that splendidly placid forked pole, the length of his legs emphasized by his short jackets.

The English music-hall star Lupino Lane, tiny, sharp-featured, bird-eyed, and a stylish acrobat, did several features in Hollywood. Jack Duffy played bespectacled old crocks with toothless grins and gnarled agility, Pantaloons in spats and, often, a jaunty top hat. Charlie Murray, whose ski-jump or sliding-pond nose antedates Bob Hope's and whose jaw lived an independent life from the rest of his face because of his immensely stretchable lower lip, came out of the Murray and Mack stage act and, after many shorts, found his way into another partnership, the Cohen and Kelly features. (Cohen was little George Sidney.) Syd Chaplin, who did not always wear a mo, is sometimes said, on slender evidence, to have been as inventive as his half-brother. He and some others, Arbuckle, Harry Depp, and Billy Reeves among them, brought fe-

---

[13] After Arbuckle had been tried for months for the murder of a starlet named Virginia Rappe, the third jury issued a strong statement affirming his innocence. But public opinion had been marshaled against him, and Arbuckle took the rap socially, if not legally. Much like the blacklisted Hollywood Ten in the Fifties, he had to find sporadic directing and other nonacting assignments under a pseudonym, William B. Goodrich—a variant of his friend Buster Keaton's suggestion, Will B. Goode.

male impersonation out of vaudeville and medicine-show tents and onto the screen. Lloyd Hamilton's are the heavy-lidded eyes, great stretch of nostrils, and baby's mouth in the "Ham and Bud" one-reelers of the early silent years; Hamilton went on into many solo roles in farces of the Twenties.

And there were more. . . .

Clair

The outstanding director of film farce in the Twenties was a Frenchman, René Clair.[14] For several years Clair served his apprenticeship as an actor and wrote critical appreciations of the early cinema, before directing his first picture in 1923, *Paris Qui Dort (The Crazy Ray)*, based on his own scenario.[15]

His silent farces differ from those of his contemporaries in the United States. Young men like Frank Capra, Leo McCarey, and George Stevens were assigned to pictures that showed off well-known comics; Clair worked independently and chose actors, rather than professional funnymen. The Americans made mostly farces of the realistic type; Clair had a predilection for fantasy, although he did make some realistic farces. Two of the latter, *An Italian Straw Hat* and *Two Timid People*, come from nineteenth-century plays by Labiche and Marc-Michel, and adhere closely to the tightly knitted dramatic texts and their beat-the-clock formula. But Clair's films don't seem as stagy as many other adaptations of the time do. And his cinematic additions harmonize with the play. In *An Italian Straw Hat*, for instance, a hot-tempered army officer waits in a bridegroom's apartment for the groom to return from the wedding, and hurls a chair out a window. Clair cuts to the chair landing outside on the pavement. A passing junkman looks at this handout from heaven and quickly loads it on his cart. Soon

---

[14] In the theater of the West, directing as a separate type of artistry dates back only to the last quarter of the nineteenth century. It did not become a recognized profession until the early years of the film industry. The birth of film and the power of its directors have often been acknowledged as enhancing the respect accorded theater directors. By way of contrast, directors have functioned in the Indian (Sanskrit) theater for over two thousand years.

[15] Clair acted for two French directors, the prolific Louis Feuillade and Jacques Protazanov, a Russian working in France. He also persuaded Jacques de Baroncelli to take him as an assistant in the making of a couple of films, and he studied the early farces of Méliès and Linder. In 1947 his film *Silence Is Golden* paid homage to the pioneers of French film.

after, some friends of the groom drop off a clock, a wedding gift. The officer hurls it too out the window. In the street, the departing friends watch as their wedding present is brutally spurned (by the groom, they think), and then as the junk dealer strolls by again and makes off with the clock. At the wedding ceremony, the groom, who knows the officer is in his apartment, pictures to himself the desecration of his property as Clair shows us a shower of furniture flying out of windows.

Two Timid People opens with an anticipation of *Rashomon:* two opposed accounts of the same events. In a courtroom during a wife-beating case, we see a drunken hog of a husband assaulting his meek little wife while the prosecuting attorney speaks. But the defense attorney conjures up a cheerful room in which the glowing, well-fed wife opens the door to her devoted husband, who brings her a bouquet, kisses her, polishes her shoes, and plays his violin for her. The defense attorney falters and stops. So does the film. He doesn't believe his own story. He begins his speech again, and again, while the film goes into fast-forward as it retells his story at top speed. Clair embellishes the play, but without violating it, when he introduces a variation on the conflicting narrative, a split-screen scene in which two rivals for a girl simultaneously imagine they are beating each other up and winning.

Clair's adopted name (his real name was Chomette) suggests light, clarity, rapidity. *The Crazy Ray* opens on top of the Eiffel Tower, where the janitor, Albert, has his quarters. He goes down into the city and finds the streets empty—even the Place de la Concorde—and people frozen into poses. A gendarme, about to seize a thief, holds a pose of reaching out in the instant before grabbing him. A beggar's arm is poised above a pail of garbage. Albert soon meets four men and a woman who have just landed in Paris from a plane and, like him, can move around freely. A scientist named Dr. Crase has released a ray that brought Paris to a halt at 3:25 A.M. Albert, on the Eiffel Tower, and the plane's five passengers were above the ray's influence when the crazy Dr. Crase pulled his lever. In the course of this early sample of science fiction, Crase turns the ray off, then on again at varying intensities, deadening all life in the city, reviving it, and speeding up its activities. The device gives Clair justified pretexts, demanded by the action, for using stop-and-go cinematography, which in earlier movies had seemed merely an arbitrary effect "to show what the camera could do." The sextet of people awake in a city asleep swiftly lose all their inhibitions. They plunder banks and stores. In a nightclub they grow boisterous over champagne, wine, and cigars in the midst of inanimate waiters and patrons, people turned into scenery. One member of the group, a businessman, puts a tip into the hand of a motionless waiter; another, a criminal, takes it out again. An exhibitionistic madness seizes them. They toss bank notes around and fold some into paper airplanes, which they launch from the Tower. One bill sails to the ground as Paris comes alive momentarily, and two men wearing sandwich boards get locked into a half-stoop, but a passerby pounces under the boards and scoops up the money.

The Imaginary Journey (1925), a farcical fairy tale, starts out at a fast clip. A young man, Jean, is followed along back streets by another man and a mutt. He begins to run; so do his pursuers. He gets to the entrance of a bank. Cut. Inside the bank there are a woman, named Lucie, an elderly branch manager, and three male tellers, one of whom is Jean. The pursuit of Jean was a dream— and so is the rest of the film. He races through a wood, is led by way of a capacious rabbit hole down a circular chute into a Lewis Carroll Land underground. He kisses some ugly crones and transforms them into attractive flappers. In gratitude, they grant his wish to have Lucie with him. But the other two tellers also find their way to the magic kingdom. Lucie and Jean dally in settings festooned with immense flowers, while the other tellers lose their clothes to a garment-gobbling monster. Later the four of them are transported on a cloud to Paris, and deposited high up on the cathedral of Notre Dame. Night comes and they find themselves in a waxworks museum where the statues of famous people are played by immobile actors. At midnight these figures come to life. The farce turns briefly horrific as the wax figures, their "open" eyes painted on closed eyelids, form a tribunal which sentences Jean to the guillotine. At the last moment he is reprieved by the wax statue of none other than Charlie Chaplin. When he wakes from his dream, Jean finally feels brave enough to propose to Lucie.

The most abstract of Clair's films, Entr'acte (1924), was exactly that: a surrealist interlude, screened during the intermission between two acts of a ballet entitled *Relâche* (*No Show Tonight*). This was another of those French evenings of *scandale*, almost comparable to the opening nights of Hugo's *Hernani* (1830) and Jarry's *King Ubu* (1896). The ballet and the twenty-two-minute film were sponsored by Francis Picabia, the Spanish-born painter, who prepared some fragmentary suggestions to build the film on. Clair incorporated nearly all of Picabia's ideas, which included the loading of a cannon by Picabia himself and the composer Erik Satie; a game of chess between Marcel Duchamp and the American photographer Man Ray; a girl dancing on a sheet of glass, viewed from below; and a funeral hearse drawn by a camel. But he amplified these shots, added many more of his own, and tied some of Picabia's ideas together without explaining them away literally.[16] He turned the funeral into an exciting chase: the hearse escapes from the camel; rolls away downhill, gathering speed, then uphill, gathering more speed (an effect achieved by tilting of the camera), while the procession of mourners tries to keep up with it. This procession circles a small model of the Eiffel Tower—a moment that brought gasps from the original audience. The hearse somehow gets on a roller coaster and travels around dizzying curves, up and down, like a preview of Cinerama.

Entr'acte is not a surrealist film drawn from free association, but a scrupulously organized, coherent farce that shoots for laughs and surprises all the way. In lieu of a conventional story, Clair offers thematic imagery (repetition is one of farce's surefire techniques), as when he keeps cutting to a legless man pushing himself along laboriously on a wheeled board. In one of the many surprises, the man later gets up off his board on two healthy legs and scampers away. Clair fortifies his treatment with so many dissolves; superimpositions (a paper boat sails across rooftops); and variations of shooting speed, focus, and angle; so much horizontal and vertical tracking and unorthodox panning and editing that he brings farce to the innovative forefront of film making. As a whole, Clair's output in the Twenties lived up to the best pictures made by the

---

[16] Picabia's eight shots to be used in the film gave way to the three hundred fifty–odd shots specified in Clair's full screenplay. The notes and the screenplay can be compared in the paperback *À Nous la Liberté* and *Entr'acte* (New York: Simon and Schuster, 1978), pp. 113–40. This edition of the film script has an introductory essay by Clair in which he modestly alludes to his contributions as "what I had added" to Picabia's notes.

best silent comics, matching their display pieces of acting with a host of novel directing techniques. He broadened the purview of film farce and helped to make it the most vital of the genres during the succeeding decades.

---◆---

EIGHT

THE TALKING THIRTIES

MRS. RITTENHOUSE: You are one of the musicians? But you were not due until tomorrow.

RAVELLI: We couldn't come tomorrow. It was too quick.

CAPTAIN SPAULDING: Say, you're lucky they didn't come yesterday.

RAVELLI: We were busy yesterday, but we charge you just the same.

SPAULDING: This is better than exploring. What do you fellows get an hour?

RAVELLI: For playing we get ten dollars an hour.

SPAULDING: I see. What do you get for not playing?

RAVELLI: Twelve dollars an hour.

SPAULDING: Well, cut me off a piece of that, will you?

RAVELLI: Now, for rehearsals we make a special rate, fifteen dollars an hour.

SPAULDING: That's for rehearsing? What do you get for not rehearsing?

RAVELLI: You couldn't afford it. You see, if we don't rehearse, we don't play, and if we don't play that runs into money.

SPAULDING: How much do you want to run into an open manhole?

RAVELLI: Just the cover charge.[1]

CHICOLINI: Monday we watch-a Firefly's house, but he no come out. He wasn't home. Tuesday we go to the ball game, but he fool us. He no show up. Wednesday he go to the ball game and

---

[1] *Animal Crackers*, Paramount, 1930.

we fool him: *we* no show up. Thursday was a double-header; nobody show up. Friday it rained all day. There was no ball game, so we stayed home and we listened to it over the radio.

TRENTINO: Then you didn't shadow Firefly?

CHICOLINI: Oh, sure we shadow Firefly. We shadow him all day.

TRENTINO: What day was that?

CHICOLINI: Shadowday.[2]

OTIS B. DRIFTWOOD (*to Mrs. Claypool*): That's why I'm sitting here with you. Because you remind me of you. Your eyes, your throat, your lips . . . everything about you reminds me of you. Except you.[3]

CUTHBERT J. TWILLIE: Whom have I the honor of addressing, Milady?

FLOWER: They call me Flower Belle.

TWILLIE: Flower Belle! What a euphonious appellation! Easy on the ears and a banquet for the eyes.

FLOWER: You're kinda cute yourself.

TWILLIE: Thank you. I never argue with a lady.

FLOWER: Smart boy. . . .

TWILLIE: I will be all things to you. Father, mother, husband, counselor, Japanese bartender.

FLOWER: You're offering quite a bundle, honey.[4]

STAN: She's got a surprise for you.

OLLIE: What else did she say?

STAN: She told me not to tell you that she had the surprise.

OLLIE: Then *don't* tell me.

STAN: I won't. I can keep a secret.[5]

The talking Thirties began, of course, in the silent Twenties. Or before. When sound came in, Chaplin moved from strength to strength; *City Lights* (1931) and *Modern Times* (1935) represent his farce at its most exquisitely sustained. W. C. Fields, who came into his own in a bundle of sound features made in and after 1932,

[2] *Duck Soup*, Paramount, 1933.
[3] *A Night at the Opera*, MGM, 1935.
[4] *My Little Chickadee*, Universal, 1940.
[5] *Twice Two*, Roach Studios, 1933.

had played a fairly slim, fairly youthful lead in the silent *Pool Sharks* as early as 1915. Laurel and Hardy paired up late in 1926; they had turned out more than thirty silent features before the "all-talking" *Berth Marks*, released in June 1929.[6] "Our Gang," with its casts constantly replaced as its actors reached puberty, knew its shining days in the Thirties when Spanky McFarland, Alfalfa Switzer, Buckwheat Thomas, Stymie Beard, and Porky Lee were the principal Gang members; but the Gang, which persisted into the Forties, had been a moneymaking staple of the Roach studios since 1922. The Marx Brothers slipped *Cocoanuts* into circulation by 1929. And many solo comedians who went intermittently farcical—among them Will Rogers, Jimmy Durante, and Edgar Kennedy—became neighborhood-movie-house faces in the Thirties, even though most of them had transferred to the cinema from vaudeville a decade or more previously.

But movie farce in these years belonged preeminently to teams, rather than to solo acts; and in place of the traditional funnyman backed by a feed, or straight man, these duos (Olsen and Johnson, Wheeler and Woolsey) or trios (the Three Stooges, the Ritz Brothers) consisted mostly of performers each of whom was a comic in his own right and looked for his featured turns and scenes. In the case of the Crazy Gang in Britain, three pairs amalgamated into a sextet: Bud Flanagan and Chesney Allen, Jimmy Nervo and Teddy Knox, Charlie Naughton and Jimmy Gold. Even a solo comic like Will Hay, another Briton, worked with two backup comics, the plump Graham Moffatt, who was like a youthful Fatty Arbuckle on a partial diet, and Moore Marriott as a prematurely aged, wizened, and toothless reincarnation of that American specialist in old men, Jack Duffy; Hay himself, a rollicking farceur, wore his glasses on the end of his nose, much as Andy Clyde or, occasionally, Jimmy Finlayson, had done, and thereby gave his gaze a peering, suspicious, schoolmasterish look. Yet another Briton, Arthur Lucan, pumped out a misbegotten series of female impersonations of Old Mother Riley, which drew on a different tradition, that of the English pantomime dame; Lucan co-starred his wife, Kitty MacShane, as Mother Riley's vapid daughter. The biggest

---

[6] Stan and Ollie had appeared together, but not in their familiar characterizations, in a two-reeler in 1919 entitled *Lucky Dog*.

box-office draw in Britain during the Thirties was the mildly farcical George Formby, whose trademarks were buckteeth and witty
songs of his own composition which he accompanied with a ukulele and a Lancashire accent. However, Formby and most other
soloists, such as Jimmy Durante of the rasping Brooklyn voice and
peninsular nose, while adding to the personality roster of farce,
did not particularly enlarge its vocabulary or resources. Nor did
most of the teams. There were, however, several exceptions. The
decade's dominant figures consist of two singles, West and Fields;
one duo, Laurel and Hardy; and one trio, the Marx Brothers.

Mae West

When she came to the screen in *Night After Night* (1932), Mae
West was thirty-nine; forty when she made *She Done Him Wrong*
and *I'm No Angel,* partnered in both by the youthful, unconvinc-
ing Cary Grant, whom she promoted to feature roles; forty-seven
by the time—the one time—she found a worthy opponent, Fields,
in *My Little Chickadee*; and going on eighty-seven when her last
picture was released showing her still magnetizing men. But by
1932 she'd been a stage star for more than twenty years, a head-
liner. Her waist and upper arms had thickened, but her legs were
still a young dancer's, just as Fields's hands, in his sixties, retained
the deftness of the young juggler's and prestidigitator's. At any age
she was one thing to all men. She decorated and flaunted what she
had with a take-it-or-leave-it air, but on the assumption that they'd
take it if they could afford it. She *said* she was always ready to give
up the game. "I'm tired of tossing the hips," she remarks to the
circus boss (Edward Arnold) in *I'm No Angel,* an adaptation of her
long-running stage show *Diamond Lil.* And soon after, to a fortune-teller: "Honey, you just tell me about my future. . . . I know
all about my past." She may be ready to reform, but is reformation
ready for her? When the fortune-teller announces, "I see a man in
your future," she comes right back with "What? Only one?"

 Her name, unlike Nathanael's, was West at birth, and she stood
alone at a point of the compass absolutely removed from Greta
Garbo, Theda Bara, Clara Bow, Margaret Dumont, Marie Dressler, Mary Pickford, Mabel Normand, Marlene Dietrich, Margaret
Hamilton, and other ones-of-a-kind. "Stood" is not quite right.

Mae, ever in movement even when her feet aren't, has shoulders and hips that lead their own restless, rotating lives.

Lolling, strolling, rolling Mae. When she likes a man, her eyes flick from his face to his knees, back to his face; one side of her mouth begins to smile, and she looks away—not at the camera but just past it, as though to say, "Did you see what I saw?"

Her ten pictures shot in the Thirties (and 1940), and the three later, mostly follow the format of getting out from under and trying to settle down with an ideal mate. The exception was *My Little Chickadee*, but in that she had to counter Fields's muddled insouciance with something new of her own, something harder-bitten: she turns into a pistol-packing mama aboard a train and picks attackers off their horses two at a time, one from each smoking fist, finally taking leave of W.C. with a kindly "Come up and see me."

And she wrote her own screenplays, the quintessence of which she distilled in majestically turned one-liners and two-liners.

To a lion who yawns: "Where were *you* last night?"

"Married five times? To you wedding bells must sound like the alarm clock."

"Did you have a haircut or get your ears moved down?"

GERTRUDE HOWARD [the Beulah of "Beulah, peel me a grape"]: I
   been under the impression you was a one-man woman.
MAE: I am. One man at a time.

CARY: I hope I haven't disturbed you.
MAE: Not so far.

EDWARD ARNOLD: I've changed my mind.
MAE: Does it work any better?

But her forte is the epigram.

CARY: You were very good tonight.
MAE: I'm always good at night. . . . When I'm good I'm very good,
   but when I'm bad I'm better.

Mae West's films are not farcical; there is in them none of the desperation and rush we look for in the genre. Yet she's so outrageously her own languid self, and her posturing is so frank, so blatantly indifferent to whether she really is the eternal feminine, so excessive for comedy (or even self-caricature) that she evidently has invented some queen of the hurly-burly that is farce's equal.

W. C. Fields

Dentists, as we know, spend bright mornings on the golf course. W. C. Fields starts his daily round in *The Dentist* (1932) by swinging mightily and hitting another player on the head with the ball just as the man breathes in luxuriously and finishes exclaiming, "This is certainly a great game for your health." Fields takes no notice of his felled victim. As the limp form is dragged away, leaving behind a dislodged set of dentures, Fields readies his next shot and snarls, "Get those teeth out of there too. They're in my line."

Fields may have rivals for the honor of funniest, most beloved, or most versatile comic of the Thirties—Will Rogers and Jimmy Durante, for example—but he is the only single comic of the period who owed his appeal to being raffish, curmudgeonly, untrustworthy. (Groucho Marx did not go off on his own until the Fifties, and then as the abusive M.C. of *You Bet Your Life* on television, and not as an outright farceur.) Fields perfected the indirect insult, a scarcely audible, sometimes bewildered aside that emerges from a corner of his mouth, glances off its target, and may then boomerang. "I don't know why I ever come in here," he says of a disagreeable restaurant. "The flies get the best of everything." When a child splatters him with food, he cannot decide "whether to eat from my coat or my plate." He will confess that a tough moll once beat him up, but he insists that "she had another woman with her, an elderly lady with gray hair."

Fields was not especially large or portly, but he moved as if he were. As a dentist, barber, or pharmacist, cardsharp or pool shark, he carried himself imposingly, seeming to hint that he was lending his time at low interest. His face gives an impression of size, expansiveness: the lump of nose (smashed more than once in childhood fights) wedged between fleshy cheeks; when he smiles, the affable double chin belies the upper teeth, which look sharpened for a bite. He doesn't always wear vividly checked pants, or a boater with its top missing, or cutaway jacket and foulard; these garments, which recur often enough to have become a recognizable uniform, are occasionally supplanted by a tradesman's smock or an apron, which enhances his appearance of solidity.

Fields found himself in Hollywood even later in life than Langdon did. I say "found himself" because he'd appeared on screen a dozen times before the Thirties, directed twice by D. W. Griffith. But Fields was a hard man to deal with, pushing for big salaries and arguing with studio writers and directors. Producers shied away from him. Not until 1931, when he went to work for Sennett, then distributing "Mack Sennett Star Comedies" through Paramount, did Fields embark on the short and long farces for which he is chiefly remembered.

By then he was past fifty, and his characterizations relied on plotting that avoided romantic attachments, or made a mockery of them. He dispensed with the smitten hero and replaced him with a wayward toper of advanced middle age who might play up to charming damsels but could easily be distracted. In his last feature, *Never Give a Sucker an Even Break* (1941), he meets a beautiful young woman (Susan Miller) whose mother has kept her away from "deceiving men," and proceeds to teach her the game of Squidgilum, also known as Post Office, a pretext for exchanging kisses. But as soon as he learns that the mother, whom he has described as "a buzzard . . . if there ever was one," has "a bankroll so big a greyhound couldn't leap over it," he tells that redoubtable lady (Margaret Dumont), "I am here to lay my heart at your feet."

By the time he came to that film, and the one before it, *My Little Chickadee* (1940), Fields was in his sixties. Some of the testiness had evaporated from his performing and given way to the guarded and ambiguous civilities he and Mae West bandied back and forth with the flawless timing of seasoned vaudevillians. Now creating his own screenplays (or collaborating with Miss West on one of them) instead of merely contributing lines, episodes, and interruptions, he departed from the domestic sitcom patterns of the early Thirties in order to concoct outrageous semi-improvisations. He dives ten thousand feet from a plane in pursuit not of a girl, but of a bottle of whiskey that has fallen out the plane window. He lands, unharmed, on a sofa in a villa set in the mountains of Mexico, where a chorus of peasants sings "Otchi Tchorniya" ("Dark Eyes") in Russian.

In addition to having—and cultivating—a distinctive shape, style, and farcical attack, Fields acquired a voice, vocal mannerisms, continuo of flowery speech formations, and intonations fluctuating between haughtiness and disgust that made him a favorite subject for professional and amateur impersonators. Graham Greene found it "his most delightful characteristic that his lips are never, for one moment, sealed, for he fills up even the blanks in the script with his rumble of unintelligible rotundities."[7] That unceasing and unmistakable prattle may come out slurred because Fields doesn't sound—and usually isn't—quite sober. On and off the set he consumed something like two quarts of gin a day, at least according to one biographer.[8] And unregenerate drinking figures cheerfully in almost all his movies.

But the slurring is induced, purposeful. Fields worked at a throwaway technique. He broke the other professionals' rules for getting laughs. Rarely did he build to a punch line. And when he did, rather than smashing into it after allowing a significant pause, he slid over it unemphatically and pressed on. He was the great underplayer, the most reticent farceur on film before Jacques Tati.

His weakness for liquor is matched by a weakness for extravagant names, places, and expressions. Such coinages as Miss Ouliotta Hemogloben, Mrs. Cleopatra Pepperday, Mr. Woolfinger, Egbert Sousé, Greasewood City, a pet ostrich named Myrtle, the Philillo bird (which "lives in the desert" and "flies backward to keep the sand out of its eyes"), and the Pronkwonk Twins, Elwood and Brentwood ("Elwood is ten minutes older than Brentwood and has been in a hurry ever since"), decorate the surface of Fields's speech and turn it into farce in a rococo mode, spreading vines and curling tendrils of language as fantasy. He calls his beloved (Mae West) "my little, sugar-coated wedding cake" with whom he would like to discuss "some very definite, pear-shaped ideas."

Fields hardly ever resorted to wordplay, as most ex-vaudevillians did. His fame came originally from his juggling and visual gags.

---

[7] *The Spectator*, July 1936. Reprinted in *Graham Greene on Film*, edited by John Russell Taylor (New York: Simon and Schuster, 1972), p. 88.
[8] *W. C. Fields: His Follies and Fortunes* by Robert Lewis Taylor (Garden City, N.Y.: Doubleday, 1949), p. 243.

When at last he speaks to his public, it's in a strange tongue that derives more from literary than from stage traditions. He evidently liked Victorian novels, and his sentence structures betray the influence of Trollope's and Dickens' measured phraseology.

The structures of his films, on the other hand, are more likely to have been borrowed from Lewis Carroll. Fields despised—or at least, spurned—the tried-and-true story patterns used by practically all farceurs and their writers and directors. He did not pile up repetitions. He would not cap one farcical device with a bigger one. He was content to string episodes together, sometimes with a minimum of connecting material and usually, in the scripts he wrote himself, without an organic scheme. The most bizarre of his farces, *Never Give a Sucker an Even Break*, ends with a Sennett-like burst of speed as he wheels a car through dense midtown traffic in order to deliver a woman to a maternity hospital. But the mad rush has nothing whatever to do with the rest of the picture; it merely exposes the rally, or chase, as a gratuitous wrap-up ending. In somebody else's movie the woman passenger would give birth—or threaten to—in the car. But in Fields's version she gets safely to the hospital, where it turns out she is not pregnant at all.

Laurel and Hardy

From 1930 to 1940, Stan Laurel and Oliver Hardy made more than fifty films (out of a total of well over one hundred, including shorts), an average of five a year, which made them easily the most productive, and thus by audience count the most popular, comics of the time. A few, but only a few, of these pictures appear to have been carelessly shucked off onto a greedy market. Almost all contain at least one strikingly novel sequence or inventive reworking of a standard routine, as when Laurel sits clothed in a full bathtub (in *Come Clean*, 1931) and proceeds to wash the underarms of his jacket; or when Hardy, set on fire by a furious husband (in *Them Thar Hills*, 1934), leaps into a well where some moonshiners have earlier poured gallons of high-proof liquor, and is blown out again.

Most of the Laurel and Hardy movies of the Thirties take place in America, in trim homes where walls, ceilings, roofs, windows, stairs, doors, cellars, attics, chimneys, gutters, ladders, furniture, bric-a-brac, domestic appliances, and foodstuffs that are moist, powdered, or liquid function as enemies and co-stars. During their partnership the boys (Stan, meager and passive, and Oliver, rotund and overbearing, are spun from sibling rivalry) became policemen, soldiers, vagabonds, barbers, servants, detectives, and convicts, as did most other American comics. But they also ventured into fantasy, exotic terrain, and parodies of history. In *The Rogue Song* (1930) they visited a studio version of Czarist Russia. *Beau Hunks* (1931) is a skit on the French Foreign Legion antics of *Beau Geste*, set in a North African desert, and so is *The Flying Deuces* (1939). *Fra Diavolo* (1933) takes them to eighteenth-century Italy, accompanied by Auber's music; *Babes in Toyland* (1934) into a vaguely Medieval fantasy, accompanied by Victor Herbert songs; *Bonnie Scotland* (1935) into kilts; *The Bohemian Girl* (1936) into Romany campfire schmaltz and tents, with music by Balfe; *Swiss Miss* (1938) into the Alps and lederhosen and across a swinging footbridge; and *A Chump at Oxford* (1940), which ribs *A Yank at Oxford* with Robert Taylor, released a couple of years earlier, into dark-paneled British interiors and caste snobbery. In at least a couple of cases the script has a classical or mythical lineage. In *Our Relations* (1936) Stan and Oliver both play identical twins who immediately recall the twins of *The Comedy of Errors* and Molière's *Amphitryon*, as well as *their* antecedents in *The Menaechmi* and the *Amphitruo* by Plautus.

The agonies of needless effort expended in the course of their movies are Sisyphean, and most obviously in *The Music Box* (1932), in which they have gone into the moving business with a horse-drawn cart. Their first assignment is to deliver a crated player piano. Their destination is at the top of a long flight of steps, the kind that bark your shins if you fall on them. Several times, and after unpleasant encounters on the way, they get the crate close to the top only to lose the contest to gravity. When, finally, they have almost made it, a mailman observes that a road circling the house will bring them more easily to their destination, whereupon they haul the crate back to the bottom of the steps and drive it around to the top. The second part of the film consists of hoisting the crate into the house through a balcony window when nobody answers the door. After strenuous heaving and tugging, and mishaps with a hook and pulley, a ladder, and an ornamental pool, they discover that the downstairs door was open all along.

The instrument is a birthday gift from the wife of a splenetic professor (Billy Gilbert), who hates pianos and demolishes this one with an ax while the machine remonstrates by tinkling the strains of the national anthem.

As with all Laurel and Hardy films, the events in *The Music Box*, aside from being funny, acquire a special piquancy from a technique in which the pair excel: the measured reaction, a distinct improvement on the double take. When something untoward happens—a blow, the collapse of a ceiling, a cream cake in the face, a collision, a fall—the partners raise their heads slowly, sometimes supporting their chins on their knuckles; they blink as they consider and perhaps relive the preceding moments; and gradually their features harden into incomprehension or, possibly, even further irresolution. When they are hit they do not retaliate impulsively but only after thinking through the indignity and choosing the appropriate means. The device is akin to the one Buster Keaton used as a child in his vaudeville days: he found that when his father assaulted him he got a bigger laugh if he waited five or ten seconds before crying "Ouch!"

The effect is theatrical, stylized, and all the more appropriate for farce. It also represented a calculated risk on Stan Laurel's part. Laurel was the brain behind the Laurel and Hardy characterizations and routines, a gagman admired by his contemporaries (and thanked by many he helped) as one of the most prolific and imaginative in the business.[9] His partner's bulk (in his early film days Hardy was typecast as a heavy) was best suited to a heavy acting style. True, he might enliven it with an occasional mime or dance—the sort of light-leaden capering that almost every stout comic from Arbuckle to Mostel could do. But Hardy's forte was

---

[9] Laurel and Hardy called on a battalion of talent. Leo McCarey, usually credited with bringing them together, and Hal Roach, who produced most of their output, frequently supervised and sometimes directed. James W. Horne, Charles Rogers, Lloyd French, George Marshall, and James Parrott directed some of their finest films; Parrott's *The Music Box*, good though it was, won an Oscar. Laurel undoubtedly had some say in the casting, which, over the years, regularly included such expert comics as Mae Busch, Thelma Todd (until her death in the mid-Thirties), Anita Garvin, Ben Turpin, Stanley (Tiny) Sandford, Edgar Kennedy, Billy Gilbert, and Charley Chase. For a number of the films young George Stevens was the cameraman. John McCabe and Richard W. Bann illustrate Laurel's loyalty to his supporting players when they mention that Harry Bernard worked in twenty-six Laurel and Hardy pictures, Jimmy Finlayson in thirty-three, Jack Hill in thirty-four, and Charlie Hill in forty-seven. See *Laurel & Hardy* (New York: Ballantine Books, 1975), p. 385, footnotes.

deliberate movement combined with slowness on the uptake. Laurel, who had trained himself in swift-footed, knockabout antics, had to modify these drastically if he was to conform with Hardy's naturally more leisurely rhythms. Their superiority as a farce team over, say, Abbott and Costello consists largely in those matched rhythms, which give their performing a planned, visually fascinating coherence.

As a rule, Laurel and Hardy played victims. Oh, they may plot some homely, harmless prank, such as a deception on their wives, but if they do they will suffer inordinate damage or inconvenience. And when they run afoul of nasty people, they don't usually get theirs back. They are cut out, in other words, to be the objects, not the subjects, of farcical cruelty. Ollie's demeanor is very close to that of a long-winded, jowly official whose majestic complacency demands a comeuppance. Stan's foolish grin, his mouth stretched over a great slab of chin and under a Barry Fitzgerald nose into a narrow line that runs parallel to his hat brim, is an open invitation to any bully. And so these two law-abiding, respectful gents undergo fiendishly unfair penalties.

It's tempting to conclude that without Laurel, Hardy would have been just another pleasing comic who might never have made it alone to the heights. When we see the boys together our eyes do tend to focus on Laurel, the more magnetic personality, assertive in the discreet fashion of the exceptional performer. His few solos, especially his pantomimes, confirm his elegance as a funnyman. A punctilious sequence occurs in *The Bohemian Girl*. He means to siphon off into bottles a barrel of wine that is "fuzzling." But between filling the bottles and corking them, he finds that the siphon tube keeps sending out a flow of wine. To avoid spilling between bottles he parks the tube in his mouth. After several fills and spills, he is shown grappling with the siphon while corking his mouth—when two jets of wine suddenly spring from his ears. The act is not just hilarious but breathtaking in its precision.

The Marx Brothers

We can rapidly pass over Zeppo. Groucho, who had hardly a kind word to say for anybody, said that Zeppo was "very good," even after the two had not spoken for years.[10] But Zeppo, who, according to his own testimony, occasionally understudied his three elder brothers and actually stood in for Groucho and Harpo on the stage, never created a film persona of his own, other than the innocuous Blando, whom he offered in *Cocoanuts* (1929), *Animal Crackers* (1930), *Monkey Business* (1931), *Horse Feathers* (1932), and *Duck Soup* (1933). A fourth funny Marx? It was out of the question. The others needed a straight man or nothing, and Zeppo eventually elected to stay with the latter. He went into talent management, and several vocalists—including Allan Jones, Kenny Baker, and Tony Martin—replaced him.

As W. C. Fields practiced aloofness and Laurel and Hardy fraternity, Harpo, Chico, and Groucho Marx practiced upstaging. Harpo often functions as Chico's sidekick, but he becomes unmanageable. In the verbal duets between Chico and Groucho, which contain some of the most memorable wordplay on film, Groucho is continually seeking to break away, to differentiate himself, to put the interloper down. And in the most famous scene between Groucho and Harpo, the mirror act in *Duck Soup*—when Harpo, wearing a Groucho face getup and an identical nightgown and nightcap, *almost* duplicates Groucho's walk and facial gyrations—it looks as if Groucho is trying to fool his own image by instantly differentiating himself from it. Like Garbo, he wanted to be alone.[11]

In theory, then, the Marxes could each have made his own films. In practice, the studio (Paramount or MGM or RKO) wanted every film hawked as a five-plate feast: three Marx courses, a romantic and loud-singing male lead, and a girl or girls. MGM touted *A Day at the Races* (1937) as "a gag-stacked musical whopper" that "whirls to the screen . . . Hear the matchless voice of Allan Jones . . . ! Marvel at the girly-girly water-carnival!"[12] (The

---

[10] *The Marx Brothers Scrapbook* by Groucho Marx and Richard Anobile (New York: Darien House, 1973), p. 253. In this book we learn from an interview with Jack Benny that Zeppo was the funniest of the brothers offstage. Gummo, the remaining brother, left the stage act before World War I. He considered himself not much of an actor.

[11] It turns out that Garbo never spoke a line that said exactly, "I vant to be alone," but she did often vant to be. The line was spoken intact and in fact by Groucho in *A Night at the Opera*.

[12] A four-column newspaper ad for *A Day at the Races* is reproduced in Marx and Anobile, *op. cit.*, p. 234.

Marx Brothers' riot of solo turns and duos threaded on a slender story line is not very far distant from the Sennett formula of loosely gathered scenes, a rally, and bathing beauties.) The Brothers can work beautifully together, but they don't seem to need to, as Laurel and Hardy do. They are three distinct zanies who happen into the same films and pile one sort of laugh on another. They had established their separateness before they came into films, and their changing teams of writers perpetuated it.[13]

Harpo, the mute, is the most elusive member of the trio, compulsively disappearing and reappearing. He is the twentieth century's preeminent exit-and-entrance man, typically scampering across the frame after a squealing girl, and then gone. Nineteenth-century farce settings were mostly doors and windows, traps and escape hatches. Rivers of people flowed through every act. New characters sometimes sauntered in, bringing fresh complications to the plot. Absentminded souls walked on, interrupted conversations with a tag line, and hardly waited for the automatic laugh to register before vanishing again; Labiche, Feydeau, and Chekhov, among others, delighted in the effect. Harpo *uses* entrances and exits; he also has a supply of them on his person. From pockets in his shapeless coat, cloak, or cape he is liable to draw a shotgun, huge tailor's scissors, a sledgehammer, a butcher knife, an ax, a simmering blowtorch that flares into action (in *Room Service*, 1938, he wears the blowtorch on his cap), or a live turkey. Out of his sleeve falls a set of silver cutlery for twelve. When he pops large items inside the garment they drop into some capacious recess and remain there. He is a walking warehouse. But when he allows a butler to remove his cloak, he is left standing in a pair of shorts. What about all the paraphernalia? Not there. Does it exist? Probably never did. Harpo has often been called a mime. He is more like a magician.

Actually, Harpo plays two roles. One is the magician, the sprite

---

[13] The writers for the Marx Brothers included Al Boasberg, Robert Hopkins, Will Johnstone, Bert Kalmar, George S. Kaufman, George Oppenheimer, Nat Perrin, S. J. Perelman, Robert Pirosh, J. Carver Pusey, Harry Ruby, Morrie Ryskind, George Seaton, and Arthur Sheekman. Herman Mankiewicz (then a producer, later the author of *Citizen Kane*) and the various directors, such as Leo McCarey, Norman McLeod, and Sam Wood, as well as Irving Thalberg, one of MGM's two Big Wheels, also had a hand in the Marx screenplays. In addition, the Brothers, and most of all Groucho, contributed to the texts with additions, subtractions, and multiplication.

of mischief and destruction, Puck or Barrie's Lob from *Dear Brutus*. This side of Harpo projects exuberance and reaps pleasure; it carries farce to manic extremes. The other side, which is barely suggested in the early films, becomes exaggerated later, probably because of pressure from studio chiefs. This is the lovable buddy of kids and pet animals (the same goo that Harry Langdon and Danny Kaye sank into), who dances patronizingly with a horde of pickaninnies, or wears transfiguration as a mask while his hands loose glissandos on the harp. The first Harpo is a joy to remember; he cuts a pack of cards and shuffles each half-pack in a separate hand by rippling them with his thumbs. He puts the cards back together in the order they were in before, deals them with one hand, licking the thumb of the other hand. He trumps a spade, then leads with the ace of spades, three times. Just for good measure he then leads with the ace of hearts, also three times in a row (*Animal Crackers*).

As an antidote to Harpo's speechless frenzy, Chico operates in low key, sending out a steady signal of misplaced and scrambled words. One of the Marx Brothers' screenwriters, Morrie Ryskind, who collaborated with Kaufman on *Cocoanuts, Animal Crackers*, and *A Night at the Opera*, sums up Chico on film as "the Italian embezzler,"[14] and it's true that Chico undertakes Italianate pirouettes of reasoning in order to prove his point. Or, more often, disprove it. In *A Day at the Races* he's somebody's idea of a tipster at the track masquerading as a vendor of "tootsie-fruitsie ice cream." Groucho wants to put a couple of bucks on a nag called Sun Up. Chico lures him into a more promising wager on a dark horse named ZVBXRPL for only one dollar. To decipher "this optical illusion you just slipped me," Groucho needs to invest in a code book given away for free (but there's "a one-dollar printing charge"), then a master code book (no printing charge, "just a two-dollar delivery charge"), a breeder's guide which comes as a set of volumes, and then ten further volumes, all kept fresh by being stored in the ice cream cart. Groucho wants to buy only one volume, but has a ten-dollar bill, while Chico has no change. Chico swiftly places six dollars for himself on Groucho's original choice, Sun Up. Groucho, meanwhile, is grappling mentally with

[14] Marx and Anobile, *op. cit.*, p. 81.

the intelligence system he has purchased and physically with fifteen or so books. By the time he figures out the name of the
recommended horse the race is over, won by Sun Up.

In *Duck Soup*, Groucho, as newly appointed head of state in
Fredonia, thinks he may hire Chico for "a swell job" if the latter
can answer "a couple of important questions. Now, what is it that
has four pairs of pants, lives in Philadelphia, and it never rains but
it pours?" Chico extricates himself from this dilemma in the most
straightforward way: "Ats-a good one. I give you three guesses."
Groucho is stumped. Chico seizes the advantage:

CHICOLINI: What is it got a big black-a mustache, smokes big black-
    a cigar, and is a big pain in the neck?
FIREFLY: . . . Just for that you don't get the job I was going.to give
    you.
CHICOLINI: What job?
FIREFLY: Secretary of War.
CHICOLINI: All right, I take it.
FIREFLY: Sold!

Chico has a guarded attitude when he sits for a piano solo.
Whereas Harpo ends up wringing body and soul from his instrument, Chico plays his like a typist typing, watching his fingers
without surprise as they dance along the keyboard—now flicking
the right index finger indecisively between two notes, now sliding
the thumb up a couple of octaves, concluding with a reverse dive
of the same index finger onto the right note, the thumb pointing
at a right angle to the finger so as to make a pistol—Groucho
called it "shooting the keys."

Chico throws his lines away; he doesn't act them. When he isn't
"on" we don't notice him. When we don't notice him we wonder
why. What has happened to the next batch of excruciating puns?
Then somebody mentions the word "eliminate" and Chico immediately wants some. Some what? "Eliminate. A nice cool glass
eliminate." This is *Duck Soup* again. When Groucho, at the conclusion of the confusion of the "party of the first part" nonsense in
A Night at the Opera, declines to give up the sanity clause in a
contract, Chico insists he's too old to be fooled, because "there
ain't no Sanity Clause." This stage Italian, with an accent that

splays out into Yiddish, Ukrainian, Spanish, and other corruptions, plays around the edges of the storm that is Marx Brothers farce.

At the febrile center of that storm crouches Groucho. Why does he crouch? Is he hiding something? His identity, say? Many of his aliases have a secretive middle initial (Henry W. Schlemmer, Rufus T. Firefly, Otis B. Driftwood, Wolf J. Flywheel, Ronald J. Kornblow). In *The Marx Brothers Go West* the initial rides up front: S. Quentin Quale. But in no case does the initial correspond to the one in his passport, Julius H. Marx. Groucho is a mine of withheld information. He presents himself as a horse doctor in *A Day at the Races*, a hotel manager in *Cocoanuts*, an explorer with a captain's rank in *Animal Crackers*, a college president and professor in *Horse Feathers*, a theater producer in *Room Service*. He confides in an interlocutor, but instead of telling about himself throws doubts on what was already believed. "I worked myself up from nothing to a state of extreme poverty" (*Monkey Business*). Or: "Oh, Susannah, if you only knew how much I need you! Not because you have millions—I don't need millions. I'll tell you how much I need you. Have you got a pencil? I left my typewriter in my other pants" (*At the Circus*). Notice the *how much* here, spoken twice, to avoid a hard number, amount, or comparison. Groucho, even more vociferously than Fields, is the pretender. Fields was once told by the director Gregory La Cava that his instinct as a comic was for counterpunching.[15] So is Groucho's, only more so. In case shielding himself from the inquisitiveness of others doesn't frighten them off, he socks them with affronts. "Why don't you bore a hole in yourself and let the sap run out?" (*Horse Feathers*). "I wouldn't put a pig among those barrels. . . . No, not even if you got down on your knees" (*Monkey Business*). "I wish you were in your other suit and your other suit was being pressed. No, mangled" (*At the Circus*). "I'd horsewhip you if I had a horse" (*Horse Feathers*).

It was not much less than collective genius on the part of the Marx Brothers and their associate creators that kept Groucho dangling in front of Margaret Dumont. She did not appear in all their films, but she was, as Groucho himself once remarked, "practically

---

[15] Robert Lewis Taylor, *op. cit.*, p. 199.

the fifth Marx Brother."[16] Dumont lends a serene, staid beauty to every film she appears in. She has a bemused countenance, not exactly baffled by the proceedings, because she knows she remains above them, but tolerant, even when she hasn't the remotest idea of what is going on. Her resonant, unchanging society voice and perfectly modulated pro forma replies to Groucho's outrageous impertinences attest to her confidence that, given time, all mis-understandings will be ironed out. Above all, she is devastatingly credulous and forgiving. Nobody else could be taken in by Groucho's jack-in-the-box eyebrows, fibrillating eyeballs, and sal-acious leer, but Dumont falls with such rapturous majesty, such unflappability; accepts him so graciously as a combination errant swain and prodigal son, that she becomes a priceless part of his act.

Groucho is the most deliberately self-conscious film farceur be-fore Woody Allen. When in *Animal Crackers* he steps out from between Dumont and Margaret Irving and the two women "freeze" as he does his takeoff of Philip Moeller's staging of O'Neill's *Strange Interlude,* he is in his element ("How happy I could be with either of these girls if both of them went away"), the Lothario who has bitten off more than he can screw and doesn't care who knows it. He was a funny man onstage, but he was made for films—for the italicized aside to the lens and that scrupulous disregard for the rest of the cast that would be intolerable in the theater. He was a soliloquist with an obsession for wordplay. When the Captain in *Monkey Business* threatens to throw him in irons, he comes back with "You can't do it with irons. It's a mashie shot. It's a mashie shot if the wind's against you. And if the wind isn't, I am." Sometimes he drives like a tourist through the landscape of his own utterances, studying the tracks he has just made, backing up, circling, and heading off in new directions: "No wonder you can't get out of college," he reproaches Zeppo, who plays his son in *Horse Feathers,* and has been seeing the college widow. "Twelve years in one college! I went to *three* colleges in twelve years and fooled around with *three* college widows. When I was your age I

---

[16] Marx and Anobile, *op. cit.,* p. 75. For an entertaining biography of the Marx Brothers see *Groucho, Harpo, Chico, and Sometimes Zeppo* by Joe Adamson (New York: Simon & Schuster, 1973; paperback, Pocket Books, 1976).

went to bed right after supper. Sometimes I went to bed before supper. Sometimes I went without my supper and didn't go to bed at all. A college widow stood for something in those days. In fact, she stood for plenty. . . ."

Some of his best moments occur, then, when he picks at words. His remaining best moments come up when he dances and sings, relaxing out of his jocular irascibility. In *Horse Feathers* he strums on a guitar, as if to show his contempt for his brothers' harp and piano turns, both of which he privately loathed. As he breaks into an arm-swinging rhythm or takes up a braying legato that discolors his naturally musical voice, he suggests that the essence of Marx Brothers farce is discord, willful discord, every instrumentalist a virtuoso but each following his own melody line.

NINE

ANIMALS AND ANIMATION

Picture an oversized mouse with a passion for music. The mouse treats a cow's lower cylindrical teeth as a xylophone, rapping out notes that rise visibly across the screen, accompanied by sounds that add up to a melody. The mouse descends to the cow's udder and wrings out more notes. He squeezes a tune out of a goat by twisting its tail; out of an unwilling cat, pigs, a duck. We are still in the world of farce, where art is a product of pain and humiliation; but the characters are now animals, and the animals are drawn instead of being photographed, and the drawings generate their own musical sound track.

In one of the exhibits at Walt Disney World in Orlando, Florida, visitors are shown short film classics from the beginning of Disney's career. One, *Steamboat Willie* (made in 1928, the same year as Keaton's *Steamboat Bill Jr.*), is a landmark in the history of animation and of synchronized sound. It also features the third performance of Mickey Mouse. *Willie* shows us a Mickey who seems unusually impish compared with the worried, nagging good citizen he became in the 1930s.

The late French mime Étienne Decroux once told me that he considered Walt Disney to be the greatest mime of this century. Decroux conceived of mime as a formal interpretation of the movements of the body in relation to the ground. One had to distinguish mime from dance, in which bodies move in relation to the space, the air, *above* ground level. Dancing, he believed, aspires upward. It defies gravity: the dancer attempts to realize man's ancient yearning to fly. But mime is anchored to the earth's surface. The mime's body never loses touch with the ground, although it may disguise its grips and footholds by rolling, sliding, or alternating its moorings from the feet to the back to the trunk to the hands, as in a "tumblesault."

Disney did abstract mime with animals, even with plants, as when a tree or flower bends over to listen to a remark and cocks its head. He captured and transposed essential movements of the human body to animals and other things. Whether this is regarded as akin to mime or mere caricature, Mickey and Minnie Mouse, Pluto, Goofy, Horace, Clarabelle, Willie the operatic whale, Donald and Donna and Daisy Duck, the Duck nephews, a later uncle of Donald's named Ludwig von Drake, and the rest of the humanized bestiary have broadened the purview of farce. And these additions are, in both senses of the word, animated.

Early Animators

Disney is to animated farce roughly what Sennett is to acted film farce: not its originator, but its most energetic and determined creator and its outstanding popularizer. The birth of animated farce predates Disney by more than twenty years—beginning in France with Georges Méliès and Émile Cohl (1857–1938) and in the United States with James Stuart Blackton (1875–1941)—while the history of film animation in general goes back to the 1830s.[1]

Méliès, the cinema's most vivid dreamer, blended artwork with live scenes staged and shot in his studio. A painter by training and temperament, as well as a professional conjuror, he developed whatever artistic devices he deemed necessary and could master. The moon's face in *A Journey to the Moon* (1902) is a beautifully rendered orb with glittering eyes and a mobile mouth. The mouth

---

[1] Early pre-movie inventions are mentioned in most film histories, and dealt with at more length in *The Animated Film* by Roger Manvell (London: Sylvan Press, 1954) and *The Animated Film* (same title) by Ralph Stephenson (New York: A. S. Barnes, 1973) as well as in a number of specialized studies devoted to particular artists, full-length animated features, computer animation, experimental animation, and so on.

gets wrenched into an upside-down W that registers convincing pain and chagrin when a space explorers' rocket slams into the right eye.[2]

Méliès' fellow countryman Cohl, who worked for Pathé, and Blackton, one of the founders of Vitagraph in New York, independently and at roughly the same time introduced to the cinema pure animated line drawings, or moving cartoons. (By further coincidence, both men had been newspaper artists, and both had farcical aptitudes. Stick-and-circle figures of the kind re-created for films by Cohl in heavy black crayon or white chalk liken the flatness of the movie screen to the flatness of the newspaper page.) An early, very short Cohl farce entitled *Phantasmagoria* (1908) opens with a hand that chalks figures in a frame. They then begin to move—a motion picture within a motion picture. Like some of Keaton's pictures of the Twenties, they are theatricalist film farce, cinema commenting on its own properties. In *The Dentures* (1909) a set of false teeth insists on chomping inside the mouth of the woman fitted with them. She gets rid of the teeth, but they clamp on to anybody who picks them up, gnashing angrily when placed on a desk by some cautious and heavily armed gendarmes. *The Automatic Moving Company* (1910), a piece of bravura film making, depicts the furnishing of an apartment by chairs, tables, rugs, draperies, wardrobes, china, and other chattels that move themselves in and shuffle about until they have arranged themselves. In one shot some empty crates and hampers that are about to descend a staircase move politely aside to make way for other furniture still coming in.

Blackton's first animation, in *Humorous Phases of Funny Faces*, released in 1906, the year before Cohl's first picture, *The Pumpkin Race*, also featured blackboard cartoons that grimaced and changed expression. *The Magic Fountain Pen* (1909) goes into pen-and-ink drawings as Blackton, photographed from life, is seen caricaturing famous historical personages one after another by

---

[2] Méliès had already practiced visual trickery in his playhouse. In his publicity material for *Mesmer's Castle*, he describes a spectacle, first put on in 1894, that included: "animated furniture, hats flying through space, turning tables, musical instruments that play themselves, human bodies that are lighter than air." Jacques Deslandes, *Le Boulevard du Cinéma à l'époque du cinéma* (Paris: Éditions du Cerf, 1963), p. 45.

converting each into the next. *The Haunted Hotel* (1907) pixilates its images by stop motion in order to animate inanimate objects, much as *The Automatic Moving Company* was to do several years later. Cohl may indeed have been inspired by Blackton's film in which, among other marvels, an enterprising knife slices salami and bread without human assistance. It will be noticed that this pixilation technique, which Cohl dubbed *le mouvement américain,* carries one step further the humanization of objects that had long been a staple of farce in the theater.

After Méliès, Cohl, and Blackton, animated farce ramifies astonishingly.[3] Winsor McCay, another graduate from newspaper artwork, adapted stylized cartoon figures for *Little Nemo* (1911) from his comic strip about a child's dreams and imaginings. One McCay character, Flip, is a cigar-chomping clown whose low-slung crotch and short legs were to be mimicked much later, in the Forties, by Max Fleischer in his drawings of Popeye, Bluto, and Wimpy and who seems to be derived from the baggy-pants comic of vaudeville. McCay went on to compose animated shorts that starred insects, such as *How a Mosquito Operates* (1912) and *Bug Vaudeville* (1916), as well as animals, the best-remembered today being prehistoric *Gertie the Dinosaur* (probably 1914). Further borrowing thereafter from the funnies included *Bringing Up Father* by George McManus; Mutt and Jeff; Felix the Cat, drawn by Otto Messmer; and Walter Lantz's Katzenjammer Kids.

Cartoonists plundered the animal kingdom for their anthropomorphic creatures. Over the years these creatures became so "humanized" in appearance that they could hardly be distinguished from cartooned human beings. By 1942, when the Fleischer studio released *Mr. Bug Goes to Town,* an insectification of Frank Capra's *Mr. Deeds Goes to Town,* released by the same studio, the heroine, Honey Bee, was a sexy teen-ager who wore a puffed-sleeve blouse and skirt, high-heeled shoes, and hair bows. Her only bee traces were a pair of transparent wings neatly folded away behind her bottom, hardly noticeable except from the back, and two slender,

[3] These three artists had much longer, more varied, and more productive careers than is suggested here by a recital of a few of their achievements. But all three died penniless, as did Edwin S. Porter and Griffith, either from inability to keep up with the market and consequent neglect by the film world or else after being wiped out by the crash of 1929.

curved, and becoming antennae. In much the same way the features of Mickey Mouse were gradually to become less mouselike —that is, more childlike.

It has been pointed out that when cartoons came into their own they outdid the live-action farce. Drawings have almost no limitations. They can perform acts that the most reckless stunt man can't manage. They can smash through solid walls leaving behind them a silhouetted hole; fall from heights and land intact; suffer their bodies to be braided and knotted; charge off the edge of a cliff, stop in midair, look down, take fright, and by means of galvanic leg-pumping, retreat to safe ground again. In trying to account for the decline of Mack Sennett in the late Twenties and Thirties, Gene Fowler asks, "Who killed Cock Robin?" He replies, "Mickey Mouse."[4] From the time of *Gertie the Dinosaur*, animation went further with its farcical brutalities than live action did. Most of the animal and bug heroes (with the notable exception of Mickey) tended to be less sympathetically presented, more ruthless and violent than their live counterparts. Once cartoons grew more competitive as the major studios went after different series, or animated new series,[5] one could observe a desperation on the part of animators to exceed their rivals. The animals dropped five-ton boulders on the enemy and left him looking like a diet wafer baked in earth or like a rug, or they dynamited him or cut him to pieces. The sternest punishments were meted out by Bugs Bunny, Tom and Jerry, and Beep and Wile E. Coyote in the "Road Runner" films. However, the distraught, if not destroyed, creature followed the tradition of live farce. He reflated himself or reassembled his parts, his eyeballs whirled in opposed circles, bells rang on the sound track, and he lived to face the next fray. What really happened, then, was that animation took the possibilities of devastation and instant recuperation further than stage or film farce had attempted to go, and in doing so emphasized the nonhuman aspects of its characters while the drawings themselves stressed the opposite.

---

[4] *Father Goose* (New York: Covici and Friede, 1934), last page. Fowler may have picked up the idea that Mickey displaced Mack from a newspaper article by Philip K. Scheuer written in 1933, the year before Fowler's book was published.
[5] Universal distributed "Woody Woodpecker"; Paramount, the Popeye films; Twentieth Century-Fox, Paul Terry's "Terry Toons"; and Warners, the "Merrie Melodies."

Looking back to the start of animation, we can say that most film cartoon figures of any consequence were animals, not human beings. In the animators' pantheon all kinds of exotic beasts showed up, including some monsters, such as dragons and centaurs. The two animals most frequently animated seem to have been the most popular domestic pet, the cat, and the most unpopular domestic scourge, the mouse. The feline ancestry extends from Krazy Kat and Felix the Cat to Tom of Tom and Jerry, Sylvester, the Aristocats, Klondike Kat, and Ralph Bakshi's Fritz. The reasons for choosing the cat as a subject are not hard to fathom: it moves with slinky grace and takes up still poses every one of which is beautiful (who can stop turning the pages of a cat calendar?). It is vain about its appearance; its eyes give off an assortment of feelings and intentions, some misleading; it has more initiative, is less dependent than a dog; and it is a cruel and cunning predator. The mouse follows inevitably. Toss a mouse into a cat cartoon and you have that staple of farce, a chase, if not a rally. The two animals then swap their lifelike roles. The pet becomes the villain and the scourge a plucky little hero.

This explanation doesn't account for Mickey. But does Mickey look like a real mouse? Not remotely. I would guess that Disney and his early collaborator Ub Iwerks saw an opportunity to take a little creature that has the uncomplicated shape of half an unshelled egg and to invest it with a personality. If the cat was a natural for animation, the mouse was more of a challenge, an "unnatural." And so Disney and Iwerks reinvented the mouse.

Disney and His Rivals

After *Steamboat Willie,* Disney continued to put cartoon farce to music regularly in his "Silly Symphonies" series and sporadically in his Mickey Mouse and Donald Duck shorts. *The Skeleton Dance* (1929) compromised with the human form by crazily animating bones to a musical accompaniment by Carl Stalling (Disney's music director) and Edvard Grieg. In *The Three Little Pigs* (1933), Disney's cartoon variations corresponded as artwork to the melodic variations of "Who's Afraid of the Big Bad Wolf?" As a more complicated achievement in laying visual farce over music, *The Band Concert* (1935) presented Mickey conducting the overture to *William Tell* while Donald led the band astray into a different set of rhythms by playing "Turkey in the Straw." Similarly, in *Music Land* (1935), jazz and extracts from classics battled in graphic counterpoint. Among the farcical episodes of *Fantasia* (1940), Mickey was the sorcerer's apprentice who, to the strains of Dukas's symphonic poem, enchanted brooms so that they could sweep without his help; and mushrooms with Oriental features, thistles in cossack hats, ostriches, hippos, crocodiles, and elephants wearing ballerina skirts danced to music by Tchaikovsky and Poncielli. The "After You've Gone" segment of *Make Mine Music* (1946) animated a boxing match, a musical squabble, and a chase performed by a clarinet, bass violin, piano, and drums, the instruments that made up Benny Goodman's quartet on the sound track.

The artistry of Disney's earliest shorts sets him apart from other farce animators. They had worked mostly with simple line drawings in black and white. He used a surprising range of expressive grays in halftones. By 1932 he was experimenting with color. His bright, solid hues suited the primitive emotions evoked by farce. Pluto up on a mountain froze into a rich shade of blue. Other animals turned green, purple, or flaming red as they exerted themselves, grew angry, or blushed.

Disney humanized his animals in three principal ways. Their voices may have derived from animal sounds—squeaks, squawks, quacking, braying, growls, roars—but these *were* voices and had human articulation. The animals moved like human beings; indeed, were often inspired by the gestures, stance, and gait of celebrities. And most of them wore clothes: Donald his sailor suit, Goofy a stovepipe hat and suspenders, Mickey a pair of shorts and a jacket with oversized buttons. If the effect was cute, as well as farcical, the cuteness reflected the attitudes of the films' audiences toward animals, and especially pets.

Disney's most significant rivals, the Fleischer brothers, introduced many animals into their repertoire, but the three characters who had durable success were distortedly human figures: Koko the Clown and Betty Boop in the Twenties, Popeye (with his entourage) in the Thirties and thereafter. Betty Boop actually started out as a dog. She had floppy ears—later replaced by earrings—bulging jowls, enormous eyes, a black blob of a nose, and rosebud lips drawn on the chin line of her face, for cartoon characters based on animals usually have minimal chins, if any. Popeye, by contrast, was never an animal; his promontory of a chin occupies about fifty percent of his head. Few of the "human" cartoons by Fleischer have necks, although Popeye and Olive Oyl do; their heads swivel on what looks like short lengths of drainpipe. They stand or walk leaning forward or rolling, so that their bodies appear charged up, always kinetic.

The Fleischers tackled a narrower expanse of subject matter than Disney's, but they frequently had more farcical verve. And more violence. Popeye might curl up into a cannonball or stretch horizontally into a torpedo so as to do greater damage as he launched himself at the villainous, unshaven, dirty-fighting Bluto.

The other cartoons from the Thirties that have held up best as farce are the ones featuring Bugs Bunny and Friends, created originally at Warners by Bob Clampett, Chuck Jones, and Tex Avery before World War II and using the voices of Mel Blanc for Bugs, Porky Pig, and Elmer Fudd. Bugs Bunny is the most versatile. He sings, dances, switches his sex, impersonates a cringing, rabbit-hearted victim as energetically as he acts the king of the backwoods or a movie temptress. And he can extract an unmatched variety of farcical business out of munching a carrot.[6]

UPA *and After*

By the early 1940s, John Hubley, one of America's most imaginative animators, had raised the question how to reinvent the human being. In 1964 he explained to me that presenting the human body in cartoons had plagued him and others he had worked with at the Disney studio. There were all those species of aesthetically gratifying animal; they derived from pudgy, stoop-shouldered, gross-featured, or babyish human beings, and there-

---

[6] Bugs Bunny seems to have been modeled on a character named Oswald the Rabbit, created by Disney. Disney had been tricked into losing the rights to Oswald some years previously. But then, the imitations of Disney have been legion. Mighty Mouse is a version of Mickey, Porky Pig of the Three Little Pigs, and the fawn in Fleischer's *Rudolph the Red-Nosed Reindeer* (1944) of Disney's *Bambi* (1942). *Mr. Bug Goes to Town* (1941) and *Slick Hare* (1952) caricatured a batch of Hollywood stars much as Disney had done in *Mickey's Gala Premiere* (1933). After Disney introduced his "Silly Symphonies," Warners put out its "Merrie Melodies" and "Looney Tunes," MGM its "Happy Harmonies."

fore they offered comments on human behavior. The dilemma, as Hubley saw it, was: From what source could presentations of human beings derive in order for them to exhibit a comparable doubleness? Idealizing the human form, as the Disney people had done with Snow White and Prince Charming, and the Fleischers in *Gulliver's Travels* (especially Princess Glory and *her* prince), amounted to mere figure exercises; these juvenile leads were vapid simplifyings of live people photographed, and they could not serve a farcical or satirical purpose. As characters they lacked "character." Nor were the farcical, comic, and evil human figures created in the Thirties helpful as general models—the Seven Dwarfs with their baseball noses, Snow White's stepmother the Queen (who from a front view had no discernible nose), her metamorphosed self, the Witch, the three spies and the two kings and Gabby (a sort of eighth dwarf) from *Gulliver*, Popeye, Olive Oyl, and so on. The truth was that animators like Hubley had searched for a way not so much to redraw the human body as to reanimate it, to come up with drawings that would *move* in an unusual and interesting way.

By 1964, Hubley could look back with a certain satisfaction on some of the solutions to which he'd contributed. Among these were the efforts of United Productions of America (UPA), a group of dissident artists who had pulled out of the Disney studio after a bitter strike there in 1941. Led by Stephen Bosustow and numbering Hubley, Robert Cannon, and Pete Burness among its founders, UPA stripped its human figures down to primary shapes, and made the lovingly applied detail of most previous animation look superfluous. Mr. Magoo consists of a circle perched on a square, a heavy L and a reversed L for legs and feet, a pair of curved arms with four-finger hands at their ends. His nose, another circle, has the bloated appearance of W. C. Fields's bulb; and his eyes, two lines for slits, denote his near-blindness, the cause of his many mishaps. Gerald McBoing Boing, a circle on a narrow rectangle on waddling shoes, is the child who utters musical noises that sound like muted versions of a plucked string.

Artists employed by Disney and Fleischer in the Thirties had already built their figures from geometrical components, which were to be guidelines for the "in-betweeners," the second-string animators. Popeye or Betty Boop or Goofy could be reduced in essence to rectangles, circles, and ovals. But these analytical diagrams formed a preliminary stage only and were meant to give a sense of the bodies' "hinges," so as to standardize the movement.

The UPA cartoons also drastically economized the animation, so that the motions, as well as the graphics themselves, became stylized. No longer did they mimic human running, bending, turning; instead, they gave the impression of inert matter being propelled. These cartoon characters were like objects. The UPA artists, whether consciously or not, had returned to the ancient farce tradition in which objects take on life and living beings sometimes act as passively as objects. Thus the human cartoons found a doubleness they had lacked.

The artists had also returned to one of the methods used by Émile Cohl in his animation of, for example, Fantoche, that basic geometrical representation of a man capable of being transmuted into inert matter, such as a house, or into another form of flesh, such as a bird. In Cohl's cartoons, as in UPA's, the inanimate and animate worlds belong to one continuum. At the same time, the backgrounds occasionally become discontinuous. In place of the solid imitations of reality, settings in perspective, fully furnished interiors and whole landscapes, the UPA artists might show an isolated figure standing on a mat or next to a floor lamp or followed by a changing shadow—but otherwise dropped into open space. A washbasin and bathroom cabinet hang in midair unsupported by any traces of a wall. Surface textures like wood, fabrics, or wallpaper are hardly differentiated, if at all. This is animation of the essential, just as the theater of Beckett and Pinter is dramatization of the essential.

Ernest Pintoff and Gene Deitch, who worked for UPA for a time, took the reduction process even further. Their character Flebus (1957) has a head and body combined in one lump, a face that reaches from hat brim to knees, since the chin line marks the lower extremity of the body, which is bounded at the bottom and back by straight lines, two sides of a square. In the Cubist manner, both of Flebus's eyes, which are dots, lie on the same side of his nose. His legs, like Magoo's, are *L*'s. The stumpy, vestigial arms hang from where his ears would be if he had ears.

UPA cartoons also free sound from lip synchronization and give it a quasi-independence from the visuals. Mouths simply open and close, like Charlie McCarthy's slot. They don't articulate words, but change from squiggles to twitchy gaps and back again. The sound tracks in the Gerald McBoing Boing series are their most noteworthy feature; and the gravelly utterances of Magoo (voice-overs by Jim Backus) maintain their steady, unemotional burble while Magoo walks along the edge of a roof or into teeming traffic. Hubley and his wife, Faith, liberated the sound track from the images in other ways after they animated several films on their own, such as *Adventures of an ** (1956), *Moonbird* (1960), and *The Hole* (1963), which are respectively abstract, lyrical, and caution-ary. All three shorts reveal Hubley's formidable artistry and talent for fantastication, but they have moved away from farce.

As a whole, the UPA advances, including the use of sound as an agency of animation in its own right and improved quality in the dialogue, underwent the same processes of absorption as do most artistic experiments; as they were picked up by other animators, they became diluted.[7] There are now faint UPA-ish traces in most American cartoons made during and since the Fifties. In these years the dozens of cartoon series that have sprung up, mostly to service television's off-hours and Saturday mornings, have inter-mingled the glossy and intricate techniques of Disney and Fleischer with the more severe UPA treatments.

In the past fifteen years, animation has gone beyond humaniz-ing animals and objects. In an assortment of European films, in commercials, on the *Sesame Street* and *Electric Company* pro-grams and other television shows animators have put letters, num-bers, abstract shapes, old engravings, and still photographs of statues and sculpture through farcical gyrations by combined drawing, pixilation, and live action. In *Monty Python's Flying Cir-cus*, cutouts of Victorian etchings and physiology charts from out-dated medical manuals jerk their limbs into motion like the undead awakening or sometimes crash down onto cartoon figures and ob-literate them. A few artists have outreached Disney in the vivid-ness of their colors and their teaming up of graphics with music and sound. *The Yellow Submarine* (1968, directed by George Dun-

---

[7] Even one short made at the Disney studio, *Toot, Whistle, Plunk, and Boom* (1953), a capsule history of music, deigned to mimic the UPA style.

ning and animated by Heinz Edelman) caricatured the Beatles, stylized the other characters, and with the aid of its pulsating music attained to a new kind of farcical fantasy that was psychedelic.

◆

TEN

POPULAR FARCE AFTER FEYDEAU

Up in a hotel's bridal suite the bride has locked herself in the bathroom. Her father has attacked the door with his shoulder and crushed an arm; has tried to break in from the outside by crawling along a ledge, fourteen floors above ground level, only to find the window immovable; has been rained on by a capricious shower and a flurry of pigeons. The tails of his wedding jacket have ripped up to the collar. His wife has split a pair of stockings wailing entreaties to her daughter through the keyhole; has smashed the diamond in her ring; has suffered palpitations that visibly shake the hand that tries to still them. To add a dash of urgency, the phone keeps ringing as the groom's father inquires over and over whether everything is ready. Down in the reception room a horde of guests surrounds him; to sate their impatience they gorge on little hot dogs and gulp their way through bottles of liquor.

In *Visitor from Forest Hills*, the third one-act play of Neil Simon's *Plaza Suite*, father and mother berate each other. What's *wrong* with the goddamned girl? Did they bring her up right? Do they know—did they ever know—how to talk to her? What sort of model has their marriage provided for a young about-to-be-wed? What are the guests saying? What will the family do? Have thousands upon thousands of dollars gone down the drain? Is Mother actually undergoing a heart attack? Is Father on the edge of a seizure as he reels under the blows to his pride? to his income? The sheer gall of the girl! And between cross-harangues and counteraccusations they yell threats and hiss appeals at the bathroom door. Which does not reply.

After some attempts at inducing the bride to rap on the inside of the door (two raps for yes, one for no), in response to such leading questions as to whether she still wants to marry, and some doubts over her replies (do two spaced-out knocks mean "Yes" or "No! No!"), the groom is summoned. He comes in, calls, "Cool it," and leaves. Whereupon, to her parents' astonishment and exasperation, she emerges. It seems that she was fearful of eventually becoming like them. The alchemical formula "Cool it" somehow converts her back into sterling obedience. As father, mother, and daughter leave for the wedding ceremony downstairs, the father is still torturing himself. "That's how they communicate? That's the brilliant understanding between two people? 'Cool it'?" Is it right for him to give his little girl to "a boy like that"? No. He concludes wanly, impotently, "She was better off in the bathroom." Curtain.

Jacques is a young Frenchman whose relatives not only have the same first name (Mother Jacques, Father Jacques, Grandmother and Grandfather Jacques, and for a refreshing variant, a sister called Jacqueline) but are also more or less of one mind in trying to shunt him into marriage. He has admitted that he loves hashed-brown potatoes. Perhaps he will equally accept what goes with potatoes. Meat. The meat is a bride named Roberte, the only daughter of Mother and Father Robert, who have brought her to Jacques's house to prove that, as meat goes, Roberte is Grade A, not mere steak or beef but a veritable *charcuterie* on legs. As her father points out, she has feet that are "truffled" and "armpits for turnspits" and "a tongue the color of tomato sauce, pan-browned square shoulders, and all the meat needed to merit the highest commendation." These are novel accomplishments. Your average bride can offer only pedestrian talents such as washing socks, or ripping off Chopin minuets by moonlight, or decorating interiors. Roberte is solid meat, high and low. As meaty bonuses, she has succeeded in growing nine fingers on her left hand and two noses. The question then arises: is Jacques carnivorous? Fortunately, yes; he is even gluttonous. He wants a bride with at least three noses. Father Robert, unfazed, rushes his only daughter offstage and returns with his "second only daughter," also named Roberte. This second Roberte is played by the same actress, who has hastily donned a third nose. But Jacques is still not content. The triple-snouted woman is "not ugly enough." At this, the Jacques family and the Robert family stalk out in high dudgeon and on tiptoe, hoping that Roberte will bring Jacques to heel once they are left together.

She certainly tries. The final segment of Eugène Ionesco's *Jacques, or the Submission* consists of an extended seduction scene in which the usual roles are reversed. Roberte does the wooing. She relates several animal stories, which arouse Jacques's interest, and then his excitement, so that he can't help interrupting at the end of many of her sentences. The last story has to do with a horse that gallops into an empty "city in the Sahara Desert." He whinnies frantically with fear; there is a spark in his mane. He is on fire. As she describes the smoke, the fire, the pain ("How beautiful he is, he's turning all pink, like an enormous lampshade. He wants to fly. . . . Through his transparent hide we see the fire burning inside him . . . he's a living torch"), Ionesco's stage directions tell us that "the rhythm intensifies progressively, then slows down toward the end." This is the rhythm of a sexual climax, which reinforces, and comments on, the play's dramatic climax. Through this seduction scene or, according to the subtitle, "submission," the characters remain seated apart; they do not touch or approach each other. Jacques is seduced by words. The text runs in segments that correspond not only to the climax, but also to sexual foreplay and postclimactic relaxation. During his "orgasm," as Jacques urges Roberte to tell him more about the flaming stallion, he cries, "He's burning too fast . . . It's going to end! Make the fire last. . . ." Roberte's "orgasm," however, consists of visions of wetness that quench his fire. While he feels "parched" and "exhausted," she intones, "My necklace is made of mud, my breasts are dissolving, my pelvis is wet, I've got water in my crevices . . . in my belly there are pools, swamps. . . . Everything trickles, the sky trickles down, the stars run. . . ."

The submission over, Jacques's and Roberte's families reenter to celebrate the match with an animal dance and animal noises, which may refer back to the animal stories told by Roberte. During this caricature of a wedding party they utter "vague miaows" and "bizarre moans" and "croakings." Then they disappear. The stage blackens. Out of the darkness comes a thin, gray light which shows us Roberte. She squats alone on the stage as her three noses quiver and her nine sinister fingers move like snakes, like Medusa's tresses.[1]

"Popular" and "Intellectual"

There is little resemblance between these two recent farces, other than that they are both brief, both deal with the reluctance of a young person to go into marriage, and both end with a submission. In most other respects they are studies in contrast which come out of two distinctive strands of theater, two farcical traditions that have survived the wear and tear of history. One dates back to the New Comedy of Menander, modified by Plautus and differently by Terence, and before them, to the mime performances of Greece and Italy; the other, to Aristophanes. Or, to put a modern face on their ancestry, one to Feydeau, the other to Jarry. Broadly speaking, one is popular, the other intellectual.

Questions immediately arise. Are "intellectual" and "popular" true semantic opposites? In other words, does an "intellectual" farce have to be unpopular? Must a "popular" farce be devoid of content and implications that are worth brooding over? Is an intellectual farce superior *per se* to a popular one? To these questions the reply is no. Here are a couple of familiar labels that enable us to avoid special terminology and neologisms that might make the distinctions sound systematic, even scientific, which they assuredly are not.

Still, the two traditions, whatever we call them, do exist. Rather than composing a lengthy disquisition about them, I have tried to summarize their principal features in a table. Few plays fit either side of the table neatly or absolutely. *Visitor from Forest Hills*, for instance, does not have the "popular" resolution; its ending is bittersweet, verging on sour—but funny. And neither play (indeed, no play ever written) is farcical throughout. And many "intellectual" farces do include a debate or *agon* that is common in the "popular" farce; in fact, the *agon* was introduced by the father of "intellectual" farce, Aristophanes. Despite these and other handi-

---

[1] Neil Simon's play is printed in *The Comedy of Neil Simon* (New York: Avon Books, 1973), pp. 560–82, and Ionesco's in *Four Plays* (New York: Grove Press, 1958), pp. 79–110.

caps, the table can stand as a rough guide to the two types of farce that reappear continually in twentieth-century theater.[2]

Popular farces, the subject of this chapter, followed Feydeau's lead by confining themselves for the most part to living rooms and bedrooms, the latter usually becoming the scene of a frustrated act-three tryst in which there is much hurling of pillows, tearing of sheets, wrapping up in draperies, and diving under box springs. Now and again they venture into a kitchen where food utensils, from rolling pins to three-gallon saucepans, hang available for the battering of heads and the shattering of pride. Some of them hang unsteadily and will, without human assistance, fall and do harm to priceless china, crystal, or pottery that has recklessly stationed itself below. Such farces, calling for domestic settings, inescapably concentrate on those time-hallowed twin themes, adultery and cuckoldry—that is, adultery unconsummated and cuckoldry feared. These in turn provoke revenge from the partner who, rightly or wrongly, feels wronged. If there are grown children living at home (and parents who are troubled about a possible waning of virility and sex appeal during their middle years), the erotic skirmishes may acquire the additional edge of a conflict between generations as father and son battle over a fetching widow or graduate student, or when daughter's boyfriend compliments mother too effusively.

Chances are that at some point in the action a man, preferably an older man and even more preferably a sedate father, will find himself in a woman's clothes or, better, undergarments or, better yet, a nun's garb. At this the audience will shriek, rather than laugh, especially the married women. As a slight variant, the plot

---

[2] The differentiation between "intellectual" and "popular" farces holds up for films too, but is far less marked once we move out of the "primitive" phase populated by Sennett, Roach, and Christie. Recent film farceurs, such as Jacques Tati, Mel Brooks, and Woody Allen, have straddled the divide, as did Chaplin, Keaton, and the Marx Brothers; while Laurel and Hardy, Abbott and Costello, and Jerry Lewis remain firmly committed to the "popular" side.

We could extend the differentiation to nonfarcical films, although many critics—starting with the French *Cahiers du Cinéma* school and going on to the British and American *auteur* theorists, the sometimes impenetrable semiologists, and others (notably David Thomson in *America in the Dark* and Leo Braudy in *The World in a Frame*)—have been at pains to take the curse off the word "popular"; they have insisted, often persuasively, that many films from the big studios that were frankly commercial are also intellectually conceived in ways that critics with only literary training and feelers may well fail to apprehend.

	"Popular" Farce	"Intellectual" Farce
Basic assumption	The folly of mankind.	The cruelty of life.
Probability of action	Could have happened—realism. (But may still strike spectators as implausible.)	Could not happen in life. (But may seem convincing.)
Sources of main conflict	Psychological quirks or obsession.	Clashes of ideas.
Satirical content	Specific and descriptive—references to famous people (especially film stars, politicians and places (especially New York, Hollywood, occasionally Paris, Oshkosh) and things (especially commercial brands, home furnishings).	Unspecific and analytical—comments on types of people (film stars, politicians, philosophers as a breed), types of setting and place, social tendencies.
Language	Wit—put-downs by means of one-liners and two-liners (much as in "high comedies"). Verbal contests or *agons*.	Humor—people unintentionally make fun (and fools) of themselves, not one another.
Incidental dialogue (lines that don't impel the main plot)	Creates subplots and embroiders characterization.	Hints at larger meanings.
Physical activity	Awkwardness and vulnerability of the human body.	Metaphorical, often dancelike.
Characterization	1. Heroes, heroines, and parents are likable, understandable kooks and bumblers who know what they want. 2. Villains are either irremediably evil or not so evil or not evil at all.	1. No real heroes or heroines. Only protagonists who are not sure what they want, if they want anything. 2. No real villains, only clumsy antagonists.
Audience kept attentive by	Suspense.	Surprise, shocks.
Resolution	Rounded off, satisfying ending. Victory or truce. Threats dispersed.	Open ending. Little—if anything—resolved. New threats. Unsatisfying, disturbing.
Dramaturgical form	Conventional, predictable.	Subversive, experimental.

241

may force father or uncle into a kilt. (Women seldom land in men's clothing in either farce or comedy; the effect seems masochistic, not titillating, and has become associated with porn movies.) A thoughtful woman spectator might take this procedure as being an insult to women, but it is actually meant, like most other farcical ploys, to embarrass the hell out of men.

The allusions in popular farces to contemporary people and events—usually amounting to little more than name-dropping, rather than all-out satire—sound smart and fashionable at the time, but they help to date the plays rapidly. Popular farces hardly ever endure. A playwright whose talent enables him to keep tickling critics and audiences in the right places and to make one quick bundle of money after another has a couple of strong years at a first-run house; his plays next disperse from Broadway, the West End, or the Parisian boulevards to summer stock in the remote provinces for up to, say, another four years; and then they go under without a trace. He must either continue to supplant himself with new winners or be overtaken by newcomers who have been boning up on the formulas. Try today to collect memories of the most profitable British genre of the 1930s, the Aldwych farces. Hardly any are visible. Those potboilers have run out of steam. Not one work by Vernon Sylvaine, one of the Aldwych's staple authors, has a listing in recent Samuel French catalogues. Sylvaine's name on a script was once money in the bank as surely as was Sam Levene's name on a "Seventh Avenue comedy" in New York, and was often backed up by the British theater's equivalent of Laurel and Hardy, the now-forgotten team of tiny, prissy, thin, nervously adenoidal, bald Robertson Hare and stout, frowningly dignified, bald Alfred Drayton. Even the roles in those farces were unmemorable. Some twenty-five years ago I had a sizable part in a revival of an Aldwych farce. Looking back at the text about twenty years later I couldn't for the life of me remember which part I'd played.

The bulk of American popular farces of the early years of the century have dropped as irrecoverably as their British counterparts into what Leon Trotsky called the wastebasket of history. P. G. Wodehouse, Ben Hecht, George Abbott, and their peers from the Thirties, Twenties, and before are resuscitated now and then (mostly the musicals, which have yielded up some of the finest

American farce scenes, such as *Leave It to Jane*), perhaps as patriotic gestures by regional troupes that depend on government subsidy, but in versions pruned back with an ax, while the remaining dialogue gets intercalated with new wisecracks that will last no longer than what they displaced. Several collaborations from the Thirties, however, between George S. Kaufman and Moss Hart, have proved sturdier, and are among the choice twentieth-century examples of farce, accomplishments that bear comparison in a different genre and manner with the dramas of Eugene O'Neill and Clifford Odets. *You Can't Take It with You* (1936), *The Man Who Came to Dinner* (1939), *George Washington Slept Here* (1940), and less clearly, *Once in a Lifetime* (1930), which was a trial run for the playwriting partnership, throw together a bountiful helping of farcical and not more than two or three realistic characters who must fight their way out of desperate third-act tangles.

Once in a Lifetime takes a show-biz buffoon, who spends most of his dazed waking day quoting one line from *Variety* and munching on Indian nuts, out to Hollywood as a voice coach at the time when movies were frantically attempting to cope with the opportunities and pitfalls of sound. Every mistake committed by this chump turns golden, even his decision to purchase two thousand aircraft in order to get one free. He ends up as executive head of the Glogauer Studios, shooting (from the hip and the wrong script) a terrible film, which is hailed by the reviewers as a refreshing approach to the art of cinema. This farce laughs raucously at Hollywood decision-making, its lucky guessers, its second guessers, all-time losers, and its inept juggling with fortunes. Employees at every echelon are fired, rehired, fired again. Are they incompetent, unfortunate, unconnected? Playwrights are shipped wholesale from the East Coast, kept on handsome retainers, and abandoned in offices with their names on the doors in temporary paint, until they walk out of the place and into a sanitarium to find out whether they exist. A baffled German director has taken charge of a picture about American rural life. The biggest boob in the cast of, well, not thousands, but more than three dozen speaking roles, is the studio owner, Glogauer. The stage here is twitting film, as though plays went into production with more efficiency, taste, and convictions than films ever did. The farce in *Lifetime* works by a process of overlapping, not unlike that in Chekhov's full-length plays. Each character interrupts somebody else's sub-plot and prevents it from being resolved—so as to create suspense. The crisis eventually dominates all the subplots and piles them one on top of another.

Kaufman and Hart exercised this technique of overlapping in their subsequent farces, sometimes refining it by keeping some piece of information dark, a mystery, until the very end. For example, in *The Man Who Came to Dinner* a strangely scatterbrained lady turns out to have murdered her parents, Lizzie Borden fashion, when she was young, and the threat of bringing this scandalous brouhaha to light tames her recalcitrant brother, the last obstacle to a happy ending. Similarly, in *George Washington Slept Here* a minor character becomes important when she unearths an ancient map that saves the hero from eviction. The family in *You Can't Take It with You* had milk delivered one morning by a man who stayed on in the house for five years; nobody learned his name, so when he died they gave him Grandpa's. At the end of the play this casual piece of amusement pays off: the Internal Revenue people who have been hounding Grandpa for not paying his income tax apologize, taking him for the dead milkman, and Grandpa discovers that the federal government, in its wisdom, owes him money.

The members of this particular household nicely illustrate the dividends available from overlapping. Mother types plays on the living-room table (because somebody once left a typewriter there years ago), while daughter cooks fudge candies and practices her ballet under the instructions of a hairy bear of a Russian aristocrat; son-in-law typesets slogans such as "God is the State; the State is God" as inserts for his wife's boxes of candy; snakes nestle in a solarium nearby; and father and a friend manufacture and set off firecrackers in the cellar. In themselves these characters are mildly diverting. Jumble them together and the result is pandemonium, especially when they keep coming and going and are joined by outlandish visitors like the Grand Duchess Olga, cousin to the former Czar of all the Russias and now serving meals at Child's Restaurant and hoping to move up socially to wait on table at Schrafft's. The play asks whether the younger daughter is courting disaster when she brings home for dinner to this madhouse her boyfriend, who happens to be the son of her boss, together with his parents. Obviously, she is, but just as obviously, the play-wrights are going to contrive to brush aside all setbacks to a marriage they devoutly wish to have consummated.

The domestic setting, that favored ambience for popular farces, becomes a hostile environment for the characters in both *The Man Who Came to Dinner* and *George Washington Slept Here*. In the former, Kaufman and Hart embellish their conceit of the milkman who stayed for five years and his successor, the iceman, who moved in and hung on for eight years; they now cause a literary celebrity, Sheridan Whiteside, to come to dinner with the Stanley family in Ohio and, after falling on his host's front step, to take over the house. Whiteside, a portrayal of the spiteful and egomaniacal Alexander Woollcott, to whom the play is cheerfully dedicated, receives from sympathetic (or intimidated) friends thousands of gifts that include such wildlife as penguins in a crate and a colony of roaches. At the Stanleys' he commandeers the cook and servants for his private lunches, dinners, card parties, and soirees; insists on exclusive use of the telephone, running up tremendous bills as he maintains his gossipy conversations with the world's great, however far abroad they happen to be flung; and generally incarnates the famous, name-dropping snob as spoiled brat. In the end, when the nominal head of the house, Mr. Stanley, himself no angel, is sighing with relief as Whiteside departs, the clumsy boor falls again on the same step.

The house in *George Washington Slept Here* is situated in a lightly settled part of Bucks County, Pennsylvania, which once enticed country-loving New Yorkers (including Moss Hart), where they purchased ramshackle rural buildings with fake pedigrees, lacking water, an access road, rainproof roofs, and other amenities. By the time reckless Newton Fuller and his wife and children have depleted their assets trying to cope with the deficiencies, the house is to be taken out of their hands. Will they, on hearing about the threat of dispossession, wreck it thoroughly and leave it in a worse state than when they found it? They will, smashing every window, sawing holes in the floors, chopping openings in the roof, reintroducing a cow to the kitchen, and spreading quantities of garbage and manure over what is left of the floors. This is the finest destruction scene since *The Weavers* (1892), a demolition job worthy of Buster Keaton, and farcical to its roots as human beings take revenge on the inanimate world. But will the Fuller family lose the house after wrecking it? Absolutely not. The final curtain leaves them on an upbeat note but with the task of rehabilitating it all over again. The play, snakelike, bites its own tail, as does *The Man Who Came to Dinner*. This ending, projecting a cyclical repetition similar to that of *The Inspector General* or Ionesco's *The Lesson*, looks back with rue at typically farcical agonies of wasted effort.

Nice and Normal

Authors of popular farces, however extravagant the antics they confect, like to anchor their situations in reality. As a rule they insert into the cast at least one character who behaves moderately. The idea is to provide a norm, an external and objective viewpoint of the proceedings that roughly matches the spectator's noninvolvement, gives him a "handle" on the play. The inclusion of a normal figure dates back to the voice of the speaker in oral epics and later the writer of epic narratives. It recurs in the choruses of Greek tragedy and in the actor representing the playwright in that episode of a farce by Aristophanes called the parabasis, during which the action of the play comes to a halt while this character steps forward and addresses the audience. In Molière's plays, level-headed brothers-in-law, cousins, and friends reason diligently with the obsessed protagonists—the hypochondriac, the snob, the misanthrope, the wife-trainer, the *précieuse*, who often is also a despotic parent—in an effort to promote more acceptable social behavior.

Such reasonable characters, the raisonneurs, expound arguments that have a similar dramatic function to the parabasis of Aristophanes, for they present opinions the *audience* can accept. But I must emphasize that they differ from the parabasis in that they do not necessarily reflect the opinions of the author. Centuries of criticism have encouraged us to see Molière's raisonneurs as his spokesmen, rather than society's (the audience's). But these characters, after all, have their own stake in the outcome of the action. They are not impartial or godlike; they seek to avoid disruption in family and social life; they advocate respectability and conformity, two qualities for which Molière himself had little use.

In the modern intellectual farce, as we shall see, the spokesmen for conformity, if any, will be caricatured and ridiculed. In Kaufman and Hart, however, and in most popular farces, they are romanticized in pairs of lovers who may occasionally seem to have their heads in low-lying clouds but who crave normal surroundings and circumstances that will enable them to get on with their plans for marriage and domesticity. The younger daughter in *You Can't Take It With You* cries out, "Why can't we be like other people? Roast beef, and two green vegetables, and—doilies on the table, and—a place you could bring your friends to—without— *(Unable to control herself further, she bursts out of the room, into the kitchen)* . . ." Earlier she had expressed misgivings about her family to her boyfriend:

ALICE: . . . I love you, Tony, but I love them too! And it's no use, Tony! It's no use! *(She is weeping now in spite of herself)*
TONY *(quietly):* There's only one thing you've said that matters—that makes sense at all. You love me.
ALICE: But, Tony, I know so well . . .
TONY: My darling, don't you think other people have had the same problem? Everybody's got a family.
ALICE *(through her tears):* But not like mine.

Contrast the sensible lines of these two ciphers with the sort of dialogue spoken by a trio of unreasonable characters from the same family:

PENNY [the mother]: Ed, dear, why don't you and Essie have a baby? I was thinking about it just the other day.
ED [Penny's son-in-law]: I don't know—we could have one if you wanted us to. What about it, Essie? Do you want to have a baby?
ESSIE [Penny's older daughter]: Oh, I don't care. I'm willing if Grandpa is.
ED: Let's ask him.

Here is the same kind of disparity as we find in Molière between the "normals" and the "abnormals," between the rational, bland spokespeople and lovers on the one side and, on the other, the often fascinating eccentrics. One senses in both Molière and Kaufman and Hart some mercenary cynicism in their creation of young, tedious lovers dragged intact and guileless out of thousands of previous farces and comedies: they may help to win over the reviewers; they may swell the takings, because audiences are thought to have grown used to them and to expect them. In their last collaboration, *George Washington Slept Here*, Kaufman and Hart don't bother with lovers or spokespeople. The only nod in the direction of a love interest here is an affair, soon scotched, between a middle-aged actor from a dingy summer-stock troupe (a dig at the Bucks County Playhouse?) and an impressionable "girl in her early twenties."[3] Two of the characters do sometimes speak for conformity; a pair of acid-tongued wives, they emit lines that are smartly sarcastic but shift the farce not toward realism but closer to Broadway staginess.

Both before and since Kaufman and Hart, farce in one or another of its modes has been a favorite device of artificers of the well-made play. They like to enliven their playscripts or musical books with farcical smatterings. These shtik and numbers accentuate the negative. They crowd the stage with confusion and make the audience agreeably dizzy, even intoxicated. They discharge the same function as Sennett's rallies. If there have been, at a conservative guess, some twelve thousand well-made plays in English in this century, we are talking about at least eighteen thousand farcical bits and pieces. But a W.M.P. playwright never lets these smatterings get altogether out of hand, for the performance must conclude on a note of sentimentality, a reconciliation that energizes the spectators' tear ducts and puts lumps in their throats.

A riffle through some W.M.P. cast lists turns up the following random selection of farcical types: prudish professors or high school teachers required by the plotting to undress, although none achieves nakedness; admen who get drunk, sass their clients, and lose a big account, only to land a bigger one; publicity-fixated nuns; bankers who gamble; blackmailing lawyers; telephone, television, and washing-machine repairmen who run off at the mouth while connecting the wrong wires; idealistic playwrights, compos-

---

[3] The quotations from Kaufman and Hart are taken from *Six Plays by Kaufman and Hart* (New York: Random House, 1942), pp. 303, 263, 239, and 512.

ers, novelists, painters, poets, sculptors, screenwriters, songwriters, and inventors, each in for a rude awakening; venal movie,
television, radio, and theater producers, each with "a great idea";
larcenous corporation presidents; nearsighted, short-winded, and
quick-tempered private eyes; corrupt movie, television, and theater directors; mean-spirited movie, television, and theater inves-
tors who have a daughter or niece or young wife with ambition to
act but no talent; and dumb journalists. These are some of our
century's updatings of the commedia masks. Since the plays are
aimed at commercial theater circuits, if not targeted on Broadway,
and designed for easy adaptation into screenplays, the authors are
either snapping at the hands that feed them or trying to convince
us that they are using the system in order to opt out of it. In any
case, by the time the fun is over the system seems not so bad if it
permits—actually promotes—such healthy questioning.

American well-made plays treat adultery as the result of some
misunderstanding. Mr. A. errs when he thinks that Mrs. A. is
having an affair with a young athlete; he really *is* giving her calisthenics lessons so that Mr. A. will find her more appealing. Mrs.
B. has drawn the wrong inferences when Mr. B. and his sexy new
secretary work overtime. Miss C. doesn't realize that her boyfriend, Mr. D., has made friends with a notorious movie vamp in
order to get her a fat part in the vamp's new picture. Such plays
flirt with adultery, examples being George Axelrod's *Seven-Year
Itch* and *Will Success Spoil Rock Hunter?*, while Axelrod's *Goodbye, Charlie* flirts with homosexuality and necrophilia as the hero
falls in love with his best friend, who has died and been reincar-
nated as a woman. F. Hugh Herbert's *The Moon Is Blue* illustrates
the prudishness of self-appointed censors in this country: when
Otto Preminger made his movie version it had a hard time beating
Hollywood's Production Code because one character uttered the
word "virgin."

In French W.M.P.s, however, where there's smoke there's fire.
Adultery, and especially cuckoldry, has long been a fact of art, if
not always of life, in France. Boulevard W.M.P.s that have proved
to be distance runners visit New York almost every year by way of
London. Usually they have been greatly denatured en route so as
to mitigate material considered offensive to English-speaking play-
goers. But their suggestiveness remains, because French play-

wrights start out by being less skittish or oppressed than their counterparts in the United States and Britain.

In Britain, W.M.P.s have grown more risqué since the ending of stage censorship in the late 1960s. The plays of Alan Ayckbourn, such as *Absurd Person Singular* and the trilogy *The Norman Conquests* (both 1973), *Absent Friends* (1974), and *Bedroom Farce* (1975), set in British suburban and exurban bungalows, cottages, and "stockbroker Tudors," align themselves with Feydeau's in the tradition of marital discontent and infidelity. Ayckbourn's geometrical manipulation of scenes; his cool and sometimes callous depiction of his characters, all of whom he keeps at a satirical remove (never playing favorites); and his intelligence of a high order make him a transitional playwright between popular and intellectual farce. This straddling position, far from being a handicap, lets him enjoy the best of both worlds—his plays do well commercially and critics take him seriously—and it emphasizes that the distinctions made here between the intellectual and the popular are artificial, not categorical.

ELEVEN

STAGE FANTASY AFTER JARRY

Thérèse, a housewife married to a baker and living on the island of Zanzibar, has a yearning to make war, rather than children. Unbuttoning her blouse to let her breasts float out like balloons, she pops them, cuts her hair short, grows a beard and mustache then and there, wrestles her husband to the floor, and takes his clothes. She modifies her name to that of Greek myth's most celebrated prophet, Tiresias, the man who, for seven years, according to Ovid's *Metamorphoses*, had been a woman. Then she leaves home and within twelve hours has promoted herself to victorious general of the Zanzibar army. To match this feat her husband puts on the clothes and role she had discarded. While she (now he) makes war, he (now she) makes babies—a total of more than forty thousand of them. Thus, while the wife fights for the island and kills off its young men, the husband more than repopulates it.

The Breasts of Tiresias, written by the French poet and art critic Guillaume Apollinaire, was begun in 1903 and completed (and staged) in 1917, only a matter of months before he died of wounds suffered in World War I. It has a subtitle, "a surrealist drama," the first use of the word "surrealist," which denotes art that is not hampered by recording life, but goes beyond realism to investigate "infinite possibilities" by means of "the reasonable use of the improbable." In addition to its two principal transformations— woman into man and man into woman—the play features a character who is killed and springs back to life, and objects that come to life. Apollinaire abolishes the distinctions we draw between male and female, life and death, animate and inanimate. He fools around with time (the play's hurly-burly events happen in twelve crowded hours) and with place (his Zanzibar is a skit on France). His "reasonable use of the improbable" includes one multiple character, known as The People of Zanzibar, speaking and listening for the island's entire population; dialogue spoken through a megaphone so as to separate the characters from their own voices; and the return of Thérèse/Tiresias in the guise of a fortune-teller, with her head lit up as if her brain were an irrepressible beacon.

In this chapter and the two that follow, the farce I've called intellectual, because it tackles ideas, sometimes in abstract form, is split into three main divisions, according to type: fantastic, realistic, and theatrically self-conscious. But *The Breasts of Tiresias* immediately illustrates the artificiality of such distinctions; it subsumes all three types. It employs fantasy most obviously in its transformations and in its free-swinging, unrealistic verse, some of which goes without punctuation. At the same time, it contains big, realistic themes, such as population growth, women's liberation (known then as emancipation), and the futility of war. The play also has its share of theatricalism, as when one character steps forward and addresses the audience in a modern equivalent of a parabasis by Aristophanes; in truth, the author has Aristophanes in mind throughout this work, which could be regarded as a twentieth-century version of *Lysistrata*.[1] Nevertheless, the distinctions are useful, if only as a start, in grouping the bewildering welter of intellectual farce that our century has come up with. If compelled to pigeonhole Apollinaire's play, I'd put it with fantasies, for if it were a realistic well-made play, Thérèse would walk out on her husband for another man; in an Ibsenian type of realism, she'd leave, like Nora, to realize her identity as a woman; in a theatricalist play, she'd retain an identity, not as the character but as an aspect of the actress. As it is, she goes off to realize herself *as a*

---

[1] *The Breasts of Tiresias*, translated by Louis Simpson, is published in *Modern French Theatre*, edited by Michael Benedikt and George E. Wellwarth (New York: E. P. Dutton, 1964). For a longer exegesis of the play, see "Apollinaire's Male Heroine" by Albert Bermel, in *Twentieth Century Literature*, Vol. 20, No. 3, July 1974.

man, and such a quest makes fantastic demands on the audience —the willing suspension of belief in barriers between the genders.

Surrealism, Dada, and Fragmentation

Did Apollinaire see silent movies? Of course. Did they influence his writing? Well, as an art critic and the most prominent champion of new painting and sculpture, he must have noted the discontinuity between shots, resulting in a barrage of unlike images and fragmented sequences. The poet-playwrights of the Twenties who called themselves Surrealists in his honor not only *knew* silent movies; they were devotees, especially of Chaplin's.

Apollinaire supplied a name for a theatrical movement that had only tenuous connections with his play and with his ideas of what theater might be. Only a few years after he coined the word Surrealism, André Breton and other French writers preempted the term for their own purposes, and because Apollinaire was by then dead he could not safeguard the meaning he'd intended for it. The Surrealism of Breton and his fellows represented a technique for writing by means of which they did not exercise conscious control over their thoughts. They wished to let their unconscious dictate the flow of words; they tried to discard their training and habits as writers and simply let come whatever surfaced in their minds. This is a sort of orgasmic theory of composition. It sometimes results in fragments of ideas and images that do not cohere or contrast, as film images do, and may read like so many non sequiturs. Here is the whole of Scene One from a playlet by Roger Gilbert-Lecomte entitled *The Odyssey of Ulysses the Palmiped* (1924):

> ULYSSES (*in his aquarium* [*or "tub" in lunar dialect*]):
> MONOLOGUE OF THE PALMIPED IN QUESTION: (*He sticks his index finger in his nose, then with a sudden thrust inserts his arms to the shoulder in his appendix while shouting*): It is I the Stupefied Mystic! (*Then he augments his sibylline bellow with this phrase befitting the Kingly vocabulary of a process server's assistant.*) I'll accord no credence to the authenticity of CAUSAL LINKS until I CAN HANG MYSELF BY MEANS OF THE AFORESAID.
> A VOICE (*coming like an old camembert out of his right sock*): Nitchevo! Nitchevo!!!

Though this be madness, yet there is method in it. The "odyssey" of this particular Ulysses takes him from his aquarium to a blissful spot in "the Mystics' Paradise," but by way of a gibbet where he "hangs without pants" at the end of the causal link he referred to in his opening speech, instead of being in a noose. Material of this sort can serve as a treasure trove for literary and dramatic and mythic—as well as Freudian and Jungian—analysis. In juxtaposing random thoughts that drift up into consciousness and drag others with them, the artist may say more than he knows. It also invites comparison with other types of Surrealist artistry, especially sculpture, which often took "found objects," such as pieces of paper and wood, metal piping, rubber bands, washers, leaves, twigs, bottle tops, and so on (a mixing of the organic and inorganic) and made a collage out of them. Surreal writing also reminds us of the attempts earlier in the century of artists like Matisse and Picasso to paint like children or like untutored adults, letting impulses reign by shedding the glossiness and professionalism that are acquired with the mastery of craft. Surrealism is, in a word, antirational.

It was fathered not only by Apollinaire but also by another artistic doctrine that became confused with Surrealism, and still is much of the time because the results look similar. Christened Dada by one of its founders, Tristan Tzara, this rebellious movement gathered its impetus in Switzerland, Germany, and then France. Dada, we are told, means "hobby horse" in French. It's also a baby word, one of the first to which English-speaking infants give lip service. We can sum up the function of Dada by treating the word as an acronym for "Defame Antiquity, Debase Art." Its practitioners mocked all art of the past, especially the distant past, and reserved their richest derision for terms like "genius" and "masterpieces." The process of continually thumbing noses at the past sounds heretical, and heresy did become a prime purpose of the Dada writer. But any new and experimental art—a style, a theory, fresh content—asserts itself, clears a space for itself, by debunking what went before. The history of art is a tissue of generation conflicts and coups, one overturning after another. The originators of Dada, like other innovators, didn't want to recognize that by spurning the past they forced themselves to take it into account. An artist may build on others' monuments or on their ruins, but never on bare ground. If Dada writers thought they could escape all debts to all their forerunners, they were too ambitious. In a speech like the following one from *The Gas Heart* (1920), we notice that however arbitrary the vocabulary of the author, Tzara, his language uses traditional rhythms and touches of old-fashioned rhetoric in its repetitions. Moreover, its imagery, made up of words that reach for extended meanings, seems to derive from the poetry of Baudelaire and his successors:

> Clytemnestra, the diplomat's wife, was looking out of the window. The cellists go by in a carriage of Chinese tea, biting the air and openhearted caresses. You are beautiful, Clytemnestra, the crystal of your skin awakens our sexual curiosity. You are as tender and as calm as two yards of white silk. Clytemnestra, my teeth tremble. I'm cold, I'm afraid. I'm green I'm flower I'm gasometer I'm afraid. You are married. My teeth tremble. When will you have the pleasure of looking at the lower jaw of the revolver closing in my chalk lung. Hopeless, and without any family.[2]

I don't mean to minimize the critical and public uproars that greeted the Dada and the Surrealist plays and are occasionally echoed today, long after they have spawned imitations galore and been partially absorbed into the mainstream of twentieth-century dramaturgy. The speech above, for instance, is delivered by a character named Eye in the presence of other characters named Ear, Neck, Nose, Mouth, and Eyebrow; and it would strike a Broadway audience as weird, incomprehensible, and—the crowning put-down—boring, which is to say, unsuspenseful, if one can conceive of a Broadway producer rash enough to finance the play these days. The theatergoing public has by and large always looked for suspense in plotting and motivation as an experience it has a right to endure; without it, a performance is "not a play." The alternative device of using surprises, shocks, and the mildly unexpected is frowned upon as being somehow unfair and unmannerly by catching the audience off guard. One reason why Dada, Surrealist, and many subsequent "intellectual" playwrights do away

---

[2] This and the earlier quotation are taken from *Modern French Theatre*, pp. 219 and 135 respectively.

with suspense is that it distracts the audience's attention from what is happening to what is going to happen. Thus even when these authors introduce a powerful dramatic moment toward the end it doesn't seem like a climax, something that has grown out of the preceding material; it appears to be an addition and perhaps gratuitous. But most of the time these plays end quietly or spoofingly. After Act III of *If You Please* (1920) by André Breton and Philippe Soupault, the text says:

CURTAIN
A LONG INTERMISSION

ACT IV
NOTE: The authors of *If You Please* do
not want the fourth act printed.

Although Dada entered the drama to wreck it, while Surrealism was supposed to open it up at the seams and make it more accessible to dreams and fleeting thoughts, both movements yielded plays and playlets that were distinctly farcical in spirit, not only in their dialogue but also in the naming of the characters and in the stage directions. The cast list of René Daumal's *en gggarrrde!* (1924) has human figures who include Mygraine, "a woman in a hennin"; a "little angel" named Bubu; a "depraved young thing" named Ursule; A Sociologist; The Author; and the favorite male and female roles adopted in insane asylums, Napoleon and Cleopatra. The list is rounded out with A Leech, Some Snails, A Cigar, A Pernod with Sugar, and A Toothbrush (female), each of whom has lines to speak. Even The Public figures as an unlisted character, crying out at one point, "Encore!" and soon after, "Enough!" As for the stage directions, we are told that the characters dance a conga to the sound of "La Marseillaise"; The Pernod with Sugar "sucks greedily" at the others' feet; The Sociologist, who falls asleep, "floats several yards above the ground"; Cleopatra does a belly dance in front of The Leech; and The Cigar and The Toothbrush blow their noses.[3] These seem

---

[3] *en gggarrrde!*, translated by Michael Benedikt, appears in *Modern French Theatre*, pp. 211–16.

straightforward when compared with the instruction to the actor in *Ulysses the Palmiped*, already mentioned, to "insert his arms to the shoulder in his appendix." Could he comply accurately with such an order? How would the audience be persuaded that he was burrowing into his appendix, rather than, say, his pancreas? Very likely these are plays to be read, not staged; but it's surprising how much—with the help of some ingenuity, stylization, and a narrator—*can* be staged.

In any event, neither Dada nor Surrealism turned into a dead end. They went underground and resurfaced some forty years later in the modified guise of Happenings; these were mostly created and performed by painters who wanted to work with movement and in four dimensions, time as well as space. Members of the public walked between screens or stroked lethargic animals or operated mechanisms that sometimes failed to operate. Such improvised activities, which depended on chance (would somebody kick down a screen? trip over an artist? yell at a balky machine? get stuck on a porcupine?), might prove farcical, not always by intention; others, solemn little ceremonies, occasioned bewilderment and frustration, especially when a spectator had wanted to become a participant or when a bystander, roped into the performance, had wanted to remain a spectator.

But by that time, the Sixties, farcical fantasies had branched out amazingly. To isolate single strands—pure forms—would be as complicated as picking out the separate shoots from a storm fence overgrown with Virginia creeper. By way of illustrating the diversity of these farces I can refer to only a piecemeal sampling from plays that originated in Belgium, Poland, Russia, France, Britain, Germany, and the United States. The selection is not meant to be representative, but to show that this type of farce had grown contagious among dramatists who are now acknowledged as international resources.

Belgium, Poland

Michel de Ghelderode (1898–1962) was an avid movie fan who, in his *Pantagleize* (1929), "a farce to make you sad," loosely modeled his hero, as he thought, on Chaplin. The untramplike Pantagleize carries an umbrella "for useless protection," in place of

Charlie's twirling stick. He is a fashion writer for a magazine, an innocent astray in the turmoil of a city, a helpless clown, born illegitimate and nourished on whims, an asthmatic, dropsical, with ambitions to be a flier, a cyclist, an explorer, and a one-man band. On his fortieth birthday, the watershed of a normal life, Panta-gleize becomes "the plaything of really terrible coincidences," some gruesomely farcical in the extreme, as he gets entangled in an insurrection and an eclipse, falls in love with a woman who despises him and is killed, gets mistaken for a revolutionary and stood in front of a firing squad, dying at exactly midnight with the words "What a lovely day!" bubbling off his lips, a harmless excla-mation that was the slogan—although he never knew it—of the failed uprising.

Ghelderode set most of his plays in Medieval or Renaissance Flanders, the time and terrain of Bruegel, and peopled them with grotesques, misshapen and psychically warped giants, dwarfs, and ordinary-sized freaks. His miser Hieronymus in *Red Magic* (1931) gloats over a trunkful of gold coins (the "red magic" of the title) and urges the ones with female heads and the ones with male heads to kiss, link tongues, and thereby couple and multiply; he will then marry off their offspring and generate wealth unlimited. In *Chronicles of Hell* (1929), a "tragedy bouffe" in one long act, after one of the most powerful scenes in the modern drama, in which a dead bishop comes back to life, the bishop lurches through an episcopal palace like Frankenstein's monster at bay and falls dead again while a conclave of bizarre clerics who have witnessed the miracle dance around sniffing at one another's cloaks to see how many of their number fouled themselves in fright.[4]

Ghelderode's plays from the Twenties and Thirties didn't reach France until the late Forties and didn't break into English until the early Sixties; but those of Stanislaw Ignacy Witkiewicz (1885–1939), who was thirteen years older than Ghelderode, had to wait even longer. It's not difficult to see why. Witkacy, as he signed

---

[4] *Ghelderode: Seven Plays, Vol. 1* (New York: Hill & Wang, 1960) and *Ghelderode: Seven Plays, Vol. 2* (New York: Hill & Wang, 1964) contain most of that author's better-known plays; others have been published in various journals or included in unpublished Ph.D. dissertations. As a mystifying playwright, Ghelderode has received a lot of attention from Ph.D. candidates, much of it superior to the material that has been published.

himself (eliding and reversing his middle name and surname), had endeavored, as had Ghelderode, to do something arrestingly new with farce. He seized on its exaggerations and hallucinatory opportunities not merely for the sake of fun and laughs but also as a means of debating the mysteries of existence. Witkacy is an unabashed ontologist; his characters want to realize purposes in their lives that they cannot quite fathom. And they keep changing their minds. If they knew what those purposes were, they'd gladly (or stoically) go on living. But perhaps the purposes become clear only after death: a hypothesis that leads to the consideration of suicide —and murder, because if people make discoveries after they have died, then to kill them is an act of kindness, a blessing, an obligation even.

How can an author reconcile such solemn ponderings with farce? Well, by having the characters ridicule their thoughts at the same time as they drift through them. To do justice to both the pugnacious merriment we associate with Jarry and a sententious, horrifying melodrama like that of Seneca will baffle readers who cannot come to Witkacy with an open mind, and defeat actors and directors who look for consistent motives. These are plays that depend on surprises, not suspense; they make you jump, rather than wait. It takes some ingenuity to accommodate Witkacy's opposites, to give some conviction to, say, the tyrant who lends his name to *Gyubal Wahazar* (1921), a desperately excitable man who, when angry at his subjects, foams at the mouth so copiously that the froth soaks his jacket, who condemns even his closest advisers and admirers to death or imprisonment, and who yet can say, not without pathos, "I've completely forgotten who I used to be, and I don't know too well who I am." But Wahazar is only one of the play's cluster of characters, who each pay out their own morbid, bemused, hilarious trains of thought in lines that seldom intersect and are sometimes less lines than spirals, zigzags, or irregularly placed markers.

In *Mr. Price, or Tropical Madness* (1920, written in collaboration with Dunin-Borkowska), an employee of a cartel in Rangoon declares to his boss, "Richard, I can't stand it any longer. I'll go mad. Today I worked like an ox all day long. I tried to get hold of myself and I can't. I love your wife with a totally new, satanic kind of love. By the way—I forgot to tell you: all the rubber in Ceylon belongs to our trust. Coffee's fluctuating, but I've sent two cables to Colombo . . ." And the wife in question proposes to the employee, "Sydney! What I'm saying may seem strange to you, but why not let me kill you? Don't get mad at me for asking." After he agrees to let her kill him, and she does, her husband, the boss, reacts selfishly: "You killed him? Why? How could you do away with someone else's property? He belonged to me and to our trust . . ."

In *Metaphysics of a Two-Headed Calf* (1921) a dying mother speaks to her teen-aged son: "Our spirits will meet someday. Have you read *Allgemeine Gespenstertheorie*, the general theory of ghosts? On the basis of absolute ontology and the theory that inanimate matter does not exist, anything is possible." A siren, Mirabella, in the same play is said to be "a combination of the so-called enchanted strumpet type and the streetwalking princess type"; while her brother is "the best fellow in the world. He murdered my father for me the way you'd kill a fly." And Mirabella exclaims to the mother, "Oh! These mothers, these mothers. I'd like to have a son, just so I could make his life miserable the way you do, Aunt. Aunt! What an atrocious thing the family is! Who ever invented such a swinish mess?"

In *The Pragmatists* (1919) the following exchange takes place between a Chinese mummy and a man who passes for the hero:

MUMMY: And do you remember that night when you seduced me in the little bamboo hut in the shadow of the Ping-Fangs and drank the last drop of my blood through a straw made of dried Wu grass?

PLASFODOR: I seem to remember something like that. Yes, I think I really was somewhere near Saigon once.[5]

This mummy is only one of many Witkacy characters who are undead. As nonchalantly as Apollinaire, Witkacy strolls back and

---

[5] The quotations from Witkiewicz are taken from *Tropical Madness*, translated by Daniel and Eleanor Gerould (New York: Winter House, 1972), pp. 156, 71, 84, 87, 197, 199, 213, 228, 16. *The Madman and the Nun and Other Plays* (Seattle, Wash.: University of Washington Press, 1968) contains six more plays by Witkiewicz, translated by Daniel Gerould and C. S. Durer.

forth across borders between the natural and supernatural, male and female (a few of his androgynous people are called "masculettes"), madness and sanity, animate and inanimate (some of his characters call others automatons), life and literature (the actual and the imagined), face and mask, farce and terror, the ordinary and the grotesque, so that the action of his plays resolves itself into one transformation after another. When his men fall in love (which they do as abruptly as falling off a cliff) they feel reborn: the loved woman is a new mother. The effect of all the transformations is vertiginous; a spectator must constantly shift stance and viewpoint to keep up with one of the nimblest imaginations in dramatic literature.

Russia

Witkacy brings into collision ill-assorted types—merchants, artists, whores, scientists, autocrats, loafers, suicides, neurotics—who act unpredictably, against their typecasting. These peculiar dramatic conjunctions let him satirize the discomforts that arise from arbitrary social groupings. By contrast, the fantasies of Vladimir Mayakovsky (1893–1930) are political, rather than social. They satirize the injustices, greed, and sloth that lead to inequality. But Mayakovsky, the poet in him always ahead of the propagandist—well ahead—can write a first, full-length play that looks forward to a society run by its workers, and a second and a third play that take jabs at that society's bureaucratic bulges without displaying any inconsistency. At the same time he can create a new kind of theater in Russia that takes farcical aim at almost the same targets as Gogol did almost a century earlier.[6]

Mystery-Bouffe (1918, revised 1921) lives up to its generic title. It has some of the lineaments of a Medieval cycle in which each playlet is called a "mystery" because of its derivation from the Scriptures: *mystère* originally meant a church service and came from the Latin *ministerium*. Mayakovsky's *buffo* treatment of ma-

---

[6] Vsevelod Meyerhold, who directed the most celebrated revival yet of Gogol's *The Inspector General*, one of the outstanding productions of this century, also staged Mayakovsky's plays.

terial borrowed (very freely) from the liturgy makes the play's lessons not merely palatable but delectable. He had the first reading of his play within a year of the staging of *The Breasts of Tiresias*, and his prologue makes it clear that the author is going, like Apollinaire, to liberate his work from the straitjacket of realism and to employ farce as his principal implement. *Mystery-Bouffe* has more than sixty roles in six acts, each with a different set. It's a farcical spectacle which opens in "the entire universe" and with an apocalyptic situation. The world, a model of which stands right there onstage, has sprung a leak. People from various parts of Europe and the Mideast appear, including the prime ministers of France and the United Kingdom, Clemenceau and Lloyd George (two tigers that Mayakovsky will swiftly defang), and a couple of Eskimos, all hoping to escape the flood. These characters are divided into the Unclean (workers), the Clean (rulers and upper bourgeoisie), and sundry hangers-on, such as the Compromiser, who keeps trying to reconcile opponents, and for his pains gets beaten up, and a White Russian lady, a refugee from the Revolution, who has already adopted umpteen different nationalities. The Unclean ones build an ark and everybody sails off in search of a new Mount Ararat. Aboard the ark the politicians appoint the Negus of Abyssinia monarch; he eats up most of the provisions and is dumped overboard, to be replaced by a republican government. But the Unclean (who function as the crew) find that the food now goes to the Clean, whom they therefore jettison. The ark floats on to hell, where the Clean have already landed and are eating the devils out of house and Hades. Beelzebub and his minions put on a show of force with their tridents. They cannot intimidate the stout-hearted workers and are dismayed to learn that things are much more hellish on earth. The ark next takes the Unclean to heaven, where they run across Methuselah, Gabriel, a corps of angels, Leo Tolstoy, and Jean-Jacques Rousseau. But the angels strike them as "lazy bums," and they dislike the ethereal food, "cloud milk and cloud bread." They snatch Jehovah's thunderbolts, leaving heaven weaponless, and push on. In the country ruled by the Queen of Chaos they get down to digging for coal and oil. In the final act they reach the Promised Land, a city of lofty, transparent towers, magnificently electrified, and a delegation of personified foodstuffs, machines, and tools (the animated inanimate again), which volunteer to help them build a gorgeous future unsullied by civil servants and their paperwork.[7]

Another vision of the future lights up Mayakovsky's next farce, *The Bedbug* (1928). A young man named Ivan Prisypkin decides to boost his pedigree by changing his name to Pierre Skripkin (which sounds less funny, less vulgar, and slightly Frenchified in Russian), jilting his fiancée (who shoots herself), and marrying into a bour-geois family. At the wedding a fire breaks out, starting with the bride's veil and ending with a conflagration that reduces everything and everybody present to ashes—with the exception of the groom, who is frozen into a block of ice that has hardened from the fire-men's hose water.

Fifty years slip by. The workers' millennium has evolved. It con-sists of a worldwide association of soviets that has abolished the bourgeoisie, tobacco, alcoholic beverages, and other forms of pol-lution. The Institute for Human Resurrection unearths Prisypkin's icebound body and brings him back to life by "rapid defrigeration." His first vital signs are furious scratching. A bedbug trapped in his clothing has revived with him. Two lost species at once: *Bedbugus normalis* and *Bourgeoisius vulgaris!*

The scientists are simultaneously ecstatic and repelled, while his jilted fiancée, who recovered from her suicide attempt and has lived on to become an aged research assistant, cannot figure out what she ever saw in this filthy creature. Prisypkin pollutes his corner of the hospital with cigarette butts, empty beer bottles, complaints about being lonely, and his breath, which is dispersed by a battery of fans.

"Society," a professor tells him, "hopes to raise you to a human level." In this society arts of all kinds, from theater to fiction, have disappeared, probably because they too are looked upon as being pollutants. Prisypkin refuses an invitation to watch a substitute for a performance, "a dance performed by twenty thousand male and female workers on the city square, a rehearsal of a new work-system on the farms." The bedbug gets away but is recaptured by a posse of crawling scientists, and the two specimens go on display

[7] *Mystery-Bouffe*, in its second version, is published in *The Complete Plays of Vladimir Mayakovsky* (New York: Simon and Schuster, 1971), translated by Guy Daniels, introduc-tion by Robert Payne, pp. 39–139. I've sometimes wondered whether Mayakovsky's play inspired J. B. Priestley's serious socialist drama *They Came to a City* (1943).

in a cage at the zoological gardens. "They are different in size, but identical in essence," the zoo's director explains. "Both of them have their habitat in the musty mattresses of time. *Bedbugus normalis*, having gorged itself on the body of a human being, falls under the bed. *Bourgeoisius vulgaris*, having gorged itself on the body of all mankind, falls onto the bed. That's the only difference."

Prisypkin greets the gaping sightseers warmly, eager for love or mere recognition as their equal—isn't this supposed to be an egalitarian life to come?—but they recoil from his breath and griminess, and the cage is quickly covered up.

Audiences at the first production doubtless read into the play the moral that to affiliate with the bourgeoisie (by, say, marrying into it) was to turn into a parasite. In 1955, Khrushchev's "thaw" in Eastern Europe melted the icebound play more than two decades in advance of Prisypkin's due date, and it enjoyed a colorful revival. Critics and audiences then started looking more closely at the characters *around* Prisypkin and at the environment he awakes into. This is the obverse of the utopian collective of A.D. 2000 that Edward Bellamy foresaw in *Looking Backward* (1888). In truth, it farcically anticipates *Brave New World* (1932), Woody Allen's *Sleeper* (1973), and the many intervening portraits of a disciplined, antiseptic future promised—that is, threatened—by a heartbreaking present.[8]

In his last play, Mayakovsky, still future-minded, goes one better than H. G. Wells. *The Bathhouse* (1929) has nothing to do with bathing. A Soviet inventor comes up with a time machine that can travel backward and forward through the years at controlled speeds and select its destinations to the moment. The machine summons a woman from one hundred years away, 2029. She arrives glowing hot and phosphorescent from her velocity of one year per second. (Mayakovsky, like Shaw, was prescient in foreseeing women as political leaders, although the U.S.S.R. has not yet caught up with him.) She decrees that the machine will take back with her—that is, forward with her—a few Soviet citizens whose

---

[8] The translation of *The Bedbug* from which I am quoting is Max Hayward's in *Three Soviet Plays* (London and Baltimore: Penguin, 1966) and in *The Bedbug and Selected Poetry* (New York: Meridian, 1960).

names will go down in the honor roll of history. The machine, instead of being an elaborate mock-up of exhaust pipes, glass, and gleaming sheet metal, or even a primitive-looking cabin like the vehicle in Michael Crichton's movie *Time After Time* (1979), is . . . invisible. The actors who board it simply stand on the stage. As soon as it takes off, it disgorges a bunch of self-seeking bureaucrats whom posterity will gladly forget. They are "scattered by the centrifugal wheel of time" and sprawled across the stage floor, while the chosen few disappear into the twenty-first century. We never get to see that century, unfortunately, washed clean by *The Bathhouse* of this century's grubby opportunists. But Mayakovsky does look pitilessly at our century's public officials. These rejects of time resemble their capitalist counterparts. They stringently apply to others rules from which they exempt themselves. They fight off change unless they can claim exclusive credit for its benefits and escape responsibility for its drawbacks. They fawn over people they want favors from and snub people who need their help or permission. They pad expenses and put in heavy overtime with good-looking secretaries.

A memorable sequence occurs when one of them, visited by an obsequious "realistic painter of portraits and historic battle scenes," asks to be depicted on horseback while posing at his desk. In another sequence Mayakovsky moves into farce that's self-conscious. The play we are watching suddenly becomes a command performance for the very Chief Administrative Coordinator who is its principal satirical mark. He sits in the auditorium and suggests revisions that will enhance his image. The character named after him must be "made more wholesome, rounder, handled with greater lyricism." The actors may have secured "special permission from the State Literary Committee" to introduce a negative character as an exception, but they should "go back to the classics" and "try to learn from the great geniuses of the accursed past." They must add some "symbolic self-criticism" and some of that decadent entertainment from prerevolutionary days which everybody now despises, even though it does let an audience relax and enjoy itself.[9] Here Mayakovsky makes his own brief trip forward in

---

[9] The version of *The Bathhouse* quoted from in this chapter is Andrew MacAndrew's in *20th Century Russian Drama* (New York: Bantam, 1963), especially pp. 278–81.

a time machine to the obtuse critical reception his play will face. And did.

Not long after the production of *The Bathhouse* the author committed suicide, and gave us brutal evidence of the tortured sincerity that underlay his satire. It seems miraculous that he could have couched it in such unrelenting farce.

Farce was apparently one inevitable and apt response to the first decade of upheaval visited on Russia by the Revolution. Mayakovsky and other writers, such as his younger contemporary Yuri Olyesha (1899–1960), found themselves caught up not only in its political ferment but also in the artistic ferment of those same years.[10] As citizens, they felt they owed allegiance to a rational, businesslike redistribution of power and wealth; as artists they wanted to exploit new forms generated by free and irrational dartings of the imagination and to follow the lead of the Surrealists.

Olyesha's *The Conspiracy of Feelings* (1928) dramatizes this emotional tug-of-war in the artist's soul, even personifies it as the contrasting Babichev brothers. Andrei Babichev, the head of a food trust, is planning to serve two thousand dinners a day, plus other meals, out of a mass-production kitchen: "scientifically prepared cream of wheat" and "a sea of cabbage soup." When Andrei gets immersed in soup statistics he hears nothing that goes on around him. He is also introducing to the Russian market a new and "sensational" salami, which the crippled but not dead poet in him would like to name after "a girl in classical literature who ate too much salami and went out of her mind from love," always supposing that he can trace such a processed-meat-worshiping equivalent of Ophelia.

While Andrei's enthusiasm over his work disconcerts those around him—he phones his assistant several times during the night to argue about salami—his brother Ivan works not at all, but goes through Moscow disreputably dressed, with a dirty pillow in tow, trying to revive and stir up people's feelings which, he believes, went numb with the Revolution. Both brothers have been warped by ambition.

---

[10] Isaac Babel (1894–1941) and Evgeny Schvarts (1897–1958), two more exceptional Russian authors of this period, each felt divided by the conflicting claims of citizenship and artistry, and both wrote vivid plays with a splendid sense of comedy, Babel as a realist, Schvarts as a fantasist; but their works are not farcical.

Both are intoxicated, not to say mildly insane—Ivan from liquor, Andrei from his joyous extrapolations. Ivan is more obviously Dionysiac, although, like the Dionysos of *The Bacchae*, he is cruel, urging a woman's husband and lover to knife each other, and finally plotting to murder his brother. A feckless young man, whose name, Kavalerov, suggests his cavalier attitude toward life, will be the instrument of the murder. But in the final scene, set in a soccer stadium, Kavalerov, without knowing why he is doing it, kills not Andrei but Ivan, and with him the possibility of a counterrevolution which would have been the fruit of "the conspiracy of feelings." Nobody but Kavalerov himself seems perturbed at this turn of events. Andrei, hearing of his brother's death, calmly declares, "That's the end of the old passions . . . The new world is beginning." And the soccer game gets under way.[11]

Germany, Britain

The deft hands of a playwright like Mayakovsky or Olyesha can shape a political challenge that is cloaked, but not muffled, in a satirical fantasy. Fantasy and satire will take the curse off preaching and teaching very nicely, but if a play is also a farce, its "message" may go down more agreeably, while leaving as much sting in the aftertaste. Another author who practiced more than he preached, Yvan Goll (1891–1950), wrote several fantasies in German, although he was bilingual, born near the border of Germany and France. His play most committed to farce, *Methusalem: or, the Eternal Bourgeois* (1922–23), has for its eponymous character a bloated, goulash-swilling reincarnation of Jarry's Ubu who rules over an international shoe empire. The antagonist, a Russian-Jewish student, leads Methusalem's workers in a demonstration, courts Methusalem's daughter, and impregnates her. The play could have settled into a rhetorical conflict between these figurations of father and son, as happens over and over in German Expressionist plays and films of the period (Reinhard Sorge's *The Beggar*, Georg Kaiser's *Gas Trilogy*, Fritz Lang's *Metropolis*, and

---

[11] Quotations from *The Conspiracy of Feelings* are taken from the translation by Daniel C. Gerould and Eleanor S. Gerould, in *Avant-Garde Drama: A Casebook*, edited by Bernard F. Dukore and Daniel C. Gerould (New York: Thomas Y. Crowell, 1976), pp. 207–56.

others). But the Student, far from being a typically youthful idealist, is a power-hungry seducer, an opposite number, rather than the opposite, of his enemy.

Goll pulls out all the farcical stops with the relish of Jarry or Apollinaire. Both Methusalem and the Student, after being shot, come back to life; this bourgeois *is* eternal, a geriatric improvement over Methuselah, who lived for only nine hundred years. Objects become animate and talk. "The artificial and stuffed animals in the room" where Methusalem falls asleep—a clock cuckoo; a stuffed monkey, cat, and parrot; a bear rug; a stag's head—lambaste Man while a living dog, his best friend, can put up only a weak defense. The Monkey says, "We have been elected by God to clean the world / Of the human garbage / Who foul our rivers, / Burn up our woods, / Fart at the heavens / And who stink on earth like no other creature! / Has any animal ever had to blush? / Has any bird ever sung a false note? / Did a deer ever have gonorrhea? / Did a tiger ever have to read Nietzsche to be Dionysian? / Man is the disgrace of this earth!" Methusalem and his conscience, an image in a mirror, get into a squabble, which he ends by smashing the glass. A machine like a robot tells ethnic jokes when a coin drops into its mouth. Its counterpart, Methusalem's son, has a head made up of mechanical parts: a megaphone for a mouth, a telephone earpiece for a nose, coins for eyes, and a typewriter and antennae in place of a hat. Goll even injects some filmed sequences into the action when Methusalem drifts off into several surreal dreams that betray his obsession with his product, as he tries to hawk his footwear to all the women in his life, to the two gravediggers in a performance of *Hamlet*, and to a regiment of infantry. He also dreams the "revolution of the animals," but this scene is acted out, not filmed, and suggests that he unconsciously confuses his underpaid and rebellious workers with animals.

The dialogue and stage directions have a farcical directness:

METHUSALEM *walks up to* [*his mistress*], *immediately putting his hand into her bosom.*
METHUSALEM: Box calf leather is looking up.
VERONICA: I'm so unhappy. I need an airplane.
METHUSALEM: You're sure you haven't cheated on me?

VERONICA: Nobody has so much as looked into my eyes since
   yesterday.
METHUSALEM: And into your pants?
He completely opens up her blouse.
VERONICA: I'm so dreadfully nervous. I need a million.
METHUSALEM: Impossible. I never give less than three.

The play sustains its farcical conflict between generations
through the closing scene, when Methusalem's daughter has given
birth to the Student's son and is planning a career for him that will
resemble her father's, while the infant wails and won't stop urinat-
ing on her dress.[12]

Goll's much more famous contemporary Bertolt Brecht (1898–
1956) tucked farcical scenes into many of his plays and operas
written in Germany and (while he was in exile) Finland and the
United States.[13] Even in a brief oratorio explicitly called *The Baden
Teaching-Play* (1929) to stress its didactic nature, a farcical sketch
between the choral odes gives us two clowns operating on a third
who is named Mr. Smith (Herr Schmidt or Everyman). Smith is
in pain, and so his fellow clowns oblige him by severing his arms,
his legs, and his head until the pain has gone. This episode could
have been staged almost without alteration in ancient Greece; it
could apply to medical or legal ministrations of our own time; but
if it refers to a political climate, the spectators will "read" it as
easily as they do a newspaper headline.

Brecht's most telling political farce, *The Resistible Rise of Arturo
Ui* (1941), transforms Hitler and his cronies into Al Capone and
his henchmen and prewar Germany into the vegetable market of
Chicago. The play has often been faulted for Brecht's inability to
take a true sounding of Hitler's depths and because Brecht seems
to have lifted his Chicago jocosely from gangster movies of the

---

[12] *Methusalem*, translated by Arthur S. Wensinger and Clinton J. Atkinson, is published in
Playbook 2: Plays for a New Theater (New York: New Directions, 1966), pp. 57–100. Quotations are from pp. 67 and 95.
[13] There is farcical content in Brecht's *Baal* (1918), *Drums in the Night* (1918), *The Wedding*
(1918) and other short plays, *In the Jungle of Cities* (1923), *A Man's a Man* and its interlude
The Elephant Calf (1925), *The Threepenny Opera* (1928), *The Rise and Fall of the City of
Mahagonny* (1929), *St. Joan of the Stockyards* (1930), *The Roundheads and the Peakheads*
(1934), *Mother Courage and Her Children* (1939), *The Good Woman of Setzuan* (1940),
Puntila and His Servant Matti (1941), *Schweik in the Second World War* (1944), *The Caucasian Chalk Circle* (1945), *Trumpets and Drums* (1955).

Thirties, such as *Scarface* and *Little Caesar*, rather than from life. A staging on Broadway by Tony Richardson refueled these criticisms. One had to see how Brecht's own company, the Berliner Ensemble, handled *Arturo Ui* to appreciate that this is a farce, and a great one. Richardson's semiserious approach lost contact with the play's forcefulness and animus; whereas in Brecht's treatment the actors kept their sights on the play itself, not on its political parable or parallels. They went farcically for broke. Ekkehard Schall as Ui made his entrance at a run, tripping over a chair, a table, and a subordinate, and ended up on his back after a somersault down the length of a sofa. A version like this reminds us that despite some stouthearted forays into Brecht's stage territory, much of it remains unexplored, not to say unmapped.

A farce by another dramatist who writes in German, and lives in Zurich, Max Frisch (born 1911), had a similar fate to *Arturo Ui*'s in New York. In *The Firebugs* (1960), a householder named Biedermann (another Everyman) welcomes two incendiaries into his house together with their stock of inflammable materials, and will not turn them out even when they are obviously planning to send the place up in smoke, as they ultimately do. The Off Broadway production directed by Gene Frankel offered chills and relentless acting, but let go of the farce that would have done away with doubts about Biedermann's implausible behavior. The play's social statement is patently true: ordinary people do suffer themselves to be exploited and destroyed; they go so far as to cozy up to their parasites. But to say so on a stage by means of farce will make the point better, faster, more subtly and conclusively. Isn't there a danger, though, that the important statement will get buried under the laughter? There certainly is, and it's precisely this sort of danger that the best theater doesn't shy away from.[14]

W. H. Auden (1907–73) and Christopher Isherwood (born 1904) may have become aware too late of the special potency of farce in political drama. Of their three collaborative efforts *The Dog Be-*

---

[14] Most of Brecht's plays are available in English translations published in two series, *Works of Bertolt Brecht*, General Editor Eric Bentley, and *Brecht: Collected Plays*, edited by Ralph Manheim and John Willett. A farcical scene in *The Caucasian Chalk Circle* in which peasants keep crowding into a tiny hut has often been compared to the cabin scene in *A Night at the Opera*.

The Firebugs was translated into English by Mordecai Gorelik (New York: Hill & Wang, 1963).

neath the Skin (1935), *The Ascent of F6* (1936), and *On the Frontier*
(1938), only the first is farcical, while the others are poetic tracts
—as beautifully written as any modern English drama except
Shaw's, but didactic in a manner that doesn't win over unbelievers
and probably doesn't even unite the believers.

Most of the scenes of *The Dog Beneath the Skin: or, Where Is
Francis?* boil with parody, insolence, and outrageous happenings
in the ripest traditions of farce. Couched in a rich mix of prose,
Gilbertian doggerel, and noble verse, some of the latter aspiring to
Shakespearean heights, these vignettes take place during an epic
search on the part of a Candide-like hero named Alan for a missing
knight, Sir Francis. On his travels Alan is accompanied by a large
dog, who, he doesn't realize, is Sir Francis on all fours and
wrapped in the skin of an Irish wolfhound in order, he says, to
"see people from underneath."

Alan and Francis are present when the King of "Ostnia" courteously and regretfully executes a group of socialists and invites
their widows after the shooting to partake of champagne and
cakes. Man and man-dog visit an insane asylum in "Westland"
very like (and unlike) an interwar Nazi rally, where one lunatic
proclaims, "Let us never forget that we are Westlanders first and
madmen second." In a hospital the dog poses as a nurse; the patient dies, and assembled doctors and nurses chant a requiem from
the Church of England liturgy. On a highway while Alan sleeps,
his left and right feet engage in a conversation, the left in a Cock-
ney dialect, the right with college-educated modulations.

At the Nineveh hotel and restaurant, a patron orders one of the
chorus girls. The waiter inquires: "Will you have her roast, sir, /
Or on Japanese Toast, sir? / With Sauce Allemagne, sir, / Or
stewed in white wine, sir?" The diner replies, "Stewed," and adds,
"But I'll have the fingernails served separately as a savoury. Oh,
and don't forget to remind the Chef to stir the pot with a sprig of
rosemary. It makes all the difference." In a nightclub, a comic
remembered for edifying his audience once before by burning a
priceless Shakespeare First Folio, page by page, tries to cap this
triumph by slashing an original Rembrandt to shreds. Alan is seduced by a Miss Vipond, who happens to be a shopwindow
dummy.

But *Dog* has its scene of self-sabotage close to the end when the seven good characters from a little village line up together and march righteously off the stage and out through the audience. Auden and Isherwood recover, however, by turning this embarrassing moment back into farce, and save the day and the play as the remaining villagers don animal masks and emit "various animal noises, barking, mewing, quacking, grunting, or squeaking," becoming "more incoherent, bestial and fantastic, until at last all are drowned in deafening military chords."[15] This fabulous moment anticipates by more than a decade the end of Ionesco's *Jacques* (discussed in the previous chapter).

France After Surrealism

France, the seedbed of the Enlightenment, the nation renowned for its logic in argument and its legal orderliness, has also, perhaps out of artistic revulsion, been the twentieth century's stronghold of fantasy and farce.

Jean Giraudoux (1882–1944) is thought of as quintessentially French. Most books that allude to him mention his debt to the French neoclassicists, especially Racine, and his distance from the British theater. Yet Giraudoux has in common with British dramatists of the late sixteenth and early seventeenth centuries at least one source of inspiration: that doughty Roman, Seneca. Like Seneca and the Elizabethans, Giraudoux conceives in his plays of a seamless universe wherein humanity, animals, spirit life (the supernatural), plants, and the inanimate belong to one continuum and even conspire to cast a catastrophic, fateful pall, often a tragic pall, over events. We might compare these lines spoken by Ulysses in *Tiger at the Gates* (1935): "Doom has transfigured everything here with the colour of storm: your grave buildings shaking with shadow and fire, the neighing horses, figures disappearing into the dark of a colonnade" with these from Seneca's *Oedipus* (*ca.* A.D. 50) describing the sympathetic aspect of the cosmos during the plague of Thebes: "Apollo's sister, Moon, drifts hardly seen / Across the sky; day, overcast with clouds, / Reveals a pale dull world; the silent night / Is dark, without a star; fog, dense and

---

[15] *The Dog Beneath the Skin* and *The Ascent of F6* are published in *Two Great Plays by Auden and Isherwood* (New York: Random House, undated).

black, / Broods over all the land; the murk of hell / Has swallowed up the heavenly citadels, / The mansions of the gods on high. The corn, / That should be ripe for harvest, bears no fruit; / The golden ears that sway on spring stalks / Soon wither and the barren crop falls dead . . ." The lines also recall doom-laden portents in speeches from *Macbeth, Julius Caesar, King Lear, Henry IV, Part One,* and so on.[16]

But Giraudoux a farceur? To accommodate him here I have to invent a subgenre: gentle farce—an oxymoronic name for a species that almost defies the elasticity of the genre, stretching its confines to pretty near the breaking point. Still, this book has done just that several times already and will do so again. But the conspiracy of matter, living and nonliving, does have its lighter side and can touch on farce. Like one of Shaw's characters, Sir Colenso Ridgeon, Giraudoux might have declared that "life does not cease to be funny when people die any more than it ceases to be serious when people laugh." Or he might have claimed, with Shaw himself, that he was held up by the power of levity. *Duel of Angels* (posthumously published, 1953) is a tragedy bursting with wit and humor. A man in a restaurant stops next to a table where two women are seated to pick up a franc he hasn't dropped. While stooping he engages them in a *sotto voce* conversation that he doesn't complete because his back is killing him. Later a magistrate finds that depriving a famished wife-killer of olives, artichokes, tomatoes, and pimentos "as a form of torture" practiced in jail "seems less effective than the thumbscrew"—even though, as the court clerk remembers, a man who'd murdered his father confessed, when denied his favorite food, cabbage salad, to "the most hair-raising details." In *The Madwoman of Chaillot* (1945) a sewer worker indignantly attacks the rumors that he and his fellow employees keep "a race of girls down there who never see the light of day." However, he concedes that they "may run a beauty contest once in a while. Or crown a mermaid Queen of the May." The

---

[16] The quotation from *Tiger at the Gates* comes from *Jean Giraudoux: Plays,* Vol. 1, translated by Christopher Fry (New York: Oxford University Press, 1963), p. 134; the Oedipus quotation from *Seneca: Four Tragedies and Octavia,* translated by E. F. Watling (New York: Penguin, 1966), pp. 210–11. The Shakespeare passages are *Macbeth,* II, iii, 50–59 and II, iv, 1–20; *Julius Caesar,* II, ii, 14–26 and I, iii, 3–35; *Lear,* III, ii, 1–9; *Henry IV, Part One,* III, i, 13–41.

farcical premise of *Madwoman* is the foiling of a plot to replace
Paris with an oilfield. A lady known as the Countess convinces a
horde of businessmen, middlemen, and prospectors that the sew-
ers are thick with oil, and that they should go down and see it for
themselves. Much as Mayakovsky trapped his obnoxious bureaucrats in the present tense, Giraudoux dispatches his marauders
into a city-sized cesspool and bolts the secret entrance on them.
Once they have gone below ground, Paris, in a burst of Senecan
stoicism, revives: the air grows pure suddenly, the pigeons fly
again, grass sprouts on the streets, and strangers shake hands and
"offer each other almond bars."

Giraudoux's treatment of the supernatural is as disrespectful as
his treatment of tragedy, even while he cheerfully admits ghosts,
naiads, and other apparitions into his plays—a further Senecan
conceit. At roughly the same time as his *The Enchanted* (1933)
appeared onstage, an Italian play, *Death Takes a Holiday* by Al-
berto Cassella, was adapted into a Broadway hit and then into a
lovingly photographed, hokily written film, directed by Mitchell
Leisen. Its heroine falls in love with Fredric March, who handsomely brings Death to life and imposes himself as a houseguest
on a villa full of wealthy, titled folk. In *The Enchanted*, the heroine, Isabel, falls for a ghost, who turns out not to be a ghost until
he is shot by the local authorities. In both stories a live man com-
petes with a spook for the girl. In the film the spook wins because
he is Fredric March and proclaims with a sententiousness typical
of the dialogue that "love does transcend death"; but how exactly
it transcends it we are never shown. A burst of light as the heroine
strolls up a few steps and into Death's arms (has she passed on? or
passed out?) dissolves into the Paramount logo, that starry hillock.
In Giraudoux's play, on the other hand, the ghost loses out, and
his rival, the local Supervisor of Weights and Measures, wins Isabel farcically by tempting her to join him and share the delights of
his civil service career. The text also glitters with farcical confusions, such as two executioners who show up when one is summoned and both glibly answer every question in an improvised
quiz about famous executions of the past; and a scene in which a
police inspector hastily pulls out a letter, hands it to the mayor,
and instructs him to read it to everybody present, "particularly the
last paragraph."

MAYOR: But the last paragraph, particularly . . .

INSPECTOR: Read it. Read it aloud. I want you all to hear what the government says.

MAYOR: The government appears to be very warmly disposed toward you.

INSPECTOR: I am happy to say it is.

MAYOR: It kisses you on your adorable mouth, asks you for a hundred francs, and signs itself, yours ever, Adele.[17]

Alongside Giraudoux's strain of gentle farce there ran in France a current of brutal farce encompassing not only fantasy but also cataclysms, hideous transmutations, and what some outraged observers took to be celebrations of horror, as its authors—principally Antonin Artaud (1896–1948), Boris Vian (1921–59), and Eugène Ionesco (born 1912)—sought formal equivalents in the drama for the destructiveness of the century. Artaud's Theater of Cruelty, intended to purge theatergoers of their violent impulses, took its theoretical tenets from his *The Theater and Its Double.* The essays and the play outline published in this collection in 1938 did not appear in English until twenty years later, a decade after Artaud's death. Then they took the intellectual theater by storm and became the most influential theater documents of the modern era. But well before the book appeared Artaud had tried his hand at scenarios for the stage and screen and several playlets which, as they switch between apocalyptic melodrama and grotesque farce, are like impassioned Surrealism.

The Fountain of Blood (1923), a play at war with itself, contains one series of actions in its dialogue, another in its stage directions. The dialogue tells indirectly of a thwarted love affair as it parades farcical character types past us: a father in armor like a Medieval knight's, a mother who is a wet nurse with ballooning breasts (a mature version of Apollinaire's Thérèse, maybe), a beadle whose wife deceives him (he thinks), and the inevitable naive boy and girl. Meanwhile, the stage directions toss in a hurricane, earth

---

[17] The Shaw quotation comes from Act V of *The Doctor's Dilemma. Duel of Angels* is published in *Jean Giraudoux: Plays, Vol. 1,* quotations from pp. 158, 190–1; *The Madwoman of Chaillot* is in *Jean Giraudoux: Four Plays,* adapted by Maurice Valency (New York: Hill & Wang, 1958), quotations from pp. 40 and 70, and so is *The Enchanted,* quotations from pp. 144 and 133–34.

tremors, collapsing landscapes, and Velikovskian collisions in the heavens—and all this in five pages. In *The Philosopher's Stone* (1931), Artaud practices a few variations on stock figures out of the commedia dell'arte: a doctor who is an alchemist in search of the formula for gold and eternal life, his young wife, Isabelle, and her lover, Harlequin. The Doctor dismembers Harlequin (out of spite or revenge or as an experiment), but the clown soon comes back to life by reassembling himself while the Doctor sleeps. Isabelle then saves him from a second dismemberment and affirms her fidelity by producing from under her skirt a doll likeness of her husband. *There Is No More Firmament* (1931–32), an unfinished scenario, posits the end of everything, not just the world. It masses its characters into crowd scenes and choruses of mad inventors, pathetic politicians, the poor, the maimed, the anonymous. A director who filled in the gaps and filled out the dialogue of this outline for a play, added a fifth "movement" to the four that exist in synoptic form, and went on to stage *Firmament* could choose to make an Expressionist *Man and the Masses* out of it or to take it all the way to Aristophanic farce without distortion.[18]

Artaud's rediscovery after World War II was no fluke. During the war years Europeans had yearned for an idyllic peace. No possible resolution could have measured up to their hopes, but the peace that actually appeared proved unexpectedly bleak: the Cold War; a perpetual Big Bomb scare; and television to numb them before bed. The postwar period has been called an age of indifference or silence, but the silence betokened disappointment, which later broke down into anger and then active resistance when the postwar generation came of age. The bitterness of the Sixties had been presaged in the arts of the Cold War years, for which Artaud's writings could have served as a general manifesto.

The first full-length play by Boris Vian (1921–59) has a title in English, *The Knacker's ABC*, that is not quite as apt as the French meaning: *Knackery for All*. The knacker is an artisan who reduces horses to glue, hair, hides, and strong meat. In this country he has been supplanted by the rendering works, a collective enterprise

---

[18] Translations of these plays by Artaud can be found in *Antonin Artaud: Collected Works*, edited by Victor Corti and in versions by a number of different writers (London: Calder & Boyers, 1968).

that doesn't restrict itself to horses. *The Knacker's ABC* (1946) takes place in a little town in Normandy on June 6, 1944, the date of the Allied D-Day landings as well as the wedding of a knacker's daughter to a German soldier she's been sleeping with for four years. The invasion thus serves as the background for a domestic farce. German and American troops wander into and out of the house, play strip poker together, exchange uniforms for the hell of it. A son who has joined the American paratroopers and an older daughter who is a pinup with a Russian paratroop brigade parachute home for the wedding. The groom gets time out from battle as soon as his current maneuver, a three-yard advance, is over. Out of the contents of some American crates left on the beachhead a do-it-yourself chaplain is assembled to conduct the ceremony. The G.I.s don't realize at first why they are in France: nobody told them about the war. And all through the action, to match the killings outside, people inside the house drop by accident or with the aid of a friendly shove into the knacker's pit. All the main characters finally land in that pit; and the house, the only one left standing in the area, gets blown up by the French authorities, while "the *Marseillaise* suddenly blares out, abominably out of tune." The play, dedicated to "my close enemy, Charlemagne," the king of warriors, is subtitled "a paramilitary vaudeville in one long act." In introducing the published version, Jean Cocteau remarks that "nothing could be more serious than this farce which is not a farce and yet is one," thereby accurately generalizing about every play alluded to in this chapter.

The generals in another Vian play, *The Generals' Tea Party* (published 1965), take afternoon refreshments as they cook up an unbeatable war-game plan—but against whom? Lacking a foe, they finally settle for a second game, Russian roulette, which finishes them off. Once again Vian chooses farcical enactment over rational preaching, carefully eschewing an accusatory tone or talking down to the audience. But this play deals overtly with a collective suicide, and a suicidal tendency forms one of the dominant themes in his last play, *The Empire Builders: or, The Schmürz* (1959); indeed, it overwhelms the farce in this story of a family's flight from a tormenting, inexplicable noise. Where shall they go? Upstairs, to a smaller apartment. And then, when the noise persists, to an even smaller one another flight up. And on into the attic. Each time they move, fewer of them ascend—this family, like Brecht's Mr. Smith, is gradually dismembered—until only the Father is left in the attic, together with the Schmürz, a shuffling, passive figure got up in rags and bandages, wounded and bleeding from being repeatedly struck and kicked by the Father. The Schmürz says not a word; it is simply there like an embodied conscience. And so the Father's ambience has shrunk to an attic where fate walls him in between a noise and a Schmürz. But then the door opens and in the half-light we watch the entry of slinking silhouettes, more Schmürzes (or *Schmürzen?*).[19]

The grave and disquieting curtain effect—can Vian really be the author of those blithe multiple murders that round out his other plays?—identifies *The Empire Builders* as a farce of the Fifties written after the ascendancy—if not in the shadow—of Ionesco because that Rumanian-born Frenchman closes his farces on a somber chord. But the action of each play has, by the end, warned us that the farce is going to switch into a less breezy mood that may be tragic or lyrical, discursive, sinister, visionary, or science-fictional. The playwright works these transpositions by means of some of the most vivid stage metaphors yet contrived. He uses rows of packed chairs to simulate an overflow of guests, a blinding white light for God, and two small windows for death in *The Chairs* (1952); a seat perched on a table for the recesses of a character's memory, fancy, and ambition in *Victims of Duty* (1953); identical cowled and hooded monks for everybody-but-oneself in *Hunger and Thirst* (1965); the sky for the future with its openness/promise and clouds/threats in *A Stroll in the Air* (1963); and rhinoceroid human beings for conformity in *Rhinoceros* (1959). By refining sense out of nonsense, Ionesco has steadily pushed farce to the center of the theatrical arena and has nudged scholars into retrospective appreciation of earlier plays that employ farce as purposefully as he does.

Ionesco loves toying with language. Not even the Surrealists or Jarry or Lewis Carroll has more painstakingly checked out the fantastic and farcical possibilities of words, either as single units or

[19] *The Knacker's ABC*, *The Generals' Tea Party*, and *The Empire Builders* are published separately in translations by Simon Watson Taylor (New York: Grove Press, 1968, 1967, and 1966 respectively). *Knackery for All*, the correct title, also appears in an earlier translation by Marc Estrin in *Playbook 2* (New York: New Directions, 1966).

strung together, for their meanings and the fragility of those meanings; their suggestiveness, provocativeness, obscurity, syllabifica-
tion; their very sounds. Words can enrapture, startle, repel. So can
nonwords. In *Jacques* one character reminds another that he is
"chronometrable," which is shorthand for saying he is growing
older, less eligible, and subject to time's wear and tear. The mother
in the same play calls her son a "mononster," which is a monster
of a word. At the end of *The Chairs* the eagerly awaited Orator,
who is to reveal a great message, stuns the audience when he
proves to be a deaf-mute who, after "desperate efforts," can say
only, "He, mme, mm, mm. Ju, gou, hou, hou. Heu, heu, gu gou,
gueue."

In his earliest plays Ionesco brought fantasy to bear on ordinary,
domestic settings: an "English middle-class interior" in *The Bald
Soprano* (1950), a teacher's study in *The Lesson* (1953), a run-down
living room in *Jacques*, a "petit-bourgeois interior" in *Victims of
Duty* (1952), and a "modest dining room–parlor–study" in
Amédée, or How to Get Rid of It (1953), as if to parody the traditional family farce. In his subsequent plays the fantasy overpowers
the farce or, at any rate, the farce thins out. This happens most
noticeably when Ionesco takes his plays out of doors. The exteriors
of *The Killer* (1958), *A Stroll in the Air*, and *Man with Bags* (1975)
seem to induce in the author a consciousness of man's smallness
on a landscape. Or above it. Bérenger, the hero of *A Stroll in the
Air*, first leaps and bounces several feet off the ground, then takes
flight into space on a bicycle that falls away from him (the front
wheel, the back wheel, the frame, the handlebars) to allow him to
soar down to a neat landing; he next hauls himself into the air by
the branches of an imaginary tree, then rockets off into space, up,
up, and away, as Superman was to do a few years later in Harold
Prince's musical. But the visions Bérenger encounters in the heavens include "columns of guillotined men . . . giant grasshoppers
and fallen angels . . . oceans of blood and mud . . . bottomless
pits opening over the plains . . . deserts of ice, deserts of fire
. . ." Ionesco appears to have wished to deal more explicitly than
before with certain serious implications in his drama, such as the
infinity of time and space as oppressors of finite, isolated man, and
the unreliability of words written and spoken.

But he'd also shown himself sensitive to attacks on his artistry from British critics in 1958–59 during a dispute known later as the London Controversy. Kenneth Tynan and others accused him of superficiality, scorning political and social issues, and starting a cult among what Tynan called "ostriches" of fashionable pessimism. Possibly Ionesco went further and deduced that his critics resented his dependence on a genre once considered mere entertainment. None of them leveled such a charge exactly, but if he read it into what they said I don't think he was altogether mistaken.

Tynan had written: "M. Ionesco certainly offers an 'escape from realism': but an escape into what? A blind alley, perhaps, adorned with *tachiste* murals. Or a self-imposed vacuum, wherein the author ominously bids us observe the absence of air. Or, best of all, a funfair ride on a ghost train, all skulls and hooting waxworks, from which we emerge into the far more intimidating clamour of diurnal reality." In other words, Ionesco's letting us escape from realism seals us off from reality. But realism is only a conventional and hackneyed method for representing reality, which can be represented just as cogently by other methods, Ionesco's among them. I would contend that his plays do address themselves to reality. No realistic play I can think of deals with the reality of an evening of conversation at home with friends better than does *The Bald Soprano*, which jiggles the commonplaces of parlor chitchat into a series of piercingly funny contradictions, irrelevancies, and mechanical responses, as theatrical as the aphorisms of Wilde. *The Lesson*, in which an effete old teacher catechizes a young female pupil who has a toothache, and finally knifes her, hits us with a real and terrifying lesson about the antagonism between instruction and learning. In *The Chairs* a man and woman of over ninety engage in a garbled colloquy which, if we listen attentively, touches on the real fears and unanswered questions of old age.[20]

In the nineteenth century and before, plays were mostly well shaped. The first act proposed consequences that a spectator could foresee within a narrow range of probability, as he can in today's

---

[20] *The Bald Soprano, The Lesson, Jacques (Jack),* and *The Chairs,* translated by Donald M. Allen are in *Ionesco: Four Plays* (New York: Grove Press, 1958); *Rhinoceros* is translated by Derek Prouse (New York: Grove Press, 1960); *The Killer,* translated by Donald Watson, is in *Ionesco: Three Plays* (London: John Calder, 1958); *A Stroll in the Air* is translated by Donald Watson (New York: Grove Press, 1968); *Man With Bags* is adapted by Israel Horovitz (New York: Grove Press, 1977). "The London Controversy" appears in Ionesco's *Notes and Counter Notes* (New York: Grove Press, 1964), pp. 87–108.

Broadway and television dramas. The playwright was god, a justice machine that tipped its scales one way, then the other, and eventually righted the balance so that the characters got what they deserved and the audience what it had been made to want. Reports of the death of the other God encouraged playwrights to behave in a more fickle way toward their characters. No longer feeling constrained by divine judgment, they meted out injustice with an even hand. Many villains waxed fatter; many martyrs died uncelebrated; many heroes suffered death—or worse, life.

In the fantasies of Samuel Beckett (born in Ireland, 1906) the characters themselves have changed from the usual dramatis personae. In the course of the action they seem not to change; and they seem resigned to their plight; they take whatever the playwriting god hands them. I say "seem" in both cases. When Beckett's plays are staged, if the characters don't detectably change and if they *appear* resigned, the performance becomes lethargic. If, on the other hand, a director pays heed to the characters' complaints and if they resist, actively struggle against the odds, refusing to sink into an ooze of *Weltschmerz*, if they *make the attempt* to change, not only will the play brim with vivacity, it will also prove funny.

Beckett, like Ionesco, has admittedly retreated from farce in his later, nearly depersonalized dramatic miniatures, in which the characters appear in urns and come to momentary life only when spotlit (*Play*, 1964); or a Mouth hopelessly intones while its dark, cloaked Auditor helplessly listens (*Not I*, 1971); or three undifferentiated women sit on a bench (*Come and Go*, 1968); or the characters are merely overheard whispering, groaning, muttering in certain radio plays (*Embers*, 1959; *Words and Music*, 1962; *Cascando*, 1963); or a mute man in a room is battered by an accusing female voice in the television play *Eh Joe* (1967). But there is no reason to make the earlier works conform with the near-immobility and dirgelike beauties of the more recent ones. *Waiting for Godot* (1952), *Endgame* (1956), the two mimes *Act Without Words I* (1957) and *Act Without Words II* (1960), *Krapp's Last Tape* (1959), *Happy Days* (1963), and the sprightly radio play *All That Fall* (1956) have a farcical spirit that makes their characters, no matter how oppressed, irrepressible.

Soon after *Waiting for Godot* opened, critics recognized the byplay between Vladimir and Estragon as a looping together of muffled vaudeville acts. When the play reached the United States, billed as "the laugh hit of two continents," audiences in Florida saw it played with two competing comics, Bert Lahr and Tom Ewell. For the Broadway stint, E. G. Marshall, a "legit" actor, replaced Ewell, leaving Lahr the unquestioned top banana of the show. Less than a decade later, when Alan Schneider shot Beckett's *Film* (1965), he had the inspiration of casting Buster Keaton in the double role of a character who is both the Object ("O") and the Eye ("E"), the observed and the observer, the former pursued by the latter. Keaton conferred on the short picture his set, lined, barely scrutable face (a wry comment on the handsome young Buster remembered from his film classics of the Twenties); his acute sense of self-awareness and of being watched; and a nostalgia for those farcical triumphs of the silent era, for *Film* has no dialogue.

Just as the last act of *The Empire Builders* sums up the Ionesco era, it also has affinities with Beckett. A person who has voluntarily entered the attic of his or her imagination and cannot leave and has peopled it with Schmürzes could serve as the ultimate meaning of most of Beckett's plays. The setting—whether open like the unending plain of *Happy Days*, in the dead center of which Winnie pokes up from an imprisoning mound (mind?), or the country road in *Godot*, or enclosed like the "bare interior" of *Endgame*, Hamm's home, or Krapp's den, or the "violently lit" platform in *Act Without Words II*—refracts onto the characters their own psychological state: wanting out or away, but remaining. In *Act Without Words I* the sole character does try to leave the onstage "desert" with its "dazzling light" but keeps being flung back into view; there he is tantalized by a carafe of water which, every time he goes to seize it, is withdrawn. This mime act verges on the self-conscious type of farce, theatricalism, but it illustrates as well as any of Beckett's plays the difficulty we have in laughing at the characters without an accompanying feeling that we are the watchers of our own futile antics.[21]

---

[21] *Waiting for Godot* (New York: Grove Press, 1954) and *Happy Days* (New York: Grove Press, 1961) are published separately. Beckett's other plays, including his scenario for *Film*, appear in *Endgame* (New York: Grove Press, 1958), *Krapp's Last Tape and Other Dramatic*

The United States

The broad river of farcical fantasy in this century takes its impetus, as we have seen, from several fast-running streams: A) disenchantment with politicians, warriors, businessmen, scientists, consumers, and professionals like lawyers, doctors, teachers, as well as with free-lancing artists; B) adaptations of vaudeville turns and revue numbers; C) sly borrowings and distortions from literature, philosophy, the drama, journalism, and the clichés of historians. In the United States, we find many ingenious combinations. Robert Hivnor's *Too Many Thumbs* (1947), for instance, adds A to C above in a subtle amalgam of farce, high comedy, and tragedy. Two chimpanzees occupy laboratory cages in "an unheard-of university." One, named Psyche, has only a "mediocre" brain, but the other, Too Many Thumbs, is "brilliant" and develops over three acts into Tom Smith, a "medium-sized, normal-looking young man with well-brushed hair and a charming smile." But Tom passes on up through the normal range, for he evolves into a Christ-like seer who can read the thoughts of his human instructors. Even then his evolution continues until, in panic at his new abnormality, he hangs himself. Hivnor's *The Ticklish Acrobat* (1949) locates a team of American archeologists in Europe near the Adriatic. As they dig deeper they unearth new, more remote civilizations. The farcical apposition pits modern urban sophisticates against rural folk and ancient ruins, and brash young America against mysterious old Europe, which yields up a few of its timeless treasures but not its secrets. *The Assault upon Charles Sumner* (1966), one of the most ambitious plays of the postwar years, is Hivnor's account of a divided America (long before the Kerner Report came out), in which the self-righteous and yet in many ways admirable senator from Massachusetts and foe of slavery is repeatedly flogged with a stick—even, at last, by the black man whom he proposes for admittance to heaven. The action, set in the North, the South, and Purgatory (a sort of ethereal Washington, D.C.), has a minstrel show, a jazz combo, and

---

Pieces (New York: Grove Press, 1960), and *Cascando and Other Short Dramatic Pieces* (New York: Grove Press, 1970).

a comic funeral and is a melting pot of historical and fictional characters.[22]

Arnold Weinstein's *Red Eye of Love* (1961) paints a different portrait of America, or rather, of American enterprise and consumption, whose pinnacle is a building forty-nine stories high, a department store of meat that offers varied cuts and parts on every level. A quaint triangle consisting of an indecisive hero who seeks the "key" to happiness; a heroine who dances in the street, "moving the daylight this way and that"; and a millionaire butcher (the other man) who makes up poems but can't read or write are the means and the ends of this grab bag of farcical scenes. They satirize some of the follies and excesses of the big city from the Twenties, the Depression, and the War on into the early Sixties. Significantly, among the thirty-odd characters only the rich butcher doesn't age with time.[23]

In two later shows, Weinstein went further in indulging his predilection for vaudeville and versification. For *Fortuna* (1962), which he adapted from Eduardo de Filippo's *Fortuna with a Capital F*, he wrote the book and most of the lyrics to music by Francis Thorne. He followed this excursion into the fortunes and misfortunes of a Neapolitan rogue, a distant descendant of commedia zanies, with *Dynamite Tonite* (1964), a mock-operatic performance (music by William Bolcom). *Dynamite* exploded out of a military bunker in an unidentified no-man's-land during an "unspecified war." One of its notable features was the unusually strong cast of farceurs for an Off Broadway presentation: Gene Wilder, David Hurst, and Lou Gilbert, besides several graduates of the improvisational Second City company who included Barbara Harris and Anthony Holland. Paul Sills, who codirected with the author, had been one of the organizers of the Second City. (See Chapter 13.)

By 1960 some of the innovations of European farce had begun to affect younger American dramatists. *The American Dream* (1959) by Edward Albee (born 1928), and his only farce, and *Oh*

---

[22] *Too Many Thumbs* is published separately (Minneapolis, Minn.: University of Minnesota Press, 1949); *The Ticklish Acrobat* appears in *Playbook 1* (New York: New Directions, 1956); and *The Assault Upon Charles Sumner* in *Playbook 2* (Plays for a New Theater, New York: New Directions, 1966).

[23] *Red Eye of Love* by Arnold Weinstein (New York: Grove Press, 1962).

*Dad, Poor Dad, Mama's Hung You in the Closet and I'm Feelin'
So Sad*, "a Pseudoclassical Tragifarce in a Bastard French Tradition" (1960) by Arthur Kopit (born 1937), took aim at the close-knit
family and blasted it. *Oh Dad* checks a domineering American
matron, Madame Rosepettle, and her pampered, jittery son, her
silver piranha, and two famished Venus Flytraps into a plush hotel
suite in Havana. There Madame scares the wits out of a millionaire
reckless enough to woo her, while her seventeen-year-old son
smothers a girl to death with her own uplifted skirt after she, a
daylight succubus, tries to undress him. During this last sequence
the stuffed corpse of the late Mr. Rosepettle, which Madame takes
on tour with her, falls off the closet hook where she'd hung it and
onto the young couple, hampering their movements. Did the play
constitute an attack on overprotective motherhood? On absent
fatherhood? On American interferences in Cuba before Castro or
"containment" after Castro? Or, more broadly, on the brutalities
of imperialism?

Without writing off these and other possibilities, I'd guess that
Kopit is having a good, grim time at the expense of *The Rose
Tattoo* (1950) by Tennessee Williams. In that tear-stained tale the
middle-aged heroine, who is something of a blown rose herself,
wears a rose-colored dress and a rose in her hair, carries a rose-
decorated fan, and lives amid rose-patterned wallpaper. Her lover
tames his hair with oil of rose brilliantine. Her daughter, Rosa
delle Rose, is named after her late husband, Rosario delle Rose,
who had a rose tattoo on his chest. Just before the play ends, a
glass of wine is poured for the heroine, but the author doesn't say
whether it's red, white, or rosé. Kopit's farce also plays roses, roses
all the way. Madame Rosepettle calls her pet piranha Rosalinda,
after another Rosalinda, her late husband's secretary. The millionaire she flirts with and terrifies calls himself Commodore
Roseabove, and the girl throttled by Young Rosepettle is named
Rosalie.

Kopit has Ionesco's knack of braiding grotesquely amusing incidents into a grotesquely fearsome ending. In *Chamber Music*
(1962) eight bizarre women who belie the innocent-sounding title
of the piece present themselves respectively as Gertrude Stein,
Joan of Arc, Amelia Earhart, Pearl White (or sometimes Theda
Bara), Susan B. Anthony, Queen Isabella of Spain, the explorer

Osa Johnson, and Frau Mozart, wife of Wolfgang Amadeus. And they dress accordingly. The action rumbles along brightly even after we gather that they are in an insane asylum; but then we learn that they are meeting to forestall an attack by the male patients. One of them, they decide, must kill herself and be deposited outside the men's ward with all their signatures attached to the body as a warning. When no one volunteers to become the corpse, they set upon "Amelia Earhart" and murder her. After that, their minds drift away from the rest of the plan, as though the ritual murder had drained them. (This play also looks forward indirectly to Kopit's much later *Wings*, 1978, in which a former pioneer aviatrix, much like Amelia Earhart, is recovering from brain surgery.) [24]

Bruce Jay Friedman's plays avoid the mechanistic plotting of well-made farces, but have in common with them ample references to big names and the stuff of gossip columns, the fodder and detritus of pop culture. Friedman writes good-natured fantastications, rather than satire. The male characters have hang-ups about the impressions they make on their bosses, their subordinates, and women. The dialogue looks loose and scatterbrained, crammed with inconsequentialities, but is actually polished to a high glaze, with the consequential word in each sentence cunningly placed for maximum laughs so that the lines become a boon for actors. *Scuba Duba* (1967) takes an American advertising man, Harold Wonder, on vacation to the South of France, where he risks losing his wife to a skin diver and himself to a skin-ornamenter, a teen-aged girl with flower designs painted in the generous gap between the two parts of her bikini. But Wonder can be seen as a narrator-nebbish, who serves to introduce a series of bravura solos enacted by the other characters. A similar structure governs *Steambath* (1972). Sweaty men, their loins toweled, wait their turn to go through a door to oblivion. The tiled premises are an anteroom to death, and the Puerto Rican attendant is God. When challenged, He can work up a colorful miracle or two with lighting to confirm

---

[24] *Oh Dad, Poor Dad* is published separately (New York: Hill & Wang, 1960). *Chamber Music* appears in *The Day the Whores Came Out to Play Tennis and Other Plays* (New York: Hill & Wang, 1965), which also contains *The Conquest of Everest*, a cheerfully farcical one-act; *The Hero*, a farcical mime; and the title play, which is closer to comedy than to farce.

His divinity. The doomed men protest and plead to fight off the inevitable: they have unfinished business and appointments; they need time to prepare a winning defense; other people need them. They are simply not about to die if they can help it. Not yet. Their defensive maneuvers are, once again, a lineup of farcical turns by characters who have updated Ben Jonson's humors.[25]

As the Sixties wore on, farce saturated the American drama of New York's Off Off Broadway stages, a scene of youthful dreams, tryouts, showcases, fads, unpaid professionals and overapplauded novices, vitality, shlock, and uncontrolled talent. This fresh farce vented some of the grudges and hopes of the under-thirties, both players and spectators. Written rapidly and staged with a minimum of rehearsal, it deliberately provided for insertions of asides, jokes, political (often antiwar) commentary, audience participation, and bursts of spontaneity. The times felt chaotic. Too many electronic outlets bombarded people with news that was good, bad, and un- believable, but mostly unbelievably bad; and farce struck the Off Off enthusiasts as an appropriately chaotic response. Many of the plays brought together characters who were strangers and talked at, not to, one another, never listening; a common structure was the series of confessional tirades only tenuously linked. A few of the most entertaining and glistening of these farce-fantasies came from Rosalyn Drexler. Her *Hot Buttered Roll* and *Home Movies* (both 1963–64) alternated poetry, slang, and dignified sentences that sound like quotations, and sometimes are: another technique that goes back to Jarry.[26]

Two of the most sumptuous farcical fantasies since Witkiewicz and Giraudoux have come from an unexpected source, Dostoev- sky. Robert Montgomery, in his *Subject to Fits* (1971) and *Stavro- gin's Creatures* (1973), plucks armfuls of characters out of *The Idiot* and *The Possessed* respectively, and bulls them through situ- ations analogous to the ones in the novels. Adaptations of prose fiction, sometimes sponsored by producers, rear up all the time on Broadway, and are a Hollywood staple. Montgomery's plays, though, are not adaptations, but reminiscences or reinventions,

---

[25] Bruce Jay Friedman: *Scuba Duba* (New York: Simon and Schuster, 1967) and *Steambath* (New York: Knopf, 1971).
[26] *Hot Buttered Roll* appears in *Theater Experiment: An Anthology of American Plays,* edited by Michael Benedikt (New York: Doubleday, 1967), pp. 182–213.

what he calls "responses." *Subject to Fits*, as staged by A. J. Antoon, crackled with music and dancing and bombastically funny acting, like a wild playing out of Dostoevsky's subtext. The play's scenes cut one another short; each tramples on the one before. A stage direction pictures the hero—Prince Myshkin, that radiant innocent—as "bouncing and being bounced" into and out of several scenes at great speed. Myshkin is an epileptic surrounded by crazies. One can visualize the crush of events and encounters he's oppressed by as a dramatizing of compressed images that dart through his mind in the course of an epileptic fit. Phrases and clauses explode out of the ones that precede them: "IPPOLIT: . . . I dreamed you had an epileptic fit and fell down a staircase. And I crawled over to you and you looked at me kindly, then more kindly, and more and more, until finally you were looking at me so kindly your forehead cracked. Then you took my hand and put it kindly through the crack and looked at me with great honesty as I lay there with my hand around your brain . . ."

Sentences crowd together and chop one another down:

NATASHA *(embracing Myshkin)*: Prince! I'll be your princess. I shall impose tariffs! Prince! We shall rule the stew and read children's stories. We shall come true . . .
(Myshkin is cold, confused. . . . Natasha breaks away.)
OFF WITH HIS HEAD!

Speeches fly away from each other:

IVOGLIN: Ganya was thirteen, Ippolit was playing under the rug like he always did. My wife had just stabbed me in the shoulder with a meat knife. I had a terrible headache. The weather outside was awful. We were having potato soup and tongue again for dinner. I was in a bad mood.
LEBEDEV: Sitting on babies' faces, sticking ear wax in your neighbor's beer, and pulling down your pants in front of grandma!

The effect is of Chekhov imposed on Ionesco, or Seurat on Goya. It's American *and* international in flavor, new *and* traditional. And it's farcical, despite the rich mix of emotions that ferment in Montgomery's text.

TWELVE

Stage Realism After Chekhov and Shaw

At the end of the third and last act of *Tango* (1965) by Slawomir Mrożek (born 1930), one character clasps his partner in the unorthodox hold of the tango and they perform tango variations to the melody of "La Cumparsita." Their movements appear grotesque because the dancers are both men, and as they go through their intricate footwork they thread their way across and around two dead bodies.

The dance intrudes into what looks on the face of it like a domestic farce. For *Tango* has a lineup of characters who correspond to the ones in a routine TV series expanded from a Broadway comedy. The young hero, Arthur, brims with ideals, while those of his father have wasted away. Arthur's fadedly attractive mother has lapses of memory. His grandmother and great-uncle are anachronisms. The love interest consists of Ala, Arthur's dumb and sexy cousin of eighteen. But for a TV series *Tango* has peculiarities. Arthur doesn't get the girl. He doesn't win the friendship of his rival. He doesn't close the generation gap between his father and himself. The generation gap, as a matter of paradox, has been turned upside down by the author. Instead of a son who rails at his parents for their middle-class manners, caution, worship of money, and disgusting conventionality, we have an impeccably tailored young man who yearns for an orderly, harmonious life. Instead of parents who nag their son to clean up his room and person, we have a pair of middle-aged slobs who exist as though there were no tomorrow. Instead of a happy ending for Arthur, he is murdered. The family's living room, far from being one of those expensively decorated and furnished stage parlors, looks like the aftermath of a white-elephant sale. Uneaten food lies about. So do a catafalque, a wedding dress, and Arthur's baby carriage (he is now twenty-five).

His mother and father were certified members of the avant-garde before they married. They danced the tango when, as Father says, it took courage to do that in public. Mother now wears slacks and suspenders, which were outrageous for a woman in the 1930s. Father rarely bothers to change out of his pajamas. The two older members of the family, Grandmother and her brother, Great-uncle Eugene, go along with the general informality. Grandma wears a jockey cap and sneakers; Uncle Eugene, khaki shorts and plaid knee socks. But these last two are not entirely happy about conditions in the home; as a mild protest, Uncle Eugene sports a swallowtail coat, a dirty stiff collar, a wide tie, and a pearl stickpin. Then there's Eddie, the outsider from nobody-knows-where, a heavily built redneck. He scratches his backside, belches aggressively, and from time to time runs a comb through his greased hair. He eats up all the sugar in the house. He borrows Uncle Eugene's toothbrush to shine his shoes. He's an easygoing soul and comes in handy for various tasks around the house, such as making up a fourth for bridge.

Of that house we see only the living room and part of a small room off it. Father has taken over all the other rooms for his artistic experiments, one of which he stages, a surrealistic puppet show about Adam and Eve in Paradise. Father and Mother have grown slothful and complacent. Long ago the two of them fought for, and helped to win, the battles for free thought, free love, eccentric clothing, and general permissiveness. In 1928, before they were married, they undressed and made love "in the first row of the orchestra at the opening night of Tannhäuser," while her parents looked on, dumbfounded. Now they have raised a son who wants to be a doctor and respectable. Mother is heartbroken. She always dreamed Arthur would become an artist. "When I was carrying him in my womb, I ran through the woods stark naked, singing Bach. All for nothing!"

The situation is worse than she thinks. Arthur has decided to start a counterrevolution against his parents. He enlists Uncle Eugene, who still sometimes dreams of "the good old days," as we might guess from the swallowtail jacket. As for Ala, the alluring teen-ager who has just moved in but already glides around like a temptress in her nightgown, she doesn't know why she came or how long she will stay; and Arthur appears unsure whether to recruit her for his counterrevolution or seduce her. He begins by enunciating lofty principles about restoring "the right kind of values," but suddenly breaks off, "flings himself at Ala, and tries to kiss her." Ala would sooner be made love to, without the principles. But he gains all her attention when he proposes marriage. They will have "a genuine old-fashioned wedding with an organ playing and bridesmaids marching down the aisle." Ala will get to wear a wedding gown as "white as snow." Father will "at long last be forced to button his fly."

Next Arthur implicates his father in the counterrevolution. To rid the family of Eddie, whom Arthur finds "repulsive" and an "idiot" and a "pig," Father must assert his manhood and shoot him. But why? Arthur hands his father the revolver used in the Adam and Eve puppet show, and explains, "He sleeps with Mother." Which Eddie does. Father is not pleased about being cuckolded. Neither is he a killer. But after his son taunts him for being "a hero in pajamas," he shouts, "You know what I'll do? I'll take care of this whole thing tomorrow." Arthur accuses his father of being "stuck in a farce." Very well, Eddie must die. Father admits, "I've had it in for that bastard for a long time." He marches into the room where Mother and Eddie have gone. Arthur waits. Nothing happens. Finally he flings open the door. Grandma, Mother, and Eddie have roped Father into their bridge game. They needed a fourth.

Arthur sees no point in delaying his coup any longer. He snatches the revolver from his father, orders him to fasten his fly; calls in Ala, makes her promise to marry him the next day; sends Eddie out to the kitchen; secures Grandma's blessing on his marriage.

Next day the room looks like a middle-class parlor from about 1910. It has been straightened up and cleaned for the wedding. So have the characters. Father, forsaking his pajamas, wears a suit, white spats, a stiff collar; his hair is "combed, pomaded, and parted in the middle." Eddie, in a valet's "crimson vest with black stripes," is addressed as Edward. The scene would indeed be Edwardian if there were such an era in the history of Poland, where the play was written. Uncle Eugene, in charge of the ceremony, stands prepared to photograph the wedding group with an ancient tripod plate camera that doesn't work. But where is the bridegroom?

When he turns up, Arthur is drunk, untidy, listless. He got drunk out of despair. He can't go back to the old life but doesn't know how to proceed with the new one. Before long Grandma comes in, leaning on a cane, and announces that she's going to die. She clambers up on the catafalque and dies. Her strange, willed death galvanizes Arthur. Now he realizes what he needs: power, the supreme power over the life and death of others. He begins to rant boozily; calls the family "unthinking cattle" and himself "the act, the will, and the way." By this time he has lifted a chair onto the table and sits on it like an emperor surveying his minions. But he means business. He will assert his power over life and death with an act of murder: "First we're going to rub out Uncle Eugene." His chosen executioner, Eddie, chases the old fellow around the room and has trapped him—when Ala drops a bombshell.

She cries out to Arthur, "I've been unfaithful to you. With Eddie." It had happened that morning. She didn't think Arthur would mind. He does mind. After momentarily losing control of his voice and limbs, he stumbles in search of the revolver. Eddie has it. He hits Arthur in the back of the neck with the butt. Then he clasps his hands and "swings them down on Arthur's head like an axe."

Did Eddie mean to kill Arthur? He seems surprised. But since he has assumed the power over life and death, he's now the leader. He reassures his followers: he's a regular guy, easy to get along with, provided they do what they're told. He puts on Arthur's jacket—a tight fit, but he gets into it. Father and Mother are allowed to leave the room, although Eddie warns them, "Be ready to come running when I call." Ala goes out too, uttering a war widow's line from a B movie: "Arthur loved me, nobody can take that away from me." Eddie next celebrates his accession to power. He removes Mendelssohn's Wedding March from a tape recorder and replaces it with "La Cumparsita." He clasps Uncle Eugene around the waist and "they dance all the figures of the tango." The curtain falls. "La Cumparsita" is still heard . . . "from numerous loudspeakers throughout the house" as the lights go up.[1]

If the surreal, or fantasy, makes what Apollinaire calls a "reasonable use of the improbable," realism in the drama makes a reasonable use of the probable. We can believe in the characters; they seem like real people during the performance, and afterward we still feel they could have existed or even that they did *and do* exist. The events they took part in could have happened. The settings they lived in remind us of actual interiors and exteriors we've seen, or seen illustrated, or read or heard about. The play amounts to an organized but plausible facsimile of life. Still, the pioneers and monarchs of nineteenth-century realism—Ibsen, Strindberg, Becque, Hauptmann, Verga, Chekhov, and Shaw—chose this mode not only because it gave their plays the appearance of life captured in flight and compressed, but also because realism is absorbent; it can soak up parables, myths, allegories, and other types of parallel story and it can keep them partially concealed. So too can fantasy, but the parallel stories in a fantasy are generally easier to detect. For the farces of Oscar Wilde and Shaw one must extend the definition. They make not a reasonable, but a slightly unreasonable use of the probable. Their dialogue doesn't limit itself to mimicry of natural speech; it rises to levels of paradox and rhetoric that real people could not achieve spontaneously. On through this century the dialogue of realistic farces has often alternated between the lifelike, homely, stammering incertitudes of Chekhov's characters and the heightened, polished speechifying sustained by Wilde's and Shaw's.

Tango has both. In addition to its lighthearted household squabbles, Arthur and his father engage in aesthetic and political arguments over artistic form and violence; whether they are living out a tragedy or a farce; whether it's desirable, or even possible, to turn back the clock to a more orderly era (if any era *was* more orderly). The characters remain plausible for the most part; they are hardly more kooky than the family in *You Can't Take It with You*. Yet

---

[1] The English translation of *Tango* is by Ralph Manheim and Teresa Dzieduscycka (New York: Grove Press, 1968).

their behavior forces us to ask questions—questions of the sort, questions of motive, that wouldn't occur to us during or after the Kaufman and Hart play. Why does Arthur appoint Uncle Eugene his deputy during the coup but then change his mind and decree that the old man must be the first to die? Why does he urge his father to kill Eddie, whom he detests, who has slept with his mother and, a further provocation, sleeps with Ala, and then invite Eddie to be his executioner, "the right arm of my spirit, my word made flesh"? Why does Eddie round on Arthur and kill him? And why doesn't Eddie use the gun? What is the purpose of the aesthetic and other disputes? Why the tango at the end? And why that title?

Inside the domestic farce several parallel stories are agitating to get out. One is a literary parody; the play rings with echoes of *Hamlet*, of Aeschylus' trilogy *The Oresteia*, and of plays and novels by an assortment of Polish writers: Mickiewicz, Slowacki, Wyspianski, Witkiewicz, and Gombrowicz, some farcical, some not.[2]

---

[2] I gladly yield the explication of the Polish and Greek allusions to some hardworking Polish and classical exegetes. But since we are all *Hamlet* specialists, here come a few tentative conjectures for the general reader, based on *Tango*'s analogies with *Hamlet*.

In the first place, we have to recognize the rise of Fortinbras in postwar Poland. A number of recent Polish plays have opposed a Hamlet character, a spiritual man, to a Fortinbras, or a man of action—literally, a "strong in arm." The Norwegian prince, often omitted from English-language productions for the sake of brevity or a smaller cast (*vide* Laurence Olivier's movie) or simply out of ignorance, has become an emblematic figure in Polish drama of the Fifties and Sixties. It may be that Fortinbras' objective in *Hamlet*, to launch a war against Poland, has made him seem to the Poles like a personification of their national and eternal enemy, Germany and Russia rolled into one.

In *Tango*, Eddie plays Fortinbras to Arthur's envious Hamlet. (Hamlet's envy of Fortinbras is voiced in that magnificent speech "How all occasions do inform against me," which, like Fortinbras, sometimes gets shorn away in production.) This particular Fortinbras is present throughout the play; that is because Eddie doubles as the other powerful opponent of Hamlet, Claudius, who sleeps with Gertrude, Hamlet's mother. Arthur's father, the derivative artist and coward, stands in for the Ghost of Hamlet senior (Arthur: "I used to have a father. Not anymore"), but it's Arthur who pushes his father toward revenge, not the other way around, as in *Hamlet*. Uncle Eugene also has two roles: as the Polonius of the household who becomes the unimaginative Horatio when he befriends Arthur. With Ala as an Ophelia who has sex constantly in mind, but does not have to go mad to reveal it, the principal parts are filled, save for Laertes. Grandma is an outsider. I would speculate that she is a personified country. Mrożek has not overtly placed *Tango* in Poland, but as Jan Kott has said, its locale is unmistakably "Poland, that is, Everywhere," a tweaking of Alfred Jarry's famous remark that his *Ubu Roi* takes place in "Poland, that is, Nowhere." Thus, Grandma is the old Poland, or Denmark, or Everywhere. She doesn't want to face any more storms; after the coup she lies down and dies.

Arthur-Hamlet tries to put the time back into joint. He must do so over the opposition of his family (the Court in *Hamlet*, including Rosencrantz and Guildenstern). He is killed

A second is a political parable, and has to do with the futility of theoretical challenges (Arthur's, his father's, Uncle Eugene's) when they come up against brute force (Eddie). A third, an aesthetic allegory, tells of a critic, Arthur, who is a purist; opposes the decadent art of his time, the worn-out Surrealism still espoused by his parents; and would like to swap it for art that's traditional, orderly, harmonious, and therefore susceptible to his kind of criticism. But after gaining the allegiance of the fickle public, Ala, and overthrowing the art he dislikes, he has nothing to replace it with; he's a critic, after all, not an artist. At that point when, intoxicated with his new, aimless power, he tries to impose himself as a sheer arbiter who will say what goes and what doesn't (who lives and who dies), the State in the person of Eddie steps in. So far the State has been content to stand by quietly but watchfully. Now it wipes out the impotent critic, and establishes *its* order and harmony, in the form of a tango. Aesthetic considerations, Mrożek seems to be saying, are ultimately political too, for the tango is foreign to Poland. Foreign to everywhere. Where does it come from? Africa? Perhaps. Latin America? Unlikely, despite the Spanish-sounding name. Out of the mind or off the feet of some promoter of the Twenties, when it enjoyed a vogue in the United States? Who knows? In contemporary Poland, at any rate, the government— or, to borrow Harold Laski's phrase, the ultimate coercive power in the State—is also foreign and imposed, even if its human apparatus is native-born. Insist on orderly art, then, and with the help of the State you'll get it. But it may not correspond to the order you wanted, and you may get it over your dead body.[3]

Tango happens to be a first-rate play which, even with its freight of parallel stories, maintains its impetus as a farce. On the boards its primary action is what counts. There are farces that swing as

---

trying. And much as Fortinbras strides in at the end of Act V, after the principals have slaughtered one another, and scoops up Denmark, so Eddie the strong in arm doesn't show his muscle until the closing scenes of *Tango*.

[3] Mrozek's short plays, some of them collected in *Six Plays by Slawomir Mrozek*, translated by Nicholas Bethell (New York: Grove Press, 1967), are also parables under the guise of farces written in a mixture of realistic and fantastic styles. *Out at Sea*, for example, has three men adrift on a raft and debating over which one of them will allow himself to be eaten by the others. Just when one capitulates, the other two discover some food, but they decide to let him go ahead anyway, because he feels he is making a noble gesture and has found his "true freedom."

much intellectual baggage as *Tango* does but have a primary action
that isn't funny, or not funny enough. Günter Grass's *The Wicked
Cooks* (1961), for example, which is part realism, part fantasy. Six
cooks try to wrest a secret recipe for "gray soup" out of a man
called the Count who makes the soup but doesn't quite know how
he does it. The cooks are not really cooks, but crooks; the recipe is
not a recipe exactly: it stands for something like the secret of life,
a DNA-ish formula plus; and the soup-maker is not a count but a
commoner, who turns into a martyr. Behind or beneath the primary action lurks a tissue of secondary stories and implications
waiting to be uncovered and unraveled. But *The Wicked Cooks*
could be enacted with verve and its primary action, the farce,
would still seem labored and arbitrary.[4]

The Bourgeois "Hero"

Grass is one of a line of German-writing dramatists from all over
Central Europe who have shown a loathing sort of respect, a repelled fascination, for their culture, for what they perceive to be a
specifically German materialist and military rapacity, for bloated
speech patterns inherited from four or five philosophers and the
Strum und Drang playwrights, and for a sense of innate superiority
inherited from Wagner and cultivated during the Hitler years to
counteract the malaise and depression of the Twenties.[5] Similar
feelings of patriotic disgust have actuated most other modern playwrights since Ibsen; but the targeting of Germany has been especially vehement.

In a previous chapter I referred to Yvan Goll's distaste for the

---

[4] *The Wicked Cooks*, translated by James Rosenberg, is published in *The New Theater of
Europe 2*, edited by Robert W. Corrigan (New York: Dell, 1964).
[5] The line of "German anti-German" playwrights, some of them doubling or tripling as
novelists and/or poets, begins as far back as the "Prussian anti-Prussian" Heinrich von Kleist
(1777–1811), and continues through the nineteenth and twentieth centuries with Grabbe
and Georg Büchner, Friedrich Hebbel, Gerhart Hauptmann, Hermann Sudermann, Frank
Wedekind, Carl Sternheim, Georg Kaiser, Reinhard Sorge, Paul Kornfeld, Ernst Toller,
Walter Hasenclever, Karl Krauss, Reinhard Göring, Oskar Kokoschka (better known as a
painter), Wolfgang Borchert, Friedrich Dürrenmatt, Max Frisch, Heinar Kipphardt, Peter
Weiss, and (more doubtfully) Rolf Hochhuth and Peter Handke. This list should be supple-
mented by a succession of Germany-chastising film directors from Robert Wiene, Fritz
Lang, Robert Siodmak, and Billy Wilder to Alexander Kluge, Rainer Werner Fassbinder,
Wim Wenders, and Werner Herzog.

"eternal" German bourgeoisie, or *Bürgertum*, in his *Methusalem*. The narrowing of the target to that sizable chunk of the populace had actually started more than ten years earlier with a volley of seven plays by Carl Sternheim (1878–1942) collectively titled "From the Heroic Life of the Bourgeoisie." Three of these plays trace the fortunes—and accumulating fortune—of Theobald Maske and his descendants. In *The Underpants* (1908) young Maske, married for twelve months, will not start a family until he feels financially sound. When the play opens he is yelling at his wife, Luise, and beating her head on the table for letting her panties drop in public during a parade starring the Kaiser. But Luise's treacherous elastic affords Maske a boon. A barber and a poet, both of whom saw the accident, have followed the panties' example and fallen for Luise. They apply to her husband for lodgings, and he crams the two of them into his tiny apartment. The big question during the four acts is, Which lodger will get Luise? But Maske has the luck of the damnable. The poet, who subscribes to Nietzsche's "master morality" and has promised the charming young Frau, "This night shalt thou be with me in paradise," is snared by a hooker on the street. And while Luise sits combing her hair in the parlor, the barber in the next room sleeps and answers her yearning with his snores; later he will go out to the park and pick up a "tremendous" young lady during a fireworks display. By act four, Maske, having signed a lease with the barber, calculates that he can live rent-free *and* put by one hundred thalers a year *and* afford to have a child *and* enjoy free sex with a bony lady named Gertrud who lives across the courtyard and one flight up.

In the succeeding play *The Snob* (1912), the anticipated child, Christian Maske, has grown to manhood and moves considerably further up than one flight. The title is an accurate use of the word snob, somebody who apes his social superiors (not somebody who imagines himself to *be* superior, although Christian does foresee a high destiny for himself and is right about that). Accordingly, he marries into an aristocratic family, becomes his father-in-law's partner, and scales to the summit of German rugged individualism.

The following year Sternheim rounded off his Maske trilogy with *1913*, in which Christian, now seventy and a baron, attempts to keep control of his armaments business out of the hands of his predatory daughter Sophie by lining up his two other children against her. But his son can think of little but English custom tailoring and haberdashery, while his younger daughter dotes on Christian's secretary; this young man dreams and writes, twenty years before Hitler's elevation to the German chancellorship, about a movement with himself as its *Führer*, founded on a post-Bismarckian "holy all-German fraternity, all-German ideas." Sophie has been working hard to consummate a large arms sale to Holland, but her father doesn't want it. If an imminent war breaks out (as a real war did a year later), he'll be able to make more money selling the munitions to his own government. Let his competitors "tie their hands" with the Dutch transaction. Sophie, no slouch, has already given a donation to Protestant charities in Holland, to emphasize (but discreetly) that the competitors are Catholic. Whereupon old Christian scotches the deal and defeats her by himself converting, with much public brouhaha, to Catholicism. After which he dies.

A number of false critical opinions about Sternheim have circulated in Germany and elsewhere. According to one such judgment, he has little interest in psychology or in personality differences; he aims to define social types. The plays refute this. He catches with precision the rancor, jealousy, and rivalry that ebb and flow among members of a family, and the sometimes halting, sometimes headlong advances and retreats made by strangers who are sounding each other out. *The Strongbox* (1912), another masterly farce in his Bourgeoisie canon, illustrates how, in his driven men, the love of property is sexual, as it is in the misers of Molière and Ghelderode. Henry Krull, a teacher aged forty-seven, has just married a much younger woman who, Krull's daughter suggests, "has poisoned him to the core with love." Returning from a honeymoon on the Rhine and ecstatic with affection for his bride, Krull learns that her aunt has securities locked up in a box ready to be inherited. The strongbox begins to haunt him. When his bride's locket slips off her neck, he dips his hand into her blouse:

FANNY: Can you reach it?
KRULL (*Feeling his way*): I have it. (*He pulls it out.*) Sweet little
  wife, sweet . . .

FANNY: Henry.
KRULL: The world, ah the world is beautiful! To sink . . . *(They
   embrace. After a moment:)* How much could she have?
FANNY: Fifty, sixty thousand at least.
KRULL: Sixty thousand. I thought so, too!

To tempt him further, the aunt gives the strongbox into his
care. It contains not sixty but one hundred forty thousand marks'
worth of stock. He hugs it to him, murmuring, "Only in bed, at
night, are you mine, do I possess you in peace." In the contest
between his lovely young wife and the ugly box with its clumsy
lock, the wife doesn't have a prayer. The play's subplot takes the
same curve. A handsome photographer who has rented a room in
the house wavers between Krull's daughter and his new wife, making plays for both. He goes so far as to climb a rope to the balcony
of the daughter's room (and loses his grip). But he never becomes
quite infatuated with either woman. When, in a parody of Juliet
looking into her garden, the daughter proposes, "We must flee
into seclusion," he replies, "Later. In the off season." He does
marry the daughter, though, once he hears about the strongbox;
goes on a honeymoon with her to Italy; drinks in the masterpieces
of Florence; and resolves to give up his profession in order to turn
bohemian painter. But one look, granted by his father-in-law, at
the contents of the box, and Bohemia gives instant way to
Bürgertum. At the play's end, as Krull and his son-in-law gloat
over the twentieth-century treasure—not precious metals or min-
erals, not coin of the realm, not bank bills, but paper—neither
knows that the rich aunt has rewritten her will leaving all her assets
to a local church.

Another misapprehension about Sternheim has it that his up-
ward-bound heroes expand their freedom to its outer limits. So far
so good. However, this interpretation, as enunciated by Wilhelm
Emrich, for example, goes on to see the ruthless exploitation of
one's freedom (at the expense of the freedom of others) as being a
trait admired by the author. If we extend this notion a bit, Sternheim is defending the expansionism of that period and later,
whether it be the financial graspings of Maske or the Wagnerian,
"all-German" politics of his secretary. We could even isolate certain lines from, say, *1913* in order to view Maske as a man con-

cerned more with serving the people than with helping himself. When he quarrels with his daughter Sophie he grumbles about the "uniform mass-produced crap that we palm off" on the public. He believes consumers will at last rebel, and says that he himself always tried to produce "quality." Sophie replies, "Such sentiments coming from you are astonishing." Maske retorts that he "never quite lost" those sentiments. But as Sophie asks unanswerably, "Who accumulated capital, monopolized it, ceaselessly consolidated it?" Maske's demand for high quality, mouthed after a life of stepping on others and "knocking together millions," and shortly before his death, when it's too late for him to atone, makes beautiful dramatic sense. It fits his character at that point in the trilogy, and it consorts well with his Christian mask of a name. It also tallies with the play's farcical outlook. Sternheim's heroes—that is, hypocritical villains—are heroic in the modern, ironic vein of Ibsen's and Shaw's. Those playwrights demonstrated that he who works his villainy best is the most persuasive of men, and often the most endearing. Until the mask drops away.

Sternheim's farce makes itself evident too in his heroes' language. Sometimes their words grow exalted and sententious, a mockery of themselves: "A day of fearful magnificence is dawning in my soul." Or a high-flown idea plummets into bathos: "It was the range of your imagination that impressed me the night you fell onto my balcony." At other times Sternheim chops up his sentences into quick exclamations, the so-called telegraphic style, preempted a few years later by the Expressionists:

CHRISTIAN (*Enters*): Good day, my dears! (*Embrace.*) Charmant that you have come. All goes well? Sophie looks dazzling. Nothing to tell me? When shall I be Grandpa? (*He laughs.*) Soon now. Our giant (*he claps Otto on the shoulder*) will look to it. Seen the children?

These clipped locutions sit well in the farcical atmosphere of doors opening and slamming, rush, rush, rush, a bewildering replenishment of the stage's occupants. A Sternheim living room is as unsettled as a traffic circle. Its bourgeois heroes frantically come and go, the young displacing the old, continually regenerating themselves.[6]

In France too, the bourgeoisie—the word is, after all, French —has come in for its doses of theatrical slaps. But the novels and plays of Jules Romains (1885–1972) spoof all the social classes without discrimination, although not without sympathy. Early in his career, Romains, who studied and taught philosophy, wrote poems and prose about "the unanimous life" of groups; his Unanimism proposed that individuals can feel a higher-than-personal identity and find a larger-than-personal fulfillment when they're among others. This is not a sociological adumbration of group-think, mob psychology, or interpersonal dynamics. It has something in common with all of these, but Romains doesn't seem to think of it as a synonym for unanimity. Rather, it insists that we recognize a quasi-mystical sense of unity in community, and that the "me" can be somehow enhanced by the collectivity of the "us." Does Unanimism mean no more, then, than that people are affected by others in whose presence they find themselves—on the street, in a store, at dinner, at work or worship, during a rally? If so, it belongs in the theater, for it corresponds to a cardinal law of the stage, learned or discovered by actors everywhere: that one doesn't act purely out of private impulses but reacts to circumstances, which include the other actors. (In this respect it resembles one of the basic principles of Naturalism, that people in life are conditioned by their background, their upbringing.) Perhaps Unanimism has broader and subtler meanings, too; after reading Romains and some of his critics, I'm not sure. It could certainly apply to the feelings and behavior of audiences, as well as those of casts, and we might expect the performance of a play by Romains to provide a sort of religious experience. As it turned out, he preferred in the Twenties to devote himself to farces and farcical

---

[6] For *The Underpants*, translated by Eric Bentley, see *The Modern Theater*, Vol. 6, edited by Bentley (Garden City, N.Y.: Doubleday, 1960); *The Snob*, translated by Bentley, is in his anthology *From the Modern Repertoire, I* (Denver, Colo.: University of Colorado Press, 1949); Bentley has also translated *1913* in *Canto*, Vol. 1, No. 1, Spring 1977. *The Strongbox*, translated by Maurice Edwards and Valerie Reich, is in *An Anthology of German Expressionist Drama*, edited by Walter Sokel (Garden City, N.Y.: Doubleday, 1963). Wilhelm Emrich's article, "Carl Sternheim's Comedy," is published in German in *Der deutsche Expressionismus* (1965).

comedies. (In collaboration with Stefan Zweig he also adapted Jonson's *Volpone* in an ill-advised effort to make that play more acceptable to French audiences; all the adapters succeeded in doing was tame the characters and leach the play of Jonson's verbal and conceptual extravagances.)

Explicating the plays of Romains by using Unanimism as an analytical tool, as some critics have done, doesn't open them up much; it merely tosses Romains into the unanimistic company of all those dramatists who've written crowd scenes. The plays show that he *is* interested in individual personalities, and that his stronger characters can overwhelm the others. One personage, Monsieur Le Trouhadec, appears in three farces, *M. Le Trouhadec Seized by Debauchery* (1923), *M. Le Trouhadec's Marriage* (1925), and the semifantasy *Donogoo-Tonka* (1931), dramatized from Romains's own novel. And in Romains's best-known play, *Knock, or The Triumph of Medicine* (1923), the leading character functions as playwright-within-the-play, planning and bringing to prosperous fruition his mischievous scheme.

Knock, who has just won a medical degree after years of practicing without one on a ship, buys out a country doctor. After twenty-five disappointing years, this doctor has decided to set himself up in the big city, Lyon. The people in the rural locality of St. Maurice are affluent enough, but he was too candid with them; he shrugged off their complaints. After a time, scorning professional help, they learned to live with their ailments or got better or died. Knock changes all that. By offering free consultations for two hours on Monday (market day, when everybody is in town), publicized by a drum-thumping town crier, he achieves every doctor's dream: a crowded waiting room. Like an Antichrist, he has converted apparently fit people into dependent patients. Within three months his office clientele soars from ten a week to over one hundred fifty, and some two hundred fifty other inhabitants of the surrounding area, including the town crier, are laid up in bed with unmistakable symptoms of one kind or another. The hotel in town has become an infirmary for taking care of visitors from farther afield. The local pharmacist and the hotel proprietor could never have imagined such prosperity. When the original doctor returns for a visit, congratulating himself on having unloaded this dog of a practice, he learns a two-edged lesson in medical ethics. Within minutes he offers to move back into his old office and let Knock take over his new, "fat" one in Lyon. The local people won't hear of it. They are wallowing in Knock's ministrations. In the old days an epidemic took them by surprise. Now, with drug supplies choking their closets and with two hundred fifty rectal thermometers entering them promptly and simultaneously at ten o'clock daily and nightly, they are seasoned, dedicated invalids, prepared for the worst. Knock has accomplished what he calls "medical penetration" of the region and what the pharmacist calls "pharmaco-medical penetration."

It may be an accident that the name Knock, when reversed in English, sounds like "con." The character would be less fascinating if he merely operated a medical mill. He's a zealot, a diabolical force let loose. He abominates the word "healthy"; he knows more about his patients' incomes than the tax collector does; and he speaks to his predecessor about "the subterranean fire of our art." At night, he says, "the noninvalids sleep in the dark. They're blotted out. But the invalids have kept on their night lights" and the entire landscape "turns into a sort of firmament of which I am the creator."

Louis Jouvet, who created the role of Knock and directed the play, revived it as often as his troupe needed to finance new, experimental plays. *Knock* was always a sellout. A knockout. It has survived all the plays it helped onto the boards. Jouvet's assumption of the role seems inevitable now. One can look at the film version he made, *Doctor Knock* (1937), and marvel at the inflections of his craggy face, the foamy little rituals when he washes his hands, the feat that is his underplaying of Knock's cold feverishness. But the play marches on by itself and is one of the funniest farces ever written. Here is how Knock deals with two young roughnecks who come into his office during the free consultations, laughing raucously and pushing to the front of the line. After ordering one of them to strip down, Knock examines him meticulously with hands and bright lights and instruments, then asks: "Your father still alive?"

MAN: No. Dead.
KNOCK: Sudden death?
MAN: Yes.

KNOCK: Of course. He couldn't have been very old?
MAN: No. Forty-nine.
KNOCK: That old?
(He unrolls two large, colored diagrams that reproduce the organs of an advanced alcoholic and those of a normal person.)
MAN: Maybe I ought to stop drinking?
KNOCK: You do whatever you wish.
MAN: Any cure possible?
KNOCK: None worth trying. (To the second man) Now you.

But both bullies are now "haggard and terrified." In no time flat they have fled. As the play's payoff, Knock will not let his predecessor travel back to Lyon yet. He must rest for twenty-four hours. Knock insists that the hotel/hospital's proprietor find a room right away. The other doctor turns pale. He has just finished hinting that Knock is a charlatan, but now, with his own health threatened, he has become a patient and as gullible as the rest of Knock's clientele. Clinging to what is left of his professional authority, he wonders whether certain misgivings he's had lately about his own condition coincide with Knock's observations. Knock, as cryptic as ever, avoids a direct answer by setting up an appointment for the following day.[7]

Local Humor

Of the three dramatists just discussed, Mrożek writes unlocalized plays about Nowhere or Everywhere, while Sternheim and Romains write plays that are distinctively German and French without calling on regional humor. But thousands of realistic dramas and melodramas by other modern playwrights capitalize on local dialects, history, associations, and manners. Like local wines, not all of them travel well. Many of the ones that do include figures with farcical idiosyncrasies. There are good reasons for their inclusion. They act as extreme examples of certain regional characteristics.

In *Juno and the Paycock* (1922) by Sean O'Casey (1880–1964), a

[7] *Knock* has been translated by James Gidney (New York: Samuel French Acting Edition, 1935).

serious play that the author names a tragedy, a poor family of tenement dwellers seems to undergo a run of devastatingly bad luck. But this is not quite the case. The principal male characters are all betrayers. A young English lawyer leaves the daughter pregnant. An idealistic labor leader then declares his unalterable love for her but retracts it swiftly when he finds out about the pregnancy. Her brother rats on a comrade in the republican "army." Her father promises her mother, Juno, that he's going out to look for work, but sneaks off all the time to a "snug" where he drinks up any money he's found at home. His boozing companion, a sponger, rounds on him whenever he runs out of cash.

These last two, "Captain" Jack Boyle, the peacock of the title, and Joxer Daly, his fair-weather friend, are Irish reincarnations of the bragging soldier and the parasite from the Roman plays of Plautus. They lighten and energize what would otherwise be a grim and soulful tale of the downtrodden being trodden harder down. O'Casey hustles them onstage just before the last curtain and keeps them there till it falls, as if he'd foreseen that his play would be remembered most vividly not for the decent, put-upon mother and daughter but for these drunken, verbose, tremulously self-absorbed, contemptibly futile, life-sustaining rascals, the vaudeville comic and his feed.

Farcical caricature creeps into the portraits of certain O'Casey characters in his other early tragedies (*The Shadow of a Gunman*, 1920–21, and *The Plough and the Stars*, 1925), as well as into a succession of nonrealistic plays. In his writing career O'Casey moved unsteadily, always the venturer, away from realism (which, he said late in life, he'd never had any regard for) and toward fantasy shot through with farce, and from characterizations toward cartoons. *Purple Dust* (1938), *Cock-A-Doodle-Dandy* (1949), *The Bishop's Bonfire* (1955), and *The Drums of Father Ned* (1958) have the verbal zest we find and relish in the six volumes of autobiography O'Casey published between 1939 and 1954. These farces burlesque censorious state and church officials in Ireland—authority-loving, love-denying sourpusses who repress young people —and those who kowtow to them. With these plays O'Casey brings us the message of joy. But urging joy in life, like urging moderation, is still urging. As he gave farce more license O'Casey began to push too hard. He was well over seventy by the time he com-

pleted the last two plays. Even so, that advanced age may not
account for his forcing the Dionysiac response and fishing for
laughs, drawing out the comic situations till they grew thin and
planting comic names on the imperious characters (Father Domi-
neer, Bishop Mullarky). He'd lived away from Ireland for close to
forty years, and the late plays are set not in his Dublin but in Irish
villages with multisyllabic names like Ballyoonagh, Doonavale,
Nyadnanave, and Clune na Geera, which represent double or
triple plays on Gaelic words but are abstractions as settlements.
They lack the specific regional flavor of Dublin which had fortified
the early drama.[8]

Brendan Behan (1923–64), another celebrant of Dublin, shares
with O'Casey a grudging fondness for blatherers who pull the
words over your eyes, as well as the habit of letting his cast forget
the action momentarily and break into song, either a familiar ditty
or an invention of the author's. Behan's exuberance approaches
farce in its language and some of its characterizations, but with its
infusions of singing it also resembles ballad operas of the eighteenth century. The early, short radio plays, *Moving Out* and *A
Garden Party* (both 1952 and both adapted later for the stage), and
the first of his two completed full-length plays, *The Quare Fellow*,
are samples of qualified realism, the qualification being the dealing
out of mood-enhancing songs.

In *The Hostage* (1954) and the unfinished *Richard's Cork Leg*
(1964), Behan shifts out of realism most of the time and into theatricalism, although there are doubts about how much of that shift
we owe to his own intentions and how much to his directors'. Joan
Littlewood, who opened *The Quare Fellow* and *The Hostage* in
London, had a reputation for substantially remaking most plays
she staged; and Alan Simpson, Behan's Irish director and friend,
trimmed *Richard's Cork Leg*, cut out repetitions, rearranged sequences, and provided additional material before he felt he could
produce it. Behan, who wrote and overwrote and poured out wonderfully careless speeches without looking back, didn't object.
(Sean O'Casey did; he called Littlewood's "improvements" tamper-

---

[8] Many of O'Casey's plays have been anthologized. The ones written before 1949 appear in
The Collected Plays of Sean O'Casey (New York: St. Martin's Press, 1949); the subsequent
ones are published separately.

ing, and was "of the opinion that she took far too much upon herself in the ways of handling the work of playwrights.") In the early Sixties I asked Behan whether he would give *Richard's Cork Leg* to Joan Littlewood to direct. He replied, "Of course" and drained his beer glass. No further questions.

The Quare Fellow investigates the life of a jail and ends with the hanging of a man, the "quare fellow." The prisoners and wardens talk about this event in a mixture of disinterested time-passing and cheerful horror:

DUNLAVIN: . . . Do you know who feels it worst going out to be topped?

PRISONER A: Corkmen and Northerners . . . they've such bloody hard necks.

After the hanging, the Chief Warden tells a prisoner to chisel the dead man's identification on his gravestone: E.777. "It should be E.779, according to the book," the Chief adds, "but a '7' is easier for you to do than a '9.' " In *The Hostage*, the Irish Republican Army captures a young British soldier doing his "national service" in Ireland and holds him in a brothel. If the British kill an IRA prisoner, the English soldier will die in reprisal. They do, and the soldier is shot, although he rises, dead, at the end and sings: "The bells of hell / Go ting-a-ling-a-ling / For you but not for me. / Oh death, where is thy sting-a-ling-a-ling? / Or grave thy victory?"—an army song from World War I. But the guts and color of the play are in the assortment of brothel residents (a notch lower and more ribald than O'Casey's tenement types) and in their shrewdly cutting lines and unselfconsciousness, not in the action.

Richard's Cork Leg has even less formal dramatic action. But what there is, "which is in a way continuous," takes place in a cemetery, in the Dublin mountains, and in a private house belonging to a lady who's a member of "The Anti-Dancing Committee of the Female Prevention Society." This time it's an IRA man who gets gunned down (by mistake), rises, and sings a curtain number. But the play once again relies for its impact less on stage activity than on speed, impudence, raciness, and surprises in the lines.

BAWD II: And there's a lovely view. (*She points.*) Look—Wicklow Mountains and Bray Head.

BAWD I: Killiney Strand.

BAWD II: I was had be a man there. The first time. Lost my virginity. He was the prefect in charge of the Working Girls' Protection Society. He said he'd show me what I wasn't to let the boys do to me. It was on an outing.

BAWD I: The sea washes up a lot of wreckage on Killiney Strand.

BAWD II: I wonder if they ever found me maidenhead.

When one IRA man asks, "Are you a communist?" the other answers, "I detest the bastards personally, but I like their party, because it's the only one that all the big shots are terrified of." A woman complains that her husband wasn't allowed to march with the unemployed, and one of the bawds cries out, "Well, that's a bloody disgrace, so it is! Your husband with his length of service with the unemployed, there is no man in this city more entitled to march. I mean, he is a veteran of the unemployed. Years and years . . . when most of the new crowd was still working."

Dublin is to O'Casey and Behan as Naples is to Eduardo de Filippo (born 1900). Eduardo, as he is popularly known, one of Italy's leading actors as well as its preeminent playwright from the Thirties to the Sixties, has written voluminously for his own company at the Teatro San Ferdinando—comedies and farces in a dialogue heavily spiced with Neapolitan dialect and sayings. The bulk of his work hasn't been translated into English—not even some plays like *Millionaire Naples* and *These Ghosts* which are modern Italian classics. Vittorio de Sica drew his film *Marriage Italian Style* (1964) from Eduardo's most celebrated comedy—not a farce—the captivating *Filumena Marturano* (1946), and although a respectful, lively version, it suffered from being considered an exploitative sequel to Pietro Germi's *Divorce Italian Style* (1961), which starred the same actor, Marcello Mastroianni, and was much more farcical in temper.[9]

---

[9] For Behan's plays see *Brendan Behan: The Complete Plays*, edited by Alan Simpson (New York: Grove Press, 1978). *Filumena Marturano*, translated by Eric Bentley, appears in Bentley's anthology *The Genius of the Italian Theater* (New York: New American Library, 1964). We still await translations of Eduardo's farces into English.

The Strident British

Since the Fifties most British playwrights of note have been responsible for at least one farce or have splashed farcical material into plays that are protests about the place and the times. Like Sternheim, these authors use farce for its shock value as they flay the self-destructiveness of British society: the obsession, as elsewhere, with a mercantile success that numbs the principles of the middle-aged and a pop culture that numbs the wits of the young; urban decay and decadence and rural miseries; the persistent remains of a class structure that prolongs privilege, inequities, and moral complacency, all of these now complicated by racial friction; neglect of the old; the country's love-hate affairs with cars, highways, technology, scientific and statistical expansionism; the continuing faithlessness of politicians and other powers, especially of those who preached radical sermons before their election. A lifelong criminal named Adam Hepple in *Revenge* (1969) by Howard Brenton, which takes place in the 1980s, says: "My dream of a criminal England, it's all come true with the 1980s. The casino towns, the brothel villages, the cities red with blood and pleasure. Public life the turn of a card, the fall of a dice. The whole country on the fiddle, the gamble, the open snatch, the bit on the side. From Land's End to John O'Groats the whole of England's one giant pinball table. The ball running wild, Glasgow, Birmingham, Leeds, Coventry, London, Brighton. Wonderful." Postwar Britain, as watercolored by the American news media with only one disfigurement, low productivity, differs from the warty, tormented sculptures that emerge from British farce, while stridency contradicts the Briton's phony reputation for being reserved and wearing a stiff upper lip.

The targets of British dramatists correspond to the targets of artists all over the world—patriotic disgust again roars lionlike—but in Britain the plays have a special ferocity when compared with plays from elsewhere or with earlier British plays. A century ago, farces by Pinero and his contemporaries featured and spoofed the landed gentry, their heirs and assigns, and the rest of the horsey set. Recent farces, like other plays, have continued to lampoon the upper classes but have also promoted working-class peo-

ple, immigrant families, vagrants, swindlers, loafers, drug pushers
(and pullers) to the status of protagonists. This promotion has
been one sign of the new realism, even a new naturalism, in Britain, and it has been accomplished by another sign of realism: a
new dialogue that interweaves regional dialects, remnants of military and civilian oaths, explicit sex talk, and direct obscenities in
place of the old "by gad's," "Here, I say's" and "blimey's." A little
quiproquo from Howard Barker's *Alpha Alpha* (1972):

MICKEY: You piss-bucket! You shithouse turd!
MORRIE: You filthy, lowdown, stinking—
MICKEY: You bum-licker, you fat-arsed, shitting—
MORRIE: —rotten, twisted, farting—
MICKEY: —pissing, nauseating, fucking—
MORRIE: ⎱
          ⎰ Cunt!
MICKEY:

And here is a man named Gordon in *Mother's Day* (1976) by David
Storey: "I've just been fucking your wife upstairs. I fucked her
everywhere I could. I fucked her up the front, then I fucked her
up the back, then I fucked her in the throat, then I fucked
her between the breasts, then I fucked her between the thighs.
She's resting now. It's been quite a night." The reviewers in London sometimes profess to be offended by such language, saying it's
fit only for a barrack room or an outhouse. But what if a play takes
place in a barracks or an outhouse?—or, more likely, in some
respectable home that symbolizes an outhouse?

I oversimplify the form and the content of these farces by herd-
ing them into realism. Many have elements of fantasy or theatricalism. Despite—or because of—their strivings for honesty and
authenticity, they often employ a narrator, or more than one;
direct playing to the audience; role-swapping; and other tokens of
theatricalism. They are literate, too, replete with references to
myth, political circumstances, scientific novelties, the other arts,
and especially to theater and films. And they certainly don't shy
away from their convictions. What they most signally lack is irony;
but after all, irony and directness are opposites. Yet some of their
scenes recall the great ironic realists of the late nineteenth century, and may even be commenting on them.

In Peter Nichols' *Forget-Me-Not Lane* (1971) this exchange transmits echoes of scenes from Wedekind's *Spring's Awakening* (1891) between two adolescents, one girlish, the other "straight":

IVOR: Hey, man, you know when you toss off?
YOUNG FRANK: Yeah.
IVOR: Do you pretend you're a man or a woman?
YOUNG FRANK: I keep changing about. Sometimes I'm a slave girl like Hedy Lamarr and my master whips me a lot and I cringe and beg for mercy . . .

This new incidence of sexual frankness and swearing owes something to an impatience in the world at large with the old prudishness, which has rapidly given way to new forms of prudishness. But it's also due to the abolition of the Lord Chamberlain's Office, that monument to courteous, purblind censorship.

A fair number of British farces have regional settings—London, the Midlands, Yorkshire, Lancashire, Wales, Scotland, the Southwest, and so on, but especially London. Serious plays differentiate these regions from others with the aid of local dialect and customs, some of them murderous, as in David Rudkin's *Afore Night Come* (1962). Farces, however, imply that life is more or less the same as in other regions, dirtied by selfishness, corruption, and finagling —too easy and yet never rewarding enough. Parties and other get-togethers are occasions for having a bad time and inflaming friends and relatives.

Regional or general, farcical or not, British plays by women are as scarce as ever. Only two female playwrights have come to the fore since 1960, Shelagh Delaney and Ann Jellicoe (if we exclude Agatha Christie, whose last play, *The Mousetrap*, has outrun her). Britain's theater has been no more sexist than that of other countries, our own included, and some of its playwrights have gone out of their way to avoid creating stereotyped female characters. Still, the theater in Britain has had fewer trammels than that in any other country. Censorship was fought down, and died. The publicly subsidized companies like the National Theatre and the Royal Shakespeare have sedulously encouraged new plays and new translations, while the privately subsidized companies and commercial managements have taken many more chances than their counterparts elsewhere. Indeed, the focal point of the new theater in Britain was the privately supported English Stage Company, led by the incredibly adventurous George Devine, who was also instrumental in abolishing the censor's office. The outcome of this loosening of strictures was an upheaval of new dramatic writings, with farces well represented among them, and an explosion in the form, content, and variety of plays.[10] One can only guess at the consequences of a second upheaval for the theater as a whole, and for farce, once women playwrights get their overdue hearing in Britain and in other countries.[11]

And the Cool British

Three realistic playwrights, Simpson, Pinter, and Orton, have set themselves apart by tapping fat veins of irony missed by most of their contemporaries (exceptions being Ann Jellicoe and John Arden, who have written very few farces). Not one of the three practices realism in the old-fashioned style that still dominates the theater, films, and television. But their plays do require a matter-of-factness in performance that is in line with realistic acting—as

[10] Plays that contain farce or are farcical throughout, written since the turnaround in British drama in 1956–58, include: Ann Jellicoe's *The Sport of My Mad Mother* (1958, revised 1963) and *The Knack* (1961); *The Hamlet of Stepney Green* (1959) by Bernard Kops; John Osborne's *The World of Paul Slickey* (1959) and *Plays for England* (consisting of *The Blood of the Bambergs* and *Under Plain Cover*, 1962); Henry Livings' *Stop It, Whoever You Are* (1960) and *Eh?* (1964); John Arden's *The Happy Haven*, written in collaboration with his wife, Margaretta D'Arcy (1960); Bill Naughton's *All in Good Time* and *Alfie* (both 1963); Charles Wood's *Don't Make Me Laugh* (1964) and *Meals on Wheels* (1965)—Wood also wrote the screenplays for *The Knack* (1965) and for Richard Lester's *How I Won the War* (1967); David Cregan's *Transcending* (1966); Simon Gray's *Dutch Uncle* (1969); Peter Nichols' *The National Health* (1969) and *The Freeway* (1974); Heathcote Williams' *AC/DC* (1969); David Hare's *Slag* (1970) and *The Great Exhibition* (1972)—Hare also collaborated with Howard Brenton on *Brassneck* (1973), a play that, like Sternheim's Maske trilogy, is a history of a family's rise to affluence, or is a potted mock-history of capitalism; Howard Barker's *Cheek* (1970) and *Alpha Alpha* (1972); Edward Bond's *The Sea* (1973). This listing is not by any means a full record.

[11] In a recent survey by Oleg Kerensky of *The New British Drama: Fourteen Playwrights since Osborne and Pinter* (New York: Taplinger, 1978), not one of those playwrights is a woman, and no women playwrights are listed in the index. Nor do any women rate a chapter or a section of one in *Revolutions in Modern English Drama* (London, 1972) by Katharine J. Worth.

Two other books on the period, both by John Russell Taylor: *The Angry Theater* (New York: Hill & Wang, 1969) and *The Second Wave: British Drama for the Seventies* (New York: Hill & Wang, 1971). See also *The Theaters of George Devine* by Irving Wardle (London: Jonathan Cape, 1978).

if the outrageous events unrolled were everyday occurrences. In other words, the staging technique of their farces toys with those hoary notions of British coolness which have paid dividends in the merchandizing of gin-and-tonic and a cloudborne Robert Morley, and twits them from start to finish.

N. F. Simpson (born 1919) has produced a small but potent crop of farces. The first of them, A *Resounding Tinkle* (1957), announces a writer who will go out of his way to go his own way. *Tinkle* courteously confounds our expectations, even the ones we didn't think we'd have. It's a play, a revue, a dialectic, a conjuring show, an exercise in verbal fireworks that splatter off four walls of the kitchen in the little suburban home of the Paradocks, Mr. and Mrs. Its action is impossible to summarize, so here goes. The Paradocks express dissatisfaction with a pet elephant they have purchased. But this farce is not about the elephant, nor about a snake the Paradocks intend to swap it for, nor about the two comics who materialize to put on an act right there near the kitchen sink. It is about performing a farce. The comics get around to having a fairly erudite chat about irrationality and humor. A young man, the Paradocks' son, comes in as a woman. The author intervenes now and then with apologies that are unrepentant and explanations that explain nothing, and the play ends without an ending. Simpson has a sense of humor that few revolutionaries— artistic, political, metaphysical, or gymnastic—can lay claim to: he can and does laugh at himself, not only at others. A few critics have had trouble with his farces. They look for something of substance, something *important* to come through. Fooling is all very well, but where's the statement, the conclusion?[12]

One Way Pendulum: A Farce in a New Dimension (1960) consists of a series of revue turns, only instead of laying them out one at a time, the playwright has made them couple and intersect until the play takes on the thematic shape of, well, a play. Of the eccentrics who make up the Groomkirby family, father has a passion for the law and for woodwork, while his son, who is also good with his hands (he has transformed an egg timer into a cash register), has collected one hundred speak-your-weight machines which he is coaxing to sing in chorus. Making the most of the capricious

---

[12] See, for example, *The Angry Theater*, pp. 66–73.

winds of logic, Simpson sails into his second act by having Mr. Groomkirby construct a criminal court in his living room. It comes with a judge, two lawyers, and other conveniences, and it harbors a trial. The defendant, the Groomkirby son, is accused of striking forty-three victims to death with an iron bar after telling each of them a joke so that they'd die happy. Mr. and Mrs. Groomkirby take the stand as witnesses, and our narrator proves to be a police sergeant, while other members of the family persist in their domestic routines; but court procedure in the living room is strictly adhered to with some fierce cross-questioning:

PROSECUTING COUNSEL: You say you were a masochist, Mr. Groomkirby. Are you a masochist now?

MR. GROOMKIRBY (*fervently*): No, sir.

PROSECUTING COUNSEL: When did you cease your masochism?

MR. GROOMKIRBY: A month or two ago, sir.

PROSECUTING COUNSEL: And what made you give it up?

MR. GROOMKIRBY: It was taking up too much of my time.

JUDGE (*intervening*): . . . And how long had you been a masochist when you suddenly decided that your time was so valuable that you could no longer spare any of it for your masochism?

MR. GROOMKIRBY: For something like three or four years, m'lord.

PROSECUTING COUNSEL: What was it that made you take it up in the first place?

MR. GROOMKIRBY: I was at a loose end at the time, sir. . . .

PROSECUTING COUNSEL: You were at a loose end. Would you tell the court, Mr. Groomkirby, as clearly as you can in your own words, exactly how loose this end was?

MR. GROOMKIRBY: It was worn right down, sir.

JUDGE (*intervening*): Worn right down. That tells us very little. Was it swinging loose? Was it rattling about?

For a British public reared on Sunday newspapers that carry verbatim extracts from sensational trials, the examination rings with the true, finicky majesty of the courtroom and its countless imitations in plays and films. The son is found guilty as charged. Solemnly the judge warns him, "In sentencing a man for one crime, we may be putting him beyond the reach of the law in respect of those other crimes of which he might otherwise have become guilty. The law, however, is not to be cheated in this way. I shall therefore discharge you." The trial closes with a rendering of the Hallelujah Chorus by the weight machines, and the Groomkirbys' family life continues in its abnormal way.

Pendulum verges on theatricalism. But *The Hole* (1957), staged two years earlier than *Pendulum*, is a realistic play, a junction box of metaphysical conjectures along German idealist, almost Kantian, lines, in which some sidewalk superintendents stand and speculate on the nature, contents, and ultimate purposes of a hole in the roadway. Yet when we concede that the play ventilates the various fantasies of its characters—is the hole for playing in? for keeping fish or other wildlife in? for incarcerating prisoners?—we must also concede that it's partly fantasy. The hole, it seems, actually goes down to a junction box. But what exactly is a junction box? One character, Cerebro the brain, ponders the meaning of this meeting (or separation) of cables. Another character, Soma the body, wants the onlookers to worship it.

And no wonder. The meaning of the device becomes amplified when, in *The Cresta Run* (1965), a junction box connects up with the rear end of an ostrich that wears a monocle. This ostrich is only one of a number of espionage wrinkles smoothed out by the farce. The head of British intelligence seeks the help of a married couple, the Fawcetts, but forgets that he's done so and sets out to capture them for suspicious behavior. Mr. Fawcett, caught in a closed circle, thinks he's an agent—he is—but the intelligence people treat him as an enemy. A beautiful Mata Hari type called Gelda, posing as Lady Godiva, invites him to her room, where she practices chiropody on him and where he is secretly photographed with incriminating bare feet. One agent holds a press conference to publicize "a new policy line" for the organization: "As a gesture of confidence in the economic system which we on this side of the iron curtain are pledged to defend, it is proposed that the whole of our intelligence and security services be handed over to private enterprise." Once again Simpson's logic strides forward unfalteringly. There is an International Secrets Exchange Control so that "you know how many of your own secrets are leaking across to the other side, and how many of theirs are finding their way back to you." When the intelligence chief is busy he wants to send his deputy on an assignment, but the deputy has to make a phone call and so the boss goes out on the job claiming to be his deputy disguised as himself. The intelligence officials are trained to trust nobody—certainly not one another, and themselves even less, since they know their own weaknesses: "I remember quite clearly," the chief remembers, "as a small boy coming over subversive one day in Woolworth's. I was watching a girl serving someone with curtain rings at the time. . . . One moment I was feeling fine, not a care in the world, dipping into a bag of mint humbugs, unless my memory plays me false, and the next thing I knew I was struggling in the grip of an overpowering impulse to undermine the legally constituted government of the country in the name of an alien philosophy. . . . During those few seconds it was all I could do not to turn to the girl behind the counter, beckon her across, and divulge an atom secret to her. And if by some catastrophic combination of circumstances I'd happened at that moment to have one on me—I really think I might have done it. In the middle of a crowded Woolworth's, with every agent within earshot waiting to make detailed notes on the back of an empty cigarette packet. That's how near we all were, had we but known it . . . to a global holocaust of the first water."[13]

Ben and Gus sit on their beds in a basement room in Pinter's *The Dumb Waiter* (1959). Ben peruses a newspaper. He's shocked to read that a man of eighty-seven crawled under a truck, the truck took off, and the man was run over; and that an eight-year-old girl killed a cat while "her brother, aged eleven, viewed the incident from the toolshed." Ben and Gus are hit men killing time until they get their orders to go out and kill people. They find the newspaper items "unbelievable" and "enough to make you want to puke . . ."

Goldberg and McCann in *The Birthday Party* (1960), two more hit men, sort of, are going to abduct a fellow from a house where

[13] *The Hole, and Other Plays and Sketches* (London: Faber & Faber, 1964) includes *A Resounding Tinkle*. *One Way Pendulum* appears in *The New British Drama* (New York: Grove Press, 1964), edited by Henry Popkin. *The Cresta Run* is published separately (New York: Grove Press, 1966). Simpson has also written *Man Overboard: A Testimonial to the High Art of Incompetence* (New York: William Morrow, 1976), a salad of prose and unattributed dialogue, with notes and appendices, narrating the fall into Mediterranean waters of one Albert Whitbrace, who remained waterbound, either dead or alive, for at least twenty-seven months, setting a new record for drowning and becoming the occasion of an international rescue mission. Which failed.

he's been hiding out from the world, or arguably from them. When they spirit him away he will look brainwashed, if not automated. But before this climactic moment Goldberg says, "Give me a blow." He elaborates: "Blow in my mouth." McCann obliges. Goldberg inhales, and asks, "One for the road?" McCann blows down his throat again. Goldberg "breathes deeply, shakes his head, and bounds from his chair," ready for action.

Mac Davies in *The Caretaker* (1960), a repellent and strangely pathetic old bum, has found a home. A room cluttered with a sink, a ladder, tools, suitcases, rubbish, it belongs to one of two brothers, either to Aston, a kindly man who gives old Davies money and does his best to make him comfortable, or to Mick, younger, shrewder, and nasty. But Davies wears out his welcome. He tries to play the brothers off against each other. He stinks. He sponges on Aston. He makes noises in his sleep; and while awake he gripes. He taunts Aston, who once went through brutal shock treatment: "You don't know what you're doing half the time. You're up the creek! You're half off! You can tell it by looking at you." Aston quietly asks Davies to leave. Davies then tries to curry favor with the sarcastic Mick. At one time Mick talked about turning the junk heap of a room into a "penthouse." Davies now volunteers to help. Mick accepts the offer provided that Davies is "an experienced first class interior decorator." The bum starts to protest.

MICK: You mean you wouldn't know how to fit teal-blue, copper and parchment linoleum squares and have those colors re-echoed in the walls?
DAVIES: Now, look here, where'd you get—?
MICK: You wouldn't be able to decorate out a table in afromosia teak veneer, an armchair in oatmeal tweed and a beech frame settee with a woven sea-grass seat?
DAVIES: I never said that!
MICK: Christ! I must have been under a false impression!
DAVIES: I never said it!
MICK: You're a bloody impostor, mate!

In *The Homecoming* (1965), Teddy, a professor of philosophy at an American college, has brought his wife, Ruth, home to meet his father, a butcher, and his two unmarried brothers, a pimp and a construction worker who wrestles for an avocation. When Teddy and Ruth are about to leave, his father and brothers offer to keep Ruth. They want a woman in their motherless house. (Ruth has already spent some time upstairs on a bed with the wrestler brother, but she didn't let him "go the whole hog.") Teddy protests only mildly. Ruth isn't well. They have three sons in the United States. She *is* his wife. His father and brothers drown him out with their enthusiasm. They'll all put money into a kitty so as to treat Ruth in "the manner to which she's accustomed." Teddy can contribute to the kitty, too. He demurs. "What?" exclaims his father, "You won't help to support your own wife? I thought he was a son of mine. You lousy stinkpig." The pimp now has a better idea. He'll put Ruth "on the game" in Soho to "pay her own way" in the household. "A stroke of genius," the father cries. "You mean she can earn the money herself—on her back?" But of course. They will limit her to four hours of work a night. The question is: will she be "up to the mark"? The pimp believes so, in his "professional opinion." He suggests, "Listen, Teddy, you could help us, actually. If I were to send you some cards, over to America . . . you know, very nice ones, with a name on, and a telephone number, very discreet, well, you could distribute them . . . to various parties, who might be making a trip over here. Of course, you'd get a little percentage out of it. . . . What I mean, Teddy, you must know lots of professors, heads of departments, men like that. They pop over here for a week at the Savoy, they need somewhere they can go to have a nice quiet poke. And of course you'd be in a position to give them inside information. . . . You could be our representative in the States."

Harold Pinter (born 1930) has written more than thirty scripts for revues, the legitimate stage, radio, television, and the cinema, some of them laden with farce. The scene between Teddy and his family is one of the funniest (and most harrowing) in the modern theater, a humiliation of a victim who won't fight back. It gets stronger as it goes along without any propping up by means of physical violence or even threats. But after *The Homecoming* the farce in Pinter's theater dwindles. In *Landscape* (1967), *Silence* (1968), *Old Times* (1971), *No Man's Land* (1975), and *Betrayal* (1979) we catch glints of the old humor, or variations on it, but Pinter has proceeded into more openly lyrical forms of drama.

These test the fragility of memory, much as Beckett's plays do. The characters turn nostalgic, regretful as they look backward, mull over time elapsed, and make of it what they can. In *Old Times* a man and a woman sing a duet made up of lines from pop love numbers of the Thirties, prompting each other back into the past. Pinter has also, as though following a destiny, condensed that most thoroughgoing of all memory writings, Proust's seven-volume *Remembrance of Things Past*, into *The Proust Screenplay* (1973), an evocative adaptation that has been published (New York: Grove Press, 1977) but not filmed.[14] However, for the characters in Pinter's earlier plays, time is an opponent still to tangle with. They play waiting games; they look forward. The events they take part in will be active, suspenseful, and come to a head. Along with this suspense goes farce, but not as embroidery. The farce Pinter doles into plays like *The Dumb Waiter*, *The Birthday Party*, *The Caretaker*, and *The Homecoming* (all those double-jointed nouns!) feeds the suspense and builds its sinew.

The deaths reported near the opening of *The Dumb Waiter* bear on the final confrontation. When the orders come through for Gus and Ben, a man will enter the door to the basement room and face Ben, who holds a gun. The man will turn out to be Gus. The play will end before a shot is fired, but it does look like curtains for Gus. Much as the old man crawled under a truck (to hide? to take shelter? to die? to commit suicide?), so Gus has gone into this underground retreat to be rubbed out. In *The Birthday Party*, what does McCann breathe down Goldberg's throat? Not oxygen. Carbon dioxide. Goldberg than springs up revived. Funny, but sinister. Very nearly inhuman, but apt for an abductor. Similarly, Mick's exotic requirements for his remade attic in *The Caretaker* —teal-blue, copper and parchment linoleum squares and afromosia teak veneer—give off hilariously precise echoes of catalogue specifications, but also torment Davies with the reminder that he found a haven, lived there while it was an overloaded dump, and is to be expelled before its transformation into a dream-decorated

---

[14] Pinter's plays resemble Beckett's in other ways too, some of them carefully detailed in Martin Esslin's *The Peopled Wound: The Work of Harold Pinter* (New York: Doubleday, 1970). It also happens that at twenty-five Beckett wrote a precocious monograph on Proust in which he proposed "to examine in the first place that double-headed monster of salvation and damnation—Time": *Proust* (New York: Grove Press, 1957, seventh printing).

penthouse. In *The Homecoming*, the project for taking Ruth from her husband and children and putting her "on the game" arises from a tissue of earlier circumstances. Teddy has been the oldest son who got everything—an education, a wife and family, a tenured job, a luxurious house in America (with pool), and a leg up out of the working class. And, as his uncle mentions, he was his mother's favorite. But this mother, now dead, slept with his father's best friend, and there is some doubt whether Teddy and his brothers are the father's sons. The father gets revenge on the mother by appropriating her favorite son's wife to replace her and revenge on the friend who betrayed him by punishing his son. The brothers take revenge for Teddy's having been indulged, as they think, at their expense. Their sense of deprivation is suggested in another funny exchange between the pimp, who's looking for a cheese roll he made for himself, and Teddy, who ate it. And Teddy himself? His passiveness is open to several interpretations, but it points to his sense of fatality, as though he knew he had this punishment coming and went to meet it, putting up only a token resistance.

The farce in Pinter, although it goes to nearly fantastic lengths at times, stays within reach of the unreasonably probable. His audiences must get a glimmering of this. Even when baffled by apparent lashings of information or when searching for motives more firmly delineated than the ones Pinter gives his characters, audiences remain gripped by the plays. Perhaps they infer that when the characters provide dubious or even contradictory information, they're attempting to conceal themselves as they unwittingly reveal themselves—something we all do.[15]

British films, plays, novels, and tours have familiarized Americans with those clichés of exactitude, conversational transitions that clog up the speech of all classes in Britain (actually, mind you, it stands to reason, in fact, in point of fact, as a matter of fact, the fact is that . . .). Modern British writers reproduce them in quantity for the sake of authenticity. Pinter has a remarkable ear for them and for odd formalities of speech. When Ben mentions the

---

[15] Pinter's plays are published by Grove Press, some separately, some in collections, and a few are included in anthologies. His writings for the cinema—no farces among them—are collected in *Five Screenplays by Harold Pinter* (New York: Grove Press, 1973).

old man who crawled under a truck, Gus wants to know, "Who advised him to do a thing like that?" Goldberg reminisces about his Uncle Barney: "Of course, he was an impeccable dresser. One of the old school. He had a house just outside Basingstoke at the time. Respected by the whole community. Culture? Don't talk to me about culture. He was an all-round man, what do you mean? He was a cosmopolitan." This pretentious language grows farcical when vernacular creeps in. Teddy's pimp brother speaks: "One night, not too long ago, one night down by the docks, I was standing alone under an arch, watching all the men jibbing the boom, out in the harbor, and playing about with the yardarm, when a certain lady came up to me and made me a certain proposal. This lady had been searching for me for days. She'd lost track of my whereabouts. However, the fact was she eventually caught up with me, and when she caught up with me she made me this certain proposal. Well, this proposal wasn't entirely out of order and normally I would have subscribed to it. I mean I would have subscribed to it in the normal course of events. The only trouble was she was falling apart with the pox. So I turned it down. Well, this lady was very insistent and started taking liberties with me down under this arch, liberties which by any criterion I couldn't be expected to tolerate, the facts being what they were, so I clumped her one." He is mimicking his older brother, the philosophy professor, and parodying academic talk with its double negatives ("this proposal wasn't entirely out of order") and qualifying phrases ("by any criterion . . . the facts being what they were . . . in the normal course of events"), but the upshot is a language at odds with what the speaker is talking about.

N. F. Simpson has a similar trick of easing artificial stiffeners into his dialogue. In *The Cresta Run*, Mr. Fawcett finds it hard to imagine that "within twenty-four hours we shall probably have every long-ranged rocket from here to Vladivostok trained on our lavatory cistern." A message received at intelligence headquarters from Agent Q-16 reads: "Excuse scrawl. Gagged, handcuffed, drowning. Trust all is well." But the playwright who exploited this mannerism so extensively and intensively that it forced a farcical discrepancy between the content and the style of his speeches was Joe Orton (1933–67). Orton's plays for the stage and television acquired a cult following during and after his short life. They have something in common with Oscar Wilde's burnished paradoxes and something else in common with Camp and the American Theater of the Ridiculous; but Orton wished fervently to dissociate himself from what he called "the fag and drag" and "the Great American Queen," which he rightly perceived to be the New York theater's responses to homosexuality.[16]

Entertaining Mr. Sloane (1964), Orton's first play to be performed, has excessively formal lines, such as "I know he can be aggravating, but you mustn't resort to violence" and "If you was to ask me that, I'd give you my answer in the affirmative" and "I'm a benign influence, a source of good"—this last phrase a tautology. But the loose writing overlies a tight dramatic structure. Sloane, a good-looking youth, introduces himself into the home of the Kemps. Kath, who is blowsy and middle-aged, a former tart, wants him for herself. But so does Ed, her gay brother, who is "disturbed by birds." The third Kemp, the father of Kath and Ed, suspects Sloane of being a murderer, which he is; but as if to prove old Kemp right, Sloane kills him. Now, we think, he will terrorize the brother and sister. Instead, they show that the Kemps are a hardy breed. They agree to divide Sloane's year, each getting him for six months. For most of its length *Sloane* is a melodramatic comedy; it marches decisively into farce when we realize that the brother and sister, far from being intimidated or appalled by the slaughter of their father, welcome it as a way of blackmailing Sloane. Either can give him away to the police if he tries to escape or even fails to provide satisfaction. Some people have read this ending as a justification of homosexuality or of "AC/DC" practices; others, as a condemnation of the hypocrisy of respectable society. I see it as neither, only as a fascinating farcical and melodramatic stalemate. Kath and Ed have masochistically taken on a sex partner who's liable to do them in, one or both of them, at any time.

Loot (1967) is more or less that: a sprinkle of barbs filched from nineteenth-century farces, some with envenomed tips, aimed at religious ceremony, police venality, personal greed, medical ethics, and everything else but war. It reverses the main virtue and vice of *Entertaining Mr. Sloane*: its lines are funnier and its plot shaggier; it is, in short, more entertaining. A household made up

---

[16] Orton quotations from *The Second Wave*, p. 140.

of a Catholic gentleman named McLeavy, who has seen Paradise, but only in a photograph; his son, who's a bank robber and hopes some day to run a three-star brothel called The Kingdom Come; a nurse who has killed off her seven husbands in as many years; and the corpse of Mrs. McLeavy with its entrails removed and its artificial eyeballs insecurely socketed—this homey parlor is invaded by a police detective, Truscott by name, a travesty of those masterminds of pulp fiction who know absolutely everything but the outcome of the action. That action relies upon hundreds and hundreds of entrances and exits as the characters slip into and out of the room, the story, the coffin, and melodrama. Some of the best exchanges are generated by Truscott, who is almost as hung up on official procedures as one of Simpson's intelligence agents.

FAY: Can't he fetch the Pope's photo?
TRUSCOTT: Only if some responsible person accompanies him.
HAL: You're a responsible person. You could accompany him.
TRUSCOTT: What proof have I that I'm a responsible person?

TRUSCOTT: Do as you're told or take the consequences.
McLEAVY: I'll take the consequences.
TRUSCOTT: I can't allow that.

Orton's last play, *What the Butler Saw* (1967), produced posthumously, uncovers more, much more than its peep-show title hints at; enough to freeze the blood and frazzle the wits of a mildly kinky denizen of an English penny arcade. In its final scenes, which are laid, and laid to rest, in á psychiatric clinic, a young woman clothed as a young man, a young man clothed as an unclothed young woman, a wounded police sergeant in a leopard-spotted dress, two psychiatrists armed with pistols, and a distraught wife fight off straitjackets and the tortured complications to which Orton has cavalierly subjected them. All of a sudden Orton wipes all the complications off his slate and in their place scribbles a set of new ones. Which are very ancient. In the most revered traditions of the happy ending, the discovery of birth trinkets in a casket, the young man produces half of a brooch which proves him to be the son of the distraught wife, whom he raped the night before in a hotel linen closet. The other half of the brooch belongs

to the young woman, proving her to be the daughter of the same
lady, and also of one of the psychiatrists, who had earlier tried to
rape her, much as, years earlier, he had made love to his wife, the
distraught lady, in the same hotel linen closet chosen by his son,
each of them taking the other for a stranger. The second psychia-
trist is making mental notes like, well, like crazy for a "documentary type novelette" he intends to make a fortune on: "The final
chapters of my book are knitting together: incest, buggery, outrageous women and strange love cults catering for depraved appetites. All the fashionable bric-a-brac. A beautiful but neurotic girl
has influenced the doctor to sacrifice a white virgin to propitiate
the dark gods of unreason. 'When they broke into the evil-smelling
den they found her poor bleeding body beneath the obscene and
half-erect phallus.' . . . Society must be made aware of the growing menace of pornography." As for the casket, yes, it appears,
and contains the private parts of a statue of Sir Winston Churchill
which were blown by a gas-main explosion into the body of a
woman nearby and removed by a thoughtful undertaker. Looking
at one of the parts, the young woman takes it for Churchill's cigar.
"Ah," sighs the psychiatrist-novelist, "the illusions of youth!" Evidently the sculpture was both realistic and a representation of Sir
Winston in the altogether.

In the piling up of manic highs that is the substance of this
farce, Orton has switched his attention from one religion, Catholicism (in *Loot*), to another, psychiatric healing, not only by sophisticated parody, but also by making his two doctors into the
puppets of insane reasoning.

DR. PRENTICE: Miss Barclay is quite safe. She's downstairs. I've
just remembered.
DR. RANCE: Why did you keep the fact from us?
DR. PRENTICE: It'd slipped my memory.
DR. RANCE: Have you suffered from lapses of memory before?
DR. PRENTICE: I can't remember.
DR. RANCE: Your memory plays you false even on the subject of
its own inadequacy?

DR. PRENTICE: You're forcing the boy to undergo a repetition of a
traumatic experience, sir. He might go insane.

DR. RANCE: This is a mental home. He couldn't choose a more appropriate place.

GERALDINE: I can't go on, doctor! I must tell the truth. I'm not a boy! I'm a girl!

DR. RANCE *(to Dr. Prentice):* Excellent. A confession at last. He wishes to believe he's a girl in order to minimize the feelings of guilt after homosexual intercourse.[17]

Neurotic Americans

The excesses of Orton's two doctors, and the playwright's implied injunction "Physician, heal thyself," remind us that in twentieth-century well-made plays, portraits of psychoanalysts and addicted patients have become a growth industry that shows no sign of stagnating. American plays and films that dramatize psychoanalytic procedures seem to delight everybody. They give comfort to those tranquil souls who require no mental coddling (these belong to a church or guru and/or follow Ann Landers), while they also reassure spectators who are captives of long-term analysis, members of two- or three-shrink families who set aside for "help" a lump of the monthly paycheck, along with the mortgage, car, boat, food, heating, book club, and home-box-office dues. Most psychoanalytic plays, farces and others, fit squarely into realism. Their authors pride themselves on an authentic display of symptoms and an accurate use of the latest jargon; their stories consist of only slightly modified case histories.

The theater has always trafficked in psychic abnormalities: obsessive fears, drives, inhibitions, and hatreds, as well as inexplicable heroism. Many older plays continue to fascinate us just because we cannot pin unarguable motives on such erratic behavior, whereas the modern psychoanalytic W.M.P., which catches our attention for a while, often ends by explaining its characters' motives away, as though psychiatry provided some kind of final answer, a lenitive for all human ills.

No modern American theater studies of psychoses stand up to

---

[17] Orton's plays are published separately (New York: Grove Press, 1965, 1967, 1970). I have not dealt here with his television plays. For a full critical discussion of Orton's works see John Lahr, *Prick Up Your Ears: The Biography of Joe Orton* (New York: Knopf, 1979).

the best written elsewhere, such as *Caligula* (1945) by Albert
Camus or *Marat/Sade* (1963) by Peter Weiss or *The Ruling Class*
(1969) and *The Bewitched* (1974) by Peter Barnes, which don't
pluck out the heart of their own mysteries. America, however, has
produced quantities of fairly realistic plays about neurotics. The
more penetrating ones, all farces, have come from Jules Feiffer
and Woody Allen. Feiffer and Allen, both caricaturists, do encroach at times on fantasy and theatricalism; still, their characters
are recognizably warped urbanites of our age, and their satire rises
from realistic foundations. Feiffer is known otherwise for his
screenplays and cartoon strips, Allen for his movies, farcical essays, and solo turns as a comedian. But both have distinction as
playwrights. They carry on the literate tradition of Gilbert and
Wilde filtered through the Broadway, Jewish nonsensicality of
George S. Kaufman, Morrie Ryskind, and Abe Burrows. Their
characters really *talk*, getting off some of the funniest lines in
recent dramatic literature. And some of the wisest. Their first plays
reached Broadway the same year, 1966. Allen's *Don't Drink the
Water*, opening after some frantic recasting, persisted there for a
year and a half. Feiffer's *Little Murders*, weakly acted and directed, shut down in a week but reappeared a couple of years later
in an Off Broadway house and had a cheerful run.

Allen (born 1935) had up until then been concocting gags and
routines for comedians, himself included, besides the screenplay
for *What's New, Pussycat?* (1965) and an English sound track for
What's Up, Tiger Lily? (1966), a whodunit some optimists had shot
in Japan. *Don't Drink the Water* reveals again Allen's gift for piling
up laughable free associations. ("I paint. You'd hate my work,
though, it's all very abstract. I stand back and splash oil all over
everything and then I run all over it with my sneakers and I stick
my lunch on it—in fact, my lunch came in second at a showing in
Cape Cod.") On these lines the author imposes a wobbly play
structure about a caterer from New Jersey, his wife, and their
nubile daughter, tourists in an East European country that might
be Bulgaria or Albania. The father snaps some photos of a missile
site, and pursued by unsecret police, the family takes refuge in the
American embassy, which is governed in the ambassador's absence
by his son, Axel Magee, an agreeable incompetent. ("If there was
such a thing as the failure business, I'd have chain stores.") Magee

is the first developed version of Allen's shnook hero to whom beautiful girls unaccountably surrender. This character, disguised as himself, always drops sharp quips at his own expense and that of page-one names from *The New York Times*. As a loser who wins, he has a lot in common with the early film personae of Chaplin, Langdon, Keaton, and later comics such as Red Skelton and Bob Hope.

In his next farce, *Play It Again, Sam* (1969), Allen took over this Woody role himself, and has enacted it since then in his films, including the film of *Sam*. (He had written it into the script for *What's New, Pussycat?*, which he had a part in, but the producer and director wrote most of it out again during filming, leaving him with a few skimpy appearances.) The hero of *Sam*, Allan Felix, "who looks as if he has just stepped out of a Jules Feiffer cartoon," represents a pace or two further along the psychiatric track from Axel Magee. Axel puts his foot in his mouth so often that the taste of toe or shoe must have deadened his palate, but he is not a "case." Allan Felix is. His wife has walked out. His friends Dick and Linda, a married couple, want to rematch him. Only, how does he subdue his neuroses and become lovable? Here is where Bogart comes in, stepping out of the wall at intervals like a bogeyman to offer advice on handling women: slug them in the mouth or kiss them to bits or keep telling them they're beautiful. Allan can't quite take these suggestions because of what he is, "a mass of symptoms," but he can't ignore them, also because of what he is, a film critic who treats the memory of Bogart even more reverently than the rest of us do. Not only Bogart materializes from the scenery. Allan's departing wife and assorted girls from his past and dreams surface from that all-too-accessible unconscious of his to join in the scenes. *Sam* concludes with some upbeat flourishes. Allan has been smitten by Linda and she by him; but—a gesture of renunciation worthy of a Corneille monarch or Bogart—he sends her back to Dick by quoting from Bogart's farewell lines in *Casablanca*. Almost immediately a new girl, who's a distinct possibility for Allan because she admires his movie criticism, strolls in. But before this soggy concession to Broadway, Allan dismisses the Bogart vision: "The secret's not being you, it's being me. True, you're not too tall and kinda ugly. But I'm short enough and ugly enough to succeed by myself."

Allen's pair of one-act plays *God* and *Death* (both 1973), although replete with familiar pop-culture references, don't fit into
a realistic frame, even one with a lot of give on all sides. *God*, a
theatricalist piece, comprises a free-for-all discussion about a
Greek play that has no ending, with interjections from modern
spectators, the very text thus being a comment on itself.[18] *Death*,
a less farcical piece of writing, reminiscent of Ionesco's *The Killer*
in that a maniac wipes out victims for no reason, catches up at last
with the hero Kleinman (a Jewish little Everyman) and not only
murders him but adds suicidal insult to injury by looking like
Kleinman's double. These plays, far more venturesome in their
fragmenting of time, space, characterization, and theatrical continuity than the two Broadway entries were, show Allen, as in his
later movies *Annie Hall* and *Manhattan*, toying with dramatic
form. The more recent works, including *The Floating Light Bulb*
(1981), are more serious, yes; but the writer seems to be searching
for some structural equivalent of the non sequiturs, mixed metaphors, and crazy analogies that riddle his dialogue and, even more,
his nightclub acts.

The figures in the cartoon strips of Jules Feiffer (born 1929) have
angular shapes. Contact with their surroundings hurts them; they
blunt themselves. Like the characters in Feiffer's plays (or those in
Allen's), they seek in self-analysis, aided by ingestions of pills that
take them up and down, harmony with their defects (the precon-
dition for happiness), generally by acquiring a soul mate. Feiffer's
farces, less strained for the sake of sheer entertainment than
Allen's, and less good-natured, draw laughter for moral purposes.
And draw blood: their satire levels social and political as well as
personal criticism. *Little Murders* unfolds the story of the corruption of a family, the Newquists, in their Manhattan apartment.
The grown son, Kenny, hesitant between budding and practicing
homosexuality, and Patsy, his sister, engaged to a lethargic young

---

[18] *God*, as a play with an unfirm ending, was probably provoked in Allen's mind by his
experience with a sequence called "What Makes a Man a Homosexual?" that he wrote and
shot for inclusion in his film *Everything You Always Wanted to Know About Sex* (see
Chapter 14). The script of the sequence is reproduced in *On Being Funny: Woody Allen
and Comedy* by Eric Lax (New York: Charterhouse Books, 1975), pp. 153–64. Allen said of
the sequence, in which a black widow spider traps a spider personification of the Woody
character in her web, "It never had an ending and it never went anyplace." The script,
though, is a joy to read.

man (kissing him, she says, is like kissing white bread) to whom she proposes and whom she proposes to rule, are the products of a bossy mother and a yielding father. So much for psychoanalytic determinism. Patsy and her boyfriend will be married by a hippie priest who's been instructed not to mention God. For the New-quists the outside world is something to shun, if not flee from; but it intrudes at every opportunity. Sounds of gunfire in the streets oppress them; so do obscene phone calls. One caller, the Breather, is "the pleasantest of the lot—you should hear the ones who talk." A police lieutenant on his rounds observes that some three hundred forty-five unsolved homicides are part of "an attempt to undermine faith in law enforcement."

During the marriage ceremony, a bullet through the window kills Patsy, the bride. In the last scene the Newquists have taken to heart the priest's sermon that doesn't mention God: "Christ died for our sins. Dare we make his act meaningless by not committing them?" Like beleaguered gangsters in a Thirties movie, they are holed up in the apartment and shooting back at the world. Kenny proclaims, "Dad and I got our two," and the bridegroom-widower gets the police lieutenant. The Newquists have turned into their own fears, into the beasts that prowl inside.

God Bless (1968), with "America" signally absent from its title, has as its principal character Bill Brackman, a brackish politician aged one hundred ten and not yet senile. Like Jack Crabb, the one-hundred-eleven-year-old hero of Thomas Berger's novel *Little Big Man* (1964), Brackman is dictating his memoirs. But his life has only a metaphorical resemblance to Crabb's adventures as an alternating Indian and white man. Brackman has lived through many decades of novelty and manipulation in Washington, and now he has seen that city succumb to a revolution. But he trims his tattered sails to it as adroitly as his eighteenth-century English predecessor the Vicar of Bray adjusted to the latest wind of political change. The revolutionaries themselves are yahoos modeled on the more flatulent demagogues of the Sixties, not so much students as perennial students, what college presidents liked to call outside agitators. Feiffer, although repelled by the p.r. strategies that pass for political administration (and not only in Washington), could not welcome a new form of government that would unseat one set of power brokers only to enthrone another.

As though to insist that he had not meant to defend the System, Feiffer's next play, *The White House Murder Case* (1970), pitilessly examines the maneuverings among a President and his advisers to hold on through the next election at a time "several presidential elections hence." America is at war with Brazil, and losing. An officer in the field gave the order to use nerve gas, a weapon banned by the Geneva Convention. The President's wife, an open opponent of her husband's policies, and therefore an embarrassment to the President, his inner councils, and his party, is stabbed to death. The play's two themes intertwine. At frenzied White House meetings some attempt is made to blame antiwar protesters for the assassination and to blame the enemy for the use of the gas. Meanwhile, on the field of battle we witness in counterpoint —simultaneously on the stage—the effects of the gas on two Americans stricken when the gas, as in World War I, blew in the wrong direction. The officer who called for deploying the gas and a CIA man sent out to grill him gradually disintegrate: their limbs break off and their minds separate from their bodies. The scenes of dispute inside the White House, while stretched beyond the usual limits of realistic accusation and confession, so that they impinge on farce ("Once a Pandora's box of fear and doubt is left lying open in our midst, we will, every one of us, be sucked helplessly into its maw"), seem not at all exaggerated when compared with the dialogues of the Watergate cover-up tapes released several years later.

Feiffer's next farce shifted away from politics and from realism. The title *Knock Knock* (1976) doesn't refer to a double helping of Jules Romains's doctor but to the entry of Joan of Arc, equipped with two competing Voices, in addition to her own, into "a small log cabin in the woods" inhabited by two recluses, Abe and Cohn, who have grown bored with each other after twenty years of being together. Joan has determined that "the sky is missing and that mankind's path to heaven is at last unblocked . . . and that God calls on His Highness, the Emperor, to build a thousand spaceships and put on them two of every kind and blast off for heaven. Before the holocaust." The holocaust doesn't come, nor does the Emperor. But there is another visitor, Joan's opposite number, a Mr. Wiseman, who affects different roles, one that of the Tempter, who traditionally had a variety of faces, front and back.

At the end Joan does soar off toward heaven, leaving the earth-bound Abe her armor and Cohn her Voices. In *Knock Knock* the dialogue, much of it quasi-metaphysical give-and-take about being and nonbeing, skates lightly over Beckett terrain, leaving in its wake a lot of vaudevillian patter and a few (deliberately?) hoary gags. ("Knock knock." "Who's there?" "Joan." "Joan who?" "Joan ask me no questions and I'll tell you no lies.")

Allen and Feiffer, although contemporaries and both realistic writers to start with, differ as farceurs. Allen goes for the big laugh, and if he happens to touch on certain causes of individual and social malaise, he does so almost by happy accident. Feiffer *looks for* explanations, and if we appreciate the humor in his diagnoses —if we can laugh at his characters while recognizing our own flaws in theirs—we see that he is a naturalistic playwright in the vein of Ibsen, Chekhov, and especially Shaw in the motives and reasons he ferrets out. Yet these two authors have found, as Ibsen, Chekhov, and Shaw did, that the older forms of realism and the determinism of psychoanalysis are insufficient for their purposes. The alternative futures available to their characters can come to pass only through exertions of willpower.

THIRTEEN

THEATRICALISM AFTER PIRANDELLO

ARTIE (*out front; nervous*): My name is Artie Shaughnessy and I'm going to sing you songs I wrote. I wrote all these songs. Words and the music. Could I have some quiet, please?

Artie goes on to perform three of his numbers as a prelude to the play proper, *The House of Blue Leaves* (1972) by John Guare (born 1938). When the two acts of the play have almost concluded, Artie rounds them off; he reappears alone, steps into a blue spotlight, and sings an aftersong.

THE CONTEMPORARY: Ladies and gentlemen. You are looking at the Chinese Wall, the greatest edifice in the history of mankind. It measures (according to the encyclopedia) over ten thousand li, or—to express it more concretely—the distance between Berlin and New York. . . .

The Contemporary continues to chat for a while. He mentions the Chinese characters in the play to come, *The Chinese Wall* (1955) by Max Frisch (born 1911), and others, celebrities from history and the drama, who will also be part of the cast list. Then, like Artie Shaughnessy, he walks into the action and takes part in it.

Two trumpets and a drum sound. Mosquito enters from wherever you wish. Mosquito is a mysterious personage, part ghost, part leprechaun, part insect. He represents the joy of a free life and the wit and poetry of the Andalusian people. He carries a little trumpet of the kind sold at village fairs.

MOSQUITO: Men and women, attention! Son, shut your little mouth, and you, little girl, sit down, by all that's unholy. Now hush so the silence can grow as clear as if it were in its own spring. Hush so the dregs of the last whispers can settle down. . . .[1]

Mosquito has assumed the role of manager-director. He tells how he and his company fled from the "gold and crystal" playhouses of the city to perform in open-air country settings, from the aristocrats and bourgeoisie to "the plain people." He orates with poetic flourishes; then he vanishes until after the six scenes of *The Billy-Club Puppets* (1922), a folk farce by the young Federico García Lorca (1899–1936), when he leads a parade of all the characters and sings a farewell.

Each of these three twentieth-century farce openings, American, Swiss-German, and Spanish, sets a tone for the play that follows. Artie's lines are casual and confiding; the Contemporary's, formal and documentary; Mosquito's, mock-stern and whimsical. But they all borrow an ancient theatrical device that has become something of a mania in our time: greeting the audience. A few words that sound personal, intimate even, are meant to put the spectators on familiar terms with the author and actors, and to give them a minute or two to settle down and realize that the show is under way. When these characters or others come on at the finish of the performance they may apologize for the work's shortcomings, bring the spectators back into their own world without too much of a bump, fish for applause, and encourage everybody present to remember that this particular showing was intended for the benefit of this particular audience, a custom-crafted perfor-

---

[1] These extracts are taken respectively from *The House of Blue Leaves* by John Guare (New York: Penguin, 1972); *The Chinese Wall* by Max Frisch, translated by James L. Rosenberg (New York: Hill & Wang, 1961); and *The Billy-Club Puppets* by Federico García Lorca, translated by James Graham-Luján and Richard L. O'Connell in *Five Plays by Lorca* (New York: New Directions, 1963).

mance. A *Midsummer Night's Dream* closes with Puck's speech as the actor unwinds himself from his role:

> If we shadows have offended,
> Think but this, and all is mended,
> That you have but slumber'd here
> While these visions did appear. . . .
> Give me your hands, if we be friends. . . .

Audiences can also be addressed during the action, not only before and after it. Some of the other characters in *The House of Blue Leaves*, besides Artie, turn to the audience now and then to voice a grievance, a hope, a stray thought. Such interruptions are different in function from hellos and goodbyes. They break the spell of the production, reminding the audience that it's watching actors at work, not people to whom these events are really happening. They say in effect, "This is the life of the theater, not the theater of life." Such spell-breakers have a long history too. Until the late nineteenth century, when the first wave of realistic plays did away with them, they existed in two forms: as the aside, in which a character tells the audience something the other people onstage aren't supposed to hear, and as the soliloquy, that species of monologue which lets a character think out loud so that spectators can't help eavesdropping.

Bertolt Brecht, more tenaciously than any other playwright in this century, revived and revised the aside and the soliloquy. While other playwrights want their audiences collectively enraptured, Brecht wants his jerked now and then out of the state of "slumber" mentioned by Puck and back to the reality of their own lives— literally disconcerted: each person taken out of concert with everybody else. In this fashion he or she has a chance to catch up with the issues discussed in the play, to be separated for a moment from the play's suspense and pay attention to its meanings and implications. Brecht's interruptions make use of posters, slides, songs, and speeches. These halt the action and either summarize what has gone on so far or announce what is to come. They work with efficacy in farce, which thrives on surprises.

Speaking to the audience, whether before, during, or after the action of a play, is the most common and least complicated type of theatricalism, the self-conscious type of theater. One explanation for the prominence of theatricalism in recent years—in farces and other drama—may be the welcome relaxing of public decorum. An executive vice-president and a junior clerk call each other Fred and Charlie. Video newscasters expend more effort on palsy-walsy palavers, on presenting themselves and one another to viewers, and on signing off by name than they do on circulating the news. Everybody these days knows everybody else—well. Men and women alike hungrily kiss and clasp other women they haven't seen for twenty-four hours. Amid this conviviality and fellowship, theater people, who are among the most demonstrative in society, hello and goodbye their beloved patrons to a fare-thee-well.

Another explanation for the spread of theatricalism is that it serves to uphold the theater's identity as a medium. From once being the exclusive purveyor of dramatic entertainment, it now ranks far behind movies and television by any system of measurement, and lacks claques as passionate and stars as magnetic as those of the dance and opera. Theatricalism is a kind of assertiveness, saying, "This is theater and nothing else." When Hope or Crosby or Woody Allen looks into the camera and murmurs something about a prop man crossing the studio floor, the filmic theatricalism—for that's what it is—appears removed, impersonal, by comparison with an aside in the playhouse, where the actors are accessible and susceptible—to flying fruit as well as unexpected retorts from a spectator that may fluster them.

Off Off Broadway in New York, the size of the houses and the nature of the plays sometimes make inevitable a close relationship between the stage and the seats. In *The Hawk* (1968) by Murray Mednick and Tony Barsha, a semiserious work about drug addicts, the missing fourth wall is regarded as a mirror before which characters frequently commune with themselves as they face the audience.

Many playwrights have doubtless eyed with envy summer stock's most popular article, *Our Town* (1938), which America ought by now to rename *Our Play*. Conducted by an actor impersonating a stage manager—an experiment the author, Thornton Wilder (1897–1978), had already attempted with two short pieces, *Pullman Car Hiawatha* and *The Happy Journey to Trenton and Camden* (both 1931)—the action is not farcical; still, its apparently loose structure, cozily attractive poetry, jumps in time, acidic nostalgia, and above all, its one-way conversations with the audience have called forth imitations in farces as well as in other genres. Some authors have also taken inspiration from Beckett's *Happy Days*, in which the heroine, Winnie, speaks what might be (and usually is) taken as a monologue addressed to the audience. Actually, Winnie aims her lines throughout the play at her husband, Willie, who crawls around and below the mound where she is partially buried.

Tom Stoppard (born 1937) had a similar idea to Mednick's and Barsha's when in *Jumpers* (1972) he decreed that his hero, a professor of philosophy, dictates to "the large mirror in the fourth wall," rather than to his secretary, memorably beginning a lecture on God, zero, and prime causes with the word, "Secondly . . ." (In the next room his wife is screaming, "Murder—rape—wolves!") Stoppard's partly farcical *Night and Day* (1979) has a sarcastic, sexy lady who's continually speaking her mind in asides. In one scene she acts out a brief, imaginary love affair with a young stranger who was killed, she learns later, before the wishful scene took place. Here Stoppard goes further than making us privy to her thoughts; he dramatizes them.

Plays Within Plays

ACE: . . . Okay! Okay! Let's everyone take a seat and do something right for a change. You, you over there, be a good fellow and sit down. Let's all take a deep breath. (*Takes a deep breath*) And let's start off alive. It's getting near opening time. . . .

Ace, a black man, is one of half a dozen "minority" men and women (the others are an Oriental-American, a nihilist, a spastic, a con man, and a streetwalker) who make up the little society of *The Apple* (1961) by Jack Gelber (born 1932). They slip into and out of scenes and roles on a stage that begins as "a restaurant or coffee shop," but becomes whatever the performers want it to be. To generate conflict, a drunk named Tom keeps cutting in on the action with offensive remarks about everybody else. Tom has no use for blacks, Oriental-Americans, nihilists, spastics, con men, streetwalkers, or drunks. He turns out himself to be one of a "minority"—lunatics. The personal but businesslike greeting offered by Ace to the audience marks this farce's theatricalism. At the same time, it introduces a second type of theatricalism. When Ace says, "It's getting near opening time," he's misleading his audience. The play opened when he appeared onstage; indeed, it opened before that because "in the lobby before the play begins drunken Tom offers several members of the audience a drink from his pint bottle. He accuses them of pushing him around and makes a paranoid nuisance of himself." Ace is preparing his listeners for a performance within the performance, a play within the play.

One of the most straightforward and familiar specimens of a play within a play is the "Murder of Gonzago" melodrama, also referred to as "The Mousetrap," put on at Hamlet's request to mortify his uncle and mother. Hamlet, Claudius, Gertrude, and the Danish courtiers are characters in an "outer" play *Hamlet* who make up an onstage audience for the "inner" play "Gonzago." Another familiar instance occurs in *A Midsummer Night's Dream* when the "mechanicals" play their "Pyramus and Thisbe" melodrama, which they unwittingly turn into a farce. The onstage audience for the inner play here consists of Theseus; his bride, Hippolyta; and two pairs of befuddled lovers recruited from the outer play. Thus, while some actors in *A Midsummer Night's Dream* are playing characters who play spectators, other actors are playing characters (Bottom the weaver, Quince, Snug, Flute, Snout, and Starveling) who play actors playing secondary roles. Without getting into semantic tangles about levels, depths, or dimensions of role-playing, we can see that in this type of theatricalism the possibilities of confusion (that is to say, of farce) are promising, even in a self-contained playlet like "Pyramus and Thisbe."

Some plays within plays are not self-contained. We may be given scattered scenes, as in *The Apple*. Or a character may do convincing impersonations of somebody else from life or from fiction, as happens in Gelber's *The Cuban Thing* (1968), in which the hero, Roberto, imitates Fidel Castro. Or the inner drama may be incomplete or fragmented, as in *Six Characters in Search of an Author*. And then questions can crop up. Does a secondary role in the inner drama ever grow more important to the outer play than the primary role done by the same actor? Is the play "really" about the outer, encircling drama or the inner one? Does the inner drama in some way stand for or reflect or refract the meanings of the outer one? (I believe, for example, that understanding the farcical "Pyramus and Thisbe" helps one to appreciate the farce and the weight of A *Midsummer Night's Dream*.)

Playwrights have long been fascinated by the flux of emotions generated when actors rehearse and alternate between being versions of themselves and rough drafts of their parts. Molière studied himself and his company at work in *The Rehearsal at Versailles* (1663), catching some of the hopes, exasperation, selfishness, and group loyalty as the troupe fumbles toward a finished production and never reaches it. *The Rehearsal* (1671) by George Villiers, Duke of Buckingham, and some of his collaborators ridicules Dryden's *The Conquest of Granada*, part two of which had opened earlier that same year. To friends who are attending a rehearsal, the author brags about his bloated similes and praises his mixed metaphors; the hero of the inner play, Prince Pretty-man, worries that his beloved Cloris is not going to keep their appointment, pleads with the sun to dry his tears, and then, as Cloris comes into sight like "some blazing comet," he falls asleep; two quartets of soldiers discover they are allies, whereupon they kill each other—and spring back to life when the orchestra sounds a magical note. In Sheridan's *The Critic: or, A Tragedy Rehearsed* (1779) we have another author who directs his own play and is his own most effusive critic. Mr. Puff, a precursor of today's press agent or copywriter who composes plays during quiet hours, "applauds everything" he has written. As he coaches the actors, he explains the beauties and ingenuity of the action to a mini-audience of two theater buffs who feel grateful for the privilege of sitting in on the rehearsal.

Plays within plays and stages upon stages like these give the theater opportunities to tell "in" jokes and to laugh at itself. Luigi Pirandello (1867–1936) encouraged the theater to think about itself. He gave new currency to the play within a play as conscientiously as Brecht did to the aside and the soliloquy. Three of Pirandello's tragicomedies deal with the act of making theater: *Six Characters in Search of an Author* (1921), *Each in His Own Way* (1922), and *Tonight We Improvise* (1932). He called them his trilogy of "theater-in-the-theater," and all of them have an outer and an incomplete inner drama. In some of his other plays, which are not about the act of making theater, he nevertheless persists with this structure of inner and outer dramas. Pirandello didn't write farces as such, but his plays do have their farcical moments. Since the Twenties and Pirandello's experiments, other playwrights, among them farceurs, have borrowed his device of theater-in-the-theater or plays within plays so often, so variously, and so shamelessly that this type of theatricalism is rightly considered *the* characteristic dramatic mode of the century, theater turning in on itself, pondering its nature as a form of life and a form of art, usually by setting up a dialogue of a sort between the outer and the inner play.

The most extravagant instance of American theater-in-the-theater happens to be also the most ambitious American play yet written: *him* (1927) by E. E. Cummings (1894–1962), a prodigal piece of work that belongs with a select group of superplays. These don't give a hoot for the customary limitations of the stage; they aspire to dramatic heights never before attained.[2] Few of these plays venture into theatricalism, and none, apart from *him*, into farce, although Sartre did make one stab at a superfarcical satire with his *Nekrassov* (1955). Plays of this caliber make imposing demands on directors and producers (perhaps a cast of hundreds for some scenes) and on scenographers (an avalanche, a storm at sea, masks by the dozen). Even when these superplays are clipped or otherwise altered for a performance—and they almost always are—they require the perfervid concentration of a superaudience. The dramatists have amassed their resources of intellect and craftsmanship in such fashion that as they pry into the mysteries of human beings who are separate entities and yet members one of another, they give us more than we bargained for.

In writing *him*, Cummings packed into his outer drama ring upon ring of inner dramas—such an abundance of them that a

---

[2] Aeschylus achieved a superplay with his trilogy *The Oresteia*; Shakespeare with *King Lear*, *Timon of Athens*, and *The Tempest*; Kalidasa with the Sanskrit classic *Shakuntala*; Thomas Lovell Beddoes with *Death's Jest-Book*, even though he hadn't completed it at his death; Ibsen with *Brand*, *Peer Gynt*, and *When We Dead Awaken*; Strindberg with *A Dream Play*; Shaw with *Man and Superman* and *Back to Methuselah*; Karl Krauss with *The Last Days of Mankind*; O'Neill with *Strange Interlude* and *Mourning Becomes Electra*; Pirandello with *Tonight We Improvise*; Sartre with *The Devil and The Good Lord*; Genet with *The Screens*; Hochhuth with *The Deputy*.

fair synopsis of the play would take several thousand words. The outer drama has to do with three characters called Him, a poet composing a play; Me, his wife or lover, who is on the verge of having her first child; and Me's obstetrician, the Doctor.

ME: What's this play of yours all about?
HIM *(To himself, smiling at the ceiling)*: This play of mine is all about mirrors.
ME: But who's the hero?
HIM *(To her)*: The hero of this play of mine? *(Hesitates.)* A man. . . .
ME: Naturally. What sort of a man?
HIM: The sort of man—who is writing a play about a man who is writing a sort of a play.
ME: That's a queer hero, isn't it?

The inner dramas of *him* run through scenes from Him's playscript (probably not all of it). We deduce that he reads or relates or acts it out to her, while she, an informal, unpracticed critic, comments on the scenes and asks questions about them. These scenes endeavor to sum up the state of the world in the late Twenties: the heady social life of the rich; starvation and inflation in Germany as two legacies of World War I; the presence of America in Europe in the guise of tourists and artists; the varied fronts on which the avant-garde fought its way toward new forms that might—but never did—break definitively with the past; the atmosphere of finally, a quarter of a century late, getting into the twentieth century. About some of these scenes there is an ambiguity that doesn't allow us to say for sure whether they are part of Him's play or his past or his past as he has dramatized it. The scenes bring on a number of characters who reappear thematically. Him and the Doctor even play roles in the inner dramas. In addition, the play as a whole has an almost mystical preoccupation with the numbers three (the Fates) and nine (the Muses). It takes place between three walls, and occasional references are made to the audience beyond the missing fourth wall. The second of three acts contains nine scenes. Scenes three and six call for nine platforms onstage. Another scene has "nine black stairs leading up to a white curtain." The Fates, the spinners, appear repeatedly as three knitting ladies, a trio of commentators named Miss Stop Weird, Miss Look Weird, and Miss Listen Weird, who address gnomic or funny remarks to one another and to Him and the Doctor, many about a pet hippo who was christened It's Toasted, evidently after a widely touted brand of cigarette. Their relationship to the hero resembles that of the three witches, or "weyerd" sisters, to Macbeth. To complement these ladies there's a trio of drunk, middle-aged men whose slurry speech is reproduced phonetically as carefully as that of certain characters of Shaw. The birth of Me's child concludes her nine months of pregnancy. Late in the play, a spectacle of sideshow freaks (the not-so-new century?) introduced by a barker ranges from the Nine Foot Giant to Six Hundred Pounds of Passionate Pulchritude and the Eighteen Inch Lady. It must be coincidental that when Cummings wrote the play he was thirty-three.

His work thus has the fatalistic tone that has always typified farce (and tragedy). It shows the protagonist pitting his will against destiny and finding that he is as much a part of his destiny as his will is part of him. Cummings even puts in a character by the name of Will and his double. Will seems to die suddenly, and then his double accuses another man of having killed him. In this sequence, a further threesome, we realize that when Him said, "This play of mine is all about mirrors," he was creating characters in *his* play most of whom are aspects of Him and Me. Him and Me, in turn, are male and female images of each other in the throes of giving birth, while the time itself labors to give birth to a new world. But Him and Me also stand for aspects of one soul: Him for the artist, who lives most fiercely in his mind as he discusses loving and being and the world he has fabricated; Me for the person who *loves* and *is*, and bears a child. The final item in the freak show turns out to be a vision of Me, in white, holding the baby in her arms. Perhaps we are meant to wonder in the end whether the outer drama is something dreamed up by Him, absorbed in his play, feeling guilty at thinking too much and feeling too little, or whether the inner dramas are dreamed by Me during the nightmare of her birth pangs.

Cummings inserts into *him* scenes that conform with Apollinaire's prescription for the surreal (the fantastic), "a reasonable use of the improbable." He shows us Mussolini, who is treated as the Emperor Nero but talks gangster slang—yet another three-in-

one. An Englishman travels on the Continent carrying his unconscious in a trunk on his back. Two American ladies in a Paris
restaurant order *homme* (man) for dinner: one wants hers stewed;
the other prefers boiled. The word *homme* sounds like the first
syllable of *homard*, lobster. A gentleman in a Central European
city meets up with a mob of starving, wraithlike figures, throws
them a loaf of bread out of desperation, and starts to strip off his
clothes under the impression that he is a baby just born. Yet this
last fantasy, and others, proceed from conditions that were real in
1927: the famine, a glut of American tourists in Paris, Mussolini
settling into his *duce*-dom. Cummings draws our attention to the
realistic elements in his theatricalism when, at the end of both the
outer drama and the entire play, Me points out that people are
watching.

ME: Real people. And do you know what they're doing?
HIM *(Stares at her)*: What are they doing?
ME *(Walking slowly upstage toward the door)*: They're pretending
    that this room and you and I are real. *(At the door, turning,
    faces the audience.)*
HIM *(Standing in the middle of the room, whispers)*: I wish I could
    believe this.
ME *(Smiles, shaking her head)*: You can't.
HIM *(Staring at the invisible wall)*: Why?
ME: Because this is true.
                    (Curtain.)

Some of its exponents have claimed that theatricalism is more
real than realism is. Realism behaves dishonestly by ignoring the
substitution of the audience for a fourth wall (or, in the case of an
outdoor setting, a fourth horizon). Anyway, how can offstage life
"really" take place on a stage? Theater is more candid, more true
to its inherent artificiality, when it acknowledges the presence of
observers and the fact of pretense. This argument will carry weight
with people who agree that honesty somehow improves art. Others
are likely to shrug. The theatrical revolution we call realism came
about not because it was truer to life than the artifice it elbowed
aside, but because the old artifice had worn out and realism
brought with it many unfamiliar investigations of new motives,

settings, and forms; it opened up fresh dramatic tracts. Much the same happened when theatricalism arrived. Realism had been imitating itself into automatism, if not slow paralysis. Theatricalism then fed into the theater new motives, forms, and transformations, the offspring of realism and fantasy, some favoring one parent, some the other, some looking like adopted children. Cummings' play thus celebrates not the birth of theatricalism, because theatricalism did already exist, but its lusty rebirth.

Memories, Dreams, Travesties—and Role-Playing

So far I have mentioned three common formulations—plays within plays, inner and outer dramas, and theater-in-the-theater —as though they were synonymous. They are all useful, but Pirandello's term is the broadest of the three. Theater-in-the-theater can refer to an inner drama set in a simple framework that is not a play, or to an outer drama with one or more inserts that are fragmentary. *The Taming of the Shrew*, for example, opens with an "induction" in which the beggar Christopher Sly is gulled into thinking that he's a lord; that a pageboy in a dress is his lady; and that a performance of the Kate-Petruchio match and its subplots is being put on for his benefit. But the play ends with the inner drama, Kate's avowal of a wife's duties. Whether Shakespeare wrote in a rude awakening for Sly, when his finery, rank, and lady are taken back, or whether the author believed that rounding out the Sly induction with an epilogue would prove an anticlimax is still a matter for dispute. As it stands, the Sly episode is an outer drama that remains unconsummated and is often for this reason omitted from productions.

In *One Way for Another* (1951), a satirical one-act, Jean Tardieu (born 1903) employs a similar device. An admiral named Sepulchre walks onstage and tells about the Nameless Archipelago, where he lived for over twenty years in a "highly advanced civilization: newly built-up cities—which owed their creation to frequent bombardments; completely free citizens—thanks to an omnipresent and ever-watchful police force; peaceful customs—defended by a militia armed to the teeth; and a government solidly based on the instability of opinions—in short . . . all the things ordinarily associated with the march of progress. . . ." The Admiral walks into the inner play as a guest at a soiree on the Archipelago, where manners and conceits are a mockery of those in France. The people greet their hostess by kissing her right foot and handing her their socks for her collection. When a gentleman reads aloud "one of his worst poems," dedicated to his wife and written "on a day when I felt particularly bad," the others voice their appreciation by coughing, for which the poet thanks them. To divert themselves further, they tickle one another's noses with feathers to provoke sneezes and, in lieu of smoking, blow up whistling balloons. The hostess sends her butler around to collect jewelry and other donations, and the play ends as she is (all too willingly, feeling flattered) turned out of doors for the night. The Admiral doesn't return for an epilogue that would complement his prologue.

The Marriage (1946) by Witold Gombrowicz (1904–69) also has a prologue without a corresponding epilogue, but the effect is not, as one might suppose, that of waiting for the other shoe to fall or of seeing only one parenthesis around an interpolation; for this grim farce about role-playing takes the hero into his own fantasy and strands him there, so that he is unable to return to the realism of the opening scene. A Polish soldier named Henry in France during the early years of World War II, when the fall of Poland would be fresh in his mind, has a vision of his parents and his fiancée, Molly, and helplessly enters it, together with his comrade Johnny. The action proceeds by a series of attributions. Henry, meeting his father again, kneels to him and by making this obeisance turns the father into a king—of no specified country. With a king as father, Henry must be a prince. And when the father suspects (as does Shakespeare's Henry IV) that his son is after his crown, Henry becomes the traitor his father thinks he is, by the mere force of attribution. From traitor it's only a step to usurper. Henry is treated as the king by a drunk whom he has treated as an ambassador (in a mutual, or cross, attribution of roles), and takes over the kingdom. Now it's Henry's turn to become suspicious. As the title reminds us, if one motive underlies Henry's passiveness in fulfilling the roles attributed to him, it is his desire to marry Molly, whom everybody else looks on as a whore. And, as king at last, Henry can go through with the marriage. But the Ambassador-Drunk warns him that she has betrayed him with Johnny. In one of the eeriest colloquies ever written, Henry then instructs Johnny to "be present at my wedding and when the time comes kill yourself with this knife," after which he asks, "Well, what's new, Johnny? Tell me, are they feeding you well, at least?" and then, with numbing inconsequence, "What time is it?"

Johnny appears at the wedding, as ordered: first as his usual impersonal self; later, stabbed, as a corpse. Henry declares he's responsible for Johnny's suicide, and at the same time not responsible: isn't this a dream, after all? Yet a corpse seems to Henry to demand punishment, and so he postpones his wedding indefinitely and pronounces himself a prisoner. The play ends in a funeral procession.

With its echoes of Calderón's *Life Is a Dream* (1635), whose hero is a medieval Prince of Poland; of Prince Hal and his betrayal of his friends Falstaff and Poins; and of Kleist's dream-enveloped Prince of Hombourg . . . with its flashes of insane buffoonery, as when the Ambassador-Drunk asserts that he can make a man anybody he wants (attribute any role) by touching him with his enormous finger . . . with the strangely unemphatic companion Johnny, who at the beginning "emerges from the shadows" like a Jungian other self (what Jung calls a "shadow") of Henry's or like Horatio as a penalty-taker to Henry's transported Hamlet . . . *The Marriage* coils itself into a spiral of inner plays, each of them simultaneously tragic and farcical, and all encircled by the one continuous line of Henry's self-conscious nightmare—from which, like Christopher Sly, he never awakens.

Jack Gelber conjured up dream images of a contrasting order to Gombrowicz' in *Sleep* (1972), laid in "an experimental sleep lab" in New York. The voluntary subject, Gil, is wired up like Frankenstein's monster on his bench to instruments that calibrate his vital signs, and tossed by the tides of sleep periods into and out of deep and shallow dreams, while his Frankenstein overseers, two "sleep scientists," watch and at intervals traumatically arouse him. Gelber has grappled with one or another subtype of theatricalism and role-playing since his first play, *The Connection* (1959), which is about the making of a play about drug addicts, and which Shirley Clarke directed in its movie adaptation as the making of a film about addicts. In *Sleep*, the characters Gil collides with in his dreams are played by two "actors" and two "actresses." Gombrowicz called a dream "a discharge of the anxieties of the day."[3] In the most anxious and strikingly farcical of Gil's dreams a mugger forces him to take off his clothes in a crowded subway car. Humiliation! Yet when Gil reaches nakedness his terror transposes into joy. Stripped of everything external, he rediscovers himself and, to his own amazement, breaks into an ecstatic dream dance of freedom.

The Theater of the Ridiculous in the mid-Sixties and after, as created variously by John Vaccaro, Charles Ludlam, Ronald Tavel, Kenneth Bernard, and a host of underpaid performers and technicians, flung live farce onto stages and littered it with takeoffs of Hollywood's New Jersey–born cowhands, Brooklyn Irishmen playing Chicago's Italian mobsters, British actresses as genteel comforting molls, and tap-dancing tough nuts . . . with boobs and mcnutts from comic strips; figures torn out of plays by Strindberg, Dumas *fils*, and Sophocles; and camp-drag portraits of the Misses Swanson, Bankhead, Davis, Crawford, and Miranda. In those same years, though, the "ridiculous" theater troupes formed only a small segment of Off Off Broadway, which swarmed with rebellious revelries. They celebrated the parting of spectators from their nineteen-inch screens and their conjunction with actors in three dimensions. Only a few churls complained that these evenings of pop art in motion, of farcical hodgepodge enlivened by theatricalist communion across the proscenium line, were "not plays." In 1977, *A History of the American Film* by Christopher Durang, with music by Mel Marvin, rationalized Hollywood nostalgia and carried it into sentimental deeps. The show, with its title that sounds like a 200-level undergraduate course, strings together scenes and numbers that typify popular film genres, from Marine Corps exploits and jailbreaks to thorny romances; and it offers guest appearances by performers representing such marquee names of the Thirties and Forties as "Bette," "Jimmy," "Hank," "Eve," and "Loretta." In production, the script, which has the

[3] Quoted by Jan Kott in his introduction to *The Marriage*, translated by Louis Iribarne (New York: Grove Press, 1969), p. 10. The quotation comes from Gombrowicz' journal, *Dziennik*, 1957–61 (Paris, 1967), p. 161.

Jack Gelber's plays are published by Grove Press, New York (*The Connection*, 1960; *The Apple*, 1961; *The Cuban Thing*, 1968), and by Hill & Wang, New York (*Sleep*, 1973; *Rehearsal*, 1976).

makings of a farce, lapsed frequently into solemnity, and the audience felt constrained to hold back what might have been more laughter of recognition.

It is hard to trace a firm border between a pastiche, such as *Subject to Fits*, which lifts material from another work, rearranges it, and may grin or jeer at it; and a travesty, such as any piece of Theater of the Ridiculous, which curdles our remembrance of the originals on which it depends and has (*means* to have) hardly a scruple of artistic merit in its own right. Of three plays by Tom Stoppard that dedicate themselves to theater-in-the-theater, the earliest one, *Rosencrantz and Guildenstern Are Dead* (1967), contains a travesty of *Hamlet* among its other virtues; the second, *The Real Inspector Hound* (1968), contains a pastiche of a routine West End murder mystery; and the third, unassumingly entitled *Travesties* (1975), isn't a true travesty at all but an arduous rewriting of history which, for its own purposes, has taken over certain names and themes from *The Importance of Being Earnest*. Stoppard seasons all his plays with farce; he is also one of the few writers in English since Shaw who can marry wit to humor so that his witty characters ridicule the rest and the humorous ones ridicule themselves.

His Rosencrantz and Guildenstern bear no resemblance to the smarmy pair of spies in Shakespeare's play. Two bewildered souls, they have somehow come to life on a stage, rather like Pirandello's Six Characters, without memories to test themselves against, while behind them Shakespeare's play grinds along, occasionally sucking them, unprepared, into its scenes. They pass the time—their lives —by spinning coins and questions at each other, and worrying about what will happen next and whether it will prove dangerous. The coins come down heads ninety times in succession, implying some sort of unavoidable fate. The questions lead them into rhetorical exercises that offer no consolation. As if to threaten them more particularly, the players from *Hamlet* enact for their benefit not only the murder of Gonzago but also the murder of Rosencrantz and Guildenstern. It will happen. It does happen. Their fears come true. These two farcical characters end up at the mercy of a tragedy. But the way we see the tragedy, as the posturing of Hamlet, Ophelia, and the other principals in the background, it too becomes farce. Stoppard has devised a new form, an inversion.

Instead of having Rosencrantz and Guildenstern function as a subplot, he makes *Hamlet* the play within the play as it interrupts the action of *Rosencrantz and Guildenstern Are Dead*.

The Real Inspector Hound sets up a stage-upon-the-stage—a revisiting of the inner stage of the Elizabethan playwrights. On it a domestic interior houses an Agatha Christie type of crime story, rife with ham-handed suspense and false clues. Right in front of the performance, two reviewers, Birdboot and a second-stringer, Moon, sit and comment on their ambitions, on a pretty ingenue in the show, and on other matters that would distract and gall the people in the row behind, if such a row existed. The phone rings on the inner stage. No one answers. Moon steps forward and takes the call. It's for Birdboot. From then on both reviewers get drawn into the action, and two members of the cast of the inner play move into their seats on the "outer stage." Birdboot is now playing the part of Inspector Hound, not very astutely, while the "real Inspector Hound" watches and criticizes. The role-swapping lets Stoppard release some jabs directed both at melodramatic, surefire W.M.P.s and at theater reviewers who almost willfully misinterpret what they see and see what they have never been exposed to.

If *Rosencrantz and Guildenstern* upstaged *Hamlet*, *Travesties* seizes on three historical personages, Tristan Tzara, James Joyce, and Lenin, who all stayed and worked in Zurich during World War I; he gives them handsome but subordinate roles in a drama of which the principal role goes to Henry Carr, a reconstruction of an actual employee at the British Consulate who, at least until *Travesties*, was little more than a footnote in Richard Ellmann's biography of Joyce. Carr serves as both the protagonist and the narrator. Many years after, he delves into his memory—"which is not notably reliable," says the playwright—and places himself at the center of the events. The events themselves consist largely of impassioned debates on art, revolution, revolutions in art, and art in revolutions, argued on the soil of Switzerland, that oasis of neutrality during Europe's great wars. Despite the momentousness of the subject matter and some cogent reasoning that issues from the characters, the play keeps making fun of itself. The people in it burst into dialogue written in limericks (farcical passes at Joyce's Irishness) or Mr. Gallagher and Mr. Shean catechisms in rhyme; some lines have the pace and lilt of lyrics by Gilbert. But the most obvious, and also the most subtle, echoes are of the play that structurally underlies *Travesties* and, with one word changed in its title, could provide an epigraph for Stoppard, The Importance of Sounding Earnest. Carr's sister, who works as an amanuensis for Joyce, is named Gwendolen. Another attractive young lady, a librarian with Bolshevik ideals, goes by the name of Cecily. Carr courts and marries Cecily; Tzara admires Gwendolen; Cecily spouts Leninism by the verse. As the occasion for the explicit preemption of Wilde's play, Joyce approaches Carr, who is a bit of a dandy, and invites him to take on the role of Algernon in a Zurich production of *Importance*, for the "English Players intend to mount a repertoire of masterpieces that will show the Swiss who leads the world in dramatic art." Stoppard also goes to some pains to connect up his three revolutionary captains—Joyce exciting a revolution in the art of fiction with his writing of *Ulysses*; Tzara, the insurgent apostle of anti-art; and Lenin in exile, working out international maneuvers that will sweep him back to Russia on the crest of a public welcome and announcing that the artist in the new society must enjoy freedom, so long as he is "a strong and sincere protester against social injustice." Joyce compiles his masterpiece from notes on scraps of paper, and has bad eyesight, as well as being, as he says himself, "something of an international eyesore"; while Tzara affects a monocle and arrives at his poems by cutting up a sheetful of words, scrambling the pieces in his hat, and reassembling them. The dramaturgical principle that governs the play turns out to be anticlimax. Instead of leading up to Lenin's subsequent triumph, Joyce's acclaim, or Tzara's *succès de scandale* in Paris, Stoppard gives us Cecily contradicting Carr's accounts (and therefore most of the play's action). Carr himself closes the play with bathetic nonsense: "I learned three things in Zurich during the war. I wrote them down. Firstly, you're either a revolutionary or you're not, and if you're not you might as well be an artist as anything else. Secondly, if you can't be an artist, you might as well be a revolutionary . . . I forget the third thing. (*Blackout.*)"

Nearly all the characters brought to life by Jean Genet (born 1910) play roles, departing from their "true selves" and returning to them reluctantly as if to say, "I wouldn't want to live here." Genet alludes over and over again to playacting and pretense. One of his uniquely poetic dramas, a potent example of farcical theater-in-the-theater, applies this kind of theatricalism in locales other than the playhouse, but turns its sets into virtual performing arenas. In *The Balcony* (1956) a luxurious brothel is made up of not mere rooms but mirrored "studios," which operate like little stages, for they shelter masochists, most of whom come there to play out personal ceremonies; they magnify themselves in private by donning paraphernalia of high rank—a bishop's, a general's, a judge's—in front of the mirrors, which give them back bloated images of themselves. Prostitutes, male and female, attend to these clients and obey their whims, treating them as the images they see in the mirrors and so reinforcing the attribution of the roles, much as actors do to one another in a production. By way of apparent contrast, another masochist chooses to degrade, rather than elevate, himself by dressing as a lice-ridden beggar; and the local chief of police drops in to dream of being martyred by castration. But the other masochists, those who get themselves up as the high and mighty, do so equally in order to degrade the roles they have taken on. The "bishop" masturbates behind his cape; the "general" pretends to ride his "mare," Dove, played by a brothel girl; the "judge" crawls to the girl who acts as a thief on trial and licks her feet.

Yet these phonies, these pitiful mongrels, get to play out their roles for real. They parade before the public, which sees them in their finery and takes the uniforms for the men. The madam of the brothel is even required to act as the country's queen, and nobody questions her in that capacity; a diplomat remarks that she's better-looking than the real queen and therefore more authentic.

The play happens at a tense time. A revolution has got under way. Certain pillars of the establishment—a bishop, a judge, a general, and the queen among them—have either fled or been killed. The madam and her clients take their place as part of an attempt to make the country look stable, if not immovable. Since they pass successfully for the real thing, the brothel's inmates are as good as a bishop, judge, and general; that is, a bishop, judge, and general are no better than the inmates of a brothel, while a queen is no better than a madam. The public's scrutiny goes only as deep as clothing. The "real" high functionaries might as well be actors for all the difference it makes. Once the clients of the brothel have offered themselves to public view and been accepted, they need never do it again; images of their images, in the form of photographs, can circulate in their place to prove they exist. Possibly Genet was thinking here of the actor who impersonated Winston Churchill during World War II, or the doubles sometimes employed by statesmen to risk an assassin's bullet. In *The Balcony*, then, Genet doesn't have to resort to a theater setting. His ferocious satire casts life itself as theater, make-believe from start to finish—an idea certified by most psychologists and sociologists today, although artists, as always, had the idea first.

In *The Balcony*, Genet ties together a number of individual stories by the threat of revolution, so that the brothel clients and its madam become perforce totems of the country's power structure. He pulls a similar trick in *The Blacks: A Clown Show* (1958), but with a collective story this time. The stage, which is a stage somewhere in an Africa of the mind, an outdoorsy indoors, has an upper platform like a royal box. From here five members of "the court" observe and butt into the proceedings on the lower, main platform. The "court"—both a court in the sense of Louis XIV's, selected members of which sat on the stage directly in front of the performers, and a court in the sense of a judicial assembly—consists of five blacks each wearing a white mask "in such a way that the audience sees a wide black band [of skin] all around it." Its Queen, Governor, Judge, Missionary (another bishop), and Valet correspond to the false establishment of the brothel clients who were ratified by public acceptance in *The Balcony*. They are present to be entertained and judged. Who attributes their roles to them? None other than the performers on the platform below.. In an unexpected inversion, the actors confirm the spectators in their roles, much as, in another inversion, the court will itself be judged, instead of passing judgment. Offstage, the actors on the main platform are a cook, a sewing-maid, a curate, a medical student, a prostitute, and several others. Now they will reenact on that lower platform the murder by a black man of a white woman. To represent the corpse of the woman retroactively, a catafalque made up of two chairs stands mid-stage, draped in white and smothered in flowers. The actors seem to delay getting to the murder. Before it is repeated (offstage, as in a Greek tragedy), they strain their brains and vocabularies to come up with ways of thinking and speaking and behaving that will be their own, inherently black, arrived at independently of what white colonials have dinned into them. That performance, the inner play, which takes the form of a ritual, marks the actors' attempt to reach back to indigenous African forms. But they wish to strike deeper than the creation of their own type of non-Western drama. They grope for a language that will invest blackness with beauty and majesty, and rob whiteness of its admirable associations such as purity. Black will be the rich mystery of darkness; white a mere bleached hue, the color of death.

The ritual is thus like a child's game, and the actors' carefree manner conveys an innocence already suggested by their sonorous, multiple names (Archibald Absalom Wellington, Deodatus Village, Edgar Alas Newport News, Felicity Trollop Pardon, Stephanie Virtue Secret-rose Diop), which contrast with the stern professional or functional titles of the court quintet. The latter, after all, are playing "grown-up," responsible roles as a judge, a queen, a governor, and so on. The farce generated by the actors on the lower platform derives from banter and word-bartering, as does Giraudoux's or Wilde's. But just as children's play can deteriorate into cruelty, even enmity, so Genet's farce overlies bitter hatred, verging on rebellion. When the time comes to replay the murder, the curate, a temporizer named Diouf, is chosen for the part of the white woman and put into a wide skirt and blond wig. She'd had an affair, it seems, with Village, the man who killed her. To signify her pregnancy, five dolls are taken from below Diouf's skirts. They are two-foot miniatures of the courtiers. The murder itself thereby stands for an act much larger. The Judge says, "He killed out of hatred. Hatred of the color white. That was tantamount to killing our entire race and killing us till doomsday."

And what about punishment for the murder? Instead of having Village sentenced, Genet brings the five court members down from the upper platform and has *them* executed in ritual fashion —all except the Missionary, stained with the paternalistic sins of Livingstone and Schweitzer, who is turned into a castrated bovine. They get up, remove their masks, are thanked for their assistance and courage, and, since they too are blacks and actors, leave unharmed. But Genet hasn't completed his black-on-black design.

Just as in *The Balcony* the revolution ruled the streets while the masochists were pursuing their specialized orgasms in the brothel studios, so while the performance given for the blacks-masked-as-whites is in progress, another meeting held nearby, a parallel trial, prosecutes the leader of a black revolution, finds him to have been guilty of treachery, and executes him, replacing him with a new leader. One of the actors, Newport News, runs as a messenger between the real and the mock trials.

Can we look on *The Blacks* as a true farce? Its wishful murder of the white race—the blacks want to annihilate and supplant the whites, not simply take over from them—is reminiscent of the more openly passionate cry of Clay, the black youngster in Imamu Amiri Baraka's *Dutchman* (1964). At the white woman who taunts him in the subway he shouts that blacks in America are a "people of neurotics struggling to keep from being sane. And the only thing that could cure the neurosis would be your murder." Like the poet Clay, Genet's blacks keep from committing murder by creating art. But what is that art? The celebration of a murder that we are led to believe was actually committed, a murder that symbolizes the wiping out of all whites. When the white woman dies in effigy, Diouf, her imitator, moves onto the upper platform to join the court in its white masks. In other words, the upper platform represents death (or hell) even before the court people are ritually executed. For some critics and spectators this burden of poetry, political diatribe, and hate-spewing would be too much for a farce to bear, and yet farce is the means by which this "clown show" operates. Written at a time when colonialism still reigned in most of Africa and freedom from foreign (here French) oppression seemed like a most urgent goal, *The Blacks*, if it were not a farce, would be little more than flamboyant rhetoric today, when the peoples of Africa need, first of all, freedom from starvation caused by drought, neglect, impoverished land, and the spreading of deserts like incurable, uncontrollable scabs.[4]

---

[4] The plays of Tom Stoppard and of Jean Genet are published by Grove Press, New York (*Rosencrantz and Guildenstern Are Dead*, 1967; *The Real Inspector Hound*, 1969; *Jumpers*, 1973; *Travesties*, 1976; *The Balcony*, 1958; *The Blacks*, 1960).

Two lively American farces with tinges of theatricalism are Saul Bellow's *The Last Analysis* (New York: Viking, 1965) and *Brisburial: A Feast* by Edward Pomerantz (Weston, Ct.: Magic Circle Press, 1981). Both are ceremonial in form, like Genet's plays, but are drastically unlike Genet's in most other respects, as well as unlike each other.

Improvisation

Dr. Hinkfuss, the director, strides down the aisle on short legs and takes over the stage before the curtain rings up. In a lengthy address to the audience, Hinkfuss explains that his production will embark on a very brief work by Pirandello about a Sicilian family and will improvise on it, in an attempt to make the evening live, rather than being a recital of a completed, and therefore dead, text. Members of the audience, who've already been griping because the show didn't start on time, heckle Dr. Hinkfuss. The actors, it then turns out, don't like the idea of doing an improvisation, but as doughty professionals will do their dutiful utmost. And thus again in *Tonight We Improvise* (1931) we find Pirandello reproducing the conditions of theater-in-the-theater, with actors playing audience malcontents, the director, inner roles, and themselves.

The inner drama about the Sicilian family proves, when the actors give us some excerpts from it, to be an overheated melodrama. Its parent, the outer drama—demonstrating how the actors go about improvising the inner drama—is farcical. Some of the transitions between inner and outer drama waver between the two genres, as when the Character Actor, playing the father of the family, appears, "his face like a dead man's; his bloody hands on his stomach, where he has been wounded by a knife; his coat and trousers smeared with blood." A powerful stage image. Is he dying? The Father, yes. But the moment of death will be prorogued. The Character Actor gets into some bickering with the Director about his entrance, leaves the stage, reenters, and, when his big death speech comes up, smiles, throwing the other actors for a loop. Instead of giving his death speech as the character, he describes how the scene ought to have led up to the character's death; and then, while he is still uttering improvised lines *as the actor*, he breaks the informality brutally by slumping into death.

This is theatricalism, all right. It's also realism, a plausible construction of what might happen and, in truth, pretty close to what has happened on a controversial first night. But it is not improvisation. If, during the original rehearsals, an actress, say, had improvised on the improvisations written out for her by the author, he would undoubtedly have brought her back literally into line.

Improvisation is the third type of theatricalism, or theater that is aware of itself as theater and proclaims itself as such. The word, a bit of a misnomer, doesn't beguile most spectators into believing that the actors prepared and rehearsed *none* of the material. Most theatergoers realize that the outline or structure of improvised action has been predetermined, and that the actors have stored some lines in their memories, if only for emergencies. The likelihood of such emergencies makes improvisation the most theatrical kind of theater. It invokes danger and unpredictability. The actors are even more liable than in a normally rehearsed staging to dry up, to supply a wrong cue or the right cue at the wrong moment, to misinterpret a cue from somebody else, to repeat lines needlessly, to resort to secondhand gags and shtik. Still, knowing that the audience half-expects such slips, and may even be hoping for a few, the actors can generally count on an indulgent reception. Indeed, when audiences come to watch a work billed as improvisation they may feel disappointed if it doesn't *look* improvised. The result is a paradox: improvised acting should come across best when it doesn't look off-the-cuff; but if it doesn't look off-the-cuff it won't look genuine, and the audience may not willingly suspend its disbelief, let alone grant its indulgence. For inept or under-trained improvisatory companies, that paradox is a godsend. The impression is all. Even in a play that merely *deals with* improvisation, one in which the actors only simulate improvising, any of them who appear to be too sure of themselves are fighting the intent of the text. In *Tonight We Improvise* they must look as if they were improvising beautifully. The same goes for Thornton Wilder's *The Skin of Our Teeth* (1942): in one scene when the maid Sabina hesitates, a voice from offstage cries out, "Make up something! Invent something!"

These days actors use the word improvisation to refer neither to making up something as the performance goes forward nor to filling unlooked-for gaps with the first line or gesture that flies out of their heads or bodies ("winging it"), but to a method of rehearsing. The director or a writer will probably start them off with a synopsis of a dramatic situation; they fill in the details themselves by free association and later sort out the best bits and put them together. This procedure lends itself equally to rehearsals of non-improvised plays, and has become a favorite technique for exploring the subtext; the actors spin variations on a written scene as a means of peeling away its literal covering and digging for poetry underneath, whether there's any there or not.

Through rehearsal practices, improvisation became a force in recent American theater, and in farce. When the revue *From the Second City* arrived in 1962 in an Off Broadway house where the participants invited suggestions from the "first city" audiences, and astonished them with the topical vivacity of the sketches and the awesome versatility and machine-gun-fire wit of the performers, it represented improvisations reworked, polished, and compiled over five or six years. Nonprofessional actors at the University of Chicago, some of whom moved on into the Playwrights Theater, some of which then moved into the revues put on by the Compass Players, had rehearsed "improvs" and theater games under the guidance of David Shepherd, Paul Sills, and combinations of actor-directors, actor-writers, and writer-directors. Second City was one outgrowth of this turmoil of activity. Other spin-offs, imitations, and competitors of this type of revue went into business at various times in St. Louis, San Francisco, Boston, and New York. The farceurs who began with these companies would later amount to a generous helping of the cream of American actors in the Sixties and Seventies—about six dozen men and women who have helped to give farce new satirical momentum in theater and in films.[5]

Now, for one revue item, Alan Arkin, let us say, takes part in a skit about living the good postwar life in West Germany. His next

---

[5] The complex story of the Second City troupe before and after 1962 is related by Jeffrey Sweet in *Something Wonderful Right Away: An Oral History of the Second City and the Compass Players* (New York: Avon Books, 1978). In addition to interviews with some of the leading figures and a historical précis of the improvisational-revue movement, Sweet provides a list of the people associated with the Compass Players and the different Second City troupes—who, considered collectively, rival Mack Sennett's agglomeration of talent. Some of the better-known names are Alan Alda, Jane Alexander, Alan Arkin, Larry Arrick, Lloyd Battista, John Belushi, Robert Benedetti, Shelley Berman, Roger Bowen, Peter Boyle, Hildy Brooks, Del Close, Barbara Dana, Severn Darden, Melinda Dillon, Bob Dishy, MacIntyre Dixon, Paul Dooley, Andrew Duncan, Theodore J. Flicker, Mark Gordon, Valerie Harper, Barbara Harris, Jo Henderson, Anthony Holland, Lee Kalcheim, Irene Kane, Robert Klein, Mina Kolb, Zohra Lampert, Linda Lavin, Richard Libertini, Ron Leibman, Elaine May, Paul Mazursky, Anne Meara, George Morrison, Alan Myerson, Mike Nichols, Sheldon Patinkin, Nancy Ponder, Gilda Radner, Joan Rivers, Bernard Sahlins, Paul Sand, Diana Sands, Reni Santoni, Avery Schreiber, Omar Shapli, Cyril Simon, Viola Spolin, David Steinberg, Jerry Stiller, Eugene Troobnick, Ronald Weyand, Collin Wilcox.

appearance casts him as a Puerto Rican strolling through an art gallery in this country, disgusted by contemporary paintings. The revue draws some of its strength from his ability to differentiate his roles. Artistry may reside in concealing its artistry, according to the Latin tag, but in a revue the artistry has to stick out like a green thumb. We appreciate the contrasts between one role and the next which hint at the breadth of the actor's skills. In a play, even a farce, we usually admire an actor who can maintain consistency in one role, piecing together its contradictions and fluctuations in temper, making them plausible without losing touch with some essence of the character. We admire a solo comedian for much the same reason. During a lengthy turn we enjoy watching him project facets of the same personality. In a revue, on the other hand, we admire an actor's radical changes, his swift and clear adumbration of distinctive roles.

A revue that begins with improvisation is likely to be farcical because 1) it is full of surprises; 2) it owes its origin in large part to rehearsal procedures that tap the actors' impulses, rather than their reason, procedures that are demonstrative (carried out in front of other people), rather than reflective (written by a playwright in a one-room fifth-floor walk-up); 3) if it asks spectators to cooperate in the performance, it liberates a feeling of community, of being suddenly dropped among friends, and as a result, a feeling of abandon—nothing serious is at stake, so let the claps fall where they may; 4) each sketch has to get to its point fast and will usually go all out with verbal ridicule and exaggerated action.

The performers of the Second City and similar troupes resembled Chaplin, Keaton, Lloyd, Fields, and other movie farceurs in taking over most of the responsibility for the writing they enacted. In effect, they became, like the commedia players, their own scenarists. When the Open Theater came into being during 1963, it too had actors who "developed" their own scenes. But Joseph Chaikin and Peter Feldman, who founded the theater, and the resident playwrights, who fed the actors ideas, probably owed little to the earlier American improvisation. Chaikin had assisted Peter Brook in London and seems now, in retrospect, to have adapted to his own use improvisational techniques favored by Brook in rehearsals in his Theater of Cruelty and with some of the members of the Royal Shakespeare Company. (Later, when Brook visited

New York one sometimes saw him sitting at Open Theater rehearsals and taking notes; by this time the Open Theater was America's outstanding troupe.)

At first the Open Theater aimed at being an actors' workshop, an alternative to the "memories," "motives," and "intentions" of Method training. Subsequently it offered some of its scenes for public consumption. Its initial spectacle, *America Hurrah*, made up of three one-act plays written (in the Open Theater sense) by Jean-Claude van Itallie, had veins of farce in the second and third plays, *TV* and *Motel*, both directed by Jacques Levy. In *TV*, the working out of a sex triangle formed by three employees in the statistics-gathering department of a studio runs in parallel with fragments of television shows acted out by live performers at the rear of the stage—soap opera, horse opera, big-buck games, patronizing lectures, and other video delicacies—so that commercial life and commercial art comment on each other in counterpoint. *Motel* opens farcically as an inert, human-sized doll with a recorded voice, representing the keepers of hostelries through the ages, rambles on about the delights, history, and sanitary advantages of putting up at motels, while the masked, oversized figures of two guests, a man and a woman, vandalize a motel room with wanton abandon and the play shifts out of farce into horrific melodrama. At the end, as if to retain a note of theatricalism, the vandals stride off the stage and leave through the auditorium. (The spectators in the aisle seats give them plenty of room to pass.)

Later productions by the Open Theater, such as *The Serpent*, *Terminal*, *The Mutation Show*, and *Nightwalk*, exploited farce much more sparingly. Not only did the Open Theater reach its productions by improvisation; it also kept improvising after opening night, so that the shows had no final stages but kept altering perceptibly. Chaikin felt that an opening night was an artificial division between rehearsing and performing, and that he should encourage the actors to go on making discoveries for as long as the show in question played, rather than trying to "fix" a completed form, with the full-dress rehearsal becoming a template for a run.

If the actors in a revue show their stuff by switching roles from one character to another or go from being human into some species of animal, plant, insect, or mineral life—a footstool, a fountain, a battering ram, a corpse—the Open Theater actors pushed beyond allowing these role changes to happen as a by-product of their art; they made them into an acting principle and named it transformations. Transformations were implicit in the Second City shows; they became a governing factor in Paul Sills' later *Story Theater*, dramatized from fables and folk tales, and in *Alice*, a freely theatrical version of Lewis Carroll's two books worked up into a scenario by a group of people from New York University who were directed by André Gregory.

Transformations condense the old practice in the theater of "doubling." A production with a long list of characters can proceed with six or eight performers who take on multiple roles. Van Itallie's *TV* playlet, for instance, gets by with eight. It requires three in the foreground to play out the sex triangle: George, a forty-three-year-old with a rocky stomach, like the haunted hero of a commercial who finds gastric bliss within thirty seconds; Susan, who is a tranquilizer-popping, shrink-visiting young secretary obsessed with her hair, weight, complexion, and apartment, like the heroine of a commercial who switches from one brand (frown) to another (cute smile with head turned slightly away from camera, knowingly, in three-quarter profile); and Hal, also young, on the lookout for a better job, adept at calisthenics, like an onlooker in a commercial, dashingly dressed, whose eyes follow the buttocks of a girl in flowered jeans. Hal may be "laying" Susan—at least, George thinks so. George also fears that Hal may be after his job. The trio spend their working hours having an office party and cursing themselves over the intake of fattening foods, or else they bicker. Will Hal see Susan this evening? If not, can George "make" her? And if George gets the date, will his wife swallow the story that he's working late, even if he keeps telling her on the phone, "Listen, I love you"?

In the background the rest of the cast, five live actors, give us the merciless barrage of daytime programming. Wonderboy saves Helen from her husband, Harry, who's turned into a monster (another triangle). Sally, a Western maiden, saves Bill, her beloved but wounded cowpoke, from the villain, Steve, by shooting Steve in the back (yet another triangle). Lily Heaven bids "So long" to her viewers and every other actor and all the technicians on the *Lily Heaven* show (some sort of polygon). A British couple from World War II on the *Billion Dollar Movie* hope there will never again be war, accompanied by the last line of "The White Cliffs of Dover" (another triangle: He, She, and the villain War). Johnny Holland interviews the daughter of President Johnson, who has just got married and defends her father's prosecution of the Vietnam conflict and its atrocities (triangle again: father, daughter, interviewer, with the new husband out in the cold). An evangelist defends America and God to the strains of "Onward, Christian Soldiers!" And *My Favorite Teenager* wrestles with the question of who's taking Sis to a prom. These and other tidbits are broken into by news clips, headlines, the weather, institutional product ads, a Spanish lesson, bursts and trickles of canned laughter. During *My Favorite Teenager* the lines spoken by the soap family and those spoken by George, Susan, and Hal converge, and then coincide. The actors playing the video characters step forward, as if off the screen; invade the studio; take over some of the chairs; and Sis sits in Hal's lap. The story of George, Susan, and Hal becomes overtly a situation comedy—which, of course, it was from the beginning.[6]

The Anything-Is-Everything

As a postscript to this last type of theatricalism, I ought perhaps to improvise a few words on the subject of Happenings, which fall between performance and the fine arts of painting and architecture. Happenings can take place in a theater, and some did. Individuals or teams of artists from the fine arts set up an environment on or off a stage, in another sort of structure than a playhouse, or in the open—on a street, in a field, by the sea, up in the air . . . wherever. People entered this environment (a conveniently loose word) by invitation or accident and were observed by its creators and possibly by an audience. They might also study their own reactions. Sometimes the creators were the performers. To the extent that nobody could quite predict what the participants would do or what the spectators would make of whatever the participants did do, there was an improvised performance. Toward the end of

---

[6] The text of *America Hurrah* has been published separately (New York: Pocket Books, 1967) and anthologized. For the texts of *Terminal*, *The Mutation Show*, and *Nightwalk*, together with photographs, some critical appreciation, and a bibliography about the Open Theater see *Three Works by the Open Theater*, edited by Karen Malpede (New York: Drama Book Specialists, 1974).

the Sixties, artists altered or transformed whole landscapes, as if to found a new Stonehenge or Avebury. They bulldozed earth into mounds, barrows, and other shapes; dug holes and trenches; laid out spiral-shaped peninsulas on lakes; raised flagpoles; covered rocks with plastic sheeting; daubed paint on trees; perpetrated graffiti; constructed tunnels, arches, corridors for the performers to pass through or meditate in; piloted planes with streamers and banners; lit up the night; darkened the day. "How we perceive it," said Robert Morris, one artist, "becomes more important than what it is." Such a relativistic attitude emphasizes the role of the spectator, rather than that of the performer or artist, except insofar as the latter is his own spectator.

The theories advanced by Happenings artists, from the first one, Allan Kaprow, who gave Happenings their name and early forms in 1959, to the latest practitioner who lays rope across a beach or describes random figures on desert sand with a motorbike or other wildlife destroyer, are so various and divergent that one can ascribe almost any properties to any Happening and make a fairly good case. We could, for example, watch somebody going into an outhouse and try to visualize it as a temple. Or vice versa. Would such an attribution be farcical? In a relativistic world it might be anything. Tragic? Why not? Here life and the life of the imagination intersect in ways that hopelessly blur old definitions.[7]

---

[7] For some scenarios of Happenings by Robert Whitman, Carolee Schneeman, Allan Kaprow, and Charles Frazier, and accompanying theory, see *Theater Experiment*, edited by Michael Benedikt (Garden City, N.Y.: Doubleday, 1967; paperback edition 1968), pp. 315–70. These are not all farcical. Some of the most striking Happenings merely happened; they were never recorded.

◆

FOURTEEN

MOVIES AFTER 1940

After François, the postman of a village in central France, has watched a documentary film about the rapidity and efficiency of the American mails (this was an earlier post-office era), he resolves to Americanize his own deliveries. Vaulting like Ken Maynard into his seat, he pumps furiously at the pedals of his bicycle, then realizes that he'd left the bike leaning against a low fence and is now riding with the fence, as well as the bike, between his legs. Keaton might have played this scene, and almost did in *Our Hospitality*.

As François wobbles down a country lane, a honking motorist behind him cannot get past because a car is coming the other way. François sticks out his long arm for a left turn, then turns right. The two cars crash. Sennett might have thought up the scene.

In his haste, François rides up to the local city hall, a modest two-story structure. Either his brakes fail or he forgets to hit them. As his wheel meets a flight of steps he takes leave of his bike and flies in through the open front doors. Seconds later he reappears on a balcony of the second floor, as if he'd shot up the staircase inside and reversed himself. Deposited on the balcony, still wearing his postman's cylindrical, peaked hat, with his blank face and severe mustache, he looks for all the world like a double of General de Gaulle in his slim, World War II days, addressing the Free French army from aloft. Solemnly, automatically, François raises his right hand in a salute. His flight through space could almost have come out of a Harold Lloyd film, such as *Never Weaken*, while the salute might hearken back a few years to Chaplin in *The*

Great Dictator or in the opening statue episode of *City Lights*. More than thirty years after seeing Jacques Tati in *Jour de Fête* (1948) I recall the farcical bounties of this pre-Hulot film, which upheld the grand tradition of the clown-creator in movies. French cinema had known no triple threat of Tati's caliber since Linder and Méliès, both of whom had written their own screenplays and prevailed before as well as behind their cameras.

By 1948, Hollywood had turned up no new clowns to rival those of the Thirties and earlier. Mae West, W. C. Fields, the Marx Brothers, and Laurel and Hardy had made more features. But West and Fields collaborated as writers and stars only in *My Little Chickadee* (1940); that dazzling marriage over, they went back, divorced, into other people's pictures, although not many. As of *At the Circus* (1939), the Marx trio had new writers whom they couldn't quite overcome. Laurel and Hardy passed their watershed after *A Chump at Oxford* and *Saps at Sea* (both 1940). Keaton was doled out a few nondescript roles; *In the Good Old Summertime* (1949) has him supporting monotonous actors like S. Z. (Cuddles) Sakall and Spring Byington. Chaplin drove on but in new directions after having dropped his Charlie characterization. Resentment had built up against him. Too many people seemed to feel that no artist had the right to be so good for so long; but they attacked him for his supposedly ungrateful suspicions of the system out of which he'd forged his triumphs. Chaplin's later career has been pecked at enough. There are plentiful rewards in his late films for spectators who cherish his unexcelled acting and clowning, and are curious about not what Chaplin had been, but what he became.

By the time of Tati's advent outside France with *Jour de Fête*, film farces had split into four groups. First, there were features identified with a particular clown or team: a Bob Hope, a Hope and Crosby, an Abbott and Costello, a Red Skelton, a Danny Kaye, a Fernandel, all directed by somebody else. Second, there were farces by a director who did his own screenplay or co-opted script partners: a Sturges, a Billy Wilder, a Lester, a De Broca. These directors, who have been responsible for many of the superior farces from 1940 to 1980, for the most part served their apprenticeships as writers; in their directing they took an active hand in modeling the dialogue and honing the edges of the drama, even when the credits didn't say so. The recognition of directors as power centers, as cinematic composer-conductors, came about belatedly in the Fifties, first in France, then in Britain, then here, with the mishmash of declarations and arbitrary rankings known as auteur theory. Third, there arose, some time after Tati's early pictures, farces put out by a new generation of clown-creators. The latter included Mel Brooks, Woody Allen, Jerry Lewis (who, in quest of that elusive condition, "total control," transferred himself into the confederacy of directors), and others you can count on two fingers and a thumb. The fourth "group" is not a group at all, but a miscellany of one-shot farces. Some came from directors who usually explored other genres (Tony Richardson, Stanley Kramer, Stanley Kubrick, Luis Buñuel, Marcel Carné) or, as with Pietro Germi, came to farce relatively late in their careers; and a number of these films gave over their leading roles to actors, rather than to clowns.

Clowns

Between actors and clowns there are soft distinctions. A clown investigates the potential of one persona. An actor switches personae, complying with the script while bringing to each part certain characteristics—a set of features, a tone and range of voice, a deportment—that will not quite be shed. These characteristics may even add up to a trademark as individual as any clown's. The chalk lines between actor and clown have been dimmed by the film industry's habit of typecasting, especially in farces. All the same, actors are actors and clowns are clowns, and if the twain often meet, the distinction remains. The two most celebrated farcical actors who have come close to outright clowning, Sir Alec Guinness and Peter Sellers, have not established themselves as definable personae, even though Sellers once did a series on television, *The Goon Show*, in which he kept repeating a few roles, and was later the big draw in the Pink Panther film series as Inspector Clouseau. But then, Sellers, like Ron Moody, a master of dialects, came out of that zone between acting and clowning which we call impersonation, one of the most satisfying of the performing arts as it catches and amplifies the famous subjects' idiosyncrasies. On a television show, Sellers once did meticulous (and therefore hilarious) impersonations of Laurence Olivier as Richard III and, of all people, Guinness as the Arab leader in *Lawrence of Arabia*. Moody can uncannily impersonate every leading clown of the twentieth century.

Other film actors who have acquitted themselves in farces with consummate aplomb but have not confined themselves to farce as a genre include Eve Arden, Alan Arkin, Wallace Beery, Eric Blore, Jerome Cowan, Joan Davis, Dom De Luise, William Demarest, Albert Finney, Hugh Griffith, Jack Haley, Dustin Hoffman, Judy Holliday, Louis Jouvet, Guy Kibbee, Percy Kilbride, Jack Lemmon, Marjorie Main, Miles Malleson, Walter Matthau, Robert Morley, Eugene Pallette, Franklin Pangborn, Nat Pendleton, Joyce Redmond, Carl Reiner, Mickey Rooney, Margaret Rutherford, George C. Scott, Alastair Sim, Michel Simon, Ned Sparks, Toto, Raymond Walburn, Gene Wilder.

Clowns are a scarcer commodity. Among the few listed here, some passed rapidly through movies on their way from vaudeville to television: Joe E. Brown, Judy Canova, Jerry Colonna, Jimmy Durante, Billy Gilbert, Joyce Grenfell, Hugh Herbert, Edgar Kennedy, Bert Lahr, Zero Mostel, Jack Oakie, Martha Raye, Phil Silvers, Terry-Thomas, Ed Wynn. Almost anybody who became somebody in radio or television turned up in at least a couple of movies. Among stand-up comics, Fred Allen did five, Sid Caesar six, Ernie Kovacs ten, Milton Berle nineteen, and Jack Benny twenty. And at this time George Burns has made his second film as God, apparently embarking on a new career. The Monty Python sextet took leave of television in order to upend chivalry in a quest for the Holy Grail; they later incensed high and low dignitaries of four or five religions or sects with *The Life of Brian*.

Between the older veteran of vaudeville who strung together stories about himself, his spouse, children, acquaintances, and rivals and the clowns who came of age in the Forties and Fifties one difference stands out. The vaudevillian went to some trouble to make himself look comfortable, to embrace an audience as fellow partygoers who happened by as he was about to launch a joke. He pulled faces, raised his voice and verve. He exaggerated unapologetically—he dramatized—but rarely showed any strain, keeping well within his limits. Above all, he took his time. Jack Benny, the model for his contemporaries, many of whom paid him tribute, was actually far from being the funniest of them, but he could take a pause better than anybody. The point of his most famous "joke" is . . . silence. A man stops him and demands, "Your money or your life." Benny stands there thinking it over. One or two of those vaudevillians had such an inherently farcical presence that people laughed in joyous anticipation the instant they appeared, before they got going. Jimmy Durante, for example. And Bert Lahr, for another. Their phenomenal underplaying, hoarding their resources, rising to the occasion but never above it, marked them as naturals for the relatively new medium. Today we can only marvel and lament that nobody tried to feature Durante or Lahr in a first-rate movie farce of his own. Sennett might have relished the opportunities they needed; but by the early Forties, Sennett was ten years out of business. All we have is bits of films given over to their lesser brethren of which they manage to take momentary possession.

The later generation pressed a lot harder. Lou Costello has timing that in its own way matches Benny's, and he can *listen* (even to a carping bore like Bud Abbott) with a farcical concentration that approaches Stan Laurel's. Red Skelton mugs with his body as well as his features so imaginatively that older comics saw him as the most likely of the comers; and he was coached by Keaton, no less. (But what was Keaton doing employed as a coach?) Danny Kaye's machine-gun delivery of lyrics written by his wife, Sylvia Fine, and his courage in assaying foreign accents that are defective keep his scenes moving at a gallop. Jerry Lewis has endless vitality and a range of unorthodox vocal mannerisms. But all these clowns betray their hunger for applause. They grow shrill. They hold next to nothing in reserve. They play the lovably inept, out-of-step little boy buffeted by the gales of cold circumstance, finding motherly warmth in the girls who settle for them; but they're too late. Langdon and Laurel have squeezed most of the sap out of that personification, and done it with much less apparent exertion.

Bob Hope hovers between the older and younger groups. A verbal specialist embarrassed by physical humor because untrained for it, he is always better than his scripts. On his own in *Louisiana Purchase* (1942), *The Princess and the Pirate* (1945), *Monsieur Beaucaire* (1946), *The Paleface* (1948), or *The Lemon Drop Kid* (1951), submitted to by ravishing blondes and brunettes who don't seem to know what day it is, he puffs and shoves. Teamed up with Bing Crosby, he's lifted out of panic and forced into subtler rhythms and contrasts. Crosby doesn't exactly slow him down. Rather, the partnership dangles fresh types of response before Hope and tones down that air of self-satisfaction which Hope evinces when, say, he's bragging about his cowardice. (Crosby in *The Road to Morocco*, contemplating an armed Arab encampment: "We'll have to storm the place." Hope: "You storm. I'll stay here and drizzle.") Crosby, it will be remembered, had once worked for Sennett. He takes the camera for granted, doesn't make up to it. He's not a farceur, but he understands farce. His manner of floating through scenes and songs, like Astaire's manner of dancing, respects the need for energy but invests it with grace. He gets few of the good lines; however, like a trouper, like Oliver Hardy, he makes his partner's good lines better. As he reacts to them with an attentive nonchalance that other crooner-comics vainly tried to command, he calls up new farcical refinements from the Hope chest of grimaces and intonations. (With Jerry Lewis it's the reverse. Dean Martin's sluggishness hampers him in their films together; and Lewis, who doesn't appear to be much of a reciprocal performer in the first place, wisely liberated himself. He operates more blithely alone, even if he keeps pleading, in effect, with the audience: "See this, Mom? Hey, Mom, will you please look?")

Hope and Crosby made seven Road films, in which they journey to Singapore (1940), Zanzibar (1941), Morocco (1942), Utopia (1946—an Alaskan setting that comments on Chaplin's *The Gold Rush*), Rio (1948), Bali (1953), and Hong Kong (1962—a trip that incorporates a rocket flight). Yet all these exotic locales are the same land of Hope and Crosby. The Paramount studio. Since 1940, film farces have drawn on, and shuffled together, the four main types of drama: realism, fantasy, W.M.P., and theatricalism. The Road series seems notable today for its ventures into film theatricalism, its teasing of the medium. In *The Road to Morocco* a camel turns its head toward us and with a horrible flapping of its upper lip leers, "This is the screwiest picture I was ever in." Jouncing along on its back, the two heroes sing that everything will turn out all right by the end: "Paramount will protect us 'cause we're signed for five more years." Robert Benchley smiles paternally out of an insert in the frame, a bubble, near the start of *The Road to Utopia* and announces, "Now this is a device known as the flashback"; he returns, still smiling, from time to time to report from his bubble on how the story is progressing. A grizzly bear in the same film who crawls into bed with Bob Hope, and suffers some caresses and tender words as he's taken for Dorothy Lamour in a fur coat, understandably grumbles that he was given no lines to speak in that scene. A mountain ("All this ice," exclaims Hope, "and no ginger ale") sprouts a halo of stars and turns into the Paramount logo. An extra passes through a stokehold where Hope and Crosby are shoveling coal into a ship's entrails and remarks that he's on his way to stage number nine. In *The Road to Rio*, after Crosby exults at having won Dorothy Lamour and a fortune, Hope observes that the Brothers Warner "will be very jealous." Jerry Colonna leads a rescue party at full gallop to the strains of the *William Tell* overture but halts it in some indeterminate spot, realizing that the film's climax is past and that he is somewhere else, anyway. "Well," he says to the camera lens, his eyes popping, "we were a little too late. But it was exciting, no?" Hope and Crosby go into their pat-a-cake routine, which ends with their knocking two thugs cold, as they've done several times before, and Hope gloats, "That's what they get for not seeing our pictures."

Since the Forties, few American clowns from radio, television, and the nightclub circuits have widened the scope of film farce, for whatever reasons—low-grade writing and/or directing, miscasting, typecasting, or restricted opportunities in the new medium. Jonathan Winters took parts in a succession of farces in the late Sixties but didn't make impressions as novel or colorful as he does on the little screen. In *The Jerk* (1979), Steve Martin, who starred and wrote the script, reverts to the little-boy-lost characterization, even depicting him as an orphan, a white kid adopted by a loving black family. Martin develops fits of brashness and pathos not unlike those of Jerry Lewis, but doesn't have Lewis's accompanying physical dexterity. Richard Pryor, by contrast, is a "natural" who can be extremely funny while keeping energy in reserve, and is still waiting for a screenplay worthy of him.

Women clowns have not shown their best work on film. Some got sidetracked into the itsi-bitsiness of TV series and specials. Lucille Ball, who has had roles in more than five dozen films, among them *Room Service* (1938) with the Marx Brothers and a handful with Hope (such as *Sorrowful Jones,* 1949; *Fancy Pants,* 1950; *The Facts of Life,* 1960; *Critic's Choice,* 1963), is unwontedly good-looking for a farceur with talent. But Hollywood and television squandered her, apart from a few showstopping sketches like the candy-wrapping conveyor belt that conveys too fast and forces her to eat or stuff into her apron all the chocolate she can't wrap, until her cheeks and bosom—and eyes—are bulging. In her prime, Ball fell into countless repetitions of the scatterbrained mother of domestic W.M.P.s, the inevitable sequel to the scatterbrained, single blondes or brunettes foisted on younger woman clowns. Saddled with her then-husband, Desi Arnaz, who had little evident sense of farce and whose lines often got mercifully drowned out by canned laughter, she grew proficient beyond a fault and hardly distinguishable from other presiding ladies of video, lacking the recklessness of Marie Dressler or Martha Raye, the nervous urgency of Mabel Normand, the naive pomposity of Margaret Dumont (whom Groucho enticed into clownishness), and the vibrant suggestiveness of Mae West, all of which she had hinted at in her early films.

Carol Burnett and Phyllis Diller might also, in their unlike ways, have contributed something personal to film and stage farce, apart from revue sketches and impersonations. I didn't see Burnett in *Who's Been Sleeping in My Bed?* (1960), whose title reeks of sex formula of the sort staged in London's West End for the delectation of tourists who speak no English; but in Robert Altman's melodramatic parody *The Wedding* (1976) and in Alan Alda's *The Four Seasons* (1981), Burnett's deftness and (when needed) intensity stood out in a large cast and a fragmented action. Diller's appearances in about ten films range from a bit part in Kazan's *Splendor in the Grass* (1961) to a mistake with Bob Hope and (a compounding of the mistake) Elke Sommer called *Boy, Did I Get a Wrong Number!* (1966), and to a lead in a minimally released adaptation of Elmer Rice's play *The Adding Machine* (1969). Will there be any chance for younger women comics and impersonators like Lily Tomlin, Goldie Hawn, Gilda Radner, and Jane Curtin to enhance their individual styles? There may be, as long as the uncertainties of producers continue to deepen over what constitutes popular taste.

Every national film industry has its folk clowns, borrowed as a rule from home-bred vaudeville, prolific favorites who cough up at least a couple of pictures a year for a decade or more but make few, if any, ripples on the international scene thanks to an unproved understanding that their humor is local and an unplanned conspiracy to keep it that way. When I grew up in Britain, George Formby and his ukulele were the top box-office draw. Other perennially popular figures were Claude Dampier and Will Hay. Their films are unavailable here for distribution today, although all three clowns turned out some farces that stand up surprisingly well. For many years Cantinflas (born 1911) was one of the Mexican industry's principal meal tickets, along with Arturo de Córdova and Dolores Del Rio, but his pictures played here mostly in Mexican-American movie houses in the Southwest. However, the Todd-AO extravaganza *Around the World in 80 Days* (1956), a British-American collaboration (Michael Anderson directed; Mike Todd produced), cast Cantinflas in a semiserious role as Phileas Fogg's valet, Passepartout, who behaved with slightly more suavity than his master, played by David Niven. *The Oxford Companion to Film* finds him disappointing in that guise, but for Cantinflas this was a muted part. For the purposes of recognition, no doubt, he wore his two usual scraps of mustache above the outer reaches of his upper lip, but gave no hint in his playing either of his lunatic fervor as a clown or of his confidence when in a more congenial atmosphere of film making. I didn't see a later Cantinflas film, *Pepe* (1960); it was swiftly withdrawn from distribution.

Fernandel (1903–71) also had a part in *Around the World in 80 Days*, but a fleeting bit part, befitting his stature as one of a host of international "guest stars" encountered by Fogg and his valet. In the postwar years Fernandel became a favorite in the art-cinema houses, where you could catch up with mostly French and Italian films, sip Colombian coffee between the features, and get into arguments with strangers about Sartre. But even before World War II, Graham Greene and other discerning reviewers approvingly noted Fernandel's work in *Un de la Légion* (1936), Duvivier's *Un Carnet de Bal* (*Life Dances On;* 1937), *Ignace* (1939), and Pagnol's *Harvest* (1939). Some of his pictures didn't reach these shores until well after the war, if at all. The impression he leaves as a clown is signified by the fact that when he plays the lead one speaks of a Fernandel film, rather than, say, a Colombier or a Verneuil—two directors he's associated with. Yet the films themselves, it must be said, rarely rate high, even among Fernandel fanciers. Discussing *Ignace*, Greene more or less dismisses the film swiftly, but goes on to say: "There remains Fernandel: Fernandel of the huge teeth, the mulish face and the long ape-like arms: an animal that laughs—it sounds like somebody's definition of Man: Fernandel with the celluloid collar that always creaks and the long greasy lock of hair. Nobody has ever laughed so infectiously as Fernandel: it is like an epidemic, and yet a prim colleague has found him in close-up disgusting."[1]

A buffoonish peasant in his looks and guffawing and occasional Provençal dialect, Fernandel can glide into straight roles with no apparent dislocations. As almost always happens with such mixtures of actor and clown, he seems to land parts that don't so much broaden the spectrum of his art as present him in double exposure. His peasant image will not quite be obliterated, whether he undertakes to give us a hairdresser (in *Un Carnet de Bal*), a tremulous suitor (in *The Welldigger's Daughter*, 1940), an American salesclerk on the run (*The Most Wanted Man*, 1961), a baker (*The Wild Oat*, 1956), a *clochard* (*Hoboes in Paradise*, 1949), or, beating George Burns to the throne of thrones, God (*The Devil and the Ten Commandments*, 1962). As an Italian village priest in the Don Camillo films (including *The Little World of Don Camillo* and *The Return of Don Camillo*) he tries to protect his flock from the competitive preachings of a nasty Communist agitator, a meatier role than his and enacted with just the right degree of self-indulgence by Gino Cervi. What with the incidence of too many bland screenplays that set out to make him lovable—make the audience feel protective toward him—by trading on a superficial charm, and supporting roles that didn't stimulate his farcical energies, Fernandel had a career that didn't exploit him fully.

Yet in *The Sheep Has Five Legs* (1954) and *The Cow and I* (1961) he comes into his own with two parts he can sink his considerable teeth into. *The Cow and I* relates the escape of a French prisoner of war from a camp in southern Germany. Like Jean Gabin and Marcel Dalio before him in Renoir's *The Grand Illusion* (1937), he

---

[1] *The Spectator*, Oct. 13, 1939. Reprinted in *Graham Greene on Film*, *op.cit.*, p. 245.

walks to freedom across the border; only Fernandel does it openly by leading a cow, pretending to be the peasant he really is. Duping German soldiers and civilians, trudging along tracks and across open country and heavily guarded bridges, he is at his best here: a simpleton born to outwit systems, the quintessential farce hero. His dilated eyes with their half-dropped curtains, flapping ears, prognathous jaw (not quite as formidable as Michel Simon's, but heavy enough) below that battlement of teeth make him the aptly equine companion for his cow: two corn spirits, fertility symbols, not-so-dumb beasts. And the man's affection for and dependence upon the animal recall the partnership of Keaton and Brown Eyes in *Go West*.

Creators

A prosperous, handsome young Hollywood director and a blond starlet who is as yet "undiscovered" fall wrestling into his back-patio pool. His stately English butler accompanies them into the water; so does the English valet when he tries to fish the butler out. Could those multiple splashes denote the close of a Sennett two-reeler? It is, after all, the moment of impact with the water that prompts our laughter, the breaking of surface tension, the fake drowning, the collision in an undignified pose—upside down, limbs flailing—with a yielding and enveloping element, rather than the immersion. But no, we've gone barely halfway through *Sullivan's Travels* (1941); and the sight of Joel McCrea, Veronica Lake, Eric Blore, and Robert Greig gasping wetly means no more than a tribute to silent farce. There are other such tributes in the course of *Sullivan's Travels*. A vehicle called The Tank, a compromise between an armored convertible and a motorbike with side-car, propelled by a thirteen-year-old boy, hurls itself across bumpy countryside pursued by a luxurious bus, a "land yacht," in which all the appointments and furnishings, from chairs to china, fly about in an inertial orgy of destruction, until, when it's all over, a publicity man sits wearing a venetian blind around his neck and the chef wears the roof around his. Later, the director, hoping to make his way in the world as a hobo, performs chores for a widow who, in payment, takes him to the movies; gives him a bed for the night under the portrait of her late, frowning husband; and locks him in—but leaves unlocked the door that connects with her bed-room. He breaks out by lowering himself out the window on knot-ted sheets that guide him into a filled rain barrel. Drenched, he stops a truck driver, who asks, "What did you fall into?" The direc-tor replies, "Everything there was." The question and answer sum up the plight of farce's victims.

And yet *Sullivan's Travels*, like the previous films made by Pres-ton Sturges (1898–1959), rings in farcical interruptions in order to bolster screenplays that are essentially screwball comedies. In the Thirties the screwball comedies made by Ernst Lubitsch, Howard Hawks, Gregory La Cava, Leo McCarey, George Cukor, and oth-ers usually make a big thing out of high-society settings and their denizens' sumptuous wardrobes. In the much-quoted opening scene of *Trouble in Paradise* (1932), Lubitsch skits this sort of op-ulence. A dog sniffs at a garbage can, which is collected by a man who flings its contents into a gondola; the man breaks into "O Sole Mio" as the camera shows us the canals of romantic Venice—and pans to a fancy restaurant nearby, where two jewel thieves smoothly pass themselves off as aristocrats. Frank Capra and his screenwriter of the Thirties, Robert Riskin, worked a similar screw-ball vein but further down the social register. Their Apple Annie, Mr. Deeds, and Mr. Smith are homey folk tempted by the rich, powerful, and corrupt.

Sturges contributed to screwball comedies as the screenwriter for William Wyler's *The Good Fairy* (1935) and Mitchell Leisen's *Easy Living* (1937). Later, as director-cum-writer, he abstracted for his own purposes the satirical outlook of screwball comedies, their slickness of story line (often reworked from money-making Broadway comedies), the Capra-Riskin deviations from the subgenre—"plain" people—and the comedic, or rational, motiva-tion, instead of the absurdities and eccentricities of farce. Perhaps by 1941 he felt ashamed of merely entertaining people if, as his hero, Sullivan, says, those were "troublous times" with "death snarling at you from every street corner." Perhaps he anticipated the reservations that some reviewers, such as James Agee, would express about his seriousness as an artist. At any rate, *Sullivan's Travels* takes as its theme the social validity of making people laugh. Sturges names his hero after the nineteenth-century world heavyweight champion John L. Sullivan, and plays his title off the title of Swift's angry novel, a pictorial slab of which had been brought to the unreading public a couple of years before by Max and Dave Fleischer. Sturges "affectionately" dedicates his film to "the memory of those who made us laugh: the motley mountebanks, the clowns, the buffoons, in all times and in all nations, whose efforts have lightened our burden a little. . . ."

In the opening shots two men, perched on the top of a fast train, trade punches for possession of a pistol. Heavily orchestrated music pounds out an accompaniment. After a few wicked blows have rocked them both, Man A gets hold of the pistol and shoots Man B, who drags Man A off the car with him into a river alongside the track. The water flowers into an explosion, the music groans its climactic chords, and a title THE END rises above the submerging heads. With this theatricalist touch Sturges pulls the camera back and we are in a studio screening room. The director, Sullivan, explains to his producers that in the "symbolism" of this ending, "capital and labor destroy each other." The film, O Brother, Where Art Thou?, represents "an answer to communism, a true canvas of the suffering of humanity." It is rife with "social significance." The front-office men, unswayed, want Sullivan to dump O Brother and go to work on a musical, Ants in Your Pants of 1941, a sequel to his hit show Ants in Your Pants of 1939. They tempt him with Bob Hope, Bing Crosby, Mary Martin, Jack Benny, Rochester—any stars he'd like. But Sullivan doesn't yield, even when they convince him that he can't make a film about poverty and suffering because he has no experience of either. What he determines to do is go out into the world, dressed in rags, carrying only ten cents and a red-and-white polka-dotted handkerchief. He'll expose himself to some of that suffering in the big outside.

Trailed and monitored for a time by the lavishly equipped land yacht, he strides off toward experience; but whenever he bums a ride—he doesn't get farther east than Las Vegas—it seems to bring him back to home territory, Hollywood or Beverly Hills. It's as if, he remarks, some gravitational force were telling him, "Get back where you belong, you phony, you." En route he picks up Veronica Lake, a disappointed actress. Together they ride a freight train, stop over in a tramps' colony, catch colds and fleas. Somebody steals Sullivan's boots and leaves him another pair which, when he walks, flap open in front like laughing mouths. He wears a sand-wich board. He fumbles for food in a garbage can but turns away in disgust.

And so he gives up the quest. But the poverty he's seen moves him. Leaving Miss Lake in the care of his butler and valet, he visits the slums of Kansas City in his hobo's garb, armed with two hundred five-dollar bills, which he thrusts into the hands of star-tled down-and-outs. One recipient tails him, hits him over the head, and steals the remaining money. Thus is philanthropy re-warded. But the thief meets with prosaic justice. He drops the bills while scurrying away across some railroad tracks. Stooping to pick them up, he's run down by a train—a reference back to the train deaths that end *O Brother, Where Art Thou?*

The thief's mutilated body, with the five-dollar bills scattered nearby, is taken for the corpse of Sullivan; while the director him-self, when he comes to with temporary amnesia, is taken for a hobo. A railroad cop picks on him; he fights back; he gets a jail term. . . . Sent to join a chain gang in the South, he now learns about real suffering under the tutelage of the gang overseer, who beats him and, catching him reading about his own death in a newspaper, consigns him to the sweatbox. Sullivan contrives to break out of the gang, a ten-year sentence, and his picaresque adventures by confessing to the "murder" of the "famous Holly-wood director." Recognized, of course, as the genuine Sullivan, he's pardoned and feted. A happy resolution. But one episode in the chain gang has left a powerful impression on him. A black preacher invites the prisoners every so often to join his congrega-tion for an evening of movies in his church. The chained men march down the aisle to take their seats as the congregants lustily sing, "Let My People Go." During the screening of a Mickey Mouse cartoon, in which Pluto gets entangled in flypaper, Sullivan can't help noticing that the convicts around him love every second of the film. They're convulsed. Caught up in their enjoyment involuntarily (he asks a neighbor, "Hey, am I laughing?"), he real-izes that "there's a lot to be said for making people laugh. That's all some people have." He will give up on *O Brother, Where Art Thou?*, which, in his absence, the studio has been touting as "the greatest tragedy ever made" and which "will put Shakespeare back with the shipping news." The final sequence of *Sullivan's Travels* superimposes over the thoughtful faces of Joel McCrea and Veronica Lake a montage of the convicts in church, their mouths splitting with unaccustomed joy.

Several years later, when James Agee reviewed Sturges' *The Miracle of Morgan's Creek* and *Hail the Conquering Hero*, he praised them as the finest, most insolent and censor-defying work then being done in Hollywood, yet could not suppress doubts about the director's cynicism and nihilism; Sturges was "rejecting half his talents" and "there is nothing on earth he is temperamentally able to do about it" because he "feels that conscience and comedy are incompatible."[2] Agee interpreted Sturges' work with both sympathy and discernment (as well as some dribs and drabs of questionable psychohistory) which have remained unmatched since. Yet I believe he got hold of the wrong end of the slapstick. Sturges' handicap was that he had too heavy, not too light, a conscience. The conclusion of *Sullivan's Travels*, while informing us that it's better to make people laugh than make them worry, affirms this director's predilection for "pure entertainment," but it does so by ramming that conclusion home. As a clue to Sturges' intentions we can note that he cast a "straight" actor in the role of the hero, his surrogate self. Now, the hero of this particular film has to have intelligence and sensitivity and the other requirements of a prominent director. Therefore, the role cannot be handled by a clown. Therefore, the creator of *Sullivan's Travels* means his hero's sentiments to be taken at smiling, not smirking, face value. As additional evidence of Sturges' earnestness, we can look for a moment at Veronica Lake's part in the film. Lake is one of the most fragilely beautiful women ever seen on a screen. She has a rich, musical voice. She can (and in this picture, does) make her persona glitter with the sort of clarity, pace, and wryness that more complimented comediennes (Claudette Colbert, say, or Joan Greenwood) never equaled. Furthermore, Sturges starts her out with an appealing characterization; a sharp-tongued, compassionate, but disillusioned young actress, she gets the better of Sullivan in their terse exchanges of wit. But then he lets her decline into a lovesick hanger-on. Much as the film doesn't carry through with its premise—the unwisdom of making solemn statements about hardship,

[2] *Agee on Film* (Boston: Beacon Press, 1958), pp. 74–76, 117, 138.

such as those, perhaps, in many Warners melodramas—so her role slides into the very sentimentality against which Sturges hurled the bolts of his ridicule. Her role becomes a metonym for a very good protofarce that blunts its own edge.

Sullivan's Travels is sometimes said to be Sturges' own favorite among his films. I wonder. Certainly it must have been the one closest to his heart, and he packed it with memorable lines. (Sullivan's Butler: "The poor know all about poverty, and only the morbid rich would find the topic glamorous." Policeman: "What are you doing in those old clothes?" Sullivan: "I just paid my income tax." Sullivan's Butler again, phoning the freight yard: "Have you a freight train going out of town? The five forty-eight? Very good. Does it carry tramps? Where do they get on?") But after trying actor-comedians in his next two films, *The Palm Beach Story* (1942) and *The Great Moment* (1943), he filled the lead roles in *The Miracle of Morgan's Creek* (1943) with Eddie Bracken, a better-than-average clown when allowed the opportunity to be, and Betty Hutton, another clown who, much of the time, appears to volunteer more than she's been asked for in the way of zaniness, cute nose-wrinkling, and pathos. In casting Hutton, Sturges may have later felt that he'd overcorrected his timidity, for in his next film, *Hail the Conquering Hero* (1944), he retained Bracken but replaced Hutton with the sincere foil Ella Raines, a less extroverted Paulette Goddard and the very image of the pretty small-town girl next door. A couple of years later for *The Sin of Harold Diddlebock* (also known as *Mad Wednesday*; 1946) Sturges restlessly changed his male lead again, this time going the limit by choosing one of the four top clowns of the Twenties, Harold Lloyd (aged fifty-three).[3] This film picks up the hero of *The Freshman* more than twenty years later, and suppresses any ingenue role.

But while he wavers between comedy and farce, "light comedians" and clowns, for his central roles, Sturges remains constant to his stable of supporting Paramount actors, most of them madcap Irishmen, who give him bright vignettes, daubs of caricature that lighten the sometimes relentlessly slick pressures of the main plot, and help him to heighten his satire: Jimmy Conlin, Franklin

---

[3] Here I'm assuming that Sturges was big enough at Paramount to choose his own casts (and technicians), instead of having to take whoever happened to be available.

Pangborn, Porter Hall, and above all, William Demarest. (As a child, I thought of Demarest as the prototype of the American cop.) Sturges' burst of eleven films made in the decade 1939–49, from *The Great McGinty* to *The Beautiful Blonde from Bashful Bend*, alternately advance on and retreat from all-out farce, generally falling back on screwball-comedy formulas with happy reconciliations.

He approached a thoroughly farcical treatment most tantalizingly in *The Miracle of Morgan's Creek*, and not only because he had farceurs in the big roles and William Demarest practicing flying ass-kicks (on a teen-aged girl!) that never connected, swung him into midair, and dropped him on his back. The action takes satirical swipes at motherhood (or madonnahood), the family as portrayed in MGM films of the Thirties, the military (in wartime), truth-telling, Christmas, and other sacred cows; it even *has* a sacred cow, which wanders into a living room where Betty Hutton is sitting in the last lap of pregnancy, as if to imply that the house is a manger.

Trudy Kockenlocker (Hutton), a name to conjure with, goes out with a batch of soldiers one night, all night, borrowing a convertible ("in case the boys don't have one") that belongs to her admirer Norval (Bracken), a reject from the armed services. During high jinks, beer, champagne, and dancing, Trudy gets hoisted into the air by a partner, cracks her head against a crystal light reflector, and turns woozy. Next morning she returns the automobile to Norval with a ripped bumper and assorted dents. Now, Norval has dreamed of marrying Trudy since they both were in school, and he is eager to go ahead even when he learns that, like his car, she has been driven recklessly. He steals for her, goes in futile search of her impregnator, gets jailed, and endures torments from her permanently irate father, the town constable (Demarest). But Norval gets what he wants, and more, when Trudy gives birth to sextuplets and he is honored as their father and put into colonel's uniform. Sturges throws the bulk of the action into a flashback; it is told to the state governor and his political manager, two scheming characters and splendid actors (Brian Donlevy and Akim Tamiroff) lifted from *The Great McGinty*.

As always with Sturges, the screenplay throws off well-turned character lines and quips. When Trudy reveals to her pragmatic and bossy young sister (Diana Lynn) that Norval has always adored her and that he took cooking and sewing lessons to be in the same classroom with her, the sister says he'd be the perfect husband: "He could do all the housework." Norval, who feels bitter about not having got into the army, describes himself as an "unwilling civilian," and adds that things might be different "if they had uniforms for *them*." After Trudy's miraculous feat, Mussolini receives the news and gapes; Hitler goes into a tantrum; Canada, nation of the Dionne quintuplets, is jealous; and headlines scream, "Mussolini Resigns" and "Hitler Demands Recount."

In several sequences Sturges displays unobtrusive acuity in framing his shots, a skill for which critics don't usually give him enough credit. As Trudy walks through the town of Morgan's Creek with her sister, foraging back into her blocked-out memory, the camera tracks alongside, close and parallel to them, as they pass houses, stores, local people, and—in a reference back to the orgiastic night before—two soldiers in a jeep, drinking. The extended scene creates the same kind of agitation that Hitchcock achieved by having his camera prey on Janet Leigh in the early scenes of *Psycho* (1960). When Trudy comes home from a walk with Norval, her father brusquely sends her away so that he can conduct a man-to-man chat. He's cleaning a couple of guns as he talks to Norval about marriage. Sturges angles his camera so that the guns (as willful as the little cannon in Keaton's *The Navigator*) seem to want to aim their muzzles at Norval. When Trudy is nine months pregnant, Sturges trains his camera on her from over the shoulder of a high wing chair, and so avoids provoking the censor, and at the same time lets his audience imagine her girth for themselves: she is, after all, about to break the world record for childbearing. And then, in the hospital where her father and sister wait for news of the birth, a well-placed stationary perspective shot along the corridor suffices for a long scene. As nurses come rushing out of the ward with news of a boy . . . twins . . . triplets . . . four fingers held up . . . five . . . six . . . they chase to and from a closet for fresh towels. Here Sturges seems to confine and trap Kockenlocker and his daughter while forcing the urgency of the scene every time the nurses appear or disappear on the run. I wouldn't judge *The Miracle of Morgan's Creek* to be a better movie overall than *Sullivan's Travels*; but because the director has conceived it as a farce, instead of pumping farcical relief into comedy, it sets forth Sturges' credo, the one he enunciates in *Sullivan's Travels*, with more conviction.

Billy Wilder (born 1906), as if in pursuit of Sturges, wrote or co-wrote screenplays at Paramount in the middle to late Thirties, including several for a director, Leisen, with whom Sturges had worked; directed his first film, *The Major and the Minor* (1942), three years after Sturges' debut as a director (with *The Great McGinty*); used one of Sturges' favorite photographers, John Seitz, for four films (*Five Graves to Cairo*, 1943; *Double Indemnity*, 1944; *The Lost Weekend*, 1945; *Sunset Boulevard*, 1950); and inevitably drew on some of the same Paramount actors. He also quoted from Sturges' pictures. As one example, the much, and rightly, admired shot of the vast, depersonalized office in Wilder's *The Apartment*, with its checkerboard layout of desks, one of them occupied by Jack Lemmon, resembles on a more grandiose scale the long office in Sturges' *Christmas in July* (1940), where all the regimented clerks, Dick Powell included, take their seats simultaneously at nine o'clock when a buzzer sounds. As if to point up the quotation, Lemmon's name in *The Apartment* is C. C. Baxter, while the office in *Christmas in July* belongs to the Baxter company.

Wilder, like earlier Paramount directors, discloses rents, flaws, and rot in the social fabric with scornful relish. Coming after Lubitsch (for whom he wrote a couple of screenplays) and Capra, as well as Sturges, Wilder can take for granted corruption in government, private corporations, the military, and other national and local institutions at home and abroad; and he can approach it more callously than those predecessors do—reviewers often rightly call his films hard-boiled. Findings are keepings, but Wilder is more than a mere follower—partly because of his consuming tidiness as a film creator, and partly because of the pungency of his dialogue. Despite the wildness, the outlandish Wilder-ness, of his story lines, he makes every scene, every moment, fit into the patterns of his action *and count*. He is one of the most accomplished craftsmen of the medium, roughly what David Belasco, George Abbott, or Abe Burrows was to the Broadway theater: a professional's professional. In recent years his stock has risen among those *cinéastes* who take craftsmanship of such excellence for art.

Most of Wilder's earlier films and screenplays, which admit streaks and flecks of farce, are in essence satirical comedies and melodramas. In them he tries to insure himself against box-office laggardliness by recruiting superstars—Barbara Stanwyck, Bing Crosby, Marlene Dietrich, Gloria Swanson, Kirk Douglas, Humphrey Bogart, James Stewart, Gary Cooper, Charles Laughton, Tyrone Power, Marilyn Monroe—although Crosby, Stewart, and Douglas don't, in the end, pay off for him. He also lays out fortunes on refashioning landscapes and reproducing such interiors as London's Central Criminal Court, the Old Bailey. But beginning with *Some Like It Hot* (1959), he plunges into six films in a row that seethe with farce. The remaining five, all of them, like *Hot*, written in collaboration with I. A. L. Diamond and produced by Mirisch, are *The Apartment* (1960), *One, Two, Three* (1961), *Irma la Douce* (1963), *Kiss Me, Stupid* (1964), and *The Fortune Cookie* (1965). Wilder has mixed the flavors and aromas in this six-pack, but each item carries his trademarks and the farce label, sharing such features as characters who get wound in coils of circumstance that tighten wickedly; wisecracks that are both sexier and more absurd than Sturges' wise sayings; young women with hyperbolic bosoms and glowing lengths of leg which Wilder bares as nearly as he dares (Judi West is said to have refused to wear a dress cut away to the navel in *The Fortune Cookie* until Wilder consented to let her put it on back to front); and inanimate objects cast in large and small roles. The main plots of *Some Like It Hot* and *Irma la Douce* also traffic in disguises, deception, and impersonation, those other hallowed staples of farce. In *Hot*, two musicians (Tony Curtis and Jack Lemmon) who have witnessed a gangland slaying get themselves up in drag and hide from the killers by joining a girls' band. The hero of *Irma* (Lemmon again), a French cop turned pimp, masquerades in the formal jacket, derby, accent and clichés of Hollywood's idea of an English lord. When Curtis, in *Hot*, gets out from under his women's garb and cosmetics in order to make a play for Monroe, he takes on the adenoidal intonations of Cary Grant as he affects the part of a "son of Shell Oil":

CURTIS: If you're interested in whether I'm married . . .
MONROE: Oh, I'm not.
CURTIS: Well, I'm not.
MONROE: Oh, that's interesting.

And then, when he is bragging about his hobbies:

MONROE: Water polo? Isn't that dangerous?
CURTIS: Sure is. I've had three ponies drowned under me.

Wilder and Diamond like these plays on words, which are mis-understandings, rather than puns. Lemmon, as the lord, tells Irma that he caught his gardener and his Lady Chatterley–like wife "red-handed in the greenhouse," so he "threw them both out, pulled up the drawbridge, and started divorce proceedings." Irma, wishing to be kind, observes, "It's too bad." He replies, "Catastrophe. Best damn gardener I ever had."

Inconsequentialities like these bob up too infrequently out of the terse logic and efficiency of Wilder's scripts, five of which come directly or otherwise from Broadway and boulevard theater. His choice of actors, rather than clowns, means that he, not his performers, dominates each picture. Under so programmatic a regime the farce sometimes hampers its own practitioners, while the visuals grow explanatory and unnecessarily emphatic. Wilder doesn't allow for the oddities and quirks we treasure in the antics of earlier creator-clowns. Any sudden fizzing of farcical inspiration must be forgone for the sake of adhering to preconceptions. (We can notice a comparable stifling effect in the explanatory melodramas of Hitchcock.) As a result, Wilder's farces seem pared down too ruthlessly to bone and gristle when measured against the more leisurely screwball comedies he wrote for Lubitsch and Hawks in the late Thirties and beginning Forties. *Kiss Me, Stupid* and *The Fortune Cookie*, in particular, have some of the panicky drive of Capra's *Arsenic and Old Lace* (1945), a forcing of the pace that sooner or later deadens our ability to respond with initiative.

Two further farce writer-directors, Frank Tashlin (1913–71) and Blake Edwards (born 1922), allayed the sting of their often-fresh satire and parody with stale well-made-play techniques and resolutions. Tashlin had a loftier reputation in France than here; one saw marquees on the Left Bank, but never in Greenwich Village, bearing that ultimate accolade, the name above the title: "Un Film de Frank Tashlin"—the film in question being a Jerry Lewis (when Lewis didn't occupy his own director's chair), such as *The Geisha Boy* (1959), *Cinderfella* (1962), or *The Disorderly Orderly* (1966). French critics admire Tashlin's way with a visual gag; with objects that are slippery, breakable, or sexually suggestive; and with substances that can be dribbled, dumped, or splashed onto the human form; they also like Lewis as a galumphing summary of American idiocy. Tashlin wrote for the Marx Brothers and directed Bob Hope in the Forties and early Fifties, but even before those days he'd worked in the animation business for Fleischer, Disney, Warners, and several cartoon independents. Tashlin thus came to farce cinema as well prepared as anybody in its history; but toward the end of his life he rode the well-made-play tracks nearly into oblivion.

Edwards, who detests the treacheries of Hollywood (witness his *S.O.B.*, 1981), where he began as a writer, turned out some nicely written scripts for other directors, among them *My Sister Eileen* (1955), adapted from the Broadway show, and *Operation Madball* (1957), a diverting exercise in lunacy, both for Richard Quine. As a onetime actor, he had the discernment to lure Peter Sellers into one Inspector Clouseau film after another (not all of which he directed), starting with *A Shot in the Dark* and *The Pink Panther* (both 1965). As Clouseau fumbles forward, he enrages his boss, played with fine, insensate fury by Herbert Lom, and eventually drives him insane, supplants him, and turns him unintentionally into one of those world-wrecking archvillains who recklessly oppose James Bond, Superman, Clouseau, and other saviors of mankind. Sellers adopts a French pronunciation for certain English words, speaking the open *o* sound as if it had an umlaut over it ("the steuve is queulled" means "the stove is cold"), so as to mock the very idea of putting on an accent. He favors penetrable disguises: a nose that melts, a beard that falls away, a wig that revolves on his scalp. With a dopey hero's panache he blunders into his successes and gains the bed-warmth of slinky beauties. In *The Pink Panther Strikes Back*, Lom sics the world's highest-paid specialists in assassination on Clouseau; they end up knifing, shooting, and stifling one another while he doesn't realize that any of them has even made an attempt on his life.

In the mid-Sixties, American farces remained slick according to the Paramount patterns, complying with the dramatic logic which decreed that cause must be seen to precede effect. But the industry's insularity had been breached. Wilder was occasionally shooting on location overseas, as with A *Foreign Affair* and *One, Two, Three*, both in West Germany. Edwards, Stanley Kubrick, and other Americans courted British actors like Sellers who did not belong to the Hollywood colony. Edwards, Richard Lester, Kubrick, and several Americans who'd departed during the McCarthy years (Carl Foreman, Joseph Losey, Jules Dassin) took up residence and worked in Europe. American farces had also begun to borrow one particular type of story line from British films: the outrageous scheme.

Creators Across the Ocean

Henry Holland (Alec Guinness) and his partner Alfred Pendlebury (Stanley Holloway) tear along London's Great West Road at about seventy miles per hour in a stolen police car. Holland and Pendlebury have seized bars of gold bullion that were being transferred between the Mint and the Bank of England, melted them down, made paperweights out of them in the shape of little Eiffel Towers, and exported them to France; there they can be melted down again into gold bars that are out of the reach of the British authorities. Because of the obstinacy of one schoolgirl, the elaborate plan of Holland and Pendlebury has come unraveled and the police are now after them. But the police don't know they're escaping in a police car. As they hurtle along and Holloway nervously steers, Guinness solemnly sends out instructions over the official car radio: the crooks have been spotted at Junction Road and all police cars in the area are to proceed there immediately. They do. And in the climactic rally of *The Lavender Hill Mob* (1951), police cars from all over meet at Junction Road, a blind multiple intersection, in one of the prettiest pileups since Sennett's *Kid Auto Races at Venice* (1914). Junction Road is in Ealing, not far from Ealing Studios, where the film was made.

It was for Ealing Studios that Peter Sellers, our link between

American and British film farces, did his first movie stint, *The Ladykillers*, in 1957; but that picture happened to be the last of Ealing's misnamed "little comedies." The beginning of his film career predates by a couple of years the dissolution of Ealing Studios. Sellers, who had come into movies from music hall, radio, and television, went on to tackle a diversity of parts, three in *Dr. Strangelove* alone, before Blake Edwards landed him for the first Pink Panther film. He was by then a known quantity, insofar as this can be said of any impersonator, and a valuable property. He continued with other, sometimes better roles than that of Clouseau (the king and the cabdriver in the remake of *The Prisoner of Zenda*, 1978, and the angelic simpleton in *Being There*, 1979), till his death in 1980.

The "little comedies" put Ealing Studios, led by Sir Michael Balcon, on the international map of farce. Between 1938 and 1959, Balcon's team of directors turned out nearly one hundred features that add up to an affectionate and sometimes mildly jingoistic portrait of Britain, especially working-class Britain, just before, during, and after World War II. Those directors wrote, edited, produced, and in other ways assisted with one another's films in a communal—almost a familial—enterprise, guided by a benevolent "father" and reminiscent of the Keystone setup.

Ealing grew famous for its farces, but they are a modest fraction —smaller than one-eighth—of its total output over two decades. Before its turning point in 1949, it was known as the purveyor of half a dozen George Formby films, several that starred Will Hay, and a slew of thrillers and tales of heroism.[4] And then 1949 was the

---

[4] Such as *The Four Just Men* (1939), *The Proud Valley* (1940), *Next of Kin* (1942), *Went the Day Well?* (1943), *San Demetrio London* (1943), *Dead of Night* (1945), *Pink String and Sealing Wax* (1945), *The Captive Heart* (1946), *The Overlanders* (1947), *Nicholas Nickleby* (1947), *Scott of the Antarctic* (1948).

Among the clowns and comedians in the films from Ealing were Sonnie Hale, Jimmy O'Dea, George Formby, Graham Moffatt, Moore Marriott, Gracie Fields, Gordon Harker, Tommy Trinder, Claude Hulbert, Will Hay, Miles Malleson, Basil Radford and Naunton Wayne, Alastair Sim, Alec Guinness, Margaret Rutherford, Tessie O'Shea, Max Adrian, Ian Carmichael, Benny Hill, Bernard Cribbins, Robert Morley.

Any listing of the other acting celebrities in Ealing pictures would have to include Michael Hordern, John Mills, Stewart Granger, Joan Greenwood, Jean Simmons, Frederick Valk, Flora Robson, Simone Signoret, Bernard Miles, Sybil Thorndike, Cedric Hardwicke, Francis L. Sullivan, Peter Ustinov, James Mason, Godfrey Tearle, Michael Wilding, Stanley Baker, Felix Aylmer, Françoise Rosay, Sally Ann Howes, Michael Redgrave, Peter Finch, Bernard Lee, Herbert Lom, Eric Portman, Paul Robeson, Robert Donat, Yvonne

year when it released *Passport to Pimlico, Tight Little Island*
(*Whisky Galore* in Britain), and *Kind Hearts and Coronets*. Altogether, Ealing let loose eleven films I would characterize as
farces. In addition to *The Lavender Hill Mob, The Ladykillers*, and
the three just cited, they are *A Run for Your Money* (1949), *The
Man in the White Suit* (1951), *The Titfield Thunderbolt* (1953),
High and Dry (in Britain, *The Maggie*; 1954), *Who Done It?* (1956;
the first leading role for Benny Hill), and *All at Sea* (in Britain,
Barnacle Bill; 1957).

Because some idiosyncratic character types recur, so that the
actors form something like an extensive repertory company, film
criticism has tended to lump these farces together; but the differ-
ing directors and writers give them complexions and innards that
are distinct from one another. In his astute book *Ealing Studios*,
Charles Barr finds that most of the films, especially the ones written by T. E. B. Clarke (*Passport to Pimlico, The Lavender Hill
Mob, The Titfield Thunderbolt, Who Done It?, All at Sea*), reaffirm
traditional English morality and mores, humane inefficiency, and
the cohesiveness of the community, the latter resembling the co-
hesive community that was Ealing Studios.

In resisting progress, the ordinary people in these farces, with
their developed sense of fair play, defeat attempts to alter or take
away the lives they know. As a couple of examples, the community
in *The Titfield Thunderbolt* succeeds in preserving a branch rail
line declared obsolete by the authorities; and in *All at Sea*, Alec
Guinness as a former skipper enlists the community's help in saving a decrepit pier by turning it into a sort of moored pleasure
steamer. The old in both cases wins out over the new.

However, Barr traces subversive elements at Ealing in the per-
sons of Robert Hamer (director of *Kind Hearts and Coronets*),
Alexander Mackendrick (who directed *Tight Little Island, The
Man in the White Suit, High and Dry*, and *The Ladykillers*), and
Mackendrick's several screenwriters, especially William Rose, an

---

Mitchell, George Rose, Robert Shaw, Serge Reggiani, Audrey Hepburn, Irene Worth,
Richard Attenborough, Laurence Harvey, Jack Hawkins, Dirk Bogarde, Jack McGowran,
Hugh Griffith, Aldo Ray, Maggie Smith, Donald Pleasance, David Farrar, Diana Wynyard,
Alec McCowen, Denholm Elliott, Kay Kendall, David Niven, Theodore Bikel, Paul Doug-
las, and, yes, Humphrey Bogart. . . . And I'm omitting the dozens of first-rate "character
actors" who took on bit parts and whose presence delights face-spotters like me.

American. Their views of communal solidarity and traditional preferences are more caustic. Thus, Guinness as the inventor of an indestructible synthetic thread (and fabric) in *The Man in the White Suit* encounters opposition and harassment from both management and unions, high-ups and humble folks, and finally becomes as lonely an enemy of the people as Ibsen's Dr. Stockmann.

Barr believes that Ealing's total product (not only the farces) reflects the desire of the British in that period to live and let live, to avoid being assertive, to take refuge in polite compromises, to behave condescendingly toward private acquisitiveness and initiative—to refuse, in short, to push themselves into the mid-twentieth century, so that they finally forfeit the nation's status as what is usually called a first-class power. Ealing films, he says, "will increasingly become accepted as a prime source of evidence for reading the inner history of the times"—that is, of Britain between the late Thirties and 1960.[5] He goes on to perceive some of the films as clashes between older and younger generations, in which the elders triumph and bring the youngsters into line, much as Balcon's paternalism conscribed the directors who worked for him.

Most of the farces can also be read as modern eruptions of the Dionysian spirit. In their communal scenes, the characters catch and pass on a fervor that may grow into mass delirium, as it does in certain of Aristophanes' plays, in Sennett's rallies, and in such diverse farces as *The Inspector General, Hail the Conquering Hero, The Crazy Ray,* and *Duck Soup.* In *Passport to Pimlico,* an old document unearthed from a bomb site reveals that a tiny neighborhood in London belongs to the vanished Kingdom of Burgundy. Independence from Britain! From postwar rationing! Ecstasy (of the guarded English kind)! And as if to cap the joke: allegiance to Burgundy, *the* wine province, one of the two places from which Dionysos might set out these days on an expedition to

[5] *Ealing Studios* (Woodstock, N.Y.: Overlook Press, 1977), p. 146. Barr suggests that the "Ealing dispensation" represents a search on the part of Balcon and most of his directors for "a cosy retreat, a soft option, operated not by harnessing and redirecting energies, but by denying them" (p. 107).

Another useful, if less than wholly accurate, book that covers the British films of this period is Raymond Durgnat's *A Mirror for England* (London: Faber & Faber, 1970). Roy Armes has a chapter, "Balcon at Ealing," in his valuable *A Critical History of British Cinema* (New York: Oxford University Press, 1978).

capture new followers—the other place being, naturally, California.

A higher-proof communal intoxication grips the inhabitants of Todday, the Scottish isle with a name that's an elision of toddy today, when, in *Tight Little Island*, a ship carrying vats of whisky crashes into offshore rocks. Its cargo left intact, it is accessible for plundering, at a time during World War II when Scotch was unobtainable except on the black market. In *The Titfield Thunderbolt*, the villagers safeguard their rail connection by coaxing an ancient locomotive that looks as if it predated Keaton's "General" out of a museum, down the front steps, and into motion along a rail bed, and everybody lends a hand. The high point of *All at Sea* shows visitors flocking aboard Skipper Guinness's pier-cum-steamer.

All these situations amount to a wished-for release from humdrum lives. Suddenly those lives have a purpose, reinforced by collective enthusiasm; and the participants feel like heroes and altruists. The release, which resembles a religious experience, sends them back refreshed into their old patterns of behavior. It has taught them, as the promise of heaven might do, to become tolerant, possibly of conditions that should not be tolerated. As a political and spiritual "passage" it has reactionary results.

In some of the films an individual or a limited group, rather than a community, yearns for such a release, even if it proves only temporary. Here we have variations on the year-king, or maybe only king-for-a-day, theme. Holland and Pendlebury in *The Lavender Hill Mob* will break out of their tedium and insignificance to share a million pounds or thereabouts with two burglars they've recruited, provided they can get away with stealing a vanload of gold ingots. Holland does get away with it—for a year, at any rate —while he plays the bon vivant in Rio. At the end of the year, when Guinness walks out of the film's last frame, cheerfully handcuffed, he counts the spendthrift year worth the much longer jail sentence ahead of him. The five crooks posing as genteel musicians in *The Ladykillers* and planning a big haul dwell in that dreamland of popular fiction and films, that wishfulness which is universal and yet overwhelmingly British: the desire to pull off the perfect crime.

Barr may be right in objecting to the neat endings of such films,

in which the perfect crime, having less-than-perfect consequences, either does not pay or must be paid for. And the transient
release undergone by the characters in Ealing films is a mere discharge of emotion, not a permanent conversion of the sort that
happens in *The Bacchae:* In their bliss the Thebans, egged on by
the queen mother, murder their young king and grow desperately
repentant and subdued, but can't go back to their old ways. They
remain votaries—or victims—of the new Dionysian creed. Yet a
permanent conversion may be less than convincing if not handled
with the skill of a Euripides. Take the closing scene of a film like
Topper (1937), adapted from Thorne Smith's novel and directed by
Norman Z. McLeod. Cosmo Topper (Roland Young), president
of a bank, is encouraged by the happy-go-lucky, translucent, seductive ghosts of George and Marion Kirby (Cary Grant and
Constance Bennett) to break out of his minute-by-minute routine,
enjoy life, and defy his "paternal" wife. He does so, half-willingly;
but instead of being defeated, his wife (played by the simpering
Billie Burke) comes around to his new way of living and even puts
on a shamelessly frilly slip. *Topper,* an endearing farce for most of
its distance, slumps into a reconciliatory clinch which is less funny
and less true somehow than it would be to have Topper revert to
his routine and look back fondly on his release as an episode that
couldn't last.

Barr assembles a carefully detailed and subtle, although in
places schematic, case for regarding the Ealing films as parables of
postwar England. All well and good. But when he interprets the
ideology of Balcon and his associates as a commitment to British
muddling-through, survival of the unfit, and a cherishing of
quaintness, he adopts an accusatory tone. In his analysis he
doesn't differentiate between Ealing's farces and its other films;
doesn't, indeed, treat the farces *as* farces, but instead tries sensi-
tively to separate out the contributions of some directors from
others. Farcical films, though, are a breed unto themselves. Farce,
and especially farce in the satirical vein, has always looked askance
on claims of social and technological progress; it has actually
served at times as a corrective to the belief that life automatically
gets better as history rolls forward. Aristophanes, who was a lot
more cutting as a satirist and a lot more interested in sexual hanky-
panky than the Ealing creators are, had a comparable instinct for

upholding customs and ideals in Athens that seemed precious to
him; for his reward, the authors of theater textbooks disdainfully
and reflexively call him a conservative.

There's nothing conservative, however, about the film Barr
picks—and I agree—as the best one to come out of Ealing Studios:
Kind Hearts and Coronets. This most extreme instance of Ealing's
wishfulness offers us a smooth, handsome, perspicacious hero,
Louis Mazzini, quietly refined in speech and attire, who does away
with his relatives. His late mother, he tells us, was disinherited by
her aristocratic family, the D'Ascoynes, when she married an un-
titled Italian. Scratching at the scabs of memory to provoke his
ambitions, Mazzini avenges the snub to his mother (and father) by
disposing of six of the eight remaining D'Ascoynes. A seventh, an
admiral, capsizes with his ship and saves Mazzini the expense of a
torpedo, while the eighth obligingly collapses and dies. The murders and deaths bring him the D'Ascoyne estate together with a
title, Duke of Chalfont, and the attentions of two lovely women.
Sibella, his sibilant childhood sweetheart, later the widow of his
childhood friend, wants him. So does regal Edith, the widow of
one slain D'Ascoyne, and later Mazzini's wife. Wealth, rank, love,
and symmetry. What more could there be in store for this villainous hero, this courtly upstart? Well, like Chaplin in *Tillie's Punctured Romance,* he has competing women on his hands. And then,
he has a moment of forgetfulness that may prove fatal.

The pleasure afforded by this most tight-lipped of farces lies in
the progression of the perfect multiple crime; in the presentation
of economical flashbacks by Robert Hamer, the director, who co-
wrote the screenplay with John Dighton; in the fastidious handling
of the secondary roles—Joan Greenwood purring her way through
Sibella's lines, Valerie Hobson's Queen Victorian Edith, Miles
Malleson as a deferential, versifying executioner; in Dennis Price's
deftly businesslike Mazzini; in Alec Guinness's appearances and
reappearances as one after another sacrificial D'Ascoyne, always
different, always matching, an animated family portrait gallery;
and finally in the right-angled turn taken by the story when a
complication that looked like a minor diversion turns major. Mazzini has been going about his long-term task of eliminating
D'Ascoynes with style and imagination. He directs a punt bearing
the overbearing Ascoyne D'Ascoyne and a girlfriend over a water-

fall; blows up boyish Henry D'Ascoyne, whose avocation is photography, in his own darkroom; poisons the port being sipped by the genial, quavering Reverend D'Ascoyne; introduces a plastic bomb into the club of which General D'Ascoyne is a member; sends an arrow into the balloon in which Lady Agatha D'Ascoyne, a suffragette (the period is the early 1900s), has started to ascend; and lures Duke Ethelred of Chalfont into a steel trap set for poachers on the D'Ascoyne grounds. There hunter and bewildered quarry in their correct sporting clothes (Mazzini in a Norfolk jacket) face each other briefly in a confrontation that epitomizes the film. Mazzini points his shotgun and fires. As though the D'Ascoynes were now yielding in despair, the last remaining member of the family, the father of Ascoyne D'Ascoyne, dies of a heart attack. Shortly thereafter, Mazzini, now Duke of Chalfont, is charged with murder.

But not with the murder of six D'Ascoynes. Some time before, he rebuffed Sibella's husband, Lionel, who had come to him for a loan. They quarreled. Later Lionel killed himself, leaving a suicide note. Sibella purloins the note. At Mazzini's trial for the murder of Lionel, she goes on the witness stand and gives apparently reluctant evidence against him. Then when he's jailed and desperate, she lets him know that she's willing to discover the note if he will make her his duchess. Mazzini has no choice. He agrees; the note turns up; he walks out, free and clear, a restored duke. Except for one detail. The story that he's been recounting in flashback, the manuscript of his confessions, remains in his cell and can damn him.

With this anguished realization, *Kind Hearts* comes to an end. As always in censor-prone movies, justice will be done. A warden or some other official has only to pick up the manuscript and glance at it. But wait a second. As Charles Barr correctly points out,[6] the now "innocent" Duke could ask to go back into his cell, collect that damning document right away, and destroy it. The director has left the ending open by cutting off the action so abruptly. Justice may not be done. And then, the Duke may also worm out of his marriage pact with Sibella. Given his slippery and vindictive nature, can she—can we—expect him to honor such an agreement? She played a trump card, but against a rogue who's

---

[6] *Ealing Studios*, p. 130.

ready at any time to manufacture a couple of quick aces. So if he tells her to go to hell, she has no comeback. Perhaps Mazzini does get away with his unkind heart and his coronet, after all. But there's one more catch. If the action of the film really is a Dionysian exercise, it requires a scapegoat; and that must be Mazzini, the Pentheus who pays with his life for the release enjoyed by the community—in this case, his audience: us. Mazzini has played out *our* fantasies. With him we have vicariously wiped out rich relatives who stand in the way; and for as long as we have enjoyed his scaling of the social ladder, rung by murderous rung, we have participated in his crimes and reveled in his demonstration of the superiority of lower-class or mixed-blood craftiness over blue-blooded lethargy and complacency. Therefore, he must be punished for our wishful sins, as well as his actual ones. Yet it's a mark of Hamer's guile that we don't witness the certainty of that punishment. We leave Mazzini between upturn and downfall. If we crave a hard-and-fast conclusion, we must impose our own. Does Hamer tilt us toward or away from the scapegoat interpretation by making another picture with Guinness ten years later titled *The Scapegoat?* In any case, with the advent of *Kind Hearts and Coronets* farce has opened another door to ambiguity, if not amorality.[7]

Even before his D'Ascoyne-times-eight portrayals, Alec Guinness had commanded the attention of the film public as Herbert Pocket in *Great Expectations* (1946) and as Fagin in *Oliver Twist* (1948). Aside from these Dickensian personages and his five Ealing efforts, which have linked him indissolubly in history with that organization, he did Benjamin Disraeli (a role that had seemed to belong immemorially to George Arliss); Chesterton's priest-sleuth Father Brown for Hamer; Joyce Cary's Gulley Jimson, that modern sub-Michelangelo with a mania for loading color onto outside walls; plus a galaxy of international parts: a sheikh; a Japanese suitor for Rosalind Russell; a British monarch; an intractable colonel; a diplomat in Havana; a Roman emperor; Hitler; a pope; an elder, outer-space statesman fencing with a bar of light . . . He also carried more than his weight in two farces that have wishful,

---

[7] For the screenplay of *Kind Hearts and Coronets*, see the Winter 1951 issue of *Sight and Sound* (London). It was also published as a book—which, like most other books, is now out of print.

heavenly titles: *Hotel Paradiso* (Peter Glenville's adaptation of Feydeau's play *L'Hôtel du libre échange*; 1966) and *The Captain's Paradise* (1953), the latter remembered most vividly for the reversible photograph in the captain's cabin of Yvonne de Carlo and Celia Johnson, his would-be reversible wives. Guinness's screen roles have understandably eclipsed his important, but not nearly *as* important, roles on the stage. In close-up or medium close-up he seems to mesmerize the camera. His crag of a jaw and spacious brow, sidelong eye movements and pinched smile may have made him unmistakable, but his veritable orchestra of voices and frieze of understated facial expressions variously modified by wigs, beards, mustaches, and sideburns encompass a huge tract of farce and illustrate its many-sidedness. The scene between Guinness and Stanley Holloway in *The Lavender Hill Mob* (directed by Charles Crichton) in which they hit upon the idea of how to ship gold bullion to France is, technically, an uncomplicated two-shot, but a study of the first order in dramatic tension and interacting governed by tiny, sly increments of cross-prompting.

Peter Sellers, who doesn't have Guinness's Keaton-like gravity in farce, went from his one Ealing experience into too many mediocre films—most of the Clouseau products included—which traded on his name, rather than trying to raise themselves to a level that matched this actor's dry confidence. Two exceptions were *Dr. Strangelove* and a short, *The Running, Jumping, and Standing Still Film* (1959), directed by Richard Lester and filmed in a couple of days with one camera and virtually no retakes, as a cinematic equivalent—if there could be such a thing—of the verbal acrobatics of *The Goon Show*. The "goons" included Sellers, Spike Milligan, Harry Secombe, and guest performers (such as Dennis Price)—some comics in their own right, others straight actors.

This short feature made by Lester won him several assignments: *It's Trad, Dad* (1962), *The Mouse on the Moon* (1963) with Ron Moody—a follow-up to *The Mouse That Roared* (1959) with Sellers —and the first Beatles feature, *A Hard Day's Night* (1964). Lester (born 1932), who hasn't devoted himself exclusively to farce, is an American working mostly in Britain, like William Rose, and has a light satirical touch that marks him as a successor to Lubitsch and Sturges, but also to some of the Ealing film makers like Hamer and

Mackendrick. (As if in counterpoise to Lester, Mackendrick came to the United States, where he was born, after his stint at Ealing, and directed, among other films, *The Sweet Smell of Success*, 1963, and *Don't Make Waves*, 1967.) *A Hard Day's Night* had a story line that did little more than trail John, Paul, George, and Ringo, plus that "clean old man," Paul's grandfather (Wilfrid Brambell), from one concert to the next, the highlights of the film being the director's evocation of the concerts themselves by means of jump-cut, all-angles, blazingly lit and assembled takes of the singers (much imitated since) and the enraptured faces of their fans. The critical reception was warm; but for Lester's subsequent films, apart from *The Knack* (1966), it rapidly cooled off. Did *A Hard Day's Night* win support because of its documentary qualities, its brushes with *cinéma vérité*? Lester's next Beatles feature, *Help!* (1966), strayed more recklessly into fiction, even purported to have a pretext for suspense: attempts by a nefarious and at the same time farcical Eastern cult to get possession of Ringo's ring. When the film came out, Lester took his lumps from reviewers. Suddenly they resented his razzle-dazzle camerawork and editing. What happened with *Help!*? It's true that the Beatles are hardly actors (and in the earlier film didn't need to be); this may be one reason why George Dunning animated cartoons of them for *The Yellow Submarine*. In real-life interviews they're fast, audacious, funny. In a plotted film they look amateurish when they're on screen with professional funnymen like Norman Rossington and Victor Spinetti. To relieve the strain, Lester avoids lip synchronization whenever possible. He photographs them on the move or swings his camera past them breathlessly and adds the dialogue that passes between them in voice-overs. I find *Help!* to be very much in the spirit of the Beatles, and have no sympathy for the casual opinion that this and his other farces are merely the outcome of the numerous television commercials he has shot using similar techniques. Lester is the one recent film maker who has persistently sought new, disconnected film forms that are suitable for farce. He breaks derisively with conventional camera treatments, which work more or less the same for farces as for other films. Like Ingmar Bergman; like the German directors of the Sixties and Seventies—notably Werner Herzog, Wim Wenders, and Rainer Werner Fassbinder; like Orson Welles in the Forties and Dziga Vertov in the Twenties, he gives his cameras a collective personality; they no longer function as detached observers, but as farcical co-performers. If they emphasize the contributions of the director, so what? The new forms introduced to the theater after World War II by Beckett, Ionesco, Genet, Adamov, Pinter, and Handke also draw attention to their creators, as any pioneering works of art must do.

In the course of the disheveled action, the Beatles elatedly sing their numbers in inappropriate settings: "Ticket to Ride" on a snowscape, piano and all, with ski runs, sleds, a toboggan, and a hole in an iced-over lake through which a head appears and asks for directions to the White Cliffs of Dover; "The Night Before" on a battlefield encircled by tanks and troops, apparently Salisbury Plain near Stonehenge, while in a cave below them their enemies place a charge of TNT; and "Another Girl" on a beach in the Bahamas. A skirmish with laser beams takes place in Buckingham Palace (or a reasonable facsimile), where the electricity drawn by the lasers puts the circuits out of commission; over at Battersea Power Station an engineer notices that "the royal fuse has blown" and is told, "She got a new hair dryer for Christmas." A crazy scientist who also covets Ringo's ring lowers a helicopter to near ground level while his partner in lunacy hangs on a wire below and holds a boot dipped in paint that plants red footprints meant to lure the Beatles into danger. Ringo is trapped in a cellar with a tiger that turns submissive when everybody sings it the chorale from Beethoven's *Ninth*. In addition to his customary machine-gun editing, Lester takes shots vertically, upside down, and sliding into and out of focus; at various times he fits pink, yellow, blue, and purple filters on his lens. Rarely has directorial self-indulgence teased so much phony, compelling excitement out of cinema. The acting looks sloppy, but when you have cameras that leap, pirouette, go cross-eyed, and change costume, heartfelt acting seems like an intrusion.

In the years that followed, Lester, having tested out the medium, addressed himself to stretching himself. He filmed a Broadway musical, *A Funny Thing Happened on the Way to the Forum* (1966), that collage of situations, characters, and songs from Plautus and other musicals. Two years later, *How I Won the War* brought him back into harness with Charles Wood, who'd adapted Ann Jellicoe's *The Knack* for the screen and had been one of the authors of *Help!* Like the experimental, autocratic, fearless Russian director Vsevelod Meyerhold, who in 1906 had written about his desire to interpret "tragedy with a smile," Lester turns a fatal attack on a German bridge in World War II into a ludicrous event, rather than a heart-shattering one with puffily detailed military strategies and blood-caked amputees, in the format of, say, *A Bridge Too Far* (1977). He flips back and forth from plain or tinted black-and-white (for some battle scenes) to color (for the farce), and reintroduces the farcical ploy of reviving corpses when some soldiers rise from the dead, painted green or purple, and rejoin their platoons. Lester dips into film theatricalism with disturbing effects when some of the soldiers become aware and resentful of the camera's spying on them. *The Bed Sitting Room* (1969), another opened-up screen version of a stage farce (by Spike Milligan and John Antrobus), looks at a postnuclear London, in which only a few maniacs survive and bring forth mutant offspring. These last two Lester movies about unhallowed disasters prepared him to move into the orthodox disaster industry. *Juggernaut* (1974) sends a titanic ship to the bottom with all the feverish sadism of the genre, yet manages to let us see it as a towering inferno of nonsense. *Superman II* (1981) allows him more special effects than it seems fair to confer on one director. In the two-part adventure *The Three Musketeers* and *The Four Musketeers*, made together but released separately in 1974 and 1975, Lester tosses together a salad of most of the platitudes of historical romance, from Cecil B. De Mille to Cecil B. De Mille, and drenches them in farcical mayonnaise. He updates Sennett's and Chaplin's ass-kicking by having his musketeers during their swordfights practice crotch-kicking, and inflict an anguish never contemplated in Hollywood versions of the Dumas tale by Douglas Fairbanks or Don Ameche and the Ritz Brothers. The cameras zoom like projectiles between spanned horizons and glistening eyeballs. Costumes, castles, and landscapes glow until the frames quiver with color. The labyrinthine subplots cut one another's tales off. But while Lester and his designers, photographers, and cast of worthies (Charlton Heston, Faye Dunaway, Frank Finlay, Raquel Welch, Oliver Reed, Geraldine Chaplin, Michael York, Richard Chamberlain) knock themselves out, not much in either Musketeers epic makes us laugh. The difference between the Beatles and the Musketeers pictures hangs on the difference between the rewards of trying too much and the penalties of trying too hard.

If Lester sets out to bowl us over with staccato imagery and noise, his French contemporary Philippe de Broca (born 1933) sets out to seduce us with lightfooted (but never cute) characters, toy houses in gauzy, pastel settings, and of all things, farcical lyricism; he is a Dufy or Klee to Lester's Jackson Pollock, but he shares with Lester a devotion to spontaneous-looking shifts of bodies and cameras. De Broca discovered a clown in Jean-Pierre Cassel, who can sing and dance more debonairly than Maurice Chevalier ever did and is blessedly free of Chevalier's obsequious manner; he can commit himself to lovesickness as wholly as Sacha Guitry could and not stoop to Guitry's sultriness. Stanley Kauffmann refers to this multi-performer as a Harlequin and a Pierrot;[8] and his stylized poetry of acting does unite sadness and a romping joy of life that hark back to the commedia and perhaps to Molière. De Broca featured Cassel in *The Love Game* (1960), *The Joker* (in French, significantly, *Le Farceur*; 1961), and *The Five-Day Lover* (1961) before losing him to Jean Renoir (*The Elusive Corporal*, 1963), to Hollywood (*Those Magnificent Men in Their Flying Machines*, 1965, and *Is Paris Burning?*, 1966), and eventually to Luis Buñuel (*The Discreet Charm of the Bourgeoisie*, 1972). Even in the relaxed hands of masters like Renoir and Buñuel, though, Cassel didn't recapture the exultation of his films with De Broca, simply didn't have the opportunities to let go. De Broca found a replacement of sorts in *That Man from Rio* and *Cartouche* (both 1964) with Jean-Paul Belmondo of the flattened nose, lean cheeks, and slow, reflective smile, who had become hyperactive in movies since his first role in Godard's *Breathless* (1960). Belmondo, ready for anything, proved to have an unsuspected gift for literally and figuratively tripping over his own heels. *That Man from Rio*, in which the hero chases from Paris to Brazil after his stolen girlfriend, could have been a vehicle for Keaton, for whom Belmondo is here a passable substitute, and to say that is tribute enough. The film skits those 007 espionage frolics (some of them not yet made at the time) that trace the curves of a death wish in skitting themselves as they hop around intercontinentally. The swashbuckling in *Car-*

---

[8] *A World on Film* by Stanley Kauffmann (New York: Harper & Row, 1966), pp. 234–38.

touche, together with the appearance of another seventeenth-
century cape-and-épée caper of that same year, *Cyrano and
D'Artagnan* (starring Cassel), may have put Lester on to the idea
of making his Musketeers films ten years later.

De Broca's only financial success in this country, *King of Hearts*
(1967), surfaced after a lengthy life underground in the neighborhood of college campuses. Toward the end of World War I the
German army deposits a land mine in a small French town. A
British soldier (Alan Bates), sent to defuse it, finds that the local
residents have fled. But the streets are now occupied—as they've
never been *occupied* before—by inmates of a nearby insane asylum. Like the communities in an Ealing farce, these infatuates are
glorying in their freedom from rules, their sense of release. They
welcome him and, in a sort of Dionysian ceremony, crown him
their king of hearts. Is De Broca trying to get us to envy the sanity
of the insane as they cavort in the town, and to shrink from the
madness of the sane world outside, caught up in its war-making?
Possibly. But I think he's not all that interested in pointing a moral
or positing an easy choice. Rather, we are meant to share that
sense of release until the film is over. If we wish to, we can draw
an analogy between the carefree behavior of the lunatics and the
farcically improvised self-realization of the young people in De
Broca's early films. *King of Hearts* illustrates all-out, collective
irresponsibility, but since the director doesn't preach it, only describes it, he makes the child who's the parent of the grown-up in
each of us want to practice it. In picking Bates for their "king," the
French not-so-crazies remind us of the citizens in *Hail the Conquering Hero,* who pick for their mayor Eddie Bracken, a young
man so screwily honest that when a deputation comes to beg him
to accept the nomination, he asks, "What is it, a lynching?" In
both films, the farcical treatment emphasizes the wishfulness of
finding a leader who can be loved, not merely followed.

Clown-Creators

A rattletrap of illegitimate vintage and perched on four thin
wheels, its convertible roof about as sturdy as a bed sheet, its
motor throbbing more explosively than a pneumatic drill, and its
trunk lid flapping like a shirttail on a line, squeals to a stop about

six inches from a dog splayed out asleep in the roadway. The pathetic bulb horn mounted on the spare bleats and bleats again. Wearily the dog gets itself together; goes around to the driver squinched between seat and steering wheel, chin against knees; and receives a couple of pats on the head for its magnanimous gesture. The rickety vehicle staggers forward once more, and Monsieur Hulot is on the last leg of his journey to a week at the Hôtel de la Plage on the French coast, impeded only by his method of locomotion.

Mr. Hulot's Holiday (1954) passes the seven days and nights at this resort by fluttering between lyricism and slapstick in a style new to farce except for *Jour de Fête*. Gorgeously composed shots of the beach, the cloud formations over the sea, waves lashing rocks, and visitors in swimsuits moving in unconsciously collective rhythms alternate with incidents of delicious, satirical insanity. An opening sequence lays down the film's tone. In a long shot, the motionless camera watches a crowd at a railroad station waiting on Platform One. Some unintelligible instructions are snorted out over a p.a. system. The crowd turns and runs down the steps and through the underpass to Platform Three. A train then enters the frame alongside Platform Five. The crowd rushes into the underpass and arrives on Five to find that it's a freight train. At this moment, the passenger train everyone has been waiting for pulls into Platform One. And all the time the p.a. system keeps issuing grunts and mumbles.

At the hotel, where Hulot and the crowd meet, we have the chance to observe Hulot. He is so tall and apologetic that he walks toppling forward on the balls of his feet, his trunk and head at a 120-degree angle to his legs as if to let him consort more comfortably with people of ordinary height. In his flapping jacket, trouser cuffs well above his ankles, hat brim below his eyebrows in front and pointing straight up at the back, and a pipe perkily jutting out of his teeth, he acknowledges the passing world without appearing to see it. Hulot is the soul of gentility and gentleness. In his transformation from François the mailman in *Jour de Fête*, Tati has dropped the comic De Gaullish "mo," and moves decisively out of a rural backwater into several dunkings in the ocean. Hulot's surname (he has no first name) may hint at Chaplin's nickname in France, Charlot, as numerous critics have remarked. Like Chaplin, Tati comes from vaudeville; writes, directs, produces, and stars; cherishes his independence as a film maker; and turns out pictures at his own speed. But as a performer, Tati is one of Charlie's opposites: neutrally dressed, ungainly and deliberate in motion (when he speeds up, his limbs go out of control), unaggressive and fumbling. He doesn't take on villains, as Charlie does, because there are none in his films, whose only targets are harmless hucksters, bores, and conformists.

A preliminary subtitle to *Mr. Hulot's Holiday* advises us not to look for a plot. Understandably, because the action consists of the passage of mornings, afternoons, and evenings disrupted by farcical outbreaks. Hulot goes out to sea in a kayak that folds in two and drifts away on the water like an open beak. A guest drops something into a fish tank, carefully rolls up his jacket and shirt sleeves on his right arm, notices Hulot, becomes fascinated by his curious walk, and reaches abstractedly into the tankful of water with his left arm, submerging arm, sleeves, and wristwatch. A boy focuses the sun through a magnifying glass onto a sunbather's midriff. Hulot, searching for a table-tennis ball that has bounced into another room, turns two card games into fights by accidentally swinging one player around in his chair so that he slaps down an ace on the wrong table. Carrying a lady's dead-weight suitcase up the front steps, Hulot trips at the door and lurches forward; the suitcase then carries him on through the hotel and out the back door. He unleashes a flying ass-kick at a man who appears to be peeking into a woman's bathing cabin but is actually stooping to take a photograph behind the cabin. In a room filled with bric-a-brac, Hulot, dressed to go out on horseback, straightens pictures on the wall while the riding crop under his arm knocks the other pictures crooked. When his car breaks down, he steps on the rope between his front bumper and a tow truck just as the tow truck starts up, and the rope tightens to propel him in a horizontal dive into the sea. When a dog chases him, he takes refuge in a little beach house, where fireworks are stored. Lighting a match to see where he is, he sets off the firecrackers and turns the beach into a battlefield. He tries to extinguish the blaze by turning on an outdoor faucet, but it's attached to a hose. At the other end of the hose is a sprinkler that scatters the water in circles. Holding a tiny can, he chases around after the jet of water but succeeds only in getting drenched every time it swishes past him.

In *Holiday*, Tati experiments with the sound track as a component of film with a life of its own. A few bars of chirpy cool jazz announce each new day, and a liberty bell orders the guests in for dinner. The swinging doors to the dining room let out a *thwunk!* every time their rubber edges meet; it sounds like a frog's mating call. Hulot's consumptive car, the p.a. system at the station, the firecrackers, dogs, horses, windows slamming open and shut add to the symphonic accompaniment; so do splinters of over-heard conversation—greetings and farewells, remarks about the weather, expostulations. But there is no conventional dialogue to advance the dramatic situations; and Hulot himself utters only one word, his name, which comes out as a strange diphthong until the hotel clerk removes Hulot's pipe from his face.

Tati enters and leaves the frames by fits and starts—but as with all accomplished clowns, his gawkiness is executed with a grace that becomes something like ballet when he lunges at a tennis ball or returns a table-tennis ball while retreating on one foot and holding on to his balance by means of compensatory body english.

Hulot reappears in *My Uncle* (1958), a color film[9] in which, even more than in the earlier films, inanimate objects thwart human intentions, often because they are not altogether inanimate but come to life sporadically—a stone fish, for example, that spouts fountain water only when it feels like it. The spotless contemporary house belonging to the Arpel family is fitted out with labor-saving devices that consume time, labor, and patience, and ornaments that are eyesores, and it matches Arpel's spotless factory of glistening machinery which exists to spew out red tubing. Hulot, the Arpels' poor relation, serves as their social counterpoise, the natural man, living in a quaint old warren of a house and uninterested in making money or keeping up appearances. The contrast between his easygoing ways and the sterile life pursued by the Arpels is a bit pat, but it permits Tati to venture further

---

[9] Tati had produced an earlier short film in color, *The School for Postmen* (*L'École des facteurs*; 1947), its French title a play on the title of Molière's *L'École des femmes*; it seems to have been a preliminary working of *Jour de Fête*.

into his testing of dissociated sound and loving long shots of people unwittingly composing themselves in shifting patterns.

From the countryside of the Massif Central to the coast of Brittany to the upper-crust suburbs to the metropolis: Tati's most recent two films, *Playtime* (1967) and *Traffic* (1971), close in on a cityscape of glass-sheathed structures. Car windows and bank walls, like so many translucent movie screens, throw back iconic reflections of one another. In *Playtime*, edifices like the Sacré Coeur and the Eiffel Tower swing back and forth as images fleetingly imprinted on glass doors. One such sheet of glass with an imposing brass handle gets shattered when somebody walks through it, but the doorman dutifully continues to open and shut the unattached handle and nobody notices the difference. Restaurants, hospitals, hotels, airports, office buildings—all those crystal palaces of our new ice age—are similarly polished, antiseptic, public perspectives. Their Dolby-like acoustics mean that two heels clacking toward us from the far end of a corridor give out a level drumming noise. Both films are about infestations. *Playtime* overflows with American tourists in Paris; *Traffic*, with wheels upon wheels upon asphalt. But Tati's unfailing humor thaws the environment and its glacial men and women.

In *Traffic* he reintroduces Hulot as an inventor and advertising artist for a car company called Altra, a name that has international and conglomerate resonances. With the hindrance of an American publicity woman and a truck driver and his own good nature, Hulot is required to convey a camper he has devised from Paris to an auto show in Amsterdam. The gimmick-ridden vehicle can expand in length and has a mattress-bed inside that also grows or shrinks; its parking lights come detached in order to illuminate the interior as, say, a reading lamp; faucets deliver drinking or washing water, hot or cold, from the oddest orifices in the sheet metal; the rear bumper converts into a table and chairs for dining alfresco. But the truck on which this marvel of ingenuity is mounted suffers a flat, then runs out of gas. A collision damages the fenders, which must undergo the slow ministrations of an eccentric Dutch repairman. Hulot, his companions, and his exhibit arrive in Amsterdam shortly after the exhibition is over. Some of the most vivid sequences speed us along French, Belgian, and Dutch highways jammed with tailgating cars in four or five lanes. The torrent of these glass boxes, the competing, glancing reflections, the ghostly heads of drivers, the flickering brake lights, a profile of a tiny, lacquered sports car seen from below the undercarriage and between the wheels of a truck are interspersed with glimpses of wrecked and abandoned cars and an automobile graveyard stacked with rusted shells. As Hulot stands by his truck on a narrow highway shoulder, undoing wheel nuts, his backside juts into the next lane: every time he straightens his back, a car whizzes past and misses him by millimeters and split seconds in a mechanized frustration of the revered ass-kicking routine. In another sequence reminiscent of silent farce, Hulot takes home a driver injured in a crash. The front door is locked, the doorbell doesn't work, and the man lives on an upper floor. Hulot throws gravel at the window. The wife inside doesn't respond. He starts to scale the ivy in default of an outside fire escape. A bunch of ivy breaks away and descends a foot or so. While hanging there, he tries to push it back into place. It collapses further, and he finds himself clinging to it upside down. Meanwhile, the publicity woman has met with a character who wants to make out with her in the courtyard, and Hulot must helplessly witness this scene from his precarious hold on the loosening ivy.

But in both films—and especially in *Playtime*—Tati has diminished the role played by Hulot. Can we ascribe this partial withdrawal to modesty? Or to his desire to put most of his energies and imagination at the service of his directing? To his inability—or unwillingness—to investigate the Hulot persona any further? Or to an ambition to drop anecdotes whenever possible and re-create film mime with thematic treatments? One might well ask, Why can't he give us both? We do lose Hulot and his farcical predicaments for whole stretches of the action. Tati compensates to some extent with choreography achieved by camera placement and montage. In the vast exhibition hall in Amsterdam, workers are demarcating each exhibitor's area, and the aisles between, with wires raised about twelve inches off the ground. Whenever a worker goes to another area, he must lift his feet every few yards. Nobody trips—that would be too obvious a gag—but seen from a high vantage point, the workers' walking and foot-lifting give the impression of a colony of water birds. Later, the publicity woman, the craziest driver in the film, zooms past a traffic cop, distracts him, and causes about ten cars to crash. A Volkswagen Beetle runs off the road, its hood flapping up and down like an upper lip letting out soundless cries. The drivers get out of their cars with whiplash, bending and turning their bodies slowly and in unison, as if engaging in some sacred rite. At another point, cars at a multiple intersection stop at red lights. The camera cuts from driver to driver. Every one begins pensively to pick his nose; one or two dig wells up their nostrils. In a traffic jam a driver yawns; the yawns spread in a contagion. When rain starts, head-on views of the windshields suggest that the swishing of each pair of wipers matches the driver's personality—nervous and fluttery, pompous, demure, resolute. As the rain thickens, pedestrians, crossing a wide thoroughfare with their umbrellas aloft, thread their way between stationary cars to perform an unintended ceremonial rain dance. Such shots make Hulots of everybody.

American Parody

Mel Funn, the director who drowned his distinguished career in drink, is back on the bottle. Or under it. He is staggering through the streets of Los Angeles under the weight of a bottle-shaped container that must hold ten gallons of liquor, and he was sloshed before he ever purchased it. In a downtown section he comes upon a group of panhandlers, climbs up on a stone abutment, and tips the bottle's contents over himself and them. One guy gratefully remarks, "He is truly the lord of the winos." Here, in *Silent Movie* (1976), we have Mel Brooks as Bacchus, the most explicit Dionysian signal in farce sent out by the most explicit farce-maker.

What circumstances have bumped Mel off the wagon? He'd conquered his craving for a time by devoting himself to shooting a silent movie in partnership with Dom De Luise and Marty Feldman (known in the film as Eggs and Bell). The movie, which has recruited some expensive stars, will be a novel but funny throwback to the features of silent days and will earn a terrific profit, thereby saving the studio Mel works for from the claws of a conglomerate named Engulf and Devour. The film is to be previewed; the stars have let themselves be conned into joining the cast; the boss of the beleaguered studio, played by Sid Caesar, rolls his eyes in happy anticipation and hears cash registers ringing in his brain

—and so do we, as though wired to that brain. But the prexy of Engulf and Devour comes up with a fiendish plan. He steals the master print and hires Bernadette Peters, a plump, chinny stripper, to seduce Mel, who falls for her like a ton of wet cement. Eggs and Bell then learn that she's an industrial Mata Hari, and report the fact to Mel. That's when he, brokenhearted, returns to drinking. But it appears that Bernadette actually loves "the little guy," and proves her fidelity by undressing, swinging on a curtain, and punching out a few numbers to keep the preview audience in a state of excitement. Mel is found in the lower depths of L.A., sobered up with hundreds of cups of coffee, and with his partners rescues the master print, which the previewers, warmed up by Bernadette's performance, love.

Brooks (born 1926), a fancier and collector of antique Hollywood scenes and characters, has farcically parodied six types of American picture so far: the birth of Broadway musicals in *The Producers* (1968), Eastern adventures in *The Twelve Chairs* (1970), Westerns in *Blazing Saddles* (1974), horrific sci-fi in *Young Frankenstein* (1975), Hitchcockian suspense (with special reference to *Vertigo* and *Spellbound*) in *High Anxiety* (1977), and film theatricalism in *Silent Movie*, which has farfetched affinities with Sturges' *Sullivan's Travels* and with other films about the reasons for making films, as well as with the silents of the Teens and Twenties.[10] We never get to see the picture that Funn, Eggs, and Bell have made, nor any shooting sequences, nor the script: only some of the preparatory maneuvers. But since *Silent Movie* itself has titles in place of voiced dialogue, what the preview audience in the film sees on the screen is presumably the film we are watching, with themselves in it. (Brooks played a similar trick at the end of *Blazing Saddles*.) After all, the famous stars are doing their bits right there. Sid Caesar, the bemused mogul, asks in a title, "Don't you know that slapstick is dead?"—at which moment his swivel chair swivels out from under him; he slides at gathering speed across his polished floor and hits the opposite wall. Burt Reynolds, as himself, goofs around with a gigantic figure in a cloak that

[10] Two of Brooks's collaborators have explored other types of oldie: Feldman made *The Last Remake of Beau Geste* (1977) and Gene Wilder *The Adventures of Sherlock Holmes' Smarter Brother* (1977). Brooks's *The History of the World, Part One* (1981) may or may not be a deliberate parody of D. W. Griffith's *Intolerance* (1916).

conceals Funn on the shoulders of Eggs on the shoulders of Bell. James Caan, as himself, offers some unprofessional boxing. The partners visit Liza Minnelli, who's dining in the studio cafeteria, where the thee of them, in suits of armor, fall all over her table. Anne Bancroft, surrounded by gigolos, shows up in a nightclub. Paul Newman, confined to a wheelchair, tries to escape from the trio in superfast motion, as a sort of tribute to the old rally.

Most of the gags are visual, and the titles therefore sparing. Dom De Luise goes into a pastry shop for a feed, takes waiting ticket number 88, and stands there while the salesclerk works through from number 27. The customer before De Luise, number 87, then buys out the entire remaining stock of pastry—no, he forgets one cake, but comes back for it immediately. Marty Feldman waits outside a public john for De Luise. A blind man, who also wants to relieve himself, hands Feldman the leash of his German shepherd, and another man, taking him for a dog-minder, does likewise. After they come out, the dog owners pick the wrong animals. The blind man gets dragged into heavy traffic, while the sighted man can't get his shepherd to cross against the light. When the partners steal back their master print from Engulf and Devour (an arm reaches down the chimney flue of the E and D boardroom and whisks it out of the flames), it comes unwound. They rewind it around the body of Feldman. Later, during the preview, he spins on the spot, a human spool, to feed the film at twenty-four frames a second into the projector.

Brooks has not appeared in all of his movies—and a good thing, too. He is less than a first-rate comic. He functions splendidly as a disembodied voice with a Yiddish accent in the recording of *The 2,000-Year-Old-Man* and on the sound track of Pintoff's cartoon *The Critic*. On radio and television he comes on very strong, like one of those jokers who insist on being the life of the party. He dominates interview programs, seizing the initiative from the interviewer; he shows off to the camera, goes carelessly into what look like spontaneous shtik, dialects, impersonations, raptures. In movies, though, he seems inhibited, artificial, in need of encouragement: "Let go, Mel. Be interviewed. Enjoy the camera. Forget posterity." He needs a director. But in his own directing he has brought us some of the best of Zero Mostel, Gene Wilder, Ron Moody, Peter Boyle, Kenneth Mars, and Madeline Kahn.

As a writer-director, Brooks devises humor and nonverbal wit that fluctuate wildly in quality.[11] Many reviews call him sophomoric, but he usually goes further back than his sophomore year, all the way to childhood—and not always with appalling results. Childhood is the source of the finest, as well as the corniest, farce; and Brooks has touched both extremes without seeming to feel the difference or, if he does, without caring about it. The famous scene around the campfire in *Blazing Saddles* answers the anal wordplay of the title when a passel of cowboys make a meal of beans and pump out stomach gas. It reminds me of a narrative in rhyming verses called "The Farting Contest" that went the junior high school rounds about forty years ago, and was considered too risqué at the time to recite to girls or adults. Roger Vitrac's *Victor* offended some Parisian spectators when a beautiful lady's flatulence was represented by the braying of a trombone. But that was in 1929. In swinging 1974, the literal beans scene seems just about guileless.

So do the scatological moments in *Young Frankenstein*. Frederick von Frankenstein (Gene Wilder, who pronounces the name Frongkensteen), the living descendant of Mary Shelley's inventor, has assembled a monster of his own. When it rapes his frigid, unmussed fiancée (Madeline Kahn), she thaws out instantly and shrieks a coloratura "Ah, sweet mystery of life, at last I've found thee!" Frongkensteen soon swaps her for his clinging blond lab assistant, and swaps a slice of his alert brain for the monster's private parts. The monster, deprived of his sexual sap, sits in bed next to Miss Kahn reading *The Wall Street Journal*. But when Frongkensteen mounts the blond, she lets out the same ecstatic burst of song. Most of the film ambles along devotedly in the tracks of James Whale's *Frankenstein* (1931) and its follow-ups, adapting Peter Boyle's head to a fairly faithful reproduction of the square, stitched-up cranium designed by Jack Pierce for Boris Karloff. Brooks quotes from the sunnily lit encounter in a meadow between Karloff and a child; but here, when the monster obeys the

---

[11] Pauline Kael writes: "His humor is a show-business comment on show business. Mel Brooks is in a special position: his criticism has become a branch of show business—he's a critic from the inside. He isn't expected to be orderly or disciplined; he's the irrepressible critic as clown. . . . The other side of the coin is that he isn't self-critical . . ." *Reeling* (New York: Little, Brown, 1976), p. 379.

little girl's command to sit on the other end of her seesaw (what kind of symbol is that?), she's catapulted from her garden up into her second-floor bedroom.

The film opens with a distant view of a threatening Transylvanian castle on a hill. Rain . . . thunder . . . lightning . . . and memories of uncounted earlier mid-European, studio-built *Schlösser und Türme* . . . Cut to close-up of doors, an archway, lightning flashes revealing the detail in its masonry. Crawling pan shot along a wall up to a leaded window. And inside: spacious room. Fireplace lit. Circling shot to the side of a coffin inscribed "Baron von Frankenstein" in brass lettering. The lid rises. Within, a skeleton clutches a deed box. Two fleshed, living hands take hold of the box, start to remove it. *But the skeleton pulls the box back to its bony bosom . . .* Let Brooks falter, even stumble, if he can re-create with such authenticity and affection, and all for the sake of parody.

And yet in the end, doubts and questions nag us. Is this a good picture because he kept himself out of the cast? Was it that act of renunciation which enabled him to win from Peter Boyle a wondrous monster of a performance that Karloff, in his later years when he was skitting his younger self, might have envied both for its pathos and for its farce? Is Brooks a little too anxious to please by *shtupping* nostalgia into us? That pressure forms one source of his strength, his appeal to the kid and the kidder in all of us. It also diminishes his films, which we admire less for what they are than for what they refer back to. And does he delight more in the process than in the product? He surely relishes the give-and-take of working with a team, as he did once in television with Sid Caesar, Carl Reiner, Woody Allen, Neil Simon, Larry Gelbart, and other creators of *Your Show of Shows*—only now he runs the team. In a heady atmosphere of camaraderie, not unlike the one Sennett induced, the Brooks boys' spasms of improvisation must seem inspired to the improvisers. Some are.

As a film creator, and not simply as an actor, Brooks behaves like an impersonator. His quoting of earlier pictures treats them as models, rather than targets. Not so Woody Allen, poet and pedant, who levels his sights at everything and travesties sacred texts and names, and barges through taboos, and impersonates nobody but W. Allen. But even in doing that he's not so much an impersonator as an impostor: a brave man decked out in the language of a coward, a superhero making like the rest of us at our most self-excoriating. Allen does resemble some earlier clowns, the more brittle and put-upon specimens, such as the Harold Lloyd of *Grandma's Boy* and *Why Worry* (he wears Harold Lloyd cosmetics as the fake robot in *Sleeper*) and the Eddie Bracken of *Morgan's Creek* and *Conquering Hero*, although he's more disillusioned and disingenuous than either. With his freckled complexion, reddish hair, twitching smile as his mouth widens at the corners and instantly contracts, thin frame, eyes going up and down behind his glasses and hands fluttering when he's baffled, breaking into one sentence with another or flying off it at a tangent, Allen bespeaks an impatience to be where he isn't, to move on, get away fast, find something better. A recurring formula in his pictures is the fantasy, distant and then fulfilled, and then dashed or shown to be too plain ordinary to serve as a worthwhile fantasy. He gets the girl and the *gelt*, but doesn't bask in his triumph. Probably the only really satisfying end, the most explosive and lasting orgasm, is death. He allows himself that consummation in only one film, *Love and Death* (1975), after which he skips away across a skyline hand in hand with a figure shrouded in white (not black, notice!), setting the seventh seal on his outcome. But to reach the next fantasy, wherever it lurks, he'll travel to more points of the compass, and farther out, and more hastily, and with a more generous expenditure of wit than any other recent clown—to jail (*Take the Money and Run*, 1968), to Czarist Russia with *Love and Death* (1975), to a compromise between several Latin American republics called San Marcos (*Bananas*, 1971), to the twenty-second century (*Sleeper*, 1973), to a parking lot discovered by Diane Keaton some three feet from the sidewalk in Manhattan—"It's okay," he tells her, "we can walk to the curb from here" (*Annie Hall*, 1976)—and to the interior of a testicle (*Everything You Always Wanted to Know About Sex*, 1972).

Unlike most stand-up comics, Allen doesn't revel in his own jokes and stories; he regrets them. But he has to tell them, just as he has to gallivant in quest of the ultimately disappointing fantasies. To those remote lands of the unfulfilled wish he relays 1970 New York gags, hypochondria, and self-contempt. In a Russia dredged up out of Lermontov, Turgenev, Dostoevsky, Tolstoy,

Chekhov, and the Lower East Side he tells his girl cousin: "I've got a perfect fit in clothes. I'm a twenty-eight dwarf." When she observes that sex is an empty experience, he agrees, "But as empty experiences go, it's one of the best." In the year 2173 he realizes, "I'm two hundred and thirty-seven years old. I should be collecting Social Security." To a queen in Medieval Someplace he holds out a glass of aphrodisiac: "Grab some of this potion before the fizz goes out." And when "the most jealous king" is about to discover him and the queen in her bed, he reflects, "I must think of something quickly because the Renaissance will soon be here and we'll all be painting."

This last crack typifies the new attitude toward farce in theater and movies as the characters mock their plight by momentarily stepping outside it. The older farces of Labiche, Feydeau, Chaplin, Lloyd, and Langdon imprisoned the characters in their misfortunes; they had to extricate themselves by luck, pluck, ingenuity, or ineptitude. The advent of theatricalism changed all that. Nowadays the players are likely to keep dropping their characterizations, as Groucho or Hope and Crosby did. The result: farce sabotages its own lapses into melodrama; it remains farcical throughout; it refuses to take its own plot lines seriously. Groucho's and Chico's screenwriters made a fetish of undercutting the dramatic situations they'd created: they wouldn't let their characters—or their audiences—believe in what was going on.[12] Allen has adapted this type of bathos to his dialogue, although he doesn't try to get away with the sheer wordplay and fooling around with clichés that were part of the Marxian repertory. ("I've got a waiting list of fifty people at the cemetery just dying to get in.") Occasionally one can spot a remnant of a Marx shtik in an Allen film. In *Duck Soup,* Groucho gets into the sidecar of a motorbike driven by Harpo; the bike takes off and leaves Groucho and the sidecar standing. The next time Groucho sees a bike and sidecar waiting for him, he climbs onto the bike; Harpo then speeds away in the sidecar. Allen's variation on this in *Bananas* uses a hand grenade. He pulls out the pin and hurls it at the enemy, keeping

---

[12] This is not a technique restricted to farces. Partly because of the absorption of Pirandello's, Brecht's, and Beckett's narrative structures into later writings, the so-called postmodern or postcontemporary or neonaturalistic films of Jean-Luc Godard and of recent German film makers have similarly discontinuous plot lines and self-conscious characters.

the grenade in his hand. Next time he learns better: pulling out the pin, he hurls the grenade, whereupon the pin explodes in his hand.

But the gagbook one might compile from Allen's films would be distinctively Woody Allen because of its low-key disenchantment. "God is not evil. The best you can say for Him is He's an under-achiever." Or: "My parents beat me only once. They started beating me on December 23, 1942, and stopped in the spring of 1944." What he has done in his embodiments of the Woody character is wring farce out of that American literary and dramatic device gleaned from Dostoevsky, Strindberg, and Chekhov: the confession.

It was our seminal playwright, Eugene O'Neill, who imported the confession from Europe. *Beyond the Horizon, Anna Christie, Days Without End, Strange Interlude, Mourning Becomes Electra, The Iceman Cometh, Long Day's Journey into Night,* and *A Moon for the Misbegotten,* among others, stack one confessional speech on another. Since the Twenties the confession, a modernization of the soliloquy, has become a staple of playwriting and screenwriting, especially in the climactic scenes. Thus, the confessional Seventies, the years of narcissism, attended by the spread of group mea culpas (keenly satirized in Paul Mazursky's *Bob & Carol & Ted & Alice*), the echoes through apartment-building corridors of primal screams, and other forms of pop-therapeutic self-indulgence were preceded by half a century of rehearsal on stage and screen. Allen's confessions of inadequacy summarize these rugged-individualist equivalents of the Stalinist purge trials of the Thirties. His films went over in a big way not only because they were funny, but also because a young filmgoing public, coached by its elders (who were worshiping at their TV sets) to 'fess up brazenly about feelings of helplessness, could let Woody do it for them. They watched him win out and find less than full satisfaction in the consummation; then they made a hero of him.

Allen excels, it seems to me, not in his most popular and tautly shaped films, *Sleeper* and *Annie Hall,* his nearest approaches to the well-made play, but in *Everything You Always Wanted to Know About Sex* (*But Were Afraid to Ask),* a nonadaptation of the Reuben best seller, which he wrote and directed on his own. Its separate episodes steer him away from the one-and-a-half-sided affairs between the Woody figure and a well-meaning, klutzy girl (Janet Margolin, Louise Lasser, Diane Keaton) and on a revuelike excursion to the outliers of his imagination. It also gives him the chance to parody our pseudoclinical obsession with other people's sexual appetites; to unload travesties of six types of film and one TV panel show; and to display his finesse in directing other actors for the sequences he doesn't appear in. Each episode begins with a title that resembles the "controversial" questions emblazoned on magazine covers to outsmart the competition on newsstands. After the credits flow past shots of a milling pack of angora rabbits, a close-up picks on one lonely animal, its pink eyes restless, its white fur and nose quivering anxiously, while the sound track runs through Cole Porter's "Let's Misbehave."

In episode one, "Do Aphrodisiacs Work?" Allen plays Woody as a jester smitten by his queen, Lynn Redgrave low-cut. This pitiless trip back into Hollywood history re-creates doubleted nobles with British accents who litter the sound track with thee's and thou's. After slipping her a brimming dose of the elixir and raising her temperature, he tries to dismantle her chastity belt with a sledge-hammer and a key the size of a pickax. But his hand gets trapped in the belt. When the most jealous king returns, Woody bobs under her skirt, which is as voluminous as the grandmother's in *The Tin Drum*. Caught and sentenced to death, he utters his last words as jaunty instructions to the executioner: "Just clean up the neck a little and leave the top full."

Episode two, "What Is Sodomy?" introduces us to a prosperous doctor who falls in love with an Armenian sheep named Daisy. Despite the differences in nationality ("I know this may seem strange to you, you from the hills of Armenia, me from Jackson Heights; but if we give it a chance I think it'll work"), he woos her greedily—takes her to a posh hotel suite; orders up caviar, chilled Burgundy, and "just a little grass"; and beds her down. He keeps her there, plying her with jewels and love, although when he returns home to his cold wife she can't understand why he smells of lamb chops. But one day police and photographers burst into the suite. He is tried, convicted for corrupting a minor (as the judge points out, Daisy is under eighteen), and ruined. He takes a job as a waiter in a deli, but still moons over Daisy too much to handle tippable trays of food and drink with any assurance; the boss fires him. Our last sight of him is of an unshaven bum seated on a stoop, taking long pulls from a container of Woolite. In this short story of the fall of a sugar daddy for a heroine young enough to be his daughter, Gene Wilder gives us precise and unforced portraits of a fashionable doctor, a harried waiter, and a Woolite wino that add up to his best performance so far in films. Daisy supports him with a beautiful inexpressiveness that must make Wilder the envy of older men in the auditorium.

Allen may have got the idea for episode three, "Why Do Some People Have Trouble Reaching an Orgasm?" from having written the English dialogue for a Japanese film in *What's Up, Tiger Lily?*, for its lines, spoken in Italian, have English subtitles. The Woody character's name is Fabrizio, and he's married to an icy girl. When he strokes her, searching for the erogenous zones of which her father once gave him the map, she falls asleep. He purchases an electric dildo which vibrates alarmingly enough to arouse a marble statue of Elizabeth I, but as soon as he switches it on, it catches fire. Then he finds that "she gets all hot" only in public places. So, to Fabrizio's dismay, they must consummate their marriage in locales like an art gallery, a church confessional, and under a restaurant table they happen to be sharing with an older couple. Allen has shot the segment in vast spaces with expanses of washed-out color in the background, reminiscent of the sets in a movie by Antonioni, Petri, or Bertolucci.

Episode four begins at the point of perception where domestic sitcoms give up. In just about every family comedy on film and every television series, from *The Life of Riley* and *Make Room for Daddy* to *Father Knows Best* and *All in the Family*, the head of the household is more or less an impotent. In Allen's sketch "Are Transvestites Homosexuals?" a plump, stately, mustached Lou Jacobi, an ideal stand-in for a TV dad, excuses himself from a social gathering at a friend's house, ostensibly to visit the bathroom. While the rest of the company converses about some conversation pieces, imitation-primitive wood carvings picked up cheaply in Bimini, "a steal," Jacobi is stealing through the hostess's clothes closet upstairs and primping in her stockings, hat, skirt, and blouse (over a false bosom). The host comes up in search of him—could he have locked himself in the bathroom?—and Jacobi lowers himself in his finery out the window. In the respectable, suburban street outside, a thief complicates his predicament by snatching his purse. Sympathetic passers-by insist on calling the police. There stands Jacobi in full regalia and full view, talking in a falsetto screech and covering his mustache with one hand. He doesn't want to press charges, only to vanish into the ground or thin air. Luckily, his friends and wife, with wonderful understanding, accept him for what he is; and Allen improvidently tosses away in ten minutes an aberration that, some years later, provided the producers of *Bosom Buddies* with a series that didn't confront its own implications.

From aberrants to perverts. "What Are Sex Perverts?" has the format of the old television series *What's My Line?* The M.C. of *What's My Perversion?* is Jack Barry; and a quartet of celebrities, among them Pamela Mason and Robert Q. Lewis, try to figure out the kinks of a rabbi from Muncie, Indiana. He proves to be a masochist who likes being tied up and flogged by a girl representing his childhood governess, while his wife, flown in as a special surprise for the occasion, sits at his feet during the ritual and gorges on pork.

It would seem that Allen has gone about as far on the offensive as he can go and still get bookings in most parts of the country; but he hasn't finished. Episode six, "Are the Findings of Sex Researchers Accurate?" posits Woody as the author of a book called *Advanced Sexual Positions—How to Achieve Them Without Laughing*. He drives to the laboratory of a crazy inventor (John Carradine) who was the first person to name the sound waves issuing from an erection. At the workshop Woody sees Igor, a slavering, hunchbacked, Frankensteinian monster who's "the result of a four-hour orgasm" induced by Carradine, and a man having experimental intercourse with a loaf of rye bread, and a girl journalist whose respiration will be measured while a troop of Boy Scouts gang-bangs her. Woody saves her and incidentally destroys the building and its equipment. But from the wreckage a giant breast emerges, trained to glide along the ground after male prey. It passes a billboard promoting the sale of fresh milk without so much as a sidelong glance. What can stop it? "Don't worry," Woody assures the girl, "I know how to handle tits." When the breast expresses milk he retreats before it, holding up a crucifix, and so lures it into the captivity of a bra with a size 4,000-X cup.

Allen evidently realized in making this episode that it's not possible to parody horror films, and so he uses the first part of the story, in the lab, as an introduction only, and hews once again to his sex theme by turning a neat reversal. In place of the usual American pursuit—man hungers for breast—here a breast becomes the aggressor.

The final episode, and the most venturesome in its cinematic trickery and its doubleness, mocks space exploration and, at the same time, the male fantasy of an orgasm beyond belief: a shooting into space. Tony Randall, Burt Reynolds, and other scientific-looking types in white coveralls man various levels of a mission-control station situated not in Houston but in a male body: the brain, the eyes, the stomach, the genitals. They are organizing an orgasm. Allen intercuts shots of them with close-ups of the red-head (Erin Fleming) who is the object of this grand strategy. All systems are go, and the cry runs along the transmission lines: "Prepare for penetration!" Down in the lower parts are platoons of spermatozoa dressed in white space suits and sporty tails. "Hey," says one sperm to another (a Woody sperm) who's fearful about flying out into the unknown, "we're gonna make gravy." And they do, jumping away like paratroopers, while the sound track thunders to the strains of "Red River Valley" and "The Battle Hymn of the Republic" with its martial tempo and its vision of the coming of the Lord. Ejaculation . . . Success! Miss Fleming's girl at the receiving end, who is an N.Y.U. graduate and therefore has cultivated tastes, wants a repeat performance. All the contributors to the mighty effort (except the lost cannon-fodder sperm who did the trick) cheer, clap one another on the back, and gear up for a second launching.

After coming out of *Everything You Always Wanted to Know* the public may well conclude that sex is not a very serious business, not even a serious industry. This film won't glut any appetites for knowledge. The inhabitants of America's fundamentalist deeps must have choked on the title alone if it ever threatened their neighborhood marquees. But while it's putting sex on the slow-burning griddle, it manages also to epitomize Allen's film career, that wry homage he's paid to assorted types of film, which movie critics call genres. What sets this—indeed, all of his films—apart from other people's is wit. It's true that his lines are seasoned with humor, which the characters don't intend to be funny, but is. However, wit, which those characters speak with the intention of being funny, continually breaks through in his work, at least as abundantly as it did in Sturges'. I don't wish to imply that wit is superior to humor. But it's a scarce ingredient in films, and unspiteful wit is even scarcer. Together with his collaborators—especially Ralph Rosenblum, his customary editor, and Marshall Brickman, who has sometimes shared the screenwriting with him (and has now graduated into directing on his own behalf)—Allen has wrought farce with more filmic and verbal variety and impudence than anybody else since World War II.

The Appreciable Remainder

The past forty years of cinema proved to be wildly productive for farce, especially farce conceived in the vein of satire. This chapter has mashed together directors and clowns from the period whose film farces have personal styles, themes, or other individual traces. But a dozen or more outstanding farces have gone unappreciated here. Some are farcical through and through; others bounce into and out of farce. The more I think about them, the more they each clamor for consideration, and I risk a few sleepless nights fretting over what might have been said about them when I bring this chapter to an end by merely naming them and their countries of origin.

From France: Marcel Carné's *Bizarre, Bizarre* (*Drôle de drame*; 1937), *The Scandals of Clochemerle* (1950), Jean-Luc Godard's *Les Carabiniers* (1963), Yves Robert's *The Tall Blond Man with One Black Shoe* (1973), Édouard Molinaro's *La Cage aux folles II* (1981).

From Italy: Mario Monicelli's *The Big Deal on Madonna Street* (1960), Pietro Germi's *Divorce Italian Style* (1961) and *Seduced and Abandoned* (1964), Lina Wertmuller's *The Seduction of Mimi* (1972) and *Love and Anarchy* (1973), Franco Brusati's *Bread and Chocolate* (1974).

From Britain: Tony Richardson's *Tom Jones* (1963), Stanley Kubrick's *Dr. Strangelove* (with a mostly American cast; 1964), The Flying Circus ensemble's *Monty Python and the Holy Grail* (1975) and *The Life of Brian* (1978), plus one or two films in the "Doctor" and "Carry On" and "St. Trinian's" series.

From the United States: Olsen and Johnson's *Hellzapoppin* (1940), Stanley Kramer's *It's a Mad Mad Mad Mad World* (1963), *Animal House* (1978), *Airplane* (1980). . . . Perhaps readers will do me the kindness of adding their own favorites.

FIFTEEN

THE CONSTELLATION
OF FARCE

A former professor of sociology takes over as governor of a British penitentiary. He believes in humane rehabilitation by letting the more difficult prisoners in his charge practice arts and crafts, because, as he says, "almost all crime is due to the repressed desire for aesthetic expression." One prisoner, a deranged murderer, has dreams and daytime visions of ghosts, blood, and carnage. According to the sociologist-governor, this man needs a set of carpenter's tools to work off his frustrations. A prim young chaplain named Prendergast has spoken with the murderer a number of times but refuses to take his visions seriously. Soon after the tools are delivered to the murderer's cell, Chaplain Prendergast pays another visit there. The murderer thereupon kills him.

The story is contained in Evelyn Waugh's novel *Decline and Fall* (1928), which continues with a Sunday-morning service in the prison chapel. The prisoners are forbidden to speak to one another, and so they exchange information while singing. The result is a farcical desecration of Isaac Watts's familiar hymn:

> "O God, our help in ages past,
> Where's Prendergast today?"
> "What, ain't you 'eard? 'e's been done in,
> And our eternal home."
>
> "Old Prendy went to see a chap
> What said he'd seen a ghost;

Well, he was dippy, and he'd got
A mallet and a saw."

"Who let the madman have the things?"
"The Governor; who d'you think?
He asked to be a carpenter,
He sawed off Prendy's head."

"A pal of mine what lives next door,
'E 'eard it 'appening;
The warder must 'ave 'eard it too,
'E didn't interfere."

"Time, like an ever-rolling stream,
Bears all its sons away.
Poor Prendy 'ollered fit to kill
For nearly 'alf an hour."

"Damned lucky it was Prendergast,
Might 'ave been you or me!
The warder says—and I agree—
It serves the Governor right."
                    "AMEN"[1]

In *The Battle Between Carnival and Lent* (1559), Pieter Bruegel painted an allegory of the clash between the spirit of self-indulgence and the spirit of self-denial. But he treated the conflict farcically. On the left we see the roly-poly figure of Carnival in a turquoise jerkin and fire-red tights. He's ready to do battle. His tilted lance is a skewer with a boar's head and other meat impaled on it; his helmet, a pie balanced on his head; his steed, a beer vat with a hole on top so that he looks as if he's on the toilet. His masked attendants, a retinue of them, bear wine, food, and musical instruments. One, a clownish character with serious features, pushes the vat, which rests on a sled, toward Carnival's opponent.

On the right, facing Carnival, is the cadaverous figure and ashen face of Lent, mostly hidden by his dull green cloak, dirty white scarf, and open sandals. His lance is a long-handled wooden spade; his helmet, a beehive tipping over his right ear; his chariot, a square board on four little wheels. A monk and a nun haul him on his cart toward Carnival.

---

[1] *Decline and Fall* (New York: Little, Brown, 1928), part 3, chapter 3, "The Death of a Modern Churchman."

Behind Carnival we see a tavern, a dice game, two outdoor shows—Medieval farces. Behind Lent we see a procession of black-cowled people who enter and leave a church, beggars who receive alms. In both halves of the painting there are children at play. But the separate halves blend subtly. And as if to make them match each other, Bruegel has painted Lent's board and wheels in the same colors as Carnival's tights and jerkin.

Onto the Flemish market square where the "battle" takes place the artist has spilled something like one hundred seventy human figures. They cook food, scrub house, clean fish, entreat, act, stumble, crawl, limp, go on errands, spin tops, and hassle others —a swarm, viewed in microscopic detail, as active as the bees issuing from the hive that is slipping off the head of Lent.[2]

Donald O'Connor sings and tap-dances on a piano, on a plank. He opens a blind door and bangs into the brick wall behind it; grabs a headless, altogether yielding dummy and makes it sway and whirl and kick like a live partner. He runs up a wall, twice, flips backward in a classic "180" to the floor; goes right through another wall, this one made of paper; returns through the burst paper smiling an apology; falls on his back, on his knees, on his nose. He ends the number, called "Make 'Em Laugh," lying prostrate, still singing.

Later in the same film, *Singin' in the Rain* (1953), he butts into an elocution lesson being taken by Gene Kelly. Kelly and O'Connor go into another number of dancing-as-farce, making an idiot of the speech teacher as they trip, tap, leap, and scoot around him singing, "Moses supposes his toeses are roses."

In 1973, Elliot Richardson, the Secretary of Defense in the Nixon Administration, announced that our planes had dropped on Cambodia and Laos 145,000 tons of bombs in three months. From this figure and the population of the two countries, Russell Baker has calculated that the United States had "been bombing the average Laotian/Cambodian at the rate of 116 bomb pounds

---

[2] The original painting, now in the Art History Museum of Vienna, is done in oil on a wood surface measuring about four by five and a half feet. *The Complete Paintings of Bruegel* (New York: Harry N. Abrams, 1967) has a two-page reproduction (Plates IV–V) that is just over one-fifth the size of the original.

per year" in order to save his/her heart and mind "from whatever our bombers save them from." Baker went on to deduce an equation so compact that a professional mathematician would be bound to term it "elegant." Let HM stand for hearts and minds, W for "the weight of the average body to be saved," and P for the total population of the country to be bombed. Then $HM = (4W/3)P$. That is, multiply the body weight in pounds by one-and-one-third and that sum by the size of the population and you have a formula for your bombing program. Its cost-effectiveness? Using unarguable arithmetic and a touch of algebra, Baker reveals that your average American taxpayer has "made it possible to drop 1,266 pounds of bombs (at 79 cents per pound) on Laos, thereby saving the hearts and minds of 10 and 53/58ths Laotians for a whole year."[3] Thus Baker ministers with the same somber dose of ridicule to two of our national afflictions, statistics and extreme missionary fervor, and does so with the barbed quietness and precise, sometimes poetic eloquence that are hallmarks of the most accomplished farce in prose.

Two timid gentlemen pass along a murky cobblestone alley, each nervously eyeing the other. The first one says to himself, "That man looks fierce. . . . Must be a mugger. . . . And I don't have even a small knife on me." The second one says to himself, "I'm finished. . . . He must be a killer. . . . For a little pistol I'd give ten years of my wife's life."

This tableau, reminiscent of the commedia dell'arte sketch called "the *lazzi* of fear," or the botched duel in *Twelfth Night* between Viola and Sir Andrew Aguecheek, is an 1844 cartoon published in the journal *Le Charivari*, its exquisitely flowing outlines; variegated, crosshatched shadings and shadows; and beaky, caricatured faces drawn by Honoré Daumier, who has here caught in black-and-white the farcical terror of metropolitan man in the late twentieth century.[4]

---

[3] The full essay, of which the summary above is a part, was originally one of Baker's "Observer" columns for *The New York Times*; it's reprinted in *So This Is Depravity* (New York: Congdon & Lattès, 1980), pp. 50–54. (Baker has published seven earlier collections of wisdom in farce.)

[4] The cartoon is reproduced in *Honoré Daumier, 240 Lithographs*, selected and introduced by Wilhelm Wartmann (Zurich and London: Abbey Art Series, n.d.), p. 117.

Björn Borg serves. The 1980 U.S. Open championship at Flushing Meadow is at stake. Borg has been losing to John McEnroe. He has started a comeback, though. His first serve puts the ball in; but the head of his overstrung racquet snaps off and falls to the ground.

McEnroe returns the service. Borg drops his broken handle. Then, with no hesitation, perfect timing, and a sense of impetuous, nonverbal wit for which he's never given credit, he *kicks* the tennis ball into the other court. McEnroe, equally swift-witted and accurate, kicks the ball back. The head-pivoting spectators don't quite grasp the situation. What is this? Soccer? A joke? Borg and McEnroe as funnymen? Now if one of them had been Nastase . . .

A roar goes up, laughter, relief, and exhilaration. The point was finished two shots before, as soon as Borg put his foot to the ball, but the players, after three merciless hours, have broken the tension with a momentary exhibition of unplanned farce.

Farce pulsates in our culture, not only in theater and cinema, but also in such other performing arts as radio, television, dance, and music; in the visual and literary arts—painting, photography, sculpture, the different branches of writing; and in their offspring, siblings, and cousins: opera and basketball, comic strips and newspaper columns, doggerel and clowns' tumblesaults, spontaneous happenings and rehearsed commercials. These manifestations of farce constantly reinforce one another, and are reinforced in turn by life, for, as the narrator in Walker Percy's *The Second Coming* remarks, "The world is in fact farcical."

Telefarce

The vast wasteland, as Federal Communications Commissioner Newton Minow called TV, can boast a few farces and other shows worth looking at. But considering the millions of dollars that have gone into programming, the millions of people who have watched day and night, the countless words and gestures expended, the technical and artistic expertise at the disposal of the networks, and the quality and quantity of talent on tap, one must conclude that television, clogged with sitcoms at prime time and repeats at other times, has been the most retrogressive medium in history. The more venturesome efforts at farce-making, such as *Your Show of Shows* (1950–54) with Sid Caesar, Imogene Coca, Howard Morris, and Carl Reiner and guest celebrities; or that show's spin-offs— *Caesar Invites You* (1958) and others—were polished and pleasurable, but in essence theater revues or vaudeville on a stage and constricted through a lens. Between 1951 and 1962, Ernie Kovacs' experiments succeeded in bulling television out of the theater and into movies; and his spoofing of commercial sponsorship and other kinds of television gave audiences a taste of television theatricalism. But nobody followed up on Kovacs' advances.

When Lucille Ball began filming her shows on a movie lot in 1951 and started a scramble out of New York and into the San Fernando Valley, the living-room and other farces that were pumped out still looked like filmed plays, even when, as in *You'll Never Get Rich* (1955–59), they starred performers as able as Phil Silvers. Later still, filmed sitcoms that kidded film genres, such as *Get Smart* (1965–70), "created" but not always written by Mel Brooks, Buck Henry, and Leonard Stern, or *Barney Miller* (1975– 81), created by Danny Arnold and one of the pioneers of improvisation in the Sixties, Theodore J. Flicker, were cramped into halfhours, and kept tripping over their own crowded plot lines. But they had their moments, as when Maxwell Smart, or Agent 86 (Don Adams), drives his convertible into a car wash with the top down, and his companion, Agent 99 (Barbara Feldon), cranks up the side window.

The first *Saturday Night Live* ensemble on NBC (1975–80), the most popular of the farcical TV shows in the Seventies, still hewed to an old-fashioned theatrical cabaret or revue format, its continuity and its integrity as satire compromised by an overload of commercial breaks. ABC's *Fridays* and the subsequent *Saturday Night* series on NBC, as of 1980, stayed slavishly with that format, but they lacked performers of the individual caliber of the original team: Chevy Chase, Jane Curtin, John Belushi, Dan Aykroyd, Bill Murray, Garrett Morris, and Gilda Radner; and they dwelt lip-smackingly on jokes and sketches of brutality and vulgarity, thereby vitiating the humor. No censorship was no blessing. *Rowan and Martin's Laugh-In* (1968–73) had reintroduced short takes, quick-fire gags, and tag lines ("You bet your bippy") to the revue arrangement; but these had been featured variously in Fred Allen's radio shows; *The Jack Benny Show* with Benny, Mary Livingstone, Eddie (Rochester) Anderson, and Phil Harris; the gigs of Ed Wynn, Rudy Vallee, and George Burns and Gracie Allen; and even as far back as *Amos 'n' Andy* in the Twenties, as well as in such British radio and television as *ITMA* ("It's That Man Again") with Tommy Handley and Ted Cavanagh, and in *The Goon Show* more than twenty years previously.

In Britain after the advent of commercial programming in 1955, Thames, Granada, and other producing enterprises sought out established music-hall and radio-trained entertainers—Eric Morecambe and Ernie Wise, Bernard Cribbins, Tommy Corbett (a conjuror *and* comic), the wearisome Frankie Howerd, and one or two others; they were picked up in New York by WOR and WPIX. The British comic with the largest following here was Benny Hill, whose trademarks are grinning at his own female impersonations and other puns, plucking at girls' backsides, and racing into and out of women's toilets—although every Hill show has a wonderfully purposeless chase and tumble, speeded up by the cameras, and so ends in an energetic flurry.

The noncommercial British Broadcasting Corporation tried to shed its "Auntie" image by dissecting television as a farce medium much more conscientiously than did its commercial competitors and the American networks. Incidentally, it discovered an antidote to the solemnity of its *Masterpiece Theater* (the Tupperware of high culture) in *The Two Ronnies*, Ronnie Corbett and Ronnie Barker, who sparkle without gloating over their achievements and work with a reciprocity other teams might do well to study; *The Fall and Rise of Reginald Perrin*; *Monty Python's Flying Circus*; and the *Python* spin-offs, Michael Palin's *Ripping Yarns* and John Cleese's *Fawlty Towers*. Leonard Rossiter, who plays Perrin, after years of diligently supporting others in British movies, can clamp and purse his lips for a thoughtful and funny pause in at least twenty-four different ways. The muddled, fiftyish businessman, husband, and father he plays drifts away into daydreams in which he riots in the arms of his cool-mannered secretary. He finally gets her to himself, out of his restrictive office and at home. It's Sunday. His wife has gone off to visit her mother. He blurts out an erotic commitment, almost without meaning to, and before he can catch his breath the secretary's all over him and then stripped down and ready in his bed. Something might have come of this if Perrin could collect himself; but in the Feydeau tradition visitors keep walking in on him—his son, son-in-law, neighbor—all sent by his wife to make sure he's all right when left on his own. Ambushed in his love nest, Perrin has visitors downstairs watching over him like mother hens, while upstairs the secretary waits (and clamors) for some action.

The *Monty Python* bull sessions must have been not unlike the ones conducted by Sennett in or out of his hot tubs. The writer-participants, Graham Chapman, John Cleese, Eric Idle, Terry Jones, and Michael Palin; Terry Gilliam, who conceived the astonishing animations of old engravings and paintings; and the director, Ian McNaughton, could distribute yards of their unconscious from right off the tops of their heads. Perhaps they owe something to the Goons' fecund dissociations—spies trapped in a cellar for not paying their electricity bills; a locomotive that interrupts a tennis match by steaming across the court and through the net— but while they are at least as playful, their satire cuts deeper and makes British folly international.

Some visual gags:

—"Hell's Grannies" on motorcycles.

—A scrawl on a wall: "Make tea, not love."

—A coastal invasion of troops hampered by their ballet skirts.

—A man with teeth that dance—they go up and down like piano keys.

—Hands springing up like trees on a hilly landscape—a cowboy rides by on a hand.

—A man and woman getting into bed; a montage of famous symbolic shots: crested waves dashing against rocks, towers rising and falling, a train entering a tunnel, the barrels of turning cannon, missiles being launched.

—Englishmen who quiver, raise their right arms, sprout beards and kilts, turn into Scotsmen, and march across the border until Britain has no male population left.

—British heroism: a shot of a mountaineer with full climbing tackle scaling the sidewalk of the Uxbridge Road as if it were a sheer cliff.

—The Ministry of Silly Walks employing a high-kicker, stumblers, and a civil servant with collapsing knees.

Some visual-aural gags:

—How to defend yourself against a man armed with a banana: 1) Make him drop it; or 2) Eat it; or 3) Shoot him.

—A Hungarian in a tobacco shop trying to ask a question with the aid of a phrase book: "My hovercraft is full of eels."

—A woman who, to get an emergency repair done on her stove, must first let herself be gassed.

—A man during World War II who thinks up a killing joke. He tells it to his mother. They both die laughing. It's used as a secret weapon against the enemy and wipes them out.

—A TV news stringer reporting from Bolivia on the state of storage jars during a revolution.

—A fellow who buys a pet ant in a department store. At home, his mother has got rid of his pet elephant but is having a hard time fighting off his pet tiger . . .

Sometimes there's thematic continuity in a *Flying Circus* show; sometimes as a substitute for continuity one character will brassily announce: "And now for something completely different."[5] The programs exploit three types of farce: realistic (many of the settings), fantastic, and theatricalist. A censor in military uniform may appear to deplore what is going on and cut it. Skits on film directors are, like all good satire, inspired criticism. At Sam Peckinpah's disposition to go heavy on cruelty and gore, *Monty Python* guffaws by having all the characters in a sketch of the West spurting strawberry jam or tomato paste. On a *Face the Press* spoof the Minister of Housing wears a beard and pink dress, while the case against the government is to be argued by a small brown patch of fabric.

Before they split up, the *Python* members managed to lay claws on politicians, business, the family, sex, bureaucracy, war, and especially peace. They explored the medium of television—they opened it up for subsequent artists. In this country their nearest competitors as freewheeling farceurs have been *Sesame Street* and *The Electric Company*.

---

[5] A compendium of *Python* material was assembled for movie-house release under the title *And Now for Something Completely Different*.

Music, Dance, and Mime

Gilbert and Sullivan scores, pop songs, numbers from Broadway shows, and revues from all over display elements of farcical humor. Lately Peter Schickele has exhumed the *oeuvre* of the fictitious P. D. Q. Bach in order to parody a potpourri of classics.[6] But the only composer I can think of apart from Schickele who dedicated a large slice of his work and his life to farce is Erik Satie (1866–1925).

The muse Euterpe appointed Satie her envoy to Surrealism. As the twentieth century went through its rebellious Teens and early Twenties, Satie was in the thick of most of the artistic insurrections in and around Paris. The titles of a few of his compositions may give some idea of his shock tactics as a creator: *Three Pieces in the Shape of a Pear* (1903), *Disagreeable Insights* (1908), *Things Seen to Right and Left—Without Glasses* (1912), *Sketches and Twitchings of a Big Wooden Guy* (1913), *Five Grimaces* (1914), *Bureaucratic Sonatina* (1917), *Bottle Imps* (1923). The peculiar conjunction of artists and the arts in that time and place energized Satie after some years of underactivity on his part. "He proceeded," says Roger Shattuck, "to confound everyone by composing works in a totally new style," and "came closer than most men to discovering a second youth."[7]

For Satie had had an earlier career as a composer of influence; had been a friend of Debussy and a counselor to Ravel. Later he would help to promote the fortunes of Honegger, Milhaud, Poulenc, and Roger Désormière (the last-named composed the music for Artaud's only large-scale staging, *The Cenci*); and he worked and mingled with such celebrities as Picasso, Cocteau, Duchamp, Massine, Picabia, Man Ray, and René Clair. Thanks to Clair's film

---

[6] *The Definitive Biography of P. D. Q. Bach* by Prof. Peter Schickele (New York: Random House, 1976) includes a pictorial essay, "The World of P. D. Q. Bach," with hilarious illustrations and captions; an annotated catalogue of his music (the *Concerto for Piano vs. Orchestra*; the "opera in one unnatural act" called *Hansel and Gretel and Ted and Alice*; a Schleptet; the cantata *Iphigenia in Brooklyn*; among other diversions); a list of undiscovered works; and a glossary of unusual instruments required by P.D.Q., such as the foghorn, the left-handed sewer flute, the windbreaker, and the shower hose in D—all of which goes to certify that Schickele works as deftly with words as with notes.

[7] *The Banquet Years* by Roger Shattuck (New York: Doubleday, 1961), pp. 114, 115. Shattuck has an invaluable chapter on Satie, pp. 114–85, as well as a rundown of Satie's principal works and a bibliography.

Entr'acte, we have shots of Satie cavorting in the company of several of these contemporaries. Satie's music and other writings suffered neglect for many years; but in 1979 the director of the Paris Opéra put together as a posthumous tribute "a sort of seamless, surrealistic happening." *The Complete Erik Satie* had "a cast of hundreds of diverse performers, including singers and dancers from the Paris Opéra, the Ars Nova Ensemble, actors from the Comédie Française and the boulevard theaters, the Brussels Marionettes and six gymnasts from the Paris Fire Department."[8] Satie wrote the music for ballets, among other works, and it seems fitting that Moses Pendleton of the Pilobolus dance troupe should have been invited to choreograph one Satie item for the tribute.

The Pilobolus principals (Robby Barnett, Alison Chase, Jamey Hampton, Georgiana Holmes, Pendleton, Michael Tracy, and Jonathan Wolken) form one of the two best-known companies that have taken dance into many corners of farce (solo dancers like Baryshnikov also have done so); the other is Mummenschanz. It remains open to question whether these troupes are performing dance; mime; some mixed art, such as "sculpture-in-motion"— one of the desiderata Vachel Lindsay proposed for the movies[9]— or a formalizing of movement training of the kind practiced by apprentice actors; or something else. My own leaning is toward a "something else"; but whatever that is, it has affiliations with dance (which usually requires music) and mime (which usually doesn't). Certainly the distinction once drawn by Étienne Decroux between dance and mime doesn't hold up when applied to Pilobolus: that mime shows a performer's relationships with the ground and dance a performer's attempts to escape from the ground.[10]

---

[8] "Paris Staging the Entire Erik Satie Body of Work" by Susan Heller Anderson, *The New York Times,* May 11, 1979.

[9] "Suppose the seated majesty of Moses (by Michelangelo) should rise, what would be the quality of the action? Suppose the sleeping figures of the Medician tombs should wake, or those famous slaves should break their bonds, or David again hurl the stone. Would not their action be as heroic as their quietness? Is it not possible to have a Michelangelo of photoplay sculpture? Should we not look for him in the fulness of time?" From *The Art of the Moving Picture* by Vachel Lindsay (New York: 1915 and 1922, reprinted by Liveright, 1970), p. 124.

[10] Decroux wanted mime to be abstract, not representational, and certainly not an imitation of everyday movements—perhaps a transcendence or a crystallization of them. For a teasing elaboration of his differentiation between dance and mime see Eric Bentley's *In Search of Theater* (New York: Knopf, 1953, reissued by Atheneum, 1975), pp. 184–95, especially pp. 190–91.

A solo act called *Momix* by Pendleton brings him onstage in a white suit, white running shoes, and dark glasses. He holds a brief bag in one hand; in the other a white stick, which he uses the way a singer toys with a microphone. Is he a blind man on the loose? Or do the dark glasses signify nothing more than a mask—a freezing of the features like that in many Italian and some French movies, or in the broad daylight of American life when, in cloudy weather, some people on the street like to assume inscrutability? Strutting, walking, running, leaping, staggering, Pendleton flings his body about, commenting farcically on normal modes of human locomotion and giving a display of physical virtuosity. (He reminds one of the Harlem Globetrotters, who are dance farceurs —not only sportsmen, not only gymnasts—who comment on normal basketball and make it look pale beside their virtuoso handling of a ball.) Sitting spotlit on a chair with the chair blacked out, Pendleton lets his legs and feet dance while the rest of him stays motionless or sways slightly as he simulates dancing in a crouched position.

In *Molly's Not Dead*, three couples slink like prehistoric monsters (did dinosaurs *slink?*) across the boards, one partner of each couple with bent legs, the other partner perched on his knees. Two men stand behind a third and they all flap their arms independently so that the audience watches a visual sonata for six arms— or for six legs, when they crisscross the stage in threes. In addition to the feats of balance and the matched rhythms, what Pilobolus is doing is making novel shapes out of human forms, startling us into laughter with revelations of what we are and could be under controlled patterns of light.

Mummenschanz also makes dozens of farcical shapes out of the body, resculpturing it with the active cooperation of objects and cardboard cutouts. These allow discrete limbs to poke out along their edges or to pierce them. The Mummenschanz performers mostly strike ridiculous poses; their aim is to hold a strange moment, not to evoke a sense of change or evolution, as Pilobolus does. Pilobolus is an assembly of people trained in the dance; Mummenschanz consists of a trio trained as mimes,[11] two of them

---

[11] Mummenschanz was created by two Swiss (Andres Bossard and Bernie Schürch) and an Italian (Floriana Frassetto). In New York the performers I saw were two Americans (Louis

with Jacques Lecoq, who was himself a pupil of Jean-Louis Barrault. Pilobolus displays kinetic movement; it is dynamic. Mummenschanz concentrates on potential movement; it is not static; it conveys movement barely (but not always) held under constraint.

Mime takes an integral and sometimes dominating role in many farces. But mimes themselves don't like to think of mime—and they're right—as being simply theater without dialogue. (No more do dancers like to think of themselves as simply moving rhythmically to music, actual or imagined.) The wordless episode (Act I, Scene 10) in Arnold Wesker's *Chips with Everything* (1963) in which some air-force recruits steal coke to heat their barrack room would be mime only if played with a heightened movement. Sensing this, the author says in a stage direction that the acting must be "silent, precise, breathtaking, and finally very funny." Mime as an art of caricature demands careful selection and exaggeration. In some theater farces it receives it; in farce films since the days of the silents, seldom, Jacques Tati being one of its few exponents, and less and less since his early pictures. Revues have often provided an outlet for bursts of mime, whether of the rehearsed kind (*Beyond the Fringe, The Establishment*) or the semi-improvised (*The Second City, The Premise*). Mime, at any rate, seems to function more appropriately and efficaciously in farce than in the other genres. Spike Jones used to set mime to music when his instrumentalists blew water out of their trombones or snipped the end off a clarinet with a pair of shears while somebody was playing a solo on it.

Cartoons

In the work of Bruegel, Chagall, and a few other visual artists there appear to be three characteristics that allow us to interpret some of their work as farce. First: an element of caricature, willful distortion, especially of faces and figures. This distortion passes directly into the drawings of caricaturists and cartoonists like Dau-

---

Gilbert and James Greiner) and another Swiss (Dominique Weibel). Another artist whose work can be construed as mime or dance (or mime plus dance) is Alwin Nikolais. His troupe and that of his protégé Murray Louis make unorthodox shapes out of the human form, displaying moments of farce and near-farce.

mier, Rowlandson, Cruikshank, and the hundreds of draftsmen who publish cartoons—whether satires of actual politicians and other public figures or stylizations of fictitious characters—and who distort by clever simplifying. Second: an emphasis on outlines. We judge cartoonists by the quality of their "line"—its flow, its economy, its variations of weight, its suggestiveness. And third, as with mime: arrested motion. We have the impression that the figures are about to spring into movement, as though each drawing were one frame of an animated film. A painted or drawn cartoon that doesn't have these characteristics may be amusing, cutting, extraordinary, but it will be comic, not farcical. Artists whose drawing styles are as individual as those of Charles Addams, Max Beerbohm, R. O. Blechman, Jules Feiffer, George Grosz, Herblock, Al Hirschfeld, David Levine, David Low, Pat Oliphant, George Price, Ronald Searle, Ralph Steadman, R. Taylor, and James Thurber, and range through realistic, fantastic, and theatricalist subjects, produce work in which the three characteristics stand out, especially the arrested motion—although they may produce other kinds of work as well.

The pointy figures, block lettering, geometrical landscapes, and scrolls of massed cloud by Saul Steinberg show these same characteristics, despite the abstract and dreamlike nature of this artist's drawings. For example, the solid word YEAR supports a less massive MONTH, which has a lighter DAY balanced between the M and the T, while on top of that the H of a slim HOUR holds up a thinner MINUTE on the E of which rests Second in upper and lower case. The arrangement is, to put it mildly, precarious; but it's a tiny outline of a man on top that makes this drawing, this allegorical portrait of the transience of life, quiver. He carries a banner inscribed with the word NOW! and he is stepping off the vertical stroke of the d in Second out into open space.[12]

Of the regularly published funnies only a few are farcical, and then not very. *Blondie*, which incorporates some of the best draftsmanship in the business, restricts itself to stereotypical domestic comedy and office politics with only infrequent forays into farce. *Li'l Abner* and *Pogo* had the most persistent and telling farce and

---

[12] The drawing is reproduced in Steinberg, *The Inspector* (New York: Viking, 1973), the pages of which are unnumbered.

satire in the past. *Doonesbury*, the leading satirical strip today, is
high comedy, not farce; its creator, Garry Trudeau, has a placid,
architectural drawing style, but writes dialogue more punchy and
astringent than that of most contemporary playwrights and novelists.

The most uncompromising comic strips, the ones in *Mad* magazine, are satirical from start to finish; they pull many stunts in
realistic and theatricalist farce. The writers—Dick de Bartolo, Stan
Hart, Arnie Kogen, Larry Siegel, Lou Silverstone—occasionally
grope with some desperation to come up with a smashing climax
for their skits of films and television shows, but if the journey
exceeds the arrival in enjoyment, that's not much to complain
about. Caricatures of stars and politicos by Jack Davis, Mort
Drucker, Harry North, Angelo Torres, and George Woodbridge,
and the special features by artist-writers Dave Berg, Al Jaffee, and
Don Martin, catch the insane melee of circus acts that are twentieth-century America with a sane lucidity. Marie Winn, lament-
ing the loss in *Children Without Childhood* (New York: Random
House, 1981) of a "Golden Age of Innocence" (which was also an
iron age of rank ignorance) and of a respect for parents that was
an outgrowth of fear and oppressive discipline, takes the magazine
to task for using material already "available to children in other
media, especially television and the films." Ms. Winn is no Mrs.
Grundy but a parent understandably appalled at children's exploitation by the depravity and rapacities of our culture. Yet as I read
Mad, it strikes me as being one of the most salutary counterforces
born of that same culture; and I feel sad that once again the satirist, rather than what he satirizes, becomes the target of a well-
meaning citizen with an unquiet social conscience.

As for the fine arts that are three-dimensional—sculpture, architecture, and such recent hybrids as motorized paintings, self-
destruct machines, and Christo's eleven thousand gates and nylon
panels intended to festoon Central Park—there's no reason some
of them cannot be farcical in intent or give rise to farce when
spectators approach and discuss them. Certain crafts might well
be farcical: knitting, weaving, crewelwork, origami, costume jewelry, woodworking (other than sculpture), and even manufactured
trinkets like stamped-out mantelpiece uglifiers embossed with slogans—"World's Spunkiest Uncle"—whose original had to be con-

ceived and executed by somebody. I am not so much rooting for farce in this book, or enlarging its empire, as noticing its ubiquity. There is, after all, bad farce. More bad than good.

Prose and Verse

The boundary we take for granted between fiction and nonfiction is a fiction. Novelists and short-story writers capitalize whenever they can on their experiences, and sometimes outrage their peers, their enemies, and people who took themselves for their friends by portraying them unmistakably. We admire passages of fiction that freshly but faithfully capture the look, sounds, and smells; the specialness; the soul of an actual place or the taste of a shot of liquor, a madeleine, a crust.

But nonfiction trespasses just as freely on fictitious things. We can find farce in a campaign document that harks back to an age of peace and plenty that never was; in the puffing of an advertisement; in the published results of an opinion poll. And in deliberately farcical nonfiction we can find fictitious characters and events, dreamed up for the sake of giving human warmth and color to a narrative. Woody Allen, for instance, in his *New Yorker* pieces hits us with such unlikely imaginings as a perplexed professor of philosophy.

The columns of our best-known syndicated humorists, the three B's, Baker, Bombeck, and Buchwald, include conversations with acquaintances of theirs who, if any semblance of them ever existed, couldn't have made fools of themselves so tartly. Art Buchwald has Washingtonians by the gross standing by to unravel for him the remoter implications of every move and delay perpetrated by the federal government. Fictional ladies from the suburbs, magnificently cultured and accoutered, keep descending on Erma Bombeck to shame her into heartbreak over her dress size, housekeeping discipline, child rearing, cooking utensils, and husband. La Bombeck's home tribulations, set down with amazing sensitivity to the nuances of language, are enough to shatter any sympathetic reader's funnybone. Russell Baker, in recording the penalties of living unpretentiously and minding one's own business, summons up fictional losers in the human race who are more real than real ones. Dick Orfling, for instance. Orfling, a business executive, reads a book written for business executives. From it he culls a piece of advice: when you're away from the office, phone back once in a while and ask to speak to yourself; check up on your company's efficiency at taking incoming calls. During a trip to the heartland Orfling calls his office number from Missouri and asks for Dick Orfling. To his chagrin, the voice at the other end claims to belong to Dick Orfling and nobody else. The next day he tries the tactic again, this time from Montana, with roughly the same inexplicable result. He boards the next plane out of Montana, lands, hurries to the office, and informs his secretary that if anybody calls and "it's me, tell me I'm not in." [13] We know this Orfling. He may be us.

Many of the mighty farce essayists of the near past—from Michael Frayn, Paul Jennings, Robert Benchley, S. J. Perelman, and scores of contributors to *Punch, Le Canard Enchainé, Simplizissimus*; back to Stephen Leacock, George Ade, Finley Peter Dunne and his Dooleyisms; and thence back, back, back into the far past of Juvenal and Horace—have equally called on fiction. They pull names out of hates, join each to a persona, go through the necessary selecting and exaggerating, and come up with a script based on fiction but taken by its readers for some kind of historical verity. The *Satires* of Horace, written in 35 and 30 B.C., and those of Juvenal, written about one hundred fifty years later, are forerunners of the *roman à clef.* If nonfiction farceurs rarely publish books that are officially called novels it's because they don't need to. Their nonfiction speaks in fiction's accents, and it may contain more truth per paragraph than some books that parade supposed fact and imposed interpretation of it over hundreds of pages.

Among explicit novelists of farce, Evelyn Waugh undoubtedly gets the laurel for his compendium of mostly British, mostly upper-class follies in *Decline and Fall* (1928), *Vile Bodies* (1930), *Black Mischief* (1932), *A Handful of Dust* (1934), *Scoop* (1938), *Put Out More Flags* (1942), and *The Loved One* (1948), as well as his short stories and travelogues. [14] If, in these writings, Waugh had

---

[13] The full version of Orfling's plight is told in *Poor Russell's Almanac* (New York: Doubleday, 1972), pp. 53–56.

[14] The tradition probably began with Gargantua and Pantagruel, created by Rabelais in a written work of fiction, and was carried forward by Cervantes, Sterne, and Fielding, among others.

indulged his moralist's naggings or permitted some figuration of himself to take part, as he did with Charles Ryder in *Brideshead Revisited* or Guy Crouchback in the trilogy *Men at War,* or in *The Ordeal of Gilbert Pinfold* (none of these intended to be farces), the farce might have lost out. In Waugh, as in Twain, the ice-cold prose makes for white-hot farce. Keeping a distance from his story, compelling his passions to liquefy and freeze instead of letting them go up in warm air—here we find what separates the exceptional farceur in prose from the also-ran.

Farcical characters wind into and out of the novels of another British author, Ronald Firbank (1886–1926)—farcical, that is, in what they are, not particularly in what they do—and have names that might have been adapted from the "precious" romances of seventeenth-century France (Eulalia Thoroughfare, Parvula de Panzoust, Queen Thleeanouhee). Reading Firbank's distilled prose is rather like eating meringues off bone china and whipped cream out of champagne glasses. It runs in tiny paragraphs; naughty defiances of grammar ("Neither her Gaudiness the Mistress of the Robes, or her Dreaminess the Queen were feeling quite themselves . . ."); exclamatory locutions and italicized words, with a *penchant* for the French; the retailing of minuscule points of dress, complexion, and demeanor ("Meanwhile Madame Wetme was seated anxiously by the samovar in her drawing-room. To receive the duchess, she had assumed a mashlak à la mode, whitened her face and rouged her ears, and set a small but costly aigrette at an insinuating angle in the edifice of her hair. As the hour of Angelus approached, the tension of waiting grew more and more acute, and beneath the strain of expectation even the little iced-sugar cakes upon the tea-table looked green with worry . . ."); and touches of self-deprecation that only authors like Shaw, Pirandello, Ionesco, and Firbank, whose styles are inimitable, can bring off ("I suppose I'm getting squeamish! But this Ronald Firbank I can't take to at all. *Valmouth!* Was there ever a novel more coarse. I assure you I hadn't gone very far when I had to put it down").[15]

---

[15] The quotations above are taken from *The Flower Beneath the Foot. Five Novels* (New York: New Directions, paperback edition, 1981) assembles Firbank's *Valmouth, The Artificial Princess, The Flower Beneath the Foot, Prancing Nigger,* and *Concerning the Eccentricities of Cardinal Pirelli.*

If the fiction of the eighteenth and nineteenth centuries was peppered with farce (Lesage, Smollett, Thackeray, Dickens, Twain, Chekhov), the twentieth century's has become riddled with it.[16] The book that did the most wholehearted and vivid selling job for farce in the postwar years, though, was Joseph Heller's *Catch-22* (1961). Its story of the members of a bomber squadron in 1945 brought home with soaring humor the rich stink of larceny, lunacy, hypocrisy, and other forms of bloody-mindedness that make war a dirty joke.

Farce lurks in anthologies of verse, like Geoffrey Grigson's *(The Oxford Book of Satirical Verse)* and Kingsley Amis' *(The New Oxford Book of Light Verse)* and Carolyn Wells's *(The Book of Humorous Verse* and *A Nonsense Anthology)*; in gatherings of the limerick (there are some fifty of them in and out of print); in poems expressly published or republished for our children and the children still alive and kicking in us; in dirty verses, collected or passed on by word of mouth; in parodies and travesties; and in poems of invective, for poets have always been wonderful haters, whose ammunition redeems them. The best farcical verse may well be mediocre poetry; it requires a moment of conflict or, better, a narrative, even one condensed into a quatrain or a limerick. Edward Lear, who popularized the limerick form around 1850, although it predated him, is responsible for

> There was a Young Lady from Norway
> Who casually sat in a doorway.
> When the door squeezed her flat
> She exclaimed, "What of that?"
> This courageous Young Lady of Norway.

. . . which is on the way to being farce. Swinburne, who, in addition to his gifts as a formal poet, wrote the finest blue limericks of

---

[16] Any compilation of moderns who have written farce into their fiction would have to include Thomas Berger, Anthony Burgess, Julio Cortázar, J. P. Donleavy, Stanley Elkin, Anatole France, Bruce Jay Friedman, Günter Grass, Aldous Huxley, James Joyce, Ken Kesey, Jerzy Kosinski, Sinclair Lewis, Jakov Lind, Anita Loos, Don Marquis, Aubrey Menen, Vladimir Nabokov, Flannery O'Connor, George Orwell, Anthony Powell, Raymond Queneau, Richard Stern, Dylan Thomas, Kurt Vonnegut, Nathanael West, P. G. Wodehouse.

any, adapted Lear's version, and shoved it into line with the farcical canon:

> There was a young lady of Norway
> Who hung by her toes in a doorway.
> She said to her beau:
> "Just look at me, Joe,
> I think I've discovered one more way."[17]

As with the limerick, the song lyric imposes a discipline on its writer, but gains strength from the constraints of end-stopped rhymes and an ictus that fits and dramatizes the melody line. W. S. Gilbert's verses still astound us with their metrical tricks and unorthodox rhymes taken to farcical lengths. One of the most prolific recent songwriters in farce is Tom Lehrer, who in the Fifties was performing, with cracked voice and piano, parodies of just about every kind of pop number as devoutly as Woody Allen and Mel Brooks later did with films—and less fondly. Lehrer gleefully twits glee-club songs and marches ("Fight Fiercely, Harvard" and "Be Prepared"), love waltzes ("I Hold Your Hand in Mine" and "The Wiener Schnitzel Waltz"), soulful ballads ("The Irish Ballad" and "When You Are Old and Gray" and "The Old Dope Peddler"), and regional nostalgia ("I Wanna Go Back to Dixie," "My Home Town," and "The Wild West Is Where I Want to Be"). Lehrer is particularly sharp at discerning private motives behind public behavior. In the Fifties his "National Brotherhood Week" nipped at political efforts to mask the feuding between ethnic and religious groups with a combination of outspokenness and even temper that remains unmatched.

As farcical verse skids onward, but not always upward, there is at least one development worth considering which began in the Sixties. The Librascope Division of General Precision, Inc., devised a computer named the Auto-Beatnik. Its creators ordered it to construct rhyming couplets by picking its words at random.

---

[17] Both these limericks are printed in a variety of books, but a good place to check them out is on pages 43 and 87 respectively of William S. Baring-Gould's *The Lure of the Limerick* (New York: Clarkson N. Potter, 1967), a prodigal piece of bookmaking with illustrations by Lear, Aubrey Beardsley, and André Domin.

Although lacking the classical niceties of Pope or Dryden, it may drive future Surrealists out of business:

> My corkscrew is like a hurricane
> Under a lamp the nude is vain
> Quiet is my plumber, cruel is your parade
> Yes, its bed mumbles by a barricade
> Usually does a nourishing cannon ordain
> Like salt no adulterers were insane
> Like gasoline some battlefields were volatile
> Thus their revolt will gently drill.

SIXTEEN

NOT THE LAST WORD

Dionysos and his slave Xanthias have arrived at the portals of Hades; they want to bring the god's favorite playwright back to Athens. But before they can gain admission they must get past Aiakos, the janitor of the lower regions. Now, Aiakos, for his own reasons, means to punish the slave and spare the god. That being so, both Dionysos and Xanthias claim to be the god. Aiakos tries to resolve the question of identity with an experiment. He will whip and beat them both. Whichever one lets out a cry is the slave, since gods aren't supposed to feel pain.

The torture begins. As Dionysos or Xanthias takes a kick or a lash or a thump in the gut, he howls—and then converts the noise into a gasp of surprise at not feeling hurt. In the end Aiakos gives up: "I can't tell which of you two is a god."[1]

The god and the slave, the king and the beggar, the man and the machine all suffer equality under the scourgings of farce. I reiterate this point about equality because, since the Renaissance, critics have insisted that older tragedy dealt with great ones, comedy (and farce) with the lowborn.[2] The tragic hero must fall to death or ignominy from a height. It's true that the fall of Oedipus

---

[1] *The Frogs* by Aristophanes, translated by Richard Lattimore (New York: New American Library, paperback edition, 1970), p. 64.

[2] This interpretation could be based on a misreading of what is ambiguous in the Greek of the *Poetics*. According to Gerald F. Else's meticulous translation (Ann Arbor, Mich.: University of Michigan Press, 1970), p. 18, Aristotle says that tragedy tends to imitate people who are better than the average; comedy, people who are worse than the average. "Better" and "worse" could imply social rank, moral qualities, or, less probably, intellectual or physical prowess.

is excruciating to witness, a wise and beloved ruler with a beautiful wife and four children—reduced to a blind exile. Similarly with the fall of Pentheus, a youth of impressive beauty and resolution who has inherited a future that may turn out to be as distinguished as his retired grandfather's past—butchered by Bacchae who don't even know what they are doing and are incited by his mother. But Aristophanes had also humbled great men, actual men, in his farces—not killed them off in effigy, but damaged their reputations: Kleon, Socrates, Euripides; some historians hold the dramatist partly responsible for the philosopher's trial and sentence.[3]

After the nineteenth-century plays of Hebbel, Ibsen, Strindberg, Tolstoy, Hauptmann, and others made middling citizens—the "average"—and not leaders the subjects of tragedies, farce continued to aim its barbs impartially at high and low alike, not so much to prove that the bigger they are the harder they fall as to show that the higher the rank the more conspicuous and inviting the target. In this respect at least, farce has changed less than tragedy has. But both have changed drastically in another respect. In embracing new subject matter, they have met, clashed, and become synthesized in tragifarce. Tragifarces, such as Molière's *George Dandin*, Wedekind's *The Tenor*, Ionesco's *The Lesson*, and Pinter's *A Slight Ache*, came into being because the well-made play had softened the impact of farce in commercial theater and later in the cinema. An example of this softening is Buck Henry's film *The First Family* (1980), a realistic farce with pretensions to fantasy. The President of the United States (Bob Newhart) is considered by his advisers to be a dope—which he is—without a hope of being reelected (shades of W. C. Fields, the President of Klopstokia in *Million Dollar Legs*, 1932). He then allows his daughter

---

[3] "It is doubtful whether Aristotle had any perception of the genius and imaginative power of Aristophanes. The characters of the Aristophanic drama are not fairly judged if they are thought of simply as historical individuals, who are subjected to a merciless caricature. Socrates, Cleon, Euripides are types which represent certain movements in philosophy, politics, and poetry. They are labelled with historic names; a few obvious traits are borrowed which recall the well-known personalities; but the dramatic personages are in no sense the men who are known to us from history. Such poetic truth as they possess is derived simply from their typical quality. It is not, indeed, in the manner of Aristophanes to attempt any faithful portraiture of life or character. His imagination works by giving embodiment to what is abstract." S. H. Butcher, *Aristotle's Theory of Poetry and Fine Art* (New York: Dover Publications, fourth edition, paperback, 1951), pp. 380–81. Aristophanes' human targets are as fictional as those tragic heroes, Oedipus and Pentheus.

(Gilda Radner) to couple with a stone statue of an island god; he trades her virginity, which she's eager to lose, for an island formula, human excrement, which produces giant vegetables (shades of Woody Allen in *Sleeper*, slugging a pursuer with a giant strawberry). In the last scenes, the President and his wife (Madeline Kahn) and daughter drive through the streets of Washington, acclaimed because by increasing the size of domestic vegetables he has brought the country prosperity. The President is wallowing in a happy ending. Who, then, is the target of this "satire"? Presumably the people who reelected him. They've rewarded him for bringing them the secret of shit. But they were not the film's subject: he was. That triumphant ride along Pennsylvania Avenue is not a *kordax* but a cop-out. Tragifarce doesn't slide away from its original targets, high-placed or other. Like tragedy, it closes in inexorably.

I expect many more tragifarces in the future, serving as correctives to the cop-out. But the older forms, designed strictly for laughs, are just as likely to keep percolating through the various arts. One augury is the rediscovery in Britain and America of Feydeau. Another is the swelling popularity of the genre in movies. Over a recent Christmas season the five top attractions at the box office were *Popeye*, *Seems Like Old Times*, *Any Which Way You Can*, *9 to 5*, and *Stir Crazy*[4]—none of them venturesome either as farce or as film making, but collectively, a sign of the times.

As farce continues to mock the high, mighty, and officious, the low, sluggish, and snobbish, obsessives and addicts, its opportunities look boundless. Take addictions alone. A majority of Americans, it appears from a poll, are addicted to liquor, cigarettes, or drugs. We need no polls to tell us about such other national addictions as automobiles, television, telephoning, taking exercise and relaxation, undergoing mental repairs, staying young and thick-haired, being and smelling clean, suntanning, eating out fast, eating out of doors, half-eating sundaes, drinking up calories, dieting, spending to cure the blues, saving to cure spending, investing to beat saving, gambling to recoup on futile investments, collecting antiques to avoid having cash to gamble away, finessing on taxes and laws, tweezing out "problems" from moral and political issues

---

[4] *The New York Times*, Jan. 19, 1981, p. C-13.

so that they can be subjected to "realistic" or "pragmatic" solutions, cutting budgets as a substitute for following through on social programs, making large circles of friends and yearning for privacy, breaking rules and upholding traditions, believing statistics, suspecting generalizations, and depending on polls . . .

It doesn't look as if farce will run dry.

Index